"A *tour de force*, based on diligent archival research that looks boldly at the impact of Zionism on Palestine and its people in the first part of the 20th century. The book is the first comprehensive and structured analysis of the violence and terror employed by the Zionist movement, and later the state of Israel, against the people of Palestine. Much of the suffering we witness today can be explained by, and connected to, this formative period covered thoroughly in this book."

ILAN PAPPÉ, ISRAELI HISTORIAN AND AUTHOR

Other books by Thomas Suárez

Palestine Sixty Years Later
[Americans for Middle East Understanding, 2010]

Early Mapping of the Pacific [Charles E. Tuttle, 2004]

Early Mapping of Southeast Asia [Charles E. Tuttle, 1999]

Shedding the Veil: Mapping the European Discovery of America and the World [World Scientific, 1992]

STATE OF TERROR

How Terrorism Created Modern Israel

Thomas Suárez

OLIVE BRANCH PRESS

An imprint of Interlink Publishing Group, Inc.
www.interlinkbooks.com

First published in the United States in 2017 by

OLIVE BRANCH PRESS
An imprint of Interlink Publishing Group, Inc.
46 Crosby Street, Northampton, Massachusetts 01060
www.interlinkbooks.com

Copyright © Thomas Suárez, 2017

Published simultaneously in the United Kingdom
by Skyscraper Publications

All rights reserved; no part of this publication may be reproduced, in any form or by any electronic or mechanical means, without the written permission of the publisher, except by a reviewer who may quote brief passages in a review.

Library of Congress Cataloging-in-Publication Data available

ISBN 978-1-56656-068-9

Printed and bound in the United States of America

To request our complete 48-page, full-color catalog, please call us toll free at 1-800-238-LINK, visit our website at www.interlinkbooks.com, or send us an email: info@interlinkbooks.com

> The growth of Fascism in Palestine
> at a time when the liberated nations will put it into its grave
> is a tragi-comedy.
>
> —*Physicist Wolfgang Yourgrau, a German Jew
> who emigrated to Palestine but left in 1948,
> in the journal* Orient, *February, 1943.*[1]

CONTENTS

Acknowledgments   1
Illustration credits   4
Introduction   7
Notes   17

Part I   Other People's Lands

1. The Third Temple   23
2. Zionism and the British Mandate to 1938   35
3. While the War Raged, 1939–1944   57

Part II   The Fall—and Rise—of Fascism

4. Allied Victory, 1945   103
5. Race for Fanaticism, 1946   119
6. "A Besieged Garrison," 1947   173

Part III   "Only a Beachhead"

7. Partition, the "temporary expedient," 1947–1948   235
8. Israel *sans frontières*   275
9. Postscript: Segue to Today   325

Bibliography   329
Sources used at The National Archives (Kew)   335
End Notes   339
Index   409

Dedicated to the resilient youth of Palestine,
who from their parents' unwavering
struggle for freedom
will build a future of their own choosing.

Acknowledgments

This book grew out of conversations with Ghada Karmi in the aftermath of Israel's "Cast Lead" attacks against Gaza. Documents I had come across when writing my 2010 book, *Palestine Sixty Years Later*, raised questions about Mandate-era terrorism that Ghada encouraged me to pursue. This led me to the National Archives—and to the present book. Without her encouragement and assistance, this book would not exist.

I was fortunate to have had very smart people peruse the draft and share their expertise—Laurence Dreyfus' academic rigor and acumen; Nancy Elan's attention to language and political context; Francis Manasek's organizational perspective as a scientist; Nancy Murray's historical input; John Suárez' help with detail and cohesion; and my daughter Sainatee's tenacious regard for logic and accuracy. My gratitude goes as well to Emily Dreyfus, Mirene Ghossein, Yosef Grodzinsky, Elaine Hagopian, Reem Kelani, Joseph Massad, Sami Musallam, Jamal Rjoub, Rona Sela, Chris Somes-Charlton, Rawan Yaghi, as well as the entire always-helpful staff of the National Archives in Kew.

My publisher Karl Sabbagh's encouragement, trust in my work, and extensive knowledge of the subject all helped make this book a reality. I was fortunate to have Skyscraper Publications bring the book to the light of day, joining such other works on its list as Mads Gilbert's *Night in Gaza* and Karl Sabbagh's own *Britain in Palestine*.

Three eye-witnesses to events in the 1940s shared their experiences with me. The late Hanna Braun, ex-Hagana member, met with Nancy Elan and me in London in 2007. "Max" Maxwell, Sgt Maj, 16 Field Security Section, Intelligence Corps, was present after the Austrian train bombing of August 1947, and kindly shared his documents and photos. Ted Steel, who was in Palestine with the British during the last years of the Mandate, spent an afternoon sharing memories, information, and photographs. On July 22, 1946, he delivered documents to the British headquarters in the King David Hotel and, breaking with his routine of heading straight to the canteen, left the building. As he did, it blew up. He awoke later in an oxygen tent. An unknown well-wisher visited him in the hospital and handed him a few photographs of the bombing as a souvenir, one reproduced herewith. My thanks to Camilla Saunders for making our meeting possible.

During my last two years of work on this book, I was teaching at Palestine's National Conservatory of Music, first at its exquisite ex-Ottoman home in Jerusalem, and then at what is arguably its most important branch: Gaza. However, Israel blocked me from ever meeting any of my twenty Gaza-branch violin and viola students face-to-face. Lessons by Skype video, whenever Gaza had electricity, were as close as my students and I could come. I would like to acknowledge these students, who refuse to yield their humanity, their dignity, their resolve, despite the inhumanity thrust upon them.

Among my many West Bank friends and colleagues, I would like to acknowledge in particular violinist Michele Cantoni, a tireless powerhouse of empowering diverse musical life in Palestine, and an unending source of discussion about the region and the "conflict"; and Mathilde Vittu, professor of music analysis at the Conservatoire de Paris, who devotes herself tirelessly to music and children in Palestine. My thanks as well to my flatmate in Bethlehem, guitarist Pedro López de la Osa, and my colleague across the hall in Jerusalem, violinist Vilde Alnæs.

To my mother and my late father I owe everything, not least of which was growing up with their sense of universal fairness, of healthy skepticism, and of searching for truth beyond the headlines, that has led me to all that has mattered in my life.

Finally, my partner Nancy Elan was my constant alter-ego, perceptive critic, and idea tester. I could not imagine having written the book without her. In the midst of it all, my topic proved unexpectedly prescient when her activism in the Palestinian cause led its adversaries to come knocking at the door of her professional life.

Illustration credits

1. (27) *Mappamundi*. Woodcut, published in Lübeck by Lucas Brandis, 1475. Photograph courtesy Jo Ann and Richard Casten Ltd.
2. (41) Landing place, Jaffa. Photograph by American Colony (Jerusalem); marked "between 1898 and 1914"; negative, glass, dry plate, 5 x 7 in. Library of Congress, G. Eric and Edith Matson Photograph Collection, LC-M32- D-3.
3. (51) Political cartoon, "The man of the two wives," in the Jaffa based newspaper *Falastin*, June, July, or August 1936. Image taken from Pragnell, F. A., *Palestine Chronicle, 1880-1950* [Pragnell Books, 2005]. My thanks to Fred Pragnell for his kind assistance.
4. (61) Palestine Broadcasting Service, photograph by American Colony (Jerusalem), Nitrate negative. Library of Congress, G. Eric and Edith Matson Photograph Collection; LC-M33-11118.
5. (78) "Arab recruits in Nablus, May 6, '41," Library of Congress, G. Eric and Edith Matson Photograph Collection; negative, safety film, 5 x 7 in.; LC-M34-12055.
6. (99) Jerusalem from the north. Photograph by American Colony (Jerusalem); marked "between 1898 and 1914"; negative, glass, dry plate, 5 x 7 in.; Library of Congress, G. Eric and Edith Matson Photograph Collection, LC-M32- D-17.
7. (118), Railway bombing, from *Palestine Pamphlet Terrorist Methods With Mines and Booby Traps. Headquarters, Chief Engineer, Palestine and Transjordan*. December 1946.

8. (142) Operation Agatha, June 29, 1946. TNA, CO 537/1711.

9. (144) King David Hotel; Photograph courtesy of Mr. Ted Steel, who was given it while hospitalized after the bombing. Photographer unknown. Photograph also used in *Palestine Pamphlet*...,Dec 1946..

10. (158) Partition cartoon, *The Jewish Struggle*, No. 6, London, August 1946, page 2. TNA, HO 45/25586.

11. (172) Vehicle blown up by a road mine, c1946. Photograph courtesy Mr. Ted Steel.

12. (186) Bombing of police and civilian vehicles by Lehi, 1947. Verso stamped 6th Airborne. The author and publisher have tried to find all copyright holders.

13. (203) Lehi letter bomb preserved in TNA, EF 5/12.

14. (222) Medloc train, from *British Morning News*, August 17, 1947 (Allied Commission for Austria. British Element. Political Division. Information Services Branch) TNA, FO 1020/1774.

15. (232) Irgun anti-Partition broadside, summer, 1947. My thanks to Moshé Machover for his assistance via email, November 2011, and to Yael Kahn for enabling the contact.

16. (244) Anti-Arab cartoon, Arthur Szyk, in *The Legionaire*, "Voice of the Hebrew Legion," London, February 13, 1948. TNA, KV 5/11. (Odd spelling 'Legionaire' is correct.)

17. (280) Palestinian refugees, from *Aid to the Palestine Refugees*, US Government Printing Office, 1951.

18. (294) Wadi Araba incident, TNA, FO 905/111. A similar photo was published in *The Rising Tide of Terror or Three Years of an "Armistice" in the Holy Land*, Press & Publicity Bureau, Ministry of Foreign Affairs, Amman, February 1952.

19. (302) MAC "barrel" incident, photograph by John Scofield, from Hutchison, *Violent truce* [Calder, 1956].

20 (319) Extract from a document dated April 27, 1955, from G.H.Q. Middle East Land Forces, to Ministry of Defence, London; TNA, PREM 11/945.

Introduction

Mystical Complexity, and Other Myths

A Nazi is a Nazi he be a Jew or otherwise, and it is a false sentiment of the Jewish people to condemn Nazism and condone Jewish fascism. —*Protest by the Jewish socialist group Hashomer Hatzair, March 13, 1946, at a secret meeting of the Hagana, which would become the core of the Israel Defense Forces.*[2]

We intend to attack, conquer and keep until we have the whole of Palestine and Transjordan in a Greater Jewish State. This attack is first step. —*Press statement by the Zionist terrorist group Irgun, under future Israeli Prime Minister Menachem Begin, on April 13, 1948, regarding its massacre at Deir Yassin four days earlier, in which with Hagana approval and support, men, women, and children were lined up, photographed, and slaughtered because of their ethnicity.*[3]

The ongoing "conflict" between Israel and the Palestinians is typically portrayed as the complex, indeed irreconcilable, collision between historic enemies. It is the premise of this book, based on the overwhelming evidence, that this entire tragic history, through to today's headlines, is actually the single story of the political movement known as Zionism and its determination to expropriate all of Palestine for a "Jewish" settler nation predicated on blood descent—"race". Its alleged mystical complexity is itself a weapon in this campaign, serving to obfuscate the debacle's true cause, falsely explain the failure to end it, hijack Judaism and historic Jewish persecution in its service, and present a mythical narrative as fact to the Western public whose governments empower it.

This is the essence of what Palestinians have alleged since the beginning of Zionist colonization, and what Jewish witnesses such as Alfred Lilienthal and Moshe Menuhin chronicled from the 1950s. Expanded scholarship in the 1970s added historical backbone to what should have long been self-evident from Israel's behavior, and in the following two decades Israel's "new historians" scoured Zionist archives that substantially corroborated what the Palestinians had been saying all along. Yet with notable exceptions such as Ilan Pappé, most held on to a core belief of ethnic entitlement that trumped any reckoning with the continuing injustice. Israel, meanwhile, began resealing Zionist documents that contradicted its narrative, and prevented the unsealing of others due for release.[4]

Persecution was the alleged motivation of political Zionism's early architects, and a Jewish state its solution. But whatever any individual's intentions at the time, the settler state itself became the goal, and persecuted Jews its renewable fuel. As the settler project gained momentum, so did its addiction to this fuel and the need to ensure that its wells would never run dry. Palestine's history of religious tolerance was slowly erased from the common memory as Palestinian opposition to ethnic domination was framed as anti-Semitism. World War I replaced Ottoman colonial rule in Palestine with British colonial rule, leaving the Palestinians feeling betrayed: Britain had promised them independence in exchange for fighting against the Ottomans.

The Jewish population of Palestine, estimated to have been about 1.7% in the early 1500s, increased during the nineteenth century as several nations jostled for political, religious, touristic, economic, and strategic interests in the region. They came as pilgrims, travelers, writers, or hopeful immigrants, as any person might go to another land. Beginning in the early 1880s, however, Palestine saw a new and quite distinct newcomer: European Jews who were largely secular and who championed the new ethno-nationalist movement of Zionism. The Zionists came not as immigrants, but as usurpers, and held the native Jews of Palestine in great disdain—a sentiment that was reciprocated. By the turn of the twentieth century, Palestine's Jewish population, Zionist and non-Zionist, had risen to about 6%.[5]

Even before Zionist scouts cabled Vienna in 1898 with the disappointing confirmation that Palestine was not an empty land, but was "already married" to the Palestinians, proponents acknowledged that their political goal could only be achieved by violence against the civilian population—what is commonly considered "terrorism." It is immaterial whether this is accomplished by killing or expelling the land's people, expropriating all means of livelihood and thus starving them out, by commandeering their aquifers, through laws ethnically engineered for the purpose, or simply by making life so miserable for them that they leave "of their own accord."[6]

Much is made of the meaning of this word *terrorism*. A common narrative has it that Zionist violence was not terrorism, because it targeted the British ruling establishment, not civilians. Within pre-1948 Palestine, this position would require an extravagantly narrow definition of "civilians," and by the turn of 1948 it would require declaring the entire indigenous non-Jewish population of Palestine to be non-civilian. Jews were a specific target as well: both before and after 1948, hundreds of thousands of people in Europe, North Africa, and the Middle East became fair game for Zionist violence *because* they were Jewish, since Zionism depended not just on the transfer of non-Jewish Palestinians out of Palestine, but also

---

* Because of its popularity and widespread acceptance in the US, mention should be made of the construct, popularized by Joan Peters (*From Time Immemorial*) and, following Peters, Alan Dershowitz (*The Case for Israel*), that Palestinians are Arabs who flocked to Palestine because of Zionist immigration, thus attempting to dismiss Palestinians' right to self-determination. For an analysis of this claim, "so absurd that professional historians in Israel disavowed the book" (Pappé, *The Idea Of Israel*, 23), see e.g., Norman Finkelstein, Disinformation and the Palestine Question: The Not-So-Strange Case of Joan Peters' *From Time Immemorial*, in Said and Hitchens, eds., *Blaming the Victims: Spurious Scholarship and the Palestinian Question*, [London: Verso, 1988, 33–70]; and David Hirst, *Gun and the Olive Branch*, 8-12. Before Peters, in the 1940s, the World Zionist Organization (WZO) initiated research projects in a futile attempt to make such a claim (Segev, *Complete*, 300).

on the transfer of Jews *into* Palestine. Anti-Jewish tactics included manipulating the Displaced Persons (DP) camps, thwarting safe haven opportunities in other countries, kidnapping Jewish orphans, and destroying Jewish communities in North Africa and the Middle East through propaganda and false-flag "Arab" terrorism—all to ship "ethnically correct" people to Palestine in the service of the settler state.

Is this "terrorism?" In political discourse, the word is pushed and shoved about as though the four syllables themselves had the power to condemn or vindicate. But this is a diversion: whatever one labels it, political Zionism inescapably required massive violence against non-combatants, Palestinians, Jews, and British. The fact that the Zionists' goal *also* required targeting the British colonial establishment that had nurtured it, is irrelevant.[7]

The UN has been unable to agree on a definition of terrorism, principally because of controversy over whether it should exclude the armed struggle for liberation and self-determination. This exception would have no effect on our topic, because Zionist violence sought specifically to *prevent* self-determination and impose a minority, ethnicity-based rule—"in contravention of the plainest principle of democracy," in the words of Mayer Sulzberger, a founder of the Young Men's Hebrew Association. Zionist leaders across the spectrum, from the "moderate" Chaim Weizmann to hunted terrorists like Menachem Begin and Yitzhak Shamir, uniformly denounced any suggestion of Palestinian democracy. In justification, they variously claimed that "Arabs" are inferior people and so do not deserve a vote; that all Jews are, by blood, "nationals" of Palestine, and thus Jews world-wide are its electorate; that even a Jewish vote counter to Zionism would be void, since Zionists know what is best for Jews. They claim that Jews were a majority in a vast Biblical realm two or three thousand years ago, that "they" never gave up "their" claim, and that the Zionist claim to Palestine is not subject to norms applicable to the rest of the world.[8]

Control of language's two opposing powers—its ability to communicate human thought, but more significantly for our topic its power to *dictate* human thought by stealth—is a perk of statehood, and thus one wielded by Zionism since 1948 but still denied to the Palestinians. The stroke of midnight of the May 14-15, 1948, brought an Orwellian eclipse of language under whose inverted shadow the Israeli state still escapes the scrutiny of daylight. At that moment, Zionist terrorism became Israeli "self-defense," and Palestinians attempting to live in their own homes on their own land became "infiltrators," whereas the thousands of Israelis hurriedly moved into their stolen homes were "citizens." Today, armed Israelis invading Palestinian land, commandeering the homes of non-Jews and expelling or killing their inhabitants, are not terrorists, indeed not even infiltrators, but "settlers," a term that is particularly benign to the American public whose schoolbooks use it nostalgically in their national narrative—an association that leaders like Ben-Gurion were fond of exploiting. These Israeli "settlers" are "civilians," and thus victims of any resistance, whereas the families they ethnically cleanse, should they defend themselves and their homes, are militants or terrorists.[9]

Zionist militias enjoyed wide support among the Jewish settlements, especially among the youth indoctrinated into their cause, and the British were powerless to dampen their lucrative fund-raising at home and in the US, Britain, and France. Though best remembered by the iconic Irgun and Lehi ("Stern Gang"), the Jewish Agency's Hagana was little different, and by early 1948 its elite fighting force, Palmach, terrorized the non-Jewish population with brutal ethnic cleansing campaigns that surpassed the abilities of the Irgun or Lehi.

Palestinians also committed terror attacks, and this book's focus on Zionist terror must never be misinterpreted as excusing Palestinian violence against civilians. It was Zionist terrorism, however, that ultimately dictated the course of events during the Mandate, and it is Israeli state terrorism that continues to dictate events today. Palestinian terrorism was then, and remains today, a reaction to Zionist ethnic subjugation and expropriation of land, resources, and labor. Any people attacked, will resist; and among any group there will be people who will resist in extreme ways, especially when denied any means of self-defense. An aggressor state cannot cite the resistance to its violence as a threat against which it must defend itself—otherwise all aggression would self-justify. That, however, is precisely the nature of the so-called "cycle of violence" or "conflict" in Israel-Palestine.

Palestinian terrorism during the British Mandate occurred principally during the revolts of the late 1920s and late 1930s and was the direct response to the realization that Zionism sought to cleanse non-Jews from the land. In a climate where even anti-Zionist literature was banned, Palestinian non-violent resistance—diplomacy, entreaties, strikes, boycotts—proved futile. The British response to Palestinian terror was brutal and uncompromising: suspects were summarily hung, hundreds of houses of innocent people demolished, and Palestinians were used as human shields. This, a measure of assistance on the part of the Palestinian public, and to some extent the limited and unreliable assurances of the 1939 White Paper (which attempted to regulate Zionist immigration and land expropriation), effectively stopped Palestinian terrorism a year before the outbreak of World War II.[10]

Throughout World War II and the post-war years leading up to the partitioning of Palestine, British officials frequently remarked on Palestinian restraint in the face of increasing Jewish attacks. Yet Palestinians understood full well, as did US and British intelligence, that even "moderate" Zionists would not stop until all of historic Palestine was taken as a state predicated on ethnic supremacy. In stark contrast to their treatment of the Palestinians, the British avoided strong measures against Zionist terrorism in fear of unleashing a revolt they could not control, as well as the propaganda windfall it would afford the Zionist movement, especially in the United States.[11]

As the Allies' defeat of Hitler seemed increasingly assured, Zionist violence intensified and became the defining challenge of life in Palestine. Both the terror groups and the "recognized" Zionist leaders harnessed the world's unqualified revulsion against the Nazis to frame their battle in Palestine as the new front. Pamphlets, posters, and radio broadcasts inundated the Yishuv (Jewish settlements) with the message that the British were indistinguishable from the Nazis, and their goals the same. By late 1947, as the British exit was assured, the terror militias refocused their cross-hairs, and the Nazi slander, onto the remaining obstacle to their goal of seizing all of historic Palestine: the Palestinians themselves. Emotionally scarred, vulnerable Jewish survivors of the war in Europe were indoctrinated in Zionist-run DP camps with the message that Palestine was their only hope of survival, but that it was inhabited by the heirs to their just-defeated German tormentors, hardening them against soul-searching when, three years after the defeat of the Axis, they razed village after village because of people's ethnicity. The "international community" behaved as though United Nations General Assembly Resolution 181, recommending the partitioning of Palestine into a "Jewish" (Zionist) and Palestinian state, would happen of its own accord, and had no provision to prevent the ethnic cleansing that any informed official feared was imminent. Whatever limited control they exerted slipping away, the British washed their hands of the catastrophe they had created.

Resolution 181 can fairly be labeled a scam. The US Truman Administration bullied it into passage well aware that the Jewish Agency's "acceptance" of Partition was a pragmatic move within the walls of the UN. Both British and US intelligence warned that no Israeli leader, nor the Yishuv as a whole, had any intention of honoring Partition. Indeed, in documents dating months *before* the end of the Mandate, both the British and the Americans take for granted that the British exit will yield a Jewish state not along Partition, but on however much land beyond it the Zionist militias would seize by force. Moreover, they take for granted that not even the remainder would be the Palestinian state that Resolution 181 promised, but would be absorbed into Jordan (and Egypt) awaiting, as was also assumed, Israel's next expansionist adventure. For the Zionists, Partition was a necessary inconvenience, the means to the only weapon powerful enough to conquer all of Palestine: statehood.

The Palestinians above all were painfully aware that the proposed Zionist state would be merely a beachhead to further conquest and expulsion, and this, not just their refusal to forfeit their inalienable right to self-determination, is why they would not endorse Partition. In early 1948, as Zionist leaders claimed that a Goliath of Arab armies sought to destroy their still-unborn state, their own militias swept across Palestine, razing non-Jewish villages unchallenged. It was not until after the Zionist armies had already conquered much of the Palestinian side of Partition that any Arab army entered the area, and when finally they did, the vast bulk of the war took place on, and in defense of, Palestinian soil. Little of the war took place in Israel. Yet Israel cited these armies as the existential threat against which its aggression was justified.

By the time the Armistice Line established a cease-fire, Israel had seized and ethnically cleansed not just the 56.5% of Palestine that the United Nations had designated for the state, but fully half of the Palestinians' portion as well. This Line was not a redrawn Partition and did not give Israel the extra land it had seized, but Israel hurriedly settled hundreds of thousands of new immigrants on the stolen Palestinian territory rather than in Israel, in order to make the theft irreversible. Meanwhile, the terror gangs' leaders moved on to key positions in the new Israeli government, and the most notorious of the terrorists, Menachem Begin, went to New York and openly fund-raised for the violent takeover of what remained of Palestine. Thus in January 1949, the eminent *New York Times* correspondent Anne O'Hare McCormick declared the two-state solution dead due to Israeli aggression.[12]

Crowded into what remained of Palestine were the people Israel had ethnically cleansed, both from its own side of Partition and from the land it illegally occupied to the Armistice Line. When Palestinians tried to return home at the end of hostilities, Israel blocked them and flouted the UN's demands to desist even as it sought—and won—membership in the world body. Now destitute, many of the victims were killed on sight when they tried to slip home if only to pick their harvest or retrieve savings hidden when they fled the invasion. By the end of 1953, Israeli violence against these farmers and villagers attempting to reach their homes, and its terror raids over the Armistice Line into the (Jordanian-occupied) West Bank and (Egyptian-occupied) Gaza Strip, did indeed create armed Palestinian reprisals, though minuscule in comparison to the Israeli aggression precipitating it.

By the mid-1950s, two events might have ended Israeli aggression. Israeli violence against its neighbours had become so serious that Britain set plans to neutralize the entire Israeli air force and key Israeli military and communications installations. Secondly, Israel was caught targeting British and US citizens in a botched "false-flag" operation. But at the eleventh hour, geopolitical marriages of convenience took precedence: instead of attacking Israel, Britain joined forces with Israel and France to attack Egypt, creating the so-called Suez Crisis.

This "crisis," Israel's first post-1948 war, provides a logical place for this book to end. Armed with its messianic narrative, the eight-year-old state had established the patterns of its national behaviour that continue to steer it regardless of its transient leaders. After Suez, the 'international community' gave up asking Israel to stop blocking the refugees' return and gave up asking it to end its occupation of Palestinian lands. A decade later, it failed to stop Israel from ethnically purging another three hundred thousand people in the 1967 war. The "temporary" Armistice Line became known as the 1967 borders, and even this was abrogated as Israel began expropriating yet more of Palestine: the West Bank (as well as Syria's Golan Heights), which it occupies and has annexed in all but name*; East Jerusalem, which it has openly annexed in violation of several Security Council Resolutions; and Gaza, which it occupies through a draconian siege.

Indeed it is the Gaza Strip that, at writing, is most portrayed as the purveyor of terror attacks, most visibly in the form of crude rockets sent over the Line into Israeli towns like Sderot (which is actually the Palestinian village of Najd, seized and ethnically cleansed by Israel in 1948). The Western media cite these rockets in a vacuum, as though they were the cause rather than a reaction, and depict Israel's deadly siege of Gaza not as terrorism but as the Caspian Gates keeping out the barbarian hordes. The problem itself remains unspoken: Gaza's one million refugees still waiting for the world to stop Israel from blocking their return home, Israel's cataclysmic blockade that turned their beautiful coastal enclave into a vast internment camp, its indiscriminate slaughter from the air, Gazan fishermen killed for

---

* Israel derives significant advantages by not formally annexing the West Bank. One, it enables the facade of a Palestinian "government," thereby absolving Israel of its responsibilities for occupied territories under international law; two, it enables Israel to deny Palestinians the vote yet maintain the facade of Israeli democracy, even though it is Israel, not the Palestinian Authority, that controls their lives; three, it passes on to the "international community" the expense of Israel's crippling of the Palestinian economy, "foreign aid" to Palestine thus being in truth disguised money to Israel; and four, the political repression of the Palestinians is done in the name of the Palestinian Authority, not Israel.

fishing in their own waters and Gazan farmers blown up for farming their own soil. In the words of the Israeli journalist Amira Hass, Gaza represents "the good old Israeli experiment called 'put them into a pressure cooker and see what happens'."[13]

For this book's record of Zionist attacks, I have relied chiefly on declassified source documents in the National Archives of Great Britain (Kew). Their many authors were both bureaucrats and first-hand observers on the ground, recording clinically and commenting candidly. For Zionist records I have used the terror organizations' own records when possible, translated records such as diaries and Jewish Agency documents, and the works of Israeli scholars who have scoured the limited Zionist archives made available, principally Ilan Pappé, Benny Morris, and Tom Segev. I supplement these with documents from US intelligence and from existing scholarship on the topic.

"Jewish terrorism" was the term commonly used during the Mandate, but when not quoting or paraphrasing a source, I have preferred the more accurate "Zionist terrorism," as did Arab representatives at the UN in 1947-48. When referring to the native people of Palestine, I have preferred the obvious term "Palestinians" rather than the broad ethnic term "Arabs," especially as "Arab" is used as a tool of expropriation, painting Palestinians as a nameless non-people who are merely nomadic blurs in a great Arab mass and who should be happy to vanish into that mass.[14]

Some paragraphs in the period 1944-1947 are essentially recitations of attacks without further commentary. I thought it essential to the book that these be included chronologically within the text, because their very relentlessness is integral to the context. Nonetheless, some readers may find them tedious and may prefer merely to skim some paragraphs, without loss to the larger meaning.

Tom Suárez, *London, April 2016*

Notes

Regarding the term "conflict"

The commonly used word "conflict" to denote the situation between Israel and the Palestinians is inaccurate, and has done much to stifle a wider public understanding of what is actually happening. As explained by an American Anthropological Association task force, the word "assumes that the parties involved have comparable access to resources (including material resources, freedom of movement, freedom to express oneself, as well as the forces of violence), but that they clash because their interests are mutually incompatible." Rather, "one is dealing with an occupation, which consists in one party controlling, militarily or otherwise, the territory, time, liberty, and other resources deemed to be under the rightful control of the other party." (Task Force on AAA Engagement on Israel-Palestine, Report, October 1, 2015, 7)

Regarding the terminology of "Jew," "Arab," "Palestinian," "Zionist"

In everyday usage since Zionism took hold in Palestine, the words "Jew" and "Arab" are the common, though problematic, shorthand used to distinguish the "two sides" in Israel-Palestine. Since it is blood descent that Zionism uses to distinguish its privileged class from the subjugated classes, not religion, cultural background, or birthplace, Israel is a racially predicated state, even though there are different "races" represented by this blood descent. Defining Jews by blood descent is consistent with the Nazi definition of a Jew, rather than the traditional concept of a Jew as someone who follows Judaism. Thus the anti-Semitism of the Nazis and of political Zionism differs from the conventional anti-Semitism of, for example, Ferdinand and Isabella's Spain, in which a Jew was identified as such by religion, and therefore ceased to be a Jew if s/he converted. *Arab* may be broadly defined as a pan-ethnic linguistic group that includes various religions, mainly Christians, Muslims, Jews, and Druze, spread principally across Northern Africa and the Middle East. "Zionist" and "Zionism" in this book always refer to the ethno-political movement, never to "spiritual" Zionism.

Nomenclature

Spellings of Palestinian villages and Jewish settlements is modern when their identity is clear, otherwise spelled as cited in the source documents.

The Jewish Agency

Formed in 1929 as an evolution of the Palestine Zionist Executive, the Jewish Agency was recognized by the British as the governing body of the Zionist settlements in Palestine.

The Arab Legion

This name might cause confusion today. The Arab Legion was an army formed and led by the British in 1920 to defend the Transjordan region occupied by Britain after World War I. It played an important role in the fight against the Axis powers in World War II under John Bagot Glubb, who commanded the Legion from 1939 to 1956, when it became the Jordanian army.

The Palestinian pound (£P)

Both British pounds (£) and Palestine pounds (£P) are cited. As a reference to the value of the £P, in 1929 a schoolteacher earned a minimum of £P60 and a maximum of £P340 per year. (*Report by His Majesty's Government ... Palestine and Trans-Jordan ... 1929*, 65).

Terms and abbreviations

- CID = Criminal Investigation Department
- JNF = Jewish National Fund
- Mapai = Political ('Workers') party in Israel. Merged with the Labor Party in 1968.
- OAG = Officer Administering Government
- Revisionists = Branch of the Zionist movement founded by Irgun-founder Ze'ev Jabotinsky that advocated maximal aims on both sides of the Jordan.
- TAC = Temporary Additional (or Assistant) Constable
- UNSCOP = United Nations Special Committee on Palestine
- Va'ad Leumi = General Council of Palestinian Jews
- WD = War Department
- WZO = World Zionist Organization
- ZOA = Zionist Organization of America

The National Archives in Kew, record WO 169/4334, contains a Glossary of Hebrew Terms relevant to the Mandate period.

All emphasis within quotes (underline, italics, upper-case) is original.

"*The Times*" always refers to the *London Times*. The *New York Times* is always referred to as such.

Part I
Other People's Lands

1

The Third Temple

The theory that the Jews are to come into Palestine and oust the Moslem cultivators by 'equitable purchase' or other means is in violation of principles of sound policy, [and] to this might be ascribed by future historians the outbreak of a great war between the white and the brown races, a war into which America would without doubt be drawn. —*Anstruther Mackay, The Atlantic Monthly, July 1920.*[15]

It is Doctor Weizmann, considered the most powerful of the religious foreigners, who is inducing us now to remain in Palestine ... up to the day when we sink up to our necks in a catastrophe which will no longer be in our power to rectify or correct. —*The Daily Express, November 1922.*[16]

When the League of Nations repackaged the imperialism of the past to fit the more humbled sensibilities of the post-World War I period, the Zionist "national home" in Palestine was its only overt settler project. The League's colonial ventures, such as the British Mandate that empowered that national home, were envisioned as temporary. Europe's Zionist leaders, however, held that they were not settlers, but were "returning" to Palestine to reconstitute

Biblical Israel. Their extraordinary claim—that Jews are a covenanted race whose entitlement is empowered by an ancient religious text and whose passport is genetic, a birthright passed down from a Semitic people of the ancient Middle East—put a defining mystique on what was, under its elaborate veneer, a European settler venture in an allegedly post-colonial world. "The Bible is our mandate" to take Palestine, as Ben-Gurion put it.[17]

From Weizmann and Ben-Gurion to the fanatical terror gang Lehi, the ideological pronouncements of the settler project were couched in the language of messianism. Zionism was building the Third Temple, the final kingdom, a resurrection rising from the ashes of the Second Temple and apocryphal Solomon's Temple. Its battles, its enemies, its conquests were Biblical; the state created by UN Resolution 181 was the rebirth of that created by God. Ben-Gurion all but placed himself among the Prophets, claiming that his 1948 conquest marked the third monumental event in all of Jewish history, following the Exodus from Egypt and Moses' receiving the Ten Commandments at Mount Sinai. In the United States, Christian fundamentalists were seduced by this opportunity to believe that they were living the prophecies themselves, the beginning of the end of time. "Are we not witnessing," US Congressman Albert Rossdale testified in 1922 in support of Zionist colonization in Palestine, "the truth of the words of the prophets of the return of Israel, the assurance of whose restoration gleams through the whole vista of prophecy?"[18]

As the settlers looked to the heavens to prove their divine right of return, they turned to the ground to prove their Biblical narrative. So effectively were archaeology, divine right, the collective Western subconscious, and genetics fused in the service of the settler state that today, when Israel designates archaeological sites "Israeli national heritage sites," the terminology performs a sleight-of-hand: subliminally, the ancient ruins are made artifacts not of a transient kingdom that flourished for a period in antiquity, but of the 1948 nation-state. This serves not only to spin Israel's creation as unassailable; by designating "Israeli" heritage sites that do not lie in Israel, it also "sets the stage" for further land expropriation. Israeli leaders visit these sites and speak as though the stones awaken in them a distant memory, an intrinsic familiarity, like one returning to his childhood home and clearing cobwebs from a faded photo album.

Under those cobwebs—what Theodor Herzl, in Jerusalem in 1898, called "the musty deposits of two thousand years"—were Israelites speaking Hebrew, and so that language, unspoken as a vernacular for seventeen centuries, was established as the settlers' "native" tongue. No mere historical society re-enacting pages from the past, the new settlers learned the language of the Biblical realm because they became its people.[19]

Thus when in Tel Aviv in 1938 Talmudic scholar Jacob Melnik was caught married to three women, each unknown to the other two, he successfully argued that the Torah, which contains no prohibition against polygamy, was what ruled. The prosecution as well argued on religious grounds, citing a Talmudic ban on polygamy, but the defense successfully maintained that "a Talmudic law is not as strong as one in the Torah." After both the District Court and the Court of Appeal dismissed the case, lawyers declared that the not-guilty verdict "forestalled a social upheaval in the Jewish National Home."[20]

Ben-Gurion fused his settler project onto the Old Testament by discarding the two millennia of Jewish life in between as not even part of Jewish history. Zionism, in his view, restarted Jewish life after being "paused" since the failed revolt against the Romans in 132-136 A.D. Colonel Richard Meinertzhagen, Chief Political Officer of the (British) Egyptian Expeditionary Force, went so far as to claim scientific interest in "re-establishing a race after a banishment of 2000 years," as though an ancient tribe's DNA had been frozen millennia past and Palestine was the petri dish where a bolt of lightning would bring it back to life for the fascination of anthropologists.[21]

When that precipitous bolt of lightning struck in 1948, Israel's leaders anointed their creation "the Jewish state"—not *a* Jewish state, in the sense of Judaism being a national faith that any nation might have, but rather *the* Jewish State, the exclusive ownership and metaphysical manifestation of Judaism, its people, and their history. Having armed this word-triptych with such potent symbolism, Israel wields "the Jewish state" as a talisman fending off censure: critics hesitate to fire accusatory words at such a state for fear of hitting this three-word human shield, alleging to be the embodiment of Jews and Judaism, that the state holds out in front.

This fusion of settler state and "race" (descent) reaches its inevitable conclusion with a child born to a Jewish mother in Israel, as that child is not "Israeli" but, by Israeli law and upheld in its Supreme Court, that child's *nationality* is "Jewish." Any acknowledgment of a national identity or individual voice among world Jewry would undermine Israel's messianic, tribal pretence. Zionism inverted the historic relationship between religion and colonialism, between Bible and sword: by making Jews a race and the nation-state the body and soul of that race, it used blood descent as a means of imperial control over Jews themselves. Thus Jews, Ben-Gurion asserted, were "<u>obliged</u> to settle in Palestine." Zionism freed nationalism from the constraints of geographic borders, making ethnicity itself the frontier. The Jewish "race," and nationalism, were made one and the same in the service of the settler state.[22]

Ben-Gurion told the UN that Palestine belonged to Jews because "they" never gave up "their" claim to it from Biblical times. Even if the UN accepted the extraordinary claim that he was the descendant of a particular ancient people, the argument itself would have seemed preposterous, indeed delusional, had Palestine not occupied uniquely privileged terrain in the Western cultural landscape. We, his audience, are the audience of the medieval mapmaker: Geographically and/or symbolically, post-Crusades *mappaemundi* typically flaunted Palestine at the center of the earth, the cultural womb, and even during the scientific revolutions of the sixteenth to eighteenth centuries, most European cartographers presented Palestine in a Biblical framework despite their appetite for the latest geographic data. In the nineteenth century, the Palestine Exploration Fund's British explorers moulded their surveys into the Biblical mindset, and in the twentieth century Biblical nomenclature served as *prima facie* evidence for Zionist expropriation. "Is it not absurd to turn the Hills of Judea, Samaria and the Galilee over to non-Hebrew ownership?" Irgun Commander Menachem Begin asked UN representatives in 1947 in a remarkable display of circular reasoning. "Do not the names themselves bear evidence to whom they rightfully belong?"[23]

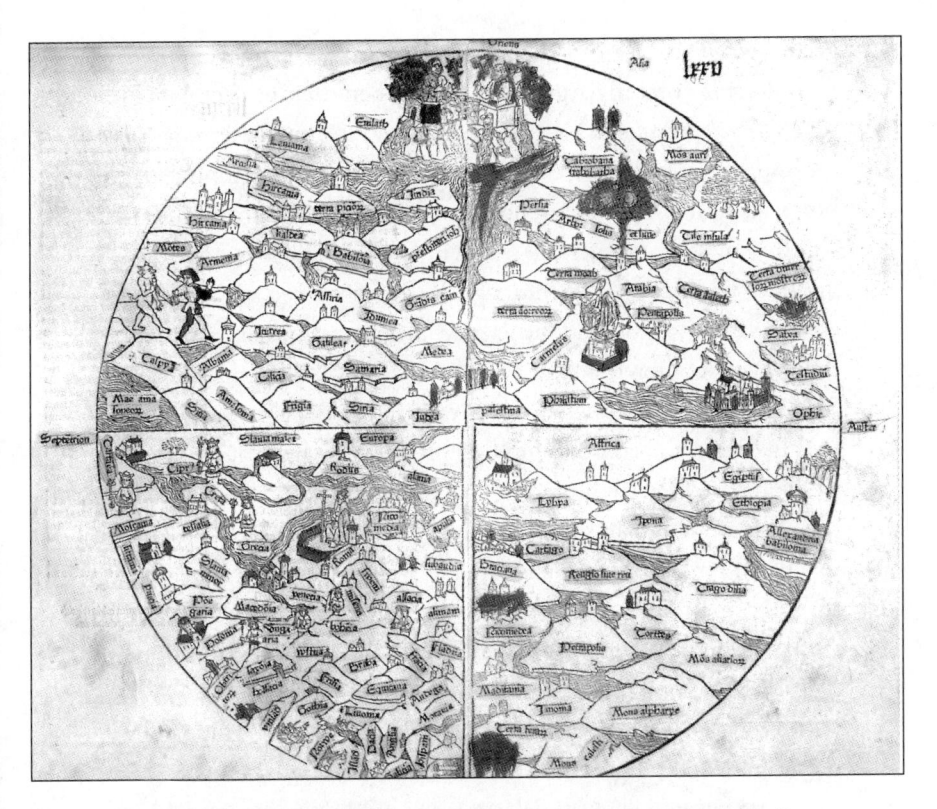

World map, 1475, typical of post-Crusades European *mappæmundi*. Oriented with east at the top. Palestine (*palestina*) is just to the upper right of the confluence of the vertical and horizontal lines, Judea to the upper left. Ophir, from whence, tradition has it, the precious materials for King Solomon's Temple were brought, is on the extreme right (south). The third place east of (above) Judea is *presbiteri joh*, the mythical Christian kingdom of Prester John, an invention of, and a catalyst for, the Crusades. Paradise, with two men holding olive branches, sits atop the map (furthest east). Just below Paradise lie India (then a broad term), Persia, and Tabrobana (Sri Lanka). Below *Tabrobana* is the Tree of the Sun and Moon from the lore of Alexander. Europe occupies the lower-left quarter (note the papal figure illustrating *Roma*), Africa the lower right. The tripartite map would represent a flat or a spherical earth according to the mindset of the viewer.

In July 1938, US President Roosevelt brought representatives of thirty-two nations to Évian-les-Bains seeking shared responsibility for the resettlement of the Jewish targets of Nazism. Yet even though Nazi intentions were already terrifyingly clear, the World Zionist Organization refused to participate because the conference was not predicated on a Zionist state in Palestine. Open safe haven for Jews, Ben-Gurion correctly argued, would weaken their project. Not even *Kristallnacht* changed his priorities: Speaking in December 1938, the month *after* that terrible night heralded the beginning of the Holocaust, Ben-Gurion assailed the idea of saving Germany's Jewish children by sending them to safety in England, a movement then in progress with the *Kindertransport*. Rather than see all the children escape safely to England, he argued that it was better to let half of them be slaughtered at the hands of the Nazis in order to get the surviving half to be settlers in his colonial project*.[24]

His were not empty words. After the war he helped sabotage well-prepared Jewish homes in England for child survivors, making the children languish in DP camps or orphanages for immigration to Palestine. Jewish orphans already well-settled were little safer: they became targets of a formal kidnapping campaign launched to snatch them from their adoptive European homes to ship them to Palestine as demographic facts-on-the-ground.

In late 1941, when Jews were being carted off to death camps by the trainload, the Irgun dismissed as "anti-Semitic" attempts to offer them safe haven outside of Palestine, and published warnings directed to dissenting Jews not to interfere with Zionists' "God-given right" to rule Palestine and Transjordan. When in 1944 President Roosevelt provisionally secured safe haven for a half million DPs, outraged Zionist leaders sabotaged it. Safe haven in the United States and other safe countries, as Roosevelt's aid Morris Ernst bitterly put it, endangered the Zionists' "pet thesis"—that Jews must go only to Palestine.[25]

Jews of North Africa and the Middle East were also needed "as cannon and demographic fodder" for the state, in the words of Hanna Braun, a Hagana member involved with bringing them into Israel, and

---

* The failure of the US and other favored countries to open their borders to Jewish immigration is cited as a principal reason why Zionists had no choice but to channel Jews to Palestine, but it is a false argument. The majority of Zionist leaders did not want Jews to have the option of any home but Palestine. They put none of their otherwise considerable energy and influence to opening borders, and tried to block such safe haven when it materialized through others' efforts. Moreover, Zionist 'immigration' to Palestine was in truth racial extra-nationalization and would have been illegal in the United States or the other Western countries whose failure to open their doors is used to justify the expropriation of Palestine.

so campaigns of misinformation, intimidation, and false-flag "Arab" terrorism were used to get them to leave their homelands. A punitive exit tax and loss of original citizenship kept many from returning home once the deceit was exposed; and especially in the case of Iraq, there was little left of "home" to which to return, as Israel's manufactured exodus had effectively destroyed the ancient native Jewish community.[26]

Zionist settlement was not immigration *per se*, but the extra-nationalization of land, resources, and labor, excised from the shared Palestinian inheritance. Baron Rothschild himself made this explicit: the new settlers' success in displacing the Palestinians from their land "had been shown when the original Zionist colonies were established," that is, since he began financing those settlements in the 1880s. Peaceful Palestinian protest against this ethnic displacement by Zionist settlers began by 1886, and in 1891 this resistance evolved into an organized petition by Christian and Muslim notables in Jerusalem.[27]

A first-hand glimpse of the pioneering Zionist settlers came from the Jewish essayist Asher Zvi Ginzberg. Visiting Palestine in 1891, he reported that the settlers "behave towards the Arabs with hostility and cruelty, trespass unjustly upon their boundaries, beat them shamefully without reason and even brag about it."[28]

The situation had become more dismal still two decades later when Dr. Paul Nathan, a prominent Jewish leader in Berlin, went to Palestine on behalf of the German Jewish National Relief Association. In a pamphlet published in January, 1914, he charged that the Zionist settlers were carrying on "a campaign of terror [against Palestinians] modelled almost on Russian pogrom models."

But there was a seductive attraction to Zionism: Dr. Nathan's friend, the political theorist Eduard Bernstein, described the ethnonationalist movement thus: Zionism is "a kind of intoxication which acts like an epidemic."[29]

The "epidemic" was displacing its host. Intensively cultivated Palestinian lands, such as one described by a visitor in 1882 as "a huge green lake of waving wheat," were acquired by the Jewish National Fund (JNF), usually from absentee (or alleged) landlords living abroad who began registering land as theirs to take advantage of the high prices being offered. Such sales, even when "legal," violated the historic norms of Palestine in which land use and occupancy rights were intertwined, and violated modern norms in that these sales were for the purpose of racially segregating the land *in perpetuum*. The displaced Palestinians were reduced to living in caves or in a "filthy tin-can settlement where the evicted Arab peasants huddle under the orange trees," as one British official described their fate.

In 1917, as the Balfour Declaration was being finessed, T. E. Lawrence "of Arabia" put it thus in a letter to Sir Mark Sykes (of the Sykes-Picot Agreement that carved up the Ottoman Empire among Britain, France, and Russia): "Do the Jews propose the complete expulsion of the Arab peasantry, or their reduction to a day-labourer class?" The ultimate absentee landlord scheme, however, failed: this was the "sale" of all Palestine to the Zionists for £20 million, payable to Abdel-Aziz Ibn Saud, first monarch of Saudi Arabia (page 85, below).[30]

The extra-national nature of Zionist land acquisition was well understood. In 1930 Sir John Hope Simpson, who became known for his involvement in refugee issues, warned that land purchases by organizations such as the JNF meant that the

> land became extra territorial. It ceases to be land from which the Arab can gain any advantage either now or at any time in the future. Not only can he never hope to lease or cultivate it, but, by the stringent provisions of the lease of the Jewish National Fund, he is deprived forever from employment on the land.[31]

This, Simpson continued, is the reason Arabs dismiss the Zionists' professions of good will. He refuted a justification for Zionist land expropriation, then already prevalent, that the settlers made the desert bloom where Arabs had left barren land.

> It is, however, unjust to the poverty stricken fellah who has been removed from these lands that the suggestion should continually be made that he was a useless cumberer of the ground and produced nothing from it. It should be quite obvious that this is not the fact…[32]

It is ironic, he continued, that this charge is made even as Zionists spend vast foreign capital to acquire the most fertile land, evict Arabs from it, and facilitate cultivation for Jews only. Yet poor productivity plagued early Zionist settlements despite their bankrolling by Rothschild, and some land formerly tilled by Palestinians fell into disuse *because of* its acquisition by Zionists, with consequences such as a plague of field mice that tormented both communities.

The invention that Palestinians let the fields lie fallow was later used by the Israel state to justify its land theft beyond the Partition. In 1955, when the US Ambassador approached PM Sharett about Israel's continued intransigence, Sharett dismissed Israel's need to return stolen Palestinian land with the extraordinary claim that no Palestinian had been fully engaged in agriculture.[33]

Ironically, the Zionists' vast infusion of European capital and rampant land speculation caused such inflation that many small Palestinian farmers fell into debt, and could only extricate themselves from it by selling their plot of land to the settlers. The tragedy of lands "temporarily abandoned because the owners have lost their cattle or other simple resources and are too much indebted to be able to replace them" was noted by Lewis French, director of the Department of Development, in 1932. "I should hate to think," Sir Charles Parkinson wrote three years later in reference to the settlers' destruction of Palestinians' livelihoods, "that ten years hence our successors ... should say that perhaps in 1935 if we had had the courage we might have saved the situation."[34]

The expropriation of land and labor, and thus of ethnic cleansing, were integral to Zionism from its beginnings. Herzl himself had proposed starving out the indigenous people by getting control of the local labor market and then denying them employment—but he cautioned that this had to be "carried out discreetly". By 1907, new Zionist immigrants, among them the young David Ben-Gurion, organized boycotts in order to starve non-Jews from the land. The JNF enforced its "only Jewish labor" regulations despite being a violation of Mandate laws forbidding discrimination based on race, religion, or language, as some British officials complained to no avail in the 1930s.[35]

When in 1924 the ban on non-Jewish labor was used to stop Orthodox Jews from having Palestinians milk their cows on Saturdays, they took their grievance to JNF director Menachem Ussishkin. If our cows are not milked they will become ill, the devout Jews explained, but it is a sin for us to do it ourselves on the Sabbath. In response, Ussishkin told them that the Zionist prohibition on Arab labor "is more sacred than Saturday".[36]

Zionism shares with all settler-colonialist projects the need to dehumanize those it seeks to displace or subordinate. When the wealthy businessman Sir Ellis Kadoorie of Hong Kong died in 1922, he willed his money to various cross-cultural causes, and one-third of his residuary trust "to the British Government for the purpose of building a School or Schools to be called after my name in Palestine or Mesopotamia [Iraq] as the said British Government shall think fit."

What the British government "thought fit" was to use the funds for "the erection and endowment of a single school which would be open to the boys of all communities in Palestine" and which would "promote mutual understanding and co-operation between the Jewish and Arab communities." The director of education in Jerusalem welcomed the inter-community project, calling it "an opportunity of bringing Jews and Arabs together on common ground." But the Jewish settlements blocked Palestinians from the school, and "allowed" them only a segregated agricultural school. After statehood, the Israeli government successfully lobbied Britain for maintenance funds from Kadoorie's estate even though all non-Jews had either been ethnically cleansed or placed under martial law.

Similarly, when Bertha Guggenheimer died in 1927, she left behind a trust fund of one hundred thousand dollars for Palestine "with special reference to playground needs," among whose projects was a new playground in Safed (Galilee). Jewish settlers, however, blocked Palestinian children from the playground, and protests from Mrs. Guggenheimer's representatives that this violated the philanthropist's intent were ignored. The presence of Arab children, the settlers retorted, was "corrupting" to Jewish children—indeed it was against "Jewish ethics" and the Torah itself.[37]

Yet even in a setting as official as the 1937 Peel Commission, Ben-Gurion claimed that the reason Arabs were against Zionist colonization was their "intolerance, which is inherent perhaps in them … in their education and upbringing. It is fanaticism," this "father" of the Israeli state testified. "It is different levels of culture."[38]

The Jewish Agency's own constitution mandated race laws in 1929, before such laws became common in Central Europe. Fundamentalists fought to preserve Jewish "purity of blood," and still today it is illegal to perform a marriage between a Jew and a non-Jew in Israel. Such parallels to German settler-colonialism in 1930s Poland continued after Israeli statehood, when it placed the property and resources of those it ethnically cleansed at the disposal of its settlers, and controlled the movements and actions of non-Jews by establishing ethnic registers.[39]

Like fascist-era Germany, Israel defined Jews as a race (blood descent), and accorded itself the right to dictate the genetic parameters of this "race" to achieve its political objectives. For Israel, this proved invaluable after its 1967 conquests, when the state needed a vast increase in settlers as human facts on the ground, and broadened its racial definition of "Jew" to suit the purpose.[40]

But Zionism's perennial problem resurfaced: not enough Jews were interested in going to Israel. When in the 1980s, during former Lehi bigwig Yitzhak Shamir's second term as Israeli Prime Minister, Russia finally allowed Jews to leave, most wanted to go to the US, and the US welcomed them to its shores. Shamir, furious, claimed extra-national "tribal ownership" over them as Jews. He called them "defectors" and successfully coerced US president Reagan to close its doors to them in order to force them to go to Israel.[41]

Zionism's treatment of Jews as a "race" apart was a hallmark of classic anti-Semitism, and "anti-Semitic" might well have been the epitaph that buried Zionism along with Herzl. But Herzl fought back by claiming world-wide Jewish allegiance to his new religion, crowning Zionism the standard by which good Jews and bad Jews are distinguished. "No true Jew can be an anti-Zionist," Herzl decreed, "only Mauschel is one," *Mauschel* (Yid, or Kike) being an offensive word for a religious Jew. "Merely to look at him," this father of Zionism said of such Jews, "let alone approach or, heaven forbid, touch him was enough to make us feel sick." The Jew, wrote Herzl, is a hideous distortion of the human character, something unspeakably low and repulsive ... We'll breathe more easily, having got rid once and for all of these people who, with furtive shame, we were obliged to treat as our fellow tribesmen...[42]

Even in its infancy, Zionism was already seen as anti-Semitic for more fundamental reasons than Herzl's own loathing of traditional Jews. "The idea of founding a modern Jewish State," the Berlin correspondent for the *London Standard* reported after the First Zionist Congress in 1897,

> which goes by the name of Zionism, finds little favour in Germany, except among the Anti-Semites. The *Kölnische* calls it one of the greatest Utopias of our time; and the *Frankfurther Zeitung* sums up an article on the subject as follows:—
>
> *In short, the degeneration which calls itself Anti-Semitism has begotten the degeneration which adorns itself with the name of Zionism.*[43]

Zionism handed anti-Semites a way of sending Jews elsewhere while looking progressive. A century ago, Gertrude Bell, the famous English writer, traveller, archaeologist, and spy, cited her diplomatic experience "to prove that the French are anxious to establish Jews anywhere [i.e., support Zionism] if only to have an excuse for getting rid of them." This was, indeed, the subtext to much of the empowering nations' adulation for Zionism. "It is very significant that anti-Semites are always very sympathetic to Zionism," C.G. Montefiore, President of the Anglo-Jewish Association, testified in 1917 in protest of the Balfour Declaration. "It is no wonder."[44]

2

Zionism and the British Mandate to 1938

[The democratic principle] does not take into account the fact that there is a fundamental qualitative difference between Jew and Arab. –*Chaim Weizmann*[45]

The fundamental difficulty over Palestine was that the Jews refused to admit that the Arabs were their equals. –*Ernest Bevin*[46]

"The time has come," Yitzhak Epstein, a delegate to the 1905 Zionist Congress wrote,

> to dispel the misconceptions among the Zionists that land in Palestine lies uncultivated for lack of working hands or laziness of the local residents. There are no deserted fields ... [And] if there are farmers who water their fields with their sweat, these are the Arabs ... Will those who are dispossessed remain silent and accept what is being done to them? In the end, they will wake up and return to us in blows what we have looted from them with our gold![47]

Keeping the dispossessed from "returning in blows" against the "looters" was one of three reasons the Zionists needed the backing of a powerful nation-state—Britain, as it happened. At the beginning, Britain's patronage was needed to give Zionist settlements political recognition and semi-autonomy. Next, Britain's military was needed to suppress the native resistance that Epstein predicted. Finally, and most importantly, British stewardship enabled Zionist settler-colonialism to juxtapose itself as an indigenous emancipation movement against foreign (British) colonizers, and thus for its 1948 war of conquest to be spun instead as one of 'independence'.

Herzl tried to "buy" Palestine from the occupying Ottomans in exchange for settling their foreign debt (1896), and when that failed he tried to get it as payment for helping Germany to extend its suzerainty to the Middle East (1898). Stepping-stones were considered: He turned to Britain and proposed to Colonial Secretary Joseph Chamberlain that a preliminary Zionist settlement be set in Cyprus, but Chamberlain suggested that this be tried somewhere "not yet inhabited by white settlers." Herzl also considered Argentina and Uganda to jump-start his project—but any land other than Palestine was what he called "auxiliary colonization" that would only attract "a few thousand proletarians" and "serve no political end." In contrast, "the very name of Palestine," Herzl argued, "would attract our people with a force of marvellous potency." Only in Palestine could Zionism's messianic narrative, racial-nationalism, and modern nation-state, metaphysically fuse.[48]

Zionism's harm to Jews was articulated by activists like *Jewish Chronicle* journalist and historian Lucien Wolf, who had at first been open to Herzl's ideas as a remedial scheme. In 1903, upon digesting the "inner meaning" of the settler movement, Wolf condemned Zionism as "a comprehensive capitulation to the calumnies of the anti-Semites." He could, he wrote in the London *Times* that year, conceive of no more serious setback for Jewish history and the Jewish struggle for equality than the Zionist scheme.[49]

For Arthur James Balfour, "the inequality of the races" was "fact." In 1905, as Prime Minister, he blocked the immigration of Jews fleeing pogroms in Czarist Russia, citing "the undoubted evils that had fallen upon" Britain from these Jews. Twelve years later, as Foreign Secretary, he signed another document that would direct Jews away from Britain, the Declaration known by his name, sixty-seven words addressed to Baron Rothschild that quickly became the claimed legal basis for turning Palestine into a Zionist settler state. The Prime Minister was Lloyd George, who "does not care a damn for the Jews or their past or their future," to quote his immediate predecessor, Herbert Asquith, but who supported Zionism for geopolitical reasons.[50]

The British honed the proposed Declaration with input from Zionist leaders, particularly Lord Rothschild and Chaim Weizmann. Both objected to its word "establishment" of "a national home for the Jewish people," wanting instead the messianic "re-establishment." "Establishment" stayed, but they succeeded in deleting a phrase protecting "Jews who are fully contented with their existing nationality and citizenship." Their discomfort over this seemingly benign phrase would become clearer as the settler project claimed global "blood ownership" of Jews. Weizmann, indeed, wanted the Declaration to refer to the Jewish "race," not "people."[51]

Opposition to the Declaration was diverse and eloquent. Claude Montefiore, president of the Anglo-Jewish Association, described as "intensely obnoxious" the invention that Jews constitute a nationality. The claim that anti-Semitism was eternal, he condemned as "a libel upon (1) the Jews and (2) human nature." Edwin Montagu, a (Jewish) MP and member of the Cabinet, expressed alarm over the premise that Jews in Palestine should be "invested with certain special rights in excess of those enjoyed by the rest of the population." Moreover, he was perplexed that his government was so distracted by Zionist demands in the midst of the Great War, and that his government's zeal to please the Zionists had to do with US participation in the war.*

---

* Some documents suggest, but do not prove, a connection between Britain and the Zionists regarding US involvement in World War I. In 1944 one James A. Malcolm even claimed that he had been the one to raise the idea with Sir Mark Sykes in the autumn of 1916. TNA folder KV 2/3171 (declassified 2010) contains a letter from Malcolm to Weizmann, at the Hotel Meurice in Paris, dated 18 June 1948, in which Malcolm tells Weizmann "I sincerely want you to recall what my friends were able to accomplish in 1916 and 1917," and he reminds Weizmann of "that fateful Saturday evening in October [1916?] in Addison Road [when you, unlike some of your] incredulous friends, manfully asked and accepted my advice..." Folder FO 371/45383 contains another paper from Malcolm in which he states that turning Palestine into a Zionist state was the "way to make American Jewry thoroughly pro-Ally." According to Jeffries (*Palestine*), Lloyd George claimed that Britain 'gave' Palestine to the Zionists in payment for influencing the US' participation in the war (the US entered the war on 6 April 1917), and for Weizmann's acetone method, though Jeffries disparages the acetone claim, noting that Weizmann's method was impractical and not widely used.

> Now will you forgive me for saying that if I am right in thinking that Jews of British birth are in the main anti-Zionist ... what can be the motive for our Government, in the midst of its great preoccupations and perplexities [World War I], doing anything in this matter? To help the Allied cause in America was one of the reasons given in the Cabinet discussion.[52]

Montagu submitted a memo on August 23, 1917, in which he bluntly charged the British government with anti-Semitism for rallying around the "mischievous political creed" of the Zionists. Fighting back, Weizmann dismissed non-Zionist Jews like Montefiore and Montagu as "Jews who by education and social connections have lost touch with the real spirit animating the Jewish people," and so spoke only for themselves, no matter their numbers. He and Rothschild, not having "lost touch," spoke for Jews world-wide.[53]

Zionism was a major topic when the Cabinet met on September 3. Montagu continued his critique, arguing that the phrase "the home of the Jewish people" for Palestine was presumptuous and prejudicial. And how, he asked, was it proposed to get rid of the land's people "and to introduce the Jews in their place?" The War Cabinet reported that a "deputation of Jews" had come to protest a segregated "Jewish Regiment" that the Cabinet had sanctioned under Zionist pressure—a prelude to the Jewish Brigade that would be created in the final months of World War II. Some 40,000 Jews, the Jewish delegation noted in indignation at the Zionists, had served with distinction in the British forces without such segregation.[54]

The Cabinet, however, was far more worried about the Zionists than the Jewish delegation. The Foreign Office had been "very strongly pressed for a long time past" by the Zionists, the Acting Secretary of State for Foreign Affairs pointed out. "Particularly in the United States," there was a "very strong and enthusiastic [Zionist] organization ... who were zealous in this matter," and it was believed that

> it would be of most substantial assistance to the Allies to have the earnestness and enthusiasm of these people enlisted on our side. To do nothing was to risk a direct breach with them [Zionists], and it was necessary to face this situation.

It was decided that the War Cabinet would explain to US President Wilson that "His Majesty's Government were being pressed to make a declaration in sympathy with the Zionist movement," asking his advice on the matter.

Rothschild and Weizmann wrote to Balfour on October 3, asking his help in countering Montagu at the next Cabinet meeting. Pressing on with their formula of inverted anti-Semitism, the two Zionist leaders assailed these "assimilated Cosmopolitan Jews" of "Haute finance" who deny that Jews constitute "a separate group" from other people, and "to whom Judaism is a mere religious formula." They reminded Balfour that it was with British approval that their "extensive propaganda for a Jewish Palestine" was carried out.

One month later, on November 2, 1917, the Declaration was signed.

Beyond its presumption that Britain had the right to give away other people's land, the Balfour Declaration's enormous power came from the combination of its claimed sacrosanct status—US Judge Joseph Proskauer called it "the law of the world"—and its calculated ambiguity. Members of the British Cabinet were the first to be confused by it and, asking for clarification, were assured that the Declaration did *not* mean the establishing of "a Jewish Republic or any other form of state in Palestine or in any part of Palestine."[55]

In the meantime Weizmann, while maintaining the modest public demeanor that became his hallmark, was pushing to create that very "Jewish Republic" immediately. He demanded that it extend all the way to the Jordan River within three or four years of the Declaration (by 1921), and then expand beyond it. Jewish settlers, Weizmann insisted, must be accorded special privileges over the Palestinians, and the British authorities must lie about the scheme.[56]

Yet even this precipitous transformation of Palestine into an ethnically predicted settler state was spoken of as a modest demand. As his supporter British Major-General William Thwaites put it, Weizmann did "not wish to push for extravagant claims," and so "the Jordan as an eastern frontier would suffice as a commencement." Meanwhile, the Zionist Organization made proposals to remove non-Jews from the region, and the words "Jewish Commonwealth" replaced the Declaration's ambiguous "national home."[57]

"Now what is a Commonwealth?" asked an exasperated Lord Curzon.

> I turn to my dictionary, and find it thus defined: 'A state.' 'A body politic.' 'An independent community.' 'A Republic' ... What then is the good of shutting our eyes to the fact that this is what the Zionists are after, and that the British Trusteeship is a mere screen..? And the case is rendered not better but the worse if Weizmann says this sort of thing to his friend but sings a different tune in public.[58]

Another of Weizmann's supporters who helped him "sing a different tune in public" was Colonel Richard Meinertzhagen, who like so many of Zionism's champions is remembered for his anti-Semitism. "The people of Palestine," Meinertzhagen argued,

> are not at present in a fit state to be told openly that the establishment of Zionism in Palestine is the policy to which H.M.G. America and France are committed.[59]

Instead, a statement was composed using "the most moderate language" that (as Meinertzhagen paraphrased it) denied "that [Jewish] immigration spells the flooding of Palestine with the dregs of Eastern Europe." Moreover, the Palestinians were explicitly and repeatedly assured, as the Cabinet had been, that the Jewish "national home" would not lead to a Zionist state. Writing to Balfour from Tel Aviv on May 30, 1918, Weizmann justified the lies as all settler projects have: by vilifying the land's native people.

> The Arabs, who are superficially clever and quickwitted, worship one thing, and one thing only—power and success ... [The British know] the treacherous nature of the Arab [who would] stab the Army in the back [and who] screams as often as he can and blackmails as much as he can.[60]

Weizmann fought the threat of democracy by claiming that Arabs are inferior people and that self-determination would (in his words) "level down the Jew politically to the status of a native," Those who objected to giving Jewish settlers special privileges denied the Palestinians were, Weizmann charged, "looking on the Jews as so many natives" and were "not conversant with the subtleties and subterfuge of the Oriental mind." After noting that German agents fostered notions of the ruthless, wealthy Jew, "the financier, the exploiter, the stock-broker," he then complained, betraying no awareness of the irony, that "the British have been strengthened in such views" by the "rich Jews of Egypt" who are "shining examples of Jewish capitalism." Weizmann railed against these "rich Jews" who "are opponents to Zionism, and so they unjustly made us suffer for the sins of our enemies..."[61]

Landing place, Jaffa, early twentieth century.

By mid-April of 1918, British officials in Jerusalem were warning of Jewish soldiers who were creating incidents "calculated to provoke the severest reprisals at the hands of the Moslems," an early mention of Zionist provocation to elicit a Palestinian reaction. There was such a pattern of this incitement that the British closed the Old City to these soldiers (not to Jewish civilians) during a religious holiday. In response, the Zionist Commission claimed persecution.[62]

Weizmann was in Palestine at the time as head of an Inter-Allied Zionist Commission organized by the British. On April 28 he gave what an official from the War Cabinet described as "a carefully worded speech" in which he again denied that Zionism heralded any move towards a state. But behind the scenes, he continued to behave (as British officials put it) "as if he were sovereign of the country" or "a sort of uncrowned King of Palestine," signing a "treaty" on Palestine's behalf with Emir Feisal (later Feisal I of Iraq) the following January (1919).[63]

January also brought the opening of the Paris Peace Conference. The pro-Zionist demands being pressed in Paris led California Congressman Julius Kahn to deliver a petition to US President Wilson on March 4, arguing that Zionism was turning back the clock on hard-won enlightened values. "For the very reason that the new era upon which the world is entering aims to establish government everywhere on principles of true democracy," the petition read, "we reject the Zionist project." Pretenses that the land's native people had nothing to fear were patently disingenuous: the Arabs deserve "neither condescension nor tolerance, but justice and equality."[64]

Kahn's petition was more prescient than he may have known. That month (March 1919) Weizmann's proposals were the subject of a meeting at which Rothschild and British officials treated the ethnic cleansing of non-Jewish Palestinians as integral to their plans, with "a comprehensive emigration scheme" (as Rothschild put it) to ship them to Egypt and Syria. Discretion was advised: this was not an issue that should be voiced in Paris, but one that would be taken up once the Mandate was settled. Neither T.E. Lawrence nor Gertrude Bell objected.

> Miss Bell and Colonel Lawrence agreed and Miss Bell added that there was scope in Mesopotamia [Iraq] for such emigrants.[65]

If their reaction is surprising to modern sensibilities, ultimately both the "pro-Arab" Bell and "Lawrence of Arabia" were, to quote Edward Said, "agent-Orientalist," whose Orient was "held in check by the White Man's expert tutelage." As these strange-bedfellows discussed other people's fates, those "Other" in the Jaffa Moslem Christian Committee appealed to London by telegram:

> What fault have we Palestinian Arabs committed ... Release us from the Zionists greed which is increasing from day to day ... Were we liberated by the Allies from the Turkish yoke to be put under the Zionist yoke?[66]

Weizmann continued to complain that "the Jews were not receiving that consideration which they had expected in a country which was to be their national home," and Rothschild as well pushed for Jewish settlers to be treated more "distinct from the other citizens of Palestine," in order to demonstrate that Britain "really intended to make Palestine the Jewish National Home." The British had already outlawed anti-Zionist publications, but Weizmann now pressed them to remove Arab iconography from the region, objecting, for example, to any Arabic inscription on postage stamps. Hebrew was pushed as Palestine's official language even though, as the British governor of Jaffa commented, most Jewish settlers were having "to sit down and learn their supposedly native tongue."[67]

Like language, music symbolized sovereignty. When Annie Landau, a paramount figure in Jerusalem education during the first half of the twentieth century, refused to stand for the Zionist "national anthem," Hatikva, at the March 1919 inauguration of a new music school, she was vilified for the defiance. Outraged, *Ha'aretz* compared her to one Dr. Ya'acov Israel de Hahn, whom the newspaper called "antisemitic scum" for his criticism of Zionism, and whom Ben-Gurion denounced as a traitor. This took on more frightening significance five years later, on June 30, 1924, when de Hahn left the synagogue on Jaffo Street in Jerusalem and was shot dead—the sixth recorded Zionist assassination attempt, and the first by the Jewish Agency's Hagana.[68]

That summer (1919), President Wilson sent a commission to survey the post-war, post-Ottoman Middle East first-hand. Heading it were Henry Churchill King, president of Oberlin College and professor of mathematics, philosophy, and theology; and Charles Richard Crane, heir to the Crane plumbing parts fortune who had contributed generously to Wilson's election campaign, but who was also considered knowledgeable on Middle East affairs and whose wide diplomatic experience included the Paris Peace Conference.

Both men reached the Middle East "with minds predisposed in [Zionism's] favor," as they put it, but that mindset did not survive "the actual facts in Palestine." Their landmark 1919 King-Crane Report should have been indispensable to the architects of Palestine's future, but it was suppressed until late 1922, when Wilson himself supplied a copy to the *New York Times*. The paper published the Report in its entirety on December 3-4, with its own introduction lamenting that the world had not seen it three years earlier, before a course had all but irrevocably been charted for the Middle East.

> The world is askew today because facts have been concealed or perverted. If in 1918-1919 the world had seen the international situation, stripped of all camouflage, with every secret treaty opened and every national condition made clear, it would have insisted on a totally different outcome of events.

The suppressed Report, indeed, corroborated the Palestinians' core allegation: that contrary to the Zionists' public protestations, they intended to purge non-Jews from the land.

> The fact came out repeatedly in the Commission's conference with Jewish representatives that the Zionists looked forward to a practically complete dispossession of the present non-Jewish inhabitants of Palestine...[69]

Zionist assertions that a Jewish, descent-based Biblical prerogative outweighed the Palestinians' desire for self-determination were dismissed outright. The claim

> submitted by Zionist representatives, that they have a 'right' to Palestine, based on an occupation of 2,000 years ago, can hardly be seriously considered.[70]

Even as King and Crane prepared their report, the Chief Administrator in Palestine, H. D. Watson, reported essentially the same. Dismissing religion as driving the Palestinians' opposition, he wrote that

> The people of the country, the owners of the land [who] have looked with eager eyes to the peaceful development of their country and the better education of their children—for their own benefit, and not for the benefit of peoples

of alien nationality ... The great fear of the people is that once Zionist wealth is passed into the land, all territorial and mineral concessions will fall into the hands of the Jews whose intensely clannish instincts prohibit them from dealing with any but those of their own religion, to the detriment of Moslems and Christians. These latter, the natives of the soil, foresee their eventual banishment from the land...[71]

Britain, he warned prophetically, "will lose the lives of many of her sons in a war which will be fought, against the principles of the League of Nations, in forcing upon a small country a population of aliens." And it was force, Sergeant Major J. N. Camp wrote from Jerusalem with obvious frustration, that would be necessary:

If we are to carry out any sort of Zionist policy we must do so with military force, [so] before you publish your mandate for Palestine with its conditions, for God's sake let us know, not your policy, but your method of putting it into effect ... if we are to proceed with energy, then send us more troops.[72]

Weizmann's friend Colonel Meinertzhagen, writing from Cairo in September of 1919, reasserted that "the determination of H.M.G. to establish Zionism in Palestine ... is still withheld from the general public," and in private correspondence he corroborated, indeed boasted, that ethnic cleansing was the plan. The "acknowledged superiority of Jewish brains and money," he wrote, will force Palestinian "land-owners and business men to realise their impotence to withstand eventual eviction." Perhaps most revealing is the word he used to describe Palestinians' objections to "the minority [Zionist settlers] ruling the majority [the Palestinians]": he dismissed these objections as "fanatical." Like Weizman, Meinertzhagen warned against "contact with the local Jew," as the Middle East's indigenous Jews remained overwhelmingly anti-Zionist.[73]

Both Weizmann and Meinertzhagen behaved as though Britain were already heir to the Ottomans in Palestine. Britain was indeed the Zionists' choice for the Mandate, but the buried King-Crane report showed that it was the United States that the Palestinians themselves wanted to assume stewardship of their land, if the promised liberation were denied them. For the Palestinians, the US was the sole great power whose history in the region was not yet tarnished, and whom they trusted to live by its ideals of justice and self-determination. For the Zionists, that was the problem: should the US take control of Palestine and institute some form of representative government, it would make their goal "infinitely more difficult," as Ben-Gurion put it, and so Zionist leaders lobbied to prevent an "American Mandate" in Palestine.[74]

Even after Britain was appointed the mandatory power and the "national home" became official policy of the League of Nations, Winston Churchill still denied that it heralded "the subordination of the Arabic population ... as appears to be feared by the Arab delegation." But the Arab delegation was no more skeptical than the British Cabinet, which complained that "the entire Mandate is built on the fallacy of attempting to reconcile the irreconcilable, [being] the creation of Jewish privileges with the maintenance of Arab rights."[75]

As "Jewish privileges" increased, the Palestinian resistance elevated from entreaties and diplomacy to strikes, boycotts, and by the late 1920s, violence, most notoriously the 1929 massacre of sixty-seven Jews in Hebron, sparked by a false rumor. The British could no longer ignore the crisis of Palestinians being "displaced from the lands which they occupied in consequence of the lands falling into Jewish hands," as a 1932 report by Lewis French put it. Weizmann nonetheless pushed to acquire another million dunams (1,000 km^2) of the Palestinians' remaining irrigable land.[76]

The increasing ethnic disenfranchisement was described by a young American named Paul Siegel in 1937, based on what he learned from "a couple of fellows" who had "been in Palestine since the beginning of Jewish colonization there." They had left Palestine because of their political beliefs and, like Siegel, were in Spain fighting against Franco's emerging fascism.[77]

"They have been giving me," Siegel wrote home, "some first-hand information about the place [Palestine] that I'm sure will interest ... the Siegel family."

> [Jewish settlers'] chauvinism towards the Arabs is even greater than that of Hitler Germany toward the Jews. No Arabs are allowed in Jewish cities—there is not a single Arab in Tel Aviv. No Arabs are permitted to work for Jews. If a Jew & an Arab are seen walking together, both are punished [by the Jewish settlers], tho the Arab is punished much more severely than the Jew. No Arabs are allowed in the Jewish Trade Unions.[78]

Siegel, who died in the fight against Franco, wrote that the "small minds [of] Hitler, Mussolini and Franco ... could not see that the people of the world will not submit to their terror and hatred any longer." That refusal to submit to terror had led to an international boycott of Germany, which faced economic ruin from poor exports—until the boycott was broken by the Zionists in 1933, just after the Nazis came to power, in a scheme formalized as the Haavara Transfer Agreement. The idea was that Jews leaving Germany for Palestine would be able to recover some of their assets by using those assets to purchase German manufactured goods, which they could then resell. It was first tried in May 1933, four months after Hitler was appointed Chancellor of Germany, by a Zionist citrus firm named Hanotaiah.

The Nazis saw a formal transfer arrangement with the Zionists as their only way to defeat the debilitating boycott. Encouraged by Germany's Gestapo, Foreign Office, and Interior Ministry, Zionist representatives lobbied to break the anti-Nazi boycott, justifying the betrayal by saying that they did not wish to take "political positions" that might compromise their settler project:

> Zionism must concern itself exclusively with the building of the National Home in Palestine, and cannot afford to take political positions against individual states.[79]

And so in August 1933, the World Zionist Congress approved the Haavara Transfer Agreement. The Agreement is spun as the result of pained soul-searching over an impossible moral dilemma: enable some Jews to leave Germany while empowering the Nazis, versus a boycott that might spare millions—or might save no one. The point of the Agreement, however, was not getting out the people themselves, but getting part of their assets out with them, much of which went to the Zionist settlement project.*

Rescue for its own sake was never part of Jewish Agency policy, and nothing in its history suggests that its decision to break the boycott was based on a tortured balancing of the moral quandary. The settler project remained the guiding factor, and so the Agreement restricted Jewish evacuation *only* to Palestine. Four years later, the Nazis still wooed a contact in the Hagana, Feivel Polkes, with the lure that they would pressure Jewish groups in Germany "to oblige Jews ... to go exclusively to Palestine, and not to other countries".[80]

Polkes met with Adolf Eichmann in Berlin and claimed that he could supply intelligence on the British, French, and Italians, as well as help the Nazis secure a source of oil—in exchange for channelling Jewish emigrants (only) to Palestine. Polkes welcomed Eichmann at Haifa's port when he visited Palestine in October 1937, but had only got so far as to give him a tour of a kibbutz when the British learned of the Nazi official's presence. Expelled from Palestine, Eichmann went to Egypt, accompanied by Polkes.

Nazi files captured by the US at the close of World War II shed some light on what Eichmann learned from his Hagana host. "In Jewish nationalist [i.e., Zionist] circles," Eichmann reported, "people were very pleased with the radical German policy," since it helped achieve "a [Jewish] numerical superiority over the Arabs." It was however difficult to get German Jews to stay in Palestine once there, as most wanted to go elsewhere. To prevent this, "those Jews coming from Germany, after taking away their capital, should be put in a communal settlement." The Hagana's records on Polkes are closed.[81]

---

* There are other flaws in the alleged "moral" rationale for breaking the anti-Nazi boycott. If at-risk Jews were the actual driving concern, and if it made sense to buy their freedom even though doing so strengthened the Nazis, the capital that the Agency received from the deal would have been put into buying the freedom of Jews without the minimum assets necessary for participation in the Haavara scheme, not building the settler state. Further, according to Brenner (*Age of Dictators*), "two-thirds of all German Jews who applied for certificates [during Nazi rule] were turned down" by the Zionists in favor of "better" settlers from the US and UK who were at no risk. He also states that between 1933-1939, fully 60% of the money invested in Zionist settlement came from breaking the anti-Nazi boycott.

It was also in 1937 that the Palestine Royal Commission, established the year before to investigate the causes of unrest in Palestine, issued its report. In stark contrast to the buried 1919 King-Crane report, the Peel Commission (as it is better known) accepted Zionists' claim of an ancient Jewish blood-"nationality" with extra-legal Biblical entitlement. Zionist settlers, the Commission's extraordinary reasoning read, "mean to show what the Jewish nation can achieve when restored to the land of its birth." Framed thus, the Commission proposed a Partition plan that gave vast Palestinian tracts to the settlers and required the forcible transfer of 225,000 Palestinians and 1,250 Jews—a ratio of 180 Palestinians for every Jew. Yet, in a premonition of today's "peace offers," the Commission presented this as though the Zionists were giving up land: "Jews," the Commission's medieval-sounding pronouncement lamented, "must be content with less than the Land of Israel they once ruled," both *Land of Israel* and, especially, *they* left begging explanation.[82]

Although the Zionist establishment welcomed the Peel Commission's implicit promise of racially segregated statehood, it rejected the plan because it did not give them all of Palestine. Ben-Gurion, speaking to the media after the hearings, invoked the Bible as Jews' unassailable legal title to (all) Palestine, and ridiculed the Arabs as being "busy with politics."[83]

In his diary, Ben-Gurion fixated on the Peel Commission's proposal of ethnic segregation, underlining "forced transfer," and "really Jewish." He then elevated his four underlined words beyond even the Biblical: Couched in a messianic, tribal use of *us* and *we* that transcended even the Peel Commission's *they*, he wrote that transfer "will give us something [ethnic purity] we never had … neither in the period of the First Temple nor in the period of the Second Temple." Interpreting the diaries of prominent people unavoidably presents the question of intent: are we voyeurs reading the writer's private, unguarded thoughts, or were the words designed for us, future autobiographical self-promotion in the guise of self-reflection? Ben-Gurion believed, or wanted us to believe that he believed, that we were indeed entering the epoch of the Third Temple, and he was its prophet.[84]

Major British papers published a "news" photograph on October 21 showing, so the caption read, Arabs rioting in Jerusalem over the Peel Commission's proposals. By the time the story was proven fraudulent (the indistinct photograph had already been circulated four years earlier, in 1933), it had fueled stereotypes of "Arabs" and provided Germany with anti-British propaganda. Nonetheless, the Peel Commission having done far more to vindicate Palestinians' fears than address the causes of unrest, the uprising that had begun in 1936 continued as Zionist terror rose. This "cycle of violence," as it is commonly understood, was driven by an underlying linear violence, the continuing racialization and expropriation of land, resources, and labor. As *NY Times* publisher Arthur Sulzberger would put it several years later, the Arabs in Palestine were opposed to Jewish domination, not to Jewish immigration.[85]

The British response to Palestinian terror was collective punishment on a massive scale, despite the fact that the Palestinian villages, in contrast to the Zionist settlements, were not organizationally complicit in empowering or shielding the terrorists. "Minesweeper Taxis," or "Arab 'bad-hat' taxis and driver," were Palestinian human shields put in trolleys in front of trains, and "used to precede all convoys" to protect the British against mines on the road, as the High Commissioner would later recall. One hundred house demolitions of innocent people, collective punishment without redress, are recorded in 1936, and when a lone Palestinian assassin murdered a British official in 1938, the British responded by levelling much of the town from which he came—Jenin.[86]

Whereas the Palestinian terrorists were loose bands of guerrillas operating in the country districts, the Zionist terrorists were organized militias operating from within urban centers and enjoying the protection of those populations. Records of Zionist gangs' early violence are sparse, "owing no doubt," the British surmised, "to the heavy penalties by which Jewish members of the organisation are bound to secrecy," and so the terror had first been explained as the work of isolated Jewish fanatics. By 1937, the British were aware of the highly organized nature of "Jewish terrorism," but—as will become apparent in the tedium of violence to come—unprepared for the extent to which that terrorism would thrive under the implicit approval and protection of the Yishuv as a whole. Already by January 1940, as World War II unfolded, the War Cabinet acknowledged that claims that the Irgun's violence was defensive "cannot now be sustained," and the terror organizations' own documents demonstrate that its carnage was indiscriminate. Zionist terror escalated in the absence of Palestinian terror, targeting anyone in the way of its political objectives—Palestinian, British, or Jewish.[87]

The man of the two wives

JOHN BULL :— My Lord, I married first an Arab woman and then a Jewess and for the last 16 years I have had no peace at home...

THE ARCHBISHOP :— How did you manage to have two wives, are you not a Christian?

JOHN BULL :— It was the pressure of the Great war, my Lord :..

THE ARCHBISHOP :— Well my son, if you are sincerely looking for peace you must divorce your second wife, because your marriage to her is illegal ...

Political cartoon from *Falastin*, summer of 1936, depicting Britain's (John Bull's) sponsoring of the Zionists as an illegal marriage resulting from the "pressure" of World War I.

Three Jews were shot on April 15, 1936, two of whom died from their wounds. Two days later, the Irgun shot dead two Palestinians "while they were sleeping in their hut in one of the plantations of the Jews in the colony of 'Ramataeem'," as the newspaper *Falastin* reported it. Palestinian shoeshine boys and peddlers were attacked on April 18, and on April 19 rumors of the murders and beheadings of Arabs in Tel Aviv set off an anti-Jewish rampage in Jaffa by unemployed Palestinians. Nine Jews were killed. As with the 1929 anti-Jewish massacre in Hebron, the number would have been higher had local Palestinians not protected would-be Jewish victims. The next day (April 20) the Irgun shot "two Arabs riding a camel west of Tel-Benyamin," killing one, and murdered a plantation worker. Irgun records cite further anti-Palestinian attacks without details.[88]

Passenger trains joined the Irgun's targets by August 17, 1936, when it attacked the Jaffa-Jerusalem line with grenades and gunfire at the bridge at Shlush Street in Tel Aviv, causing (as the Irgun put it) "great consternation among Jaffa Arabs." One passenger died on the spot, and others were critically injured. Palestinian beach-goers remained a favored target for the next decade; the terror gang murdered some in March 1937, as well as agricultural workers in the Hefer Valley.

Irgun bombings of Palestinian cafés are first documented in April 1937 in Haifa, and bombings of Palestinian buses as early as September of that year. Rehavia was hit on March 6, Yazur on March 22, Jerusalem on May 20, with further attacks on July 7 and October 20.

On November 11, the Irgun threw a bomb at a group of Palestinians on Jaffa Street in Jerusalem, "near the garage of the 'National Bus Co.'," and that month it attacked cafés in Jerusalem with semi-machine guns and grenades. Palestinian vehicles in the Galilee region were attacked in December, and on December 27 the Irgun opened fire on a Palestinian bus on the Tel Aviv - Jerusalem Road.[89]

After "two sacks containing bombs were found on the Iraq Petroleum Company's workers' train from Haifa," the British reported on April 11, 1938, a Palestinian sergeant removed the canvas sacks from the train and placed them in the Company's terminal site, where they exploded, killing two people and seriously wounding a third. As police rushed to the scene from Haifa, news came of a similar sack discovered on another train in the vicinity. That carriage was evacuated and uncoupled, and a bomb expert was summoned. Before he arrived, a sergeant and two constables ignored (or were unaware of) warnings not to risk entering the carriage and, hoping to protect the train, threw the sack out the window. It exploded, killing two of them. The British appear not immediately to have known the origin of the bombs, until the Irgun took credit for placing the "clock mines" on the trains carrying Palestinian workers. Four more people were killed that day by Irgun bombs near Kiriat Haim.[90]

The Irgun attacked what it called "mob rioters" (?) on April 17, and four days later tried to blow up a Palestinian bus, but the grenade failed to explode. "Reprisals against groups of Arabs" followed on May 17 in Jerusalem and on the Hebron-Jerusalem Road. More "mob rioters" were attacked on May 23, this time in the Tel Aviv area, and that day there were attacks against Palestinians in Haifa in response, however illogically, to the British trials of three Irgun members. The Arab market in Jaffa was hit with explosives on June 26, and on the fourth of July five more Palestinians were killed and twenty wounded in an Irgun attack on the Arab quarters (what the Irgun referred to as "concentrations of Arabs") in Jerusalem. The Irgun attacked Palestinian buses in the Ramle area on July 5.[91]

What happened on July 6 1938 was the urgent topic when the British ship HMS *Repulse* anchored in Haifa Bay two days later. The District Commissioner came aboard and explained the situation on shore:

> A large bomb had been thrown on Wednesday afternoon [July 6] in the Arab market, and had exploded causing a large number of casualties, and these had increased to about 120 before order was restored.[92]

As reported in *Falastin*, the terrorists had

> slipped up to the roof of a shop in the entrance to the bazaar market near the Aloon market and threw a bomb on a crowd of Arabs and it exploded with a terrible noise near the shop of the Jewish money changer who was killed with his son ... the sight of [the many victims] was harrowing, this one moaning, that one in pain.[93]

The attack, the British report said, "must almost certainly have been committed by Jews of the Revisionist party." It was indeed the Irgun, whose records cite both this and a similar bombing "in the Old City of Jerusalem" that day. On July 7 Irgun militants from Kfar Saba took up positions on the Tel Aviv - Haifa highway "to attack Arab traffic," but they hit Indian visitors from Tanzania instead, mistaking them for "Arabs."[94]

After a bomb "tore apart a bus filled with Arab countryfolk" (as the *NY Times* reported it) by the Jaffa Gate on July 8, killing four Palestinians immediately and wounding thirty-six, the British took four Jews into custody for the crime, among them the alleged bomb-thrower—a twelve-year-old schoolgirl. The blast was so strong that it shattered a nearby vegetable market. The Irgun, taking responsibility, boasted that the bombing had caused "great consternation in Arab quarters." For the British, it was an early indication of the Zionists' radicalization of children.[95]

To prevent further attacks, the British assigned a platoon to safeguard each of Haifa's five police districts and imposed a curfew—yet the Irgun pulled off an even deadlier terror attack on July 15. Disguised as an Arab porter, the bomber placed a booby-trapped "cucumber can" in the middle of Haifa's Arab market, killing "scores" of Palestinians and wounding many. In Jerusalem three days after that attack, another bombing by Jewish militants killed eleven Palestinians and seriously wounded three.

In Haifa, "just when the situation in the town seemed to be getting back completely to normal," a captain in the Royal Navy reported on July 25, Zionist terrorists threw a bomb into the (Arab) melon market, the same as the 6 July attack. The time chosen—six o'clock in the morning—ensured maximum civilian casualties. The bomb "did a terrible amount of damage, causing the death of 45 Arabs, wounding 45 others, and killing 3 horses and 9 donkeys." Early morning food shoppers might have thought the situation was safe, since "no more public place could have been chosen," situated by Kingsway, the Seamen's Institute, the headquarters of the landing parties, "and within easy sight of the Central Police Station."[96]

The next day (July 26), one of the Irgun's most venerated "martyrs," Jacob Rass (Yaacov Raz or Ras), tried to deposit "a particularly loathsome time-bomb in the Old City of Jerusalem," as British records put it. Dressed as an Arab, Rass hid the device in a barrow of vegetables and was wheeling it into the market when suspicious onlookers exposed the bomb and handed him over to the British. According to the Irgun, he committed suicide to avoid revealing secrets under torture.

"Arab deaths" were the goal of the militia, which inhabited an imagined Biblical 'Israel' that had never ended: it extolled Rass and its other fallen who had "saved the honor of Israel [this still a decade before the state that adopted the name] more than once during years and enlarged the number of Arab deaths in Jerusalem, Haifa and other parts of the country." To encourage what it called "right-thinking Jews" in the murder of Arabs, the Irgun exploited Biblical passages, such as the Old Testament's account of Moses.[97]

By the end of 1938, the British had served two of their three functions for Zionism: they had firmly rooted the settler movement with international political recognition and semi-autonomy, and they had squashed the Palestinian revolt against their increasing displacement from their own land. In the third phase, the British would serve as the "occupier" of the Zionist colonies, enabling the settlers to frame their war of conquest and ethnic cleansing as one of "liberation."[98]

3

While the War Raged, 1939–1944

> That he should be murdered represents the crux of the present problem, which is that the Zionists, with American backing, want the whole of Palestine and that anyone who proposes less is earmarked as their enemy. —*The Economist, November 1944, regarding the assassination of Lord Moyne* [99]

The crushing of the Palestinian uprising was one of a confluence of events in 1939 that shaped the future of Palestine. Britain issued the White Paper that spring in an attempt to put order and limits on Zionist immigration and land expropriation. The Irgun opened its US front, run by Hillel Kook under the pseudonym "Peter Bergson." And of course, in late 1939, World War II began.[100]

The Second World War dramatically strengthened Zionists' ability to commingle safe haven for Jews with a settler ethnocracy in Palestine. The incomprehensible horrors of the Holocaust engendered such universal, unqualified empathy for persecuted Jews, that it was easily coopted to the Zionist argument. Palestine was alleged to be the only answer to the suffering, and the Nazi identity was franchised onto anyone challenging this construct.

Fear of a Nazi victory led the Irgun and Hagana to moderate their terror during World War II. Not all its members agreed, however, and in 1940 a splinter group formed under Avraham Stern, just as the Irgun had been formed as a splinter group from the Hagana in 1931. The Stern Gang, as it was commonly called, or more formally Lehi, was the most fanatical of the three major organizations, claiming to be (as the Chief Secretary in Jerusalem put it), "the inheritors of the purest traditions of ancient Israel".

Lehi made little distinction between the Allied and the Axis powers, and therefore saw no reason to restrain its terror during the war. "Sensible Jews," the group reasoned, "may well look to remain in a relatively good position in Palestine after a German victory." In late 1940 Stern sought a Nazi-Lehi alliance, and when the Nazis failed to respond he sent his friend and fellow ex-Irgun member Nathan Yellin-Mor to try again. Yellin-Mor, a future Knesset member, advocated striking the British in Palestine while Britain was weakened battling the Nazis—obviously weakening that battle as well.[101]

The Italian fascists were also wooed by Lehi and, briefly, by Weizmann, who met with Benito Mussolini with the idea that a relationship with the fascists might serve as a bargaining chip against the British. Lehi, however, pursued a formal agreement with the fascists during the war, and was allegedly providing the Italian Commission in Syria with military information.

Lehi's collusion with the Italian fascists was codified in the "Jerusalem Agreement 1940." It proposed that the fascists help them overthrow the British in Palestine, and then use "all the means in its power to liquidate the Jewish Diaspora"—that is, for the fascists to destroy all non-Palestinian Jewish communities on Lehi's behalf and forcibly transfer their populations to the Zionist settlements. The agreement, dated 15 September 1940, required the signatures of the Italians and the "Provisional Jewish Prime Minister." In a comical stroke of bad luck, however, the contact through whom Lehi was negotiating was also engaged as an Irgun spy, and learning of the negotiations, the Irgun tried to secure the document to embarrass its rival. "Some hitch," a British Security Officer wrote, "the nature of which is not known," kept the document from being signed. Lehi's sympathies veered again to the Nazis.[102]

These "pro-Axis terrorists," as the London *Times* referred to Lehi, sought, in their command group's words, to "clean the city streets from every person who wears a uniform which means he is British." While "wearing a uniform" automatically marked someone as an enemy, anyone seen as an obstacle was vulnerable. Most victims of Zionist assassinations (i.e., targeted rather than indiscriminate), whether by Lehi, the Irgun, or the Hagana, were Jews.[103]

When a passenger arriving from Germany at Palestine's Lydda airport on February 22, 1939 aroused the suspicion of an immigration officer, the officer put the man under guard and left to make inquiries by telephone. The mysterious passenger escaped, and the passport he had used proved to be that of a Jew killed by Palestinians five months earlier, the photograph replaced. Four days later, Ben-Gurion rallied the Yishuv with what the British called a "manifesto ... to the Jews of Palestine." The next day (February 27) "outrages were committed by Jews in all parts of the country" against Palestinians, this still three months before the White Paper that became Zionists' new justification for terror attacks. Thirty-eight Palestinians were killed and forty-four injured. When the Va'ad Leumi (General Council of Palestinian Jews) met the day after that, even those considered moderates "spoke in the militant and uncompromising tone previously used only by the followers of Jabotinsky" (founder of the Irgun), and this new-found support for the more radical Revisionists was echoed by the Labour daily *Davar*. In May, the man who had vanished from Lydda Airport was caught boarding a flight for Haifa using a phoney identity card. He was David Raziel, Commander in Chief of the Irgun, and presumed architect of the February 27 attacks.[104]

As the text of the proposed White Paper was being aired from Tel Aviv on the evening of May 17—the broadcast delayed due to Zionists' sabotage of transmission wires—"about 1,000 Jews" attacked and sacked the District Commissioner's Office. Afterwards, Jewish gangs overpowered guards in Jerusalem's Department of Migration and deposited nine incendiary bombs, four of which exploded.

Rioting continued the next day as one thousand Jews mobbed Zionist Square and non-Jewish traffic was stoned. That evening, "youthful Jewish extremists" broke windows, looted shops, and stoned police. One policeman was shot dead. Other Jewish bands set fire to a post office in Mea Shearim Quarter, gutting it. Zionist assassinations of Jews continued with the execution of a police corporal on May 3.[105]

The White Paper was approved by the House of Commons on May 23. Two days later, "three Jews opened fire from a car on a group of Arabs near the Eastern Station Haifa," as a British Dispatch described it, wounding five Palestinians. The rebellion continued when "in the early hours of May 29 a party of unknown Jews" raided the Arab village of Biyar Adas. They shot ten Palestinians, of whom five—four women and a man—died on the spot. The attackers, who were "dressed in European clothes and talking Hebrew," planted a Zionist flag in the village and fled by motor car. "An unknown Jew" assassinated a Jewish police constable and a (Jewish) civilian who was speaking with him, and early that evening the Irgun planted four bombs in the Rex cinema in Jerusalem. Half failed, though casualties included thirteen Arabs, three Brits, and two young Jews, a boy and a girl who (as the Irgun justified it) had gone to the cinema "to enjoy themselves in the company of Arabs." In Jerusalem the next day (May 30), two Palestinians in an Arab bus were shot "by unknown Jews."[106]

On June 2-3, Irgun bombs killed fourteen Palestinians and injured thirty-five in attacks on the Arab market near Jaffa Gate, and in indiscriminate mining of Palestinian villages' orchards, roads, and footpaths. Communications were sabotaged: simultaneous explosions in telephone manholes in three sections of Jerusalem destroyed 175 telephone wires, affecting 1700 lines, and telephone booths were bombed in Jerusalem, Tel Aviv, and Haifa. When the murder "of an Arab by a Jew" in Jerusalem on June 7 "took place close to and in full view of a number of other Jews," the witnesses did nothing to stop the murder and "then refused to give evidence to the Police." In Tel Aviv that day, the telephone lines were bombed again, as was a railway line near the city. On the night of June 8, "upwards of a dozen simultaneous explosions of time-bombs destroyed five electric supply-transformers and plunged a third of Jerusalem in darkness."[107]

Palestinian musicians on the air, with girl and boy soloists at the microphone. Palestine Broadcasting Service, Jerusalem, 1940.

The next morning, a teenage Jewish girl "who is reported to have been dressed like an Arab woman, was arrested at 9:30 A.M. just after she had put down a basket containing a time-bomb set to explode at 11 o'clock among a crowd of Arabs." The arrest of the girl heightened concerns that children were being indoctrinated by the terrorists, and the capture of the unexploded device represented "the first time that incontrovertible evidence has been secured to show the long-suspected Jewish origin of these highly lethal bombs."[108]

Packages rigged with bombs, one described as an "envelope mine" (an early letter bomb), targeted the Central Post Office in June. The first exploded at about a quarter to nine on the evening of June 10. As it was being investigated by a British police officer, three Jewish additional police, and a private, a second bomb detonated, injuring them. In the morning, a postal worker clearing the debris found a suspicious heavy package; he alerted a constable, but before the constable had a chance to investigate, it exploded, killing him and injuring eight postal employees. The good news that morning was the failure of an assassination attempt against the Mayor of Jaffa.[109]

Between June 12-13, coffee houses were bombed, the post office on Herzl Street was mined and destroyed, all telephone kiosks in

Tel Aviv were bombed or otherwise sabotaged, and the Tel Aviv train station near Beth-Hadar and a Palestinian house in Jaffa were both set afire. When on the night of June 12 five Palestinians from Belad es Sheikh (Haifa) were rounded up "and shot in cold blood outside the village," the "Jewish wireless later boasted of this crime as a Jewish achievement." The road to the Arab village of Fejja was bombed, as was a Public Works Lorry, killing one Palestinian and wounding thirteen, at least one of whom soon died from his injuries. The most deadly attack of those forty-eight hours was in Tiberias, where Jewish militants planted a land mine that killed seven Palestinians and wounded fifteen. More Palestinians were killed on June 15, and British records cite continued unprovoked, random violence against Palestinians by the Jewish settlers, both by sniper fire and bombs, what the General Officer Commanding (G.O.C.) summarized as continuing "sabotage and a number of direct terrorist attacks on Arabs by Jewish extremists."[110]

Haifa was the scene of the Irgun's next major market bombing. Ethnic tension in the city, the British said, was "maintained by explosion of a large Jewish bomb in vegetable market on June 19 which killed 21 and wounded 24 Arabs." As in previous market bombings, the blast was set at the busy hour of six o'clock in the morning to maximize civilian casualties, half of whom were women and children. Lest the Irgun leave any doubt that civilians were indeed its intended targets, in its next radio broadcast the terror group bragged that they had killed far more than the British acknowledged—fifty-two Palestinian market-goers dead and thirty-two wounded in that one bombing. Three Palestinians were murdered and three wounded in Lubya village (Nazareth) the next day. When the day after that (June 21) a Jew was gunned down in Kiryat Motskin (near Haifa), the British might have first assumed that he was a victim of Palestinian retaliation, but the "secret Jewish wireless broadcast" announced that he had been executed as a "traitor."[111]

A Palestinian constable was assassinated in Haifa three days later (June 14), and more communications were sabotaged. Four Palestinians were hit by a bomb thrown at them in Haifa on June 26, two police inspectors were assassinated by a land mine outside their house in Jerusalem, and when the British put up posters in Tel Aviv condemning terrorism, all were torn down. *With blood and fire Judea will rise* typified the graffiti painted on the walls in their stead.

On the morning of June 27, the missionary-run Syrian Orphanage was bombed, wounding six Palestinians, including a boy left in serious condition. The next day, the Military Commander in Jerusalem reported a particularly "flagrant case" of the Jewish settlers "aiding and abetting terrorism": When a Palestinian man, attacked and injured by a Jewish settler west of Nahalat Shimon quarter, managed to wrest the gun from the attacker, the "Jews from the neighbourhood ... instead of assisting in the capture of the would be murderer," freed him and reunited him with his gun. Anti-Palestinian terror continued the next day (June 29) with "the killing and wounding of a number of Arabs in six separate shooting attacks by Jews this morning." Thirteen murdered and four wounded was the British tally of that morning's anti-Palestinian violence.[112]

"An Arab was shot dead this morning" again on June 30, the *Times* reported. Later that day, a Palestinian bus was attacked in Jerusalem, and a bomb "of Jewish origin" exploded in an Arab café on Mamilla Road, with eleven casualties.

"The month of July opened with two days of respite from Jewish terrorist attacks," the British reported, but on July 3 another Arab café was blown up, killing one Palestinian and injuring thirty-five. Early the next morning, "two Jews threw a bomb into an Arab truck near Rehavia quarter of Jerusalem ... the Jews escaping to Rehavia," and another Palestinian was shot "by an unknown Jew" in Jerusalem. "[Jewish] outrage succeeded outrage," a British report lamented.[113]

An indication of the "background," ongoing terror against Palestinians is found in the following extract of an Irgun diary covering a seven day period from late June to early July, 1939. It is taken principally from a fragment seized by the British, and is supplemented with Irgun records from the Israeli state.

- June 26, 1939 at 5:30 A.M. an Arab carriage was fired at by our men in the vicinity of Beit Shearim. Four Arabs were killed and one wounded and died later. On the same day, a short time after this, our men fired at four Arabs on the way of Ness Ziona to Rishon le Zion. Three Arabs were killed and one wounded. At 8:20 an Arab was killed by our men at Mea Shearim quarter, Jerusalem.

- June 17, 1939 at 7:00 a bomb thrown by our people exploded near the Shneller School in Jerusalem. Six Arabs were wounded.

- June 28, 1939 at 5 A.M. an Arab was wounded on the Nebi-Samuel Road. At noon a bomb was exploded in a lane opposite the Anglo-Palestine Bank, Haifa. At 2:30 P.M. an Arab was killed in Jurianno Square, Haifa. At 7:20 P.M. a bomb exploded in a house in Wadi Salib Quarter, Haifa.

- June 19, 1939 a few minutes part past 5 A.M. our men opened fire on two Arabs on the Petah-Tikva - Rosh-Ha-Ayin Road. Two killed and the third badly wounded. At the same time two Arabs were shot at km 78 on the Haifa-Jaffa Rd. One killed and the other badly wounded. At 5:30 A.M. an Arab was shot and killed on the Jaffa - Tel Aviv Road. At 5:30 A.M. shots were fired at an Arab cart near Sha'araim. Four Arabs killed and one badly wounded—died later. At 6:15 A.M. two mines exploded under a train between Acre and Haifa. Railway tracks were demolished. A locomotive and three coaches derailed. There were no Jews on this train. At 6:30 A.M. an Arab was killed near the Sheik-Munis orange grove. [Added at the end of the casualty tally for the day:] One of the wounded died.

- June 30, 1939 at 8 A.M. an Arab was killed by our men at Mea Shearim market, Jerusalem. On the same day a bomb was placed by our men at an Arab cafe in the corner of Mamillah Road and Julian Street exploded. Twelve Arabs were wounded. In the afternoon shots were fired at an Arab bus going from Liftah to Jerusalem. On the same day an Arab who had been wounded on June 29 by Rishon Le Zion died.

- July 4, 1939 at 5:20 P.M. a bomb exploded in the Arab cafe "Edmond" on Kingsway, Haifa, 200 meters (656 ft.) distance from the police station. Official communique said one Arab killed and forty-two wounded.

- July 5, 1939 at 5:30 A.M. a bomb was thrown at a truck carrying Arab workers. Three Arabs were wounded. At the same time Two Arabs were shot in Jaffa Str. near the Sephardi orphanage. One Arab was badly wounded.[114]

On July 20, the Irgun murdered five Palestinians and wounded eight, all "casual pedestrians" in the Jaffa and Tel Aviv area, and bombed the Lydda-Kantara Railway. "Jews demonstrating ... against cancellation of immigration decree" killed seven Palestinians and wounded six on July 22, and thirty-nine Palestinians were killed and forty-six wounded in another terror attack three days later.

When on August 2 Jerusalem's new Broadcasting House was bombed, a Palestinian engineer was killed, as was "a South African Jewess [May Weissenberg, who was] the organizer of the English Children's Hour." The British, correctly, suspected the Revisionists: the attack is confirmed in Irgun records. What the British did not know was that May Weissenberg was the Irgun's inside plant at the station, "mortally wounded by mistake," as the gang put it. The bombing rendered the new station unusable; operations were moved to Ramallah.

No group claimed credit for the attempted bombing of a cricket match in Haifa on August 5, likely targeted because one of the teams was the Haifa police. Smoke led to the discovery of the large, smouldering bomb, which malfunctioned when its timing device triggered it at 5:00 P.M. More attacks went similarly unattributed, such as the bombing of the cutter *Sinbad* on August 9, killing a police sergeant. The Irgun hit an Arab bus in Tiberias with a "clock mine," but on August 18 botched the assassination of a Jewish officer by the name of Gordon, who then fled Palestine. It was more successful on August 26, assassinating Police detective Ralph Cairns and Inspector Ronald Barker in Jerusalem, as well as bombing the Arab market in Jaffa. The gang mined an Arab truck in Tiberias in October, and on August 30 sabotaged the Jerusalem radio station. The British did have one break: police investigating a series of bombings of Palestinian houses traced the origin to a nearby Jewish settlement, thanks to police dogs and a bomb that had failed to explode.

An early, apparently unpublished, report on the Irgun comes from a *Times* correspondent in Geneva who in the summer of 1939 was approached by a man identifying himself as a member of the "Jewish Military Organization." Cell-like in structure ("each member knows only his own immediate chief on whose orders he acts"), the correspondent understood the group to be

> a pretty extensive secret organisation throughout Palestine formed on Nazi lines. Its purpose is to be in readiness to take action against the Arabs ... the organisation has plenty of money at its disposal [and] has the support of the population, without which it could not continue ... his organisation works only among the youth of Jewry, and abandoned the "oppressed" Jews as hopeless ... the ultimate aim was to seize control in Palestine at some future date [and] to colonise Palestine and Transjordan.[115]

In the event of war in Europe (which came two weeks after the meeting), Irgun recruits were to "shape their actions" with Palestine as the objective, a point that confused the correspondent at the time.

In Palestine, contradicting apologists who were attributing the terror to the desperate plight of Jews in Europe, the Irgun clarified that its attacks "were not acts of despair and not acts of revenge," but calculated campaigns of terror, "acts of persons who believe that the Jewish Kingdom will be created by force." Jews who believed otherwise were "Jews of the Ghetto, who are weak and faint-hearted and not strong enough for this revolutionary period."[116]

As World War II broke out, the Jewish Agency made a show of support for the British war effort and said that "a system of registration for service of all Jews between 17 and 50 is now in progress." By September 1940, however, the British conceded that the Agency's "so-called registration at the beginning of the war was purely a political gesture." The Agency, rather, was interested only in a segregated "Jewish" army that would further its territorial claims to Palestine.[117]

Although Palestine was experiencing an excellent orange harvest, the drive to exclude Palestinians from their own long-established trade continued. Harvests were sabotaged for using non-Jewish labor against the orders of the Labour Exchange (Histadrut), the groves at Nes Siyona (Ness Ziona) being one example. Grove owners who hired Palestinians were assaulted, and the non-Jewish workers forced off the grounds. Tel Aviv shops selling "Arab goods" were vandalized.[118]

Histadrut officials "considered that they were immune from arrest" for their violence against non-Jewish workers, and so the British detention of some of its officials under Emergency Regulations came as a shock to the settlements. Protests against the arrests ranged from "a spate of appeals" to the brutal murder of a (Jewish) constable. Histadrut refused to end its race discrimination, offering instead to "retain such Arab labor as is now in their employ" and eliminate non-Jews by attrition—an especially meaningless offer given that Palestinians continued to be violently ousted, and packing sheds burned down if their groves employed any non-Jews. Violence to starve out Palestinians further blurred any distinction between the Jewish settlements' "legitimate" institutions, and the terror gangs.[119]

As for the gangs, the Irgun in particular continued to be "responsible for the indiscriminate slaughter brought about by setting bombs in places frequented by Arab crowds and for waylaying and murdering lone Arabs," as the High Commissioner put it. Their "systematic campaign" against the police continued as well, especially in Tel Aviv, where Zionist militants planted incendiary bombs in police vehicles and murdered Jewish constables.[120]

The largest militia, the Jewish Agency's own Hagana, also remained active during the war. Although presented as a defensive army, it conducted its own terror attacks, often colluding with the Irgun and Lehi to maintain plausible deniability.[121]

Much of the terror in 1940 targeted "uncooperative" Jews. Both the Eden and Orient Cinemas were bombed on March 4, the same day that the printing equipment of the newspaper *Haboker* was attacked for failing to print a Zionist "manifesto." Police and soldiers remained particular targets: a Jewish policeman was beaten to death with iron bars on March 13 for his part in the arrest of Jewish militants, and another was "shot dead in Haifa by Jewish terrorists" on June 26. *Pum*, the Hagana's assassination department, murdered four Jewish soldiers in May as "traitors to the Jewish cause," as the British described it.

"Traitor" was also the Hagana's epitaph for a Sephardic Jew it assassinated on May 3. Printing presses serving German Jewish immigrants in their native tongue were hit by arson, one on 30 March, another on April 8. Two Egged buses were set afire by the Irgun or Lehi on August 15, and violence continued against shops selling or purchasing Palestinian goods or produce. Jews refusing payment to the JNF were threatened, and two Jews who resisted a special "tax" ("Kofer Hayishuv") imposed by the Jewish Agency had their cars bombed. The stoning of police was commonplace, but attempts to bomb police cars or public buildings were often unsuccessful as the militants' technical abilities were still evolving. Lehi, new and short of finances, devoted much of its efforts to robbery. Remnants of Arab robber gangs raided both Arabs and Jews; one attacked a Jewish milk truck on 26 March, killing the assistant driver.

Italian warplanes interrupted the internal violence, attacking Haifa on July 15 and 14, and again on September 6 and 8-9 in the Tel Aviv–Jaffa area. On the last raid the fascists dropped white, pink, and yellow propaganda leaflets in Arabic promising the Palestinians liberation; these, according to the British, were ridiculed by their intended converts. More Axis raids followed on September 21 and 26.[122]

The most deadly single terror attack to hit Palestine unfolded in November 1940, when the British transferred the passengers from three illegal immigrant vessels, the *Pacific*, the *Milos*, and the *Atlantic*, onto the ship *Patria* for the trip to Mauritius, where there were facilities for the DPs. The last refugees were put aboard on November 24. At about 9:15 the next morning, a powerful explosion (or two in quick succession) ripped open the vessel and "almost at once," a British committee headed by Supreme Court judge Alan Rose reported, "the ship listed to starboard and within fifteen minutes of the explosion she had heeled over completely" in Haifa port. An estimated 267 people were killed and 172 injured. More than 200 of the dead were Jews fleeing the war in Europe; about 50 were crew and soldiers.[123]

"Much protestation of innocence" from both the Irgun and the Jewish Agency followed the massacre. The British suspected the Irgun. The bombing was however soon proven to be the work of the Agency's Hagana under the authority of future Prime Minister Moshe Sharett (then Shertok), saddling the Jewish Agency with a public relations nightmare: how to square its mass murder of Europe's Jewish survivors with the Zionist settler project? The answer was to circulate the story that it was the DPs themselves who blew up their ship. It was a mass suicide.

Sharett argued behind Agency doors that mythicizing the *Patria* disaster into a tragic legend of heroism and sacrifice would serve the Zionist cause, both then and for future historians. Future Israeli Minister of Defense Pinhas Lavon was not convinced, but agreed that there is no "necessary link between the legend and the truth." The Yishuv's media followed suit, proposing epic plays and poetry to immortalize the victims as willing suicidal heroes who, with a logic that is not addressed, sacrificed themselves in the hope that in the future some might live. Implicit in the posthumous exploitation of the *Patria* dead was its windfall for Zionism's appetite for Biblical tie-ins: the *Patria* was a modern-day Masada.* The lie was still being spread in print nine years later by the author and journalist Arthur Koestler :

> The passengers blew up their ship. They had reached their journey's end. They were not even threatened with deportation back to Europe; only to a tropical island [Mauritius] without hope of return.[124]

The British committee investigating the tragedy was unsure "whether the loss of life was due to the saboteurs having bungled, or whether they were callously prepared to risk killing a number of the passengers in order to sink the ship" to prevent temporary safe haven for them in Mauritius. Much later, in 1957, one Monya Mardor claimed to have been the Hagana's bomber, and claimed that they intended to cripple the vessel but not sink it. Inescapably, the Jewish Agency was indeed "prepared to risk killing a number of the passengers," especially as most of the DPs were trapped in its lower level, vulnerable even if the ship remained afloat.[125]

Catastrophe struck several of these vessels bringing would-be immigrants to Palestine. The SS *Salvador* capsized in the Bosphorus in 1940 with the loss of 350 lives, and more than twice that number perished in the ageing *Struma*, whose organizers solicited immigrants through an advertising campaign whose prospectus "read like a summer camp brochure." In early February 1942 the frail vessel,

---

* According to Roman historian Josephus (first century A.D.), in ca. A.D. 73-74, 960 Jews holed up on the Masada, a high, steep mountain plateau by the Dead Sea, committed suicide or killed each other on the approach of Roman troops.

dangerously overcrowded and beset with engine trouble, reached Istanbul through the Black Sea carrying 10 crew and 781 immigrants. Landing permits for Palestine promised by the organizers did not materialize, and British attempts to facilitate the transfer to Palestine of the vessel's children aged 11-16 failed. Britain claimed to know that the Gestapo had been behind some of these immigration vessels, that Reich agents were aboard, and thus that the vessels represented a security threat. Whatever the case, Turkish authorities towed the *Struma* back through the Bosphorus Strait into the Black Sea, where its engine failed again. The vessel drifted until sinking with the loss of all aboard save for one nineteen-year-old refugee. A Russian torpedo was the likely cause.[126]

The Jewish Agency seized upon the *Struma* tragedy to reinforce its calls for Jews *not* to join the Allied struggle against the Nazis, a call it had already made during May Day festivities that year (1940). Palestine, the argument went, was the natural home of all Jews, and no Jew should fight except in defense of that home. Jews should fight only as a segregated "Jewish" army that would be a *de facto* recognition of a Zionist state, an idea dating from World War I that Ben-Gurion was presently pushing and would culminate with the creation of the so-called "Jewish Brigade."

Recent German immigrants to Palestine were outraged by Zionism's exploitation of the horrors they had just fled, and this outrage was given voice by the prominent journalist Robert Weltsch, who had been editor of the twice-weekly Berlin newspaper *Jüdische Rundschau* until it was banned by the Nazis in 1938. In a speech in Tel Aviv, Weltsch warned that Zionist leaders

> have not yet understood that the enemy seeks the destruction of the Jews ... We who have been here only a few years, we know what Nazism is.

Zionists take "part in the crash of European Jewry only as spectators," fighting the British and keeping Jews from joining the Allied struggle while getting comfortable and rich from their political project in Palestine. Recent immigrants from Germany and Central Europe know the truth in Europe but have no representation in the Zionist politic. If they did, "we would have demanded that the Yishuv should put itself at the disposal of Britain for the fight against Hitler and Nazism." But

> They do not want to fight against Hitler because his fascist methods are also theirs ... They do not want our young men to join the [Allied] Forces ... day after day they are sabotaging the English War Effort.

The Agency, he continued, wanted the *Struma* passengers only to serve the Zionist cause. "It rejected all other possibilities of saving them, [and] this was a very great crime." It had the audacity to conflate the *Struma* tragedy with that of the *Patria*, whose victims "were the fault of the Jews" (blown up by the Hagana). Sharett's and Ben-Gurion's exploitation of the *Struma* was, in Weltsch's words, "an injustice to the dead."[127]

After violence against Jews erupted in Iraq on June 1-2, 1941, an Iraqi Jewish witness, Naeim Giladi, claimed that it was a British false-flag operation designed to justify the return of British rule to Iraq. Independently, Lehi reached the same conclusion, reporting in its *Communique* that "Churchill's Government is responsible for the pogrom in Baghdad," and British documents strongly suggest this as well.* The Mufti may have been an objective: he had ensconced himself there and was colluding with the Italian fascists. The previous November, British officials had discussed "possible action against [the Mufti, and] it was decided that the only really effective means of securing control over him would be a military occupation of Iraq." Although the Foreign Office was working to "get a new Government in Iraq" in order "to clip the Mufti's wings," some officials suggested that this cleric's influence was overstated. According to documents uncovered a decade later, Zionist activity to pressure Jews to emigrate from Iraq to Palestine began about this time.[128]

British records covering a two-week period in the summer of 1941 offer a glimpse into how the Irgun dealt with those refusing

---

* TNA, CO 733/420/19, released as a result of the author's FOI request, leaves no doubt that the British conspired to create instability in Iraq in order to justify their renewed control; although none of the readable text actually states that staged anti-Jewish violence was the method used, the documents are heavily redacted.

to support it. On June 28, a bomb was thrown at the house of a Mr. Zweig of Ramat Gan, a first warning for an unpaid demand for £P.200; there would be no second warning. On July 3 a Mr. Rosner of Tel Aviv was abducted and taken to Ramat Gan, where he was tortured on account of his refusal to pay £P.400. Eight days later a bomb exploded outside his house in Tel Aviv. On July 6 a bomb was thrown at the house of a Mr. Dankner in Petah Tiqva, who was ordered to pay £P.400, and six days later his business premises at Petah Tiqva were wrecked by a bomb.[129]

"To be treated as most secret" is the red ink heading accompanying a transcript of a meeting of twenty people held in London on September 9, 1941. Present were Weizmann (who had called the meeting), Ben-Gurion, three of the Rothschilds, other Zionist leaders such as Selig Brodetsky and Simon Marks (of Marks & Spencer), and the prominent non-Zionist industrialist, Robert Waley Cohen.

Discussing the path to the proposed Jewish State, the conversation ran along the lines of George Orwell's still-to-be-published *Animal Farm*, in which all animals are equal, but some are more equal than others. Anthony de Rothschild began by stressing that there would be no "discrimination ... against any group of its citizens" in the Jewish state, not even "to meet immediate needs," as equality and non-discrimination were principles "for which Jewry has always stood". Weizmann and Ben-Gurion also assured the sceptics: "Arabs" would have equal rights. However, within that absolute equality, Jews would have special privileges. Weizmann's "equality" included the transfer of most non-Jews out of Palestine while permitting "a certain percentage of Arab and other elements" to remain in his Jewish state, the insinuation being as a pool of cheap labor. Anthony de Rothschild's vision of equality and non-discrimination ("not even to meet immediate needs") was equally compelling: it "depended on turning an Arab majority into a minority," and to achieve this, there would be "no equal rights" for non-Jews.

Cohen found the scheme dangerous "for everyone concerned," submitting that the Zionists were "starting with the kind of aims with which Hitler had started," and which "seemed to be based on one religion and one race." Cohen did not stop there: he suggested that if a state with equality for everyone were indeed intended, the state should be named with a neutral geographic term such as "Palestine," not a religious name that denoted "one the basis of race or religion." Lewis Bernstein Namier refuted Cohen: he argued that if the state had a non-Jewish name, "they would never get a Jewish majority," in effect acknowledging the use of messianism as a calculated strategy. Ben-Gurion and Weizmann, too, were adamant that the state must have a "Jewish" name, with Ben-Gurion proposing "Judea" as well as the presumed "Eretz Israel.". In another obvious but rarely spoken admission, Ben-Gurion clarified that the "Jewish state" was *not* based on Judaism, not on the Jewish faith; it was, rather, based on being a "Jew"(i.e., by his racial definition).

Asked about borders of his settler state, Weizmann continued in the same surreal manner. He replied that he would consider the Peel Commission's Partition plan, but that "the line" (the Partition) "would be the Jordan." This was nonsensical: the Jordan was the Commission's eastern border for the two states, and so Weizmann's "partition" meant 100% for his state, 0% for the Palestinians—that is, no partition. All that was left of the Commission's plan was the ethnic cleansing of non-Jews. He went further still: he would "very much" like to "cross the Jordan" (take Transjordan along with Palestine). At the end of the meeting Weizmann sought to put his proposals into effect officially in the name of all Jews worldwide. Those against his proposals were, in his word, "antisemites."[130]

The first major attack of 1942 occurred on January 20, when the police received an anonymous tip that an explosion was heard at 8 Yael Street in Tel Aviv. Five policemen responded to the lure. The bombs that ripped apart the house as they entered killed four of them on the spot, the fifth probably surviving only because twenty-nine sticks of gelignite failed to explode. All but one of the victims were Jewish. One of the dead had thwarted a Palestinian attack against Jews in 1937, and another was to testify against Lehi members for the murder of two bystanders, both Jewish, during a Lehi robbery. According to the War Office, this "cold blooded act of terrorism" was not the first time Lehi had used the trick of luring people into a house rigged to explode.

After Lehi assassinated three more police officers the following month (February 1942), the British caught its leader, Avraham Stern. Stern got no further—he was shot dead by the officer who captured him, Geoffrey Morton, when he tried to escape (some allege that Morton simply executed him while no one was looking). Morton himself proved difficult to assassinate—Lehi tried on May 1 by planting a massive mine on a roadside where Morton's car would be passing, but Morton's driver veered to the middle of the road to overtake a bicyclist just before the lethal spot. The car was not directly hit and all the occupants survived the blast.[131]

On May 11, a meeting of Zionist leaders led to the so-called "Biltmore Program" after the name of the New York hotel where the conference took place. Authored by Ben-Gurion and endorsed by Weizmann, the Biltmore platform demanded the complete and unconditional surrender of all of Palestine to the Zionists. The goals of the Revisionists were now those of mainstream Zionism. Judge Proskauer, who, though a dedicated Zionist, resisted the Biltmore's extremism, was branded "a traitor to his race" by American Zionist leaders like Stephen Wise and Abba Silver. The adoption of the Biltmore Program was denounced by the *NY Times*' publisher Sulzberger, and by such prominent rabbis as Lazaron (Baltimore) and Wolsey (Philadelphia), and led to the formation of the anti-Zionist American Council for Judaism.[132]

Compiling meticulous, comprehensive intelligence about the "Arab" areas was essential to the Jewish Agency's long-range plans, and this was accomplished through surveillance teams posing as "hiking parties" or "walking tours." In an early description of these from April 1942, the British do not yet appear to understand their actual purpose (it was presumed merely to be "illegal training"), and indeed it is mentioned only because of an accident. During the Passover holidays,

> parties of Jews consisting mainly of men and women and of students arrange extensive walking tours, frequently through Arab areas. A popular journey is to the Dead Sea. It practically invariably means taking a route through an area of Palestine that is completely Arab...

One such party consisted of 156 men and women aged 15-27, who having "completed that theoretical part of a course of pre-military training held by the HAGANA, proceeded to the Dead Sea hills in order to carry out practical training." An "exercise" was to commence at 4:00 A.M. on April 9, and so at 3:45 A.M. one group was preparing breakfast—oblivious that close to the cooking fire was a sack containing hand grenades. Six of the "hikers" were killed and ten seriously wounded. Several hours later, "thirteen Jewish Youths and five girls" returning from the Dead Sea and well-armed, were stopped by the police near Nablus. By this date the surveillance 'hikes' were already well-established: the authorities had frequently warned the Agency against the practice, "but to no avail."[133]

At about eight o'clock on the morning of April 22, 1942, as Assistant Inspector General of Police M. J. McConnell drove away from his Jerusalem residence, wires connecting a bomb to his steering column and chassis snapped. A few minutes later, his Palestinian servant noticed something strange on the ground. When he picked it up, it exploded, killing him. Three hours later, a child noticed a peculiar object on the side of the road near the house of the Inspector General. The child, fortunately, drew the attention of a passing constable to this second Lehi car bomb of that morning that had broken loose of its wires and failed to kill its intended victim—this one containing seventy sticks of gelignite and six-and-a-half pounds of rivets. Police dogs followed the scent to a nearby Jewish suburb (Rehavia), there losing the trail. According to British intelligence, had either of the assassinations succeeded, a grander terror attack awaited the funeral. A further Lehi assassination attempt on 1 May also failed. When on May 19 police attempted to seize an armoury of illegal weapons at Givat Haim, 500 settlers convened to block them, and rather than precipitate a confrontation, the police left.[134]

While Lehi, specializing in assassinations, grew slowly, the ranks of the Irgun, which focussed on large-scale destruction, swelled. Irgun recruitment records show that during a one-month period between July-August of 1942, it admitted "680 youths and girls" into the organization "after the rejection of the medically unfit."[135]

Intolerance for Jews with insufficiently Zionist views continued to tighten, and with it intolerance for any Jew using his or her native German. The problem with German was twofold: it was iconic of assimilation, and it was a rupture in the messianic imagery of a Hebrew-speaking Biblical realm. *Orient*, a German language weekly which was, as US Intelligence described it, "published by German Jews of the old liberal type," had recently been suppressed by the Zionists' Council for the Propagation of the Hebrew Language, and when on May 31, 1942 German-speaking Jewish immigrants attempted to hold a meeting of the Anti-Fascist League in Tel Aviv's Esther Cinema, it was violently broken up by thugs that included the sons of Jewish Agency officials.

Blumenthal Neuste Nachrichten was a German language daily authored by Jewish immigrants and produced by the Aliyah Hadashah (New Immigrants Party). It reflected a softer form of Zionism than the orthodoxy of the Jewish Agency and the terror gangs, and so on June 12 the newspapers were burned, and shortly after midnight Blumenthal's printing press was blown up. The blast was so strong that it injured five people in an adjoining building and started a fire that spread and seriously damaged a neighboring house.[136]

A meeting between Revisionist and Agency representatives said to have taken place about this time produced the following summary of "the enemies of Jewry": the foremost enemy was non-Zionist Jews; the second was "the democracies and their Atlantic Charter";* and lastly, "Arabs." The British foresaw the Jewish Agency's tactical reason for fuelling an alleged "Arab problem" that would never end, and an intelligence officer noted the "self-centred and patronizing attitude" to the Palestinians that "make any protestations on the part of the Zionists of desire for good relations with the Arabs seem very unreal." The Irgun had already begun the task of morphing Hitler into the Palestinians, plastering posters that warned that "Arabs"

---

* The Atlantic Charter of August, 1941, was an agreement among the Allies of post-war goals; principal among them were no territorial enlargement or territorial changes made against the wishes of the people, and self-determination. It became the basis for the United Nations.

were "making vigorous underground preparations to destroy the last of our people's hope."[137]

The role of Nazism in the Zionists' plans was on Ben-Gurion's mind when he stopped in Palestine between trips to the United States and England. In Jerusalem on October 4, 1942 he told Jewish Agency leaders that although Hitler had made Jews suffer, he also "revive[d] in assimilated Jews the feeling of Jewish nationalism, [and] we have exploited this feeling in favor of Zionism." Democracy, however, threatened to undo it. Jewish nationalism is

> slowly disappearing again because the democracies, in contrast to the dictator states, recognize the Jews as people having full rights of citizenship ... [and so] in America there now exists a strong movement away from Zionism.

Fully 85% of America's Jewry, he warned, were "assimilationists," a setback he blamed again on America's "democratic attitude." Another Agency speaker agreed, condemning the democratic countries and their Atlantic Charter as enemies of Jewry, an echo of the Agency's September meeting. Ben-Gurion then moved to oust any Agency members with diverging views, in particular anyone who voted with the socialist Hashomer Hatzair and their acknowledgment of Palestinian national rights. Meanwhile, Weizmann met with the political theorist and philosopher Isaiah Berlin in England, telling him that Jews (implicitly as a "race") were incapable of establishing roots anywhere but in Palestine, and that the "Arabs" need to "be told firmly" that they will never have a state.[138]

British pamphlets fell from the sky over Haifa on the first day of November 1942, urging people to enlist in His Majesty's Forces against the Axis powers. By the end of the year, about 9,000 Palestinian Arabs had enlisted with the Allied forces, notwithstanding reluctance to join a battle that would not bring them their own freedom. As the Haifa advocate Elias Koussa reminded the High Commissioner in an eloquent fourteen-page response to the pamphlets, Palestinians had flocked of their own accord to join the British in the previous world war, but Britain then betrayed its promise of liberation. Recruitment among the

Yishuv was hampered for quite a different reason: Zionist leaders' continuing determination that Jews enlist only as an exclusively "Jewish" army that would further the cause of Zionist statehood, not as equal soldiers in the common front.

Palestinian Allied recruits in Nablus, May 6, 1941.

The Jewish Agency maintained its opposition to Jews joining the Allied struggle against the Nazis even though the present month—November of 1942—brought hard news of the death camps, Hebrew newspapers being "flooded with reports on Nazi atrocities on the Jews in Occupied Territories, most of them appearing with black-bordered columns." One or two of the papers took up the theme that "[n]ow is the chance for Jews to join the Army and go to the rescue of our bretheren [sic]," and into December, Nazi atrocities in the Occupied Countries remained "the main item in the Hebrew newspapers almost every day."[139]

Lehi invoked the Old Testament to preach against Jews joining the Allied struggle. "The Jewish youth does not want to enlist in this Gog and Magog War," a Lehi broadcast said in December of 1941—the two apocalyptic monsters serving as Lehi's Biblical reference to the Allies and the Axis—"because it is not the war of the Jews," not one for their "national interests (a Zionist state)." The Biblical stage the ever-present prop, Lehi then decried that "a foreigner [i.e., the British High Commissioner] is placed on the seat of King David."[140]

The Jewish Agency's arsenal-building further compromised the Allied struggle. What the War Cabinet described as "a large-scale arms stealing racket [from the Allied forces] organized by the Jewish authorities" was "directly undermining the war effort" against the Axis, draining Allied resources "as if they were paid by Hitler himself." Sabotage training was also sought clandestinely from the Allies.[141]

On New Year's day of 1943, "a Jew whose integrity ... is not open to question" approached high-placed British authorities in great secrecy because he was "profoundly disquieted" by the direction of the Jewish settlements. Code-named "Z," he made an "earnest plea that Government should act now before the [Zionist] movement grew too strong; he instanced the parallel development of the Nazi movement." Settler youth, Z reported, were being enlisted *en masse*, with the greatest esteem placed on what Z called "S.S. Squads" after the Nazi death squads, a reference to the Hagana's Palmach.

1943

Z, as it turned out, was J.S. Bentwich, Senior Inspector of Jewish Schools, ironically the brother of Norman Bentwich, former attorney-general of Palestine who had helped champion the Balfour Declaration and whose actions as attorney-general caused Britain embarrassment for his unabashed favoritism to the Zionists.[142]

Henry Hunloke, Defence Security Officer in Palestine, reported in January 1943 that the Hagana was preparing to secure the Zionist state by force, but "as a feeble conscious saver for the outer world they will say that the British were unable to protect them and their settlements." Hunloke—who a year later would fall under suspicion of compromising intelligence to a Jewish mistress—said that the Jewish Agency "make one think that they have picked the strangest parts of Nazism, Fascism, Communism with a spicing of Tammany Hall* as the system best suited for the control of Jews in Palestine." Those with more moderate views are tolerated only until they become

---

* "Tammany Hall" is a reference to political patronage, graft, and corruption in the US Democratic Party in New York in the second half of the nineteenth century through the first quarter of the twentieth.

influential. "From a tender age," children are brought up to have one aim only, the fulfilment of Zionism, and children have walked out on their parents when the parents try to instil some moderation on that aim. The system "is closely akin to that adopted by the Nazis," and as history has shown, "in a comparatively short space of time, such teaching is very hard to eradicate." Mutilated bodies are found with labels tied to them stating: "This is what happens to an informer."

Immigration, Hunloke reported, was the ever-present focus, with Poland, Russia, and North Africa looked to for new settlers. But the Jews of North Africa were difficult: they "are not Zionist-minded," and so "propagandists are at present being trained in Palestine" to recruit them. "The [Jewish] Agency at the moment are exerting every effort to Zionise Jews in various North African territories," and "any method will be adopted" to achieve Zionism's political goal. Important among these methods was to "stir up anti-Semitism ... in order to force Jews ... to come to Palestine."[143]

Dr. Arieh Altman, chairman of a delegation of the New Zionist Organization (NZO, a Revisionist group founded by Jabotinsky), said much the same: anti-Semitism must "form the foundation of Zionist propaganda." Keeping alive the threat of anti-Semitism, Dr. Altman argued, would persuade Jews in Britain or America to emigrate to Palestine, and "non-Jewish support [for Zionism] in America could also be increased by emphasising the advantages" of the settler project in "reducing the number of Jews" coming into the US.[144]

Zionism's need for perpetual anti-Semitism was the essence of Irgun-founder Ze'ev Jabotinsky's message when he preached that Zionism must remain in a permanent state of emergency. In the 1940s, his son Eri was working with Peter Bergson's US organization as it attained, in the words of Israeli Defence Minister and Knesset member Moshe Arens, "unparalleled influence in many circles of American society as well as in the U.S. administration and in Congress." Some light on their operation is preserved in a letter, intercepted and copied by the British, from Eri to a friend in Jerusalem. Jabotinsky explains to his friend that they were operating under the name Committee for a Jewish Army, and that in January 1942, Bergson "hit upon a new idea."[145]

We bought a page in the 'New York Times' and advertised the Committee for a Jewish Army just the way you would advertise Chevrolet motor cars or Players cigarettes. The full page advertisement created a sensation. A coupon under the advertisement asked the public to send in their names and a contribution to cover the expenses. The results were so encouraging that we have since kept up a campaign of full page advertisements throughout the country. The advertisements have appeared in New York, Philadelphia, Washington, Chicago and Los Angeles at regular intervals. Other cities like Detroit, San Francisco, Houston (Texas), and others, have had one or two advertisements each. The results were astounding.[146]

The Committee, posing as a "non-sectarian, non-partisan, American organization," composed a letter addressing only venerable principles and sent it to one hundred men taken out of the *Who's Who*. Ten replied. New stationery was then printed containing the names of those ten prominent men (as though they were part of the organization), and a second letter was sent to a thousand people. This procedure was repeated several times.

Among their other tactics of self-promotion was what he described as "the most beautiful act of sabotage that I have ever witnessed," in which they hijacked a religious day. "Everyone got the impression that the fasting, the mourning, the pious demonstration in the synagogues ... were all a part of the Jewish Army business". But he is now, Jabotinsky tells his friend, "active in a new field: the saving of the Jews of Europe," and this banner served the terror organization's fund-raising for the next few years.[147]

Full-page Irgun fund-raising ads openly exploited anti-Semitism and dismissed any answer to the catastrophe in Europe other than a Zionist state in Palestine. Although "five million people are condemned to die," the Irgun warned in a 1943 *NY Times* ad, it quickly assured the reader that "America is not asked to open HER doors to the uprooted Jewish millions," but exclusively Palestine's doors. The New Zionist Organization of America used the same appeal to anti-Semitism: In a three-quarter page *NY Times* ad, it threatened that without a Jewish state in Palestine, "America will face increasing pressure to open her doors" to Jewish DPs. "It will be difficult for her to refuse."[148]

For those in the US who might in fact be happy to welcome Jews to their country, the propaganda threatened their own good reputations, smearing (as British intelligence described it) "those who oppose Zionist aims, and even those who do not actively support them," as "lacking in humanitarianism, failing in Christianity, anti-Semitic, by implication pro-Nazi."[149]

News of the Warsaw Ghetto Uprising led Zionist leaders to posthumously conscript its victims, like those of the *Patria*, as a mass suicide in the service of the settler state, thus trivializing their courage and hardship. Few ghetto fighters lived to speak for themselves, but one who did, Marek Edelman, condemned Zionism and refused to endorse the Israeli state as the heir to, or moral outcome of, the Holocaust. He was marginalized, and his account of the Uprising, *The Ghetto Fights*, was silenced in Israel.[150]

Zionist officials sent not a single emissary to the ghettos of Poland. Rescue, Ben-Gurion preached, was not Zionism's top priority; the top priority was furthering the Zionist state, what he referred to as "internal action." The "Jewish Conference is alive," the December 11, 1943 *Jewish Daily Forward* complained, only when it concerns Palestine, "and it is asleep when it concerns rescue work." As Hagana member and future Israeli politician Eliezer Livneh would later explain, "the rescue of Jews was not an aim in itself, but only a means." Yitzhak Gruenbaum, ironically head of the WZO's Palestinian Rescue Committee, was emphatic that calls for rescue were "dangerous to Zionism." *Can't you stop work on the Zionist state*, people would ask him, "at a time when Jews are being murdered and slaughtered by hundreds-of-thousands and by millions, at a time in which there is a need to concentrate all the efforts for their rescuing?" No,

> I do not accept such a saying. And when some asked me: 'Can't you give money from Keren Ha Yesod [a fund for building the state] to save Jews in the Diaspora?' I said: No! And again I say no! ... we do not give priority to rescue ... Zionism is over everything.[151]

Referring to those pushing for rescue as "pleaders," Gruenbaum invoked Zionism's unfailing companion, messianism, to explain why the settler project was more important than saving Europe's condemned Jews. "Whenever Jews underwent a disaster," Gruenbaum argued, "our ancestors saw the footsteps of the Messiah. Our history does not extol the pleaders ... But history extols the Messiahs, that made heroic efforts for the redemption of the nation."[152]

Just as an end to anti-Semitism was an anathema to the "redemption of the nation," so was reconstruction in Europe, since recovery from the war would make it harder to get Jewish DPs to leave (and, presumably, go to Palestine). Thus when in the fall of 1943 the British began to look ahead to post-war European development and reconstruction, Ben-Gurion and other Zionist leaders "urged the Jewish community to adopt an attitude of non-cooperation" with the Allies' reconstruction plans. The Jewish Agency's blanket opposition to post-war reconstruction brought the resignation of a Dr. Senator, its only remaining moderate member.[153]

Zionists "would have got further towards rescuing the unfortunates in Axis Europe, had they not complicated the question by always dragging Palestine into the picture"—so judged a report by US Intelligence in the Middle East, dated June 4, 1943, entitled "Latest Aspects of the Palestine Zionist-Arab Problem." It described "Zionism in Palestine" as "a type of nationalism which in any other country would be stigmatized as retrograde Nazism." The continuation of anti-Semitism was essential for the settler project, it reported; and whereas "assimilated Jews in Europe and America are noted for being ... stout opponents of racialism and discrimination," Zionism has bred the opposite mentality in Palestine, "a spirit closely akin to Nazism, namely, an attempt to regiment the community, even by force, and to resort to force to get what they want." Independently, Britain's War Cabinet as well was warning that the Jewish settlers were becoming "more and more regimented on totalitarian lines," so that "any Jew who openly opposes the 'party line' is in personal danger."[154]

The US Intelligence report cited the fate of the German language weekly *Orient* as one example. Its January 1943 issue condemned the "Yishuv Nazis" and their "super-Zionism," which it said were as bad as the super-nationalism of the German Reich; and in a February issue, the physicist Wolfgang Yourgrau attacked "the totalitarian monster" gripping the Jewish settlements, "even in the ranks of the Left parties." The periodical then fell victim itself: it closed from harassment, and a bomb was planted in the press that had published *Orient* and other non-Hebrew (German and Yiddish) publications. Kiosks were bombed for selling non-Hebrew papers to Jews, and cafés and cinemas were bombed if they did not stay closed through to the end of the Sabbath. Anti-Gentilism was rife: "Tel Aviv barely tolerates other than Jews," the US report stated, "where they even object to the use of the cross on Red Cross ambulances passing through the town" (because of its Christian symbolism).[155]

US intelligence assailed "the crude conception" being spread of the Palestinian people as "a nomad tent-dweller ... with a little seasonal agriculture," as being "too absurd to need refutation." Citing the Palestinians' priority for education and interest in modern agricultural techniques, the report noted the irony that it was from them that Zionist settlers learned the cultivation of Jaffa oranges. Whereas the Palestinians were self-sufficient, the Zionists settlements exist on massive external financing, and should Jews overseas ever tire of supporting the settlers, "the venture will collapse like a pricked balloon." The conclusion of this early US intelligence report was however naïve: now that the world "has seen the lengths to which the Nazi creed has carried the nations," it reasoned that the Zionists "are due to find themselves an anachronism."[156]

In late 1943, a campaign of meetings, plays, and songs was launched to encourage people to have more children, which was one of the Irgun's six "Commandments," but only "ethnically pure" children: presaging the "purity of blood" laws of the Israeli state, a parallel campaign more aggressively sought to prevent Jews from befriending non-Jews.[157]

It is at this point that the Irgun began to dismiss the ongoing war as a consideration in moderating its actions. As Begin would later explain, in late 1943 and early 1944 "it became obvious" that the war effort would not lead to a "Hebrew Nation" on both sides of the Jordan, and so their terror in Palestine would resume without regard for the Nazi threat.[158]

The close of 1943 also brought the rambling end of a four-year attempt to create a Zionist state by "purchasing" it for twenty million British pounds payable to Saudi Arabia's Ibn Saud, who would have become Palestine's ultimate absentee landlord. Weizmann and St. John Philby, adventurer and father of the double agent Kim Philby, were its tireless advocates. It was generally known as the "Philby Plan," though Weizmann claimed that it originated with Churchill, who suggested the idea to him in the fall of 1939. Weizmann tried to solicit support for the scheme from Roosevelt, while Philby went to tempt Ibn Saud.

Once Weizmann thought the scheme might indeed work, he regretted limiting his proposed "purchase" to the land west of the Jordan River (i.e., all of what is now Israel and Palestine), and so in a December 1943 letter to Sumner Welles, who had just retired as Roosevelt's Under Secretary of State, he tried to add Transjordan to the tab. Limiting the "purchase" to the land west of the Jordan, he complained, cut "our heritage ... down to the bone." There was another reason Weizmann wanted Jordan, a consideration he would never voice in public: owning Transjordan, he told Welles, would help in the ethnic cleansing of non-Jews from Palestine—"facilitate transfers of population," as he put it. In the end, however, Ibn Saud expressed great insult that Weizmann expected to "buy" him and betray the Palestinians. The bid was dead.[159]

A relative quiet of late 1943 was the calm before an ever-deadlier storm building to statehood. After five bombs exploded in the truck park of Steel Brothers in Jaffa on the night of January 28-29, wrecking a truck, pamphlets dropped at the scene accused the firm of being "parasites of the foreign [British] government". The Irgun claimed responsibility for the attack in a letter to the Hebrew Press. Lehi, too, had been quiet, as many of its key people had been captured; but three months earlier, on October 31, some twenty Lehi operatives in the Latrun Detention Camp slipped to freedom through a 176 foot long tunnel they had bored. The terror organization was now back in operation, and St. Georges Cathedral—where Israeli whistle-blower

Jan-Feb 1944

Mordechai Vanunu would sequester himself after his release from prison sixty years later, in 2004—was the target of a Lehi bombing on February 3. At 3:00 in the morning, alerted by a Palestinian taxi driver, police found the bombers planting an electrically triggered device (an "infernal machine," as they described it) in the Cathedral wall. They escaped, murdering a Palestinian civilian who had assisted the police.[160]

Nine days later (February 12), Lehi opened fire in Tel Aviv's Hashomer Hatzair Club in retaliation for that socialist party's favoring a binational state. The Irgun was busier that night, bombing the Immigration Offices in Tel Aviv, Jerusalem, and Haifa, using inventive methods to defeat building security. In Jerusalem, the building's guard was distracted with cries for help from a staged street "attack." In Tel Aviv, a sympathetic locksmith supplied a key to an adjoining building, by which four Irgun operatives carried sacks of explosives over the roof. The ruse was most colorful in Haifa: a decoy "couple" passed in deliberate view of the guard's post, then slipped into a nearby doorway and staged a wild sex encounter whose loud moaning was too much for the guard to resist "investigating"—at which the bombers slipped past, bombing an air raid shelter and demolishing the building. The Irgun again claimed credit in a letter to the Hebrew Press. "All non-Jewish bodies holding this country," the Irgun decreed in a pamphlet that month, "are our mortal enemies." Its terror was "a holy battle ... a sacred war, and God will help us."[161]

"We are living through a period of almost official admiration for underground activities," the Hebrew daily *Haboker* acknowledged, as the Irgun warned newspaper editors not to oppose them. But the chief rabbi of Egypt reacted angrily to the "Jewish terrorism," and refused to endorse the Zionist stance on immigration to Palestine, even as Weizmann publicly claimed again to speak for all Jews in supporting it. The Jewish Agency and the American Zionist organizations, meanwhile, were engaged in a world-wide campaign to abrogate the White Paper, which was spun as "anti-Bible," and framed any impediment to funneling Jews (only) to Palestine as the final genocide—"before it is too late to save even the remnant," in a typical phrase from the Jewish Agency. The Palestinians themselves remained tolerant, even as British Political Intelligence in the Middle East (P.I.C.M.E.) speculated that Zionists "would welcome if not actually provoke Arab reaction" to the terror, "in order that they might use the argument of self-defense against the Arabs as further justification for their own illegal acts." (*The writing is on the wall* that Palestine will be made a "Jewish state," one British official wrote in a "most secret" memo in January; *Surely Babylon*, another penciled in.)[162]

On the night of January 14-15, the Irgun bombed government buildings in Jerusalem, and Lehi murdered two more police officers, Inspector Green and Constable Ewer. Lehi's successes continued with two more police assassinations on January 16, but failed on January 24: although the bomb that the gang buried outside the garage of the Deputy Superintendent of Police exploded as he drove out, he survived inside the wrecked vehicle. Similarly, when Lehi operatives pushed a button to detonate a roadside bomb connected by wire some sixty meters (197 ft.)away, it blew up the targeted vehicle, whose four occupants included two inspectors and a sergeant, but all survived their injuries, shock, and deafness. When later in the day a third roadside device was discovered before it was tripped, the British analyzed it: it was a cocktail composed of five hand grenades made in the United States, plus thirty-three sticks of gelignite, ammunition, nuts, and bolts. Further bombings struck the Income Tax Offices in Tel Aviv, Haifa, and Jerusalem on February 26-27. The Irgun posted pamphlets in Haifa claiming responsibility.[163]

Political Terrorism Rises in Palestine, read the headline to a February 26 *NY Times* article about "terrorist activity ... in favor of extremist Jewish nationalist demands." The paper's publisher, Arthur Sulzberger, was among the prominent American Jews opposed to those extremist demands and who refused to finance the Irgun's operations. In response—for US fund-raising purposes only and in irreconcilable conflict with its ideology—Bergson's solicitations for money now distinguished between the "Hebrew nation" and the "Hebrew race." Jews could contribute to help save "stateless Hebrews from oppression" without considering themselves "Hebrew nationalists." The move appears to have helped Irgun coffers: later that year (1944), an informant for the British reported that "Bergson's group of racketeers known as the 'Hebrew Committee of National Liberation' [have] succeeded in collecting large sums of money by posing as refugee organizations and exploiting gullibility of American public."[164]

It is around this time that the Jewish Agency's "hiking parties" (surveillance teams) begin to figure more prominently in British records. Photographs taken by the "hikers" were processed by a secret photography lab fronting as an irrigation company, and mapping was led by a Hebrew University topographer who also worked as a cartographer for the British. Information collected included topographic location of each village, its access roads, quality of land, springs, main sources of income, socio-political composition, religious affiliations, names of the village leaders, ages of individual men, and an index of its hostility toward the Zionist project—everything needed to determine "how best to attack" the villages, in the words of one such "hiker." Details were expanded to encompass husbandry, cultivation, the number of trees, quality of fruit groves, average land holding per family, number of cars, names of shop owners, members of workshops, and the names of the artisans and their skills. When 1948 came, the Zionist armies already had photographs, maps, plans, and meticulous statistics about the villages and villagers they would erase.

"Hiking parties" also served two immediate needs: the data collected enabled the Hagana to conduct more accurate simulated assaults on Palestinian villages, and the "hikes" themselves camouflaged movement to and from hidden military training settlements, such as Ayelet HaShahar. Three such intelligence-gathering groups were discovered spying on Palestinian villages during the first week of February, 1944.[165]

March was marked by Jewish protests over a new Palestinian restaurant in Jerusalem. The problem was the name: "Palestine Restaurant." As reported in the then-popular paper *Hatzofeh*, an Arab business' use of the name *Palestine* was "a deliberate insult to the Jewish public."

March also brought a new spree of assassinations of policemen. One was shot in the back by Lehi in Tel Aviv on March 2, Jewish constable Zev Flesch was murdered on March 13 in Petah Tikvah, more constables were murdered on March 15 and 18, and there were

March 1944

further attacks on police on March 21. March 23 was the deadliest day: eight policemen were murdered by the Irgun in Tel Aviv, Haifa, and Jaffa. Jaffa's toll would have been much higher had a bomb not been discovered in the air raid shelter below police headquarters in time to evacuate before several explosions ripped through it, completely demolishing one end of the building. All three cities' CID (Criminal Investigation Department) offices were blown up by bombers believed to have used such guises as doctors and barbers.[166]

Thanks to an unexpected informer, the police had fifty Irgun members under arrest within the week. However, "Zionist institutions and Yishuv generally," High Commissioner MacMichael reported, "have given no (repeat no) assistance in suppressing these political fanatics partly, no doubt, through fear, but also because, to some extent, they sympathize with them." Support for terrorism was reinforced by the Jewish Agency's "intense Nationalist drive ... for years past through the education of the young, and platform propaganda." The "terrorists regard themselves as the chosen instruments" of Zionist goals. Both the Agency and the terrorists exploit the world's

> sympathy for Jewish suffering, and humanitarian urge to do everything possible to relieve it, and [the resulting] readiness to make every possible concession to [the Zionist] viewpoint.[167]

Responding to charges that the Agency shielded terrorism, Ben-Gurion accused the British of conspiracy: he claimed that the British deliberately failed to catch terrorists so that they could punish all Jews in Palestine. Yet the Jewish Agency was secretly mandating terms to the British to secure its cooperation against terror, conditions that the British found "to say the least of it, amazing," and tantamount to a "condonation of crime." The Agency demanded that the British agree neither to search for terrorists nor to search the settlements for arms; in exchange, the Agency would share only information it wished to. Zionism's supporters meanwhile continued to boast that the settler project is "a virtual gift to the Empire," in the words of the Anglo-Palestinian Club, and that the British Empire's strength "is in direct proportion to the extent of Jewish immigration."[168]

In the US, the Democrats had been the traditional guarantors of Zionist support, but the Irgun now began playing that party off against its rival Republicans, forcing a competition for more vocal support. The NZO's "Resettlement Committee" was busy enlisting US support for "the transfer of [Palestinian] populations" out of Palestine, and a NZO letter seized by the British en route to Irgun member Abraham Abrahams in London—who later would emerge as a key figure in domestic terrorism in Britain—stated that the organization's plans for forced transfer now had the endorsement of four hundred "important representatives of American public opinion" (perhaps garnered through Eri Jabotinsky's list). The Republican Party, hoping to one-up the Democrats, announced its demand for unlimited Jewish immigration into Palestine, and in the UK the Labour Party outdid the US Republicans, issuing a declaration for "the compulsory transfer of the Arab population of Palestine"—a proposal for ethnic cleansing welcomed by Zionist leaders because they were able to show that it was a British idea, not theirs. The Palestinians were, in MacMichael's words, "genuinely shocked" that "the chosen representatives of a large segment of the British public" could advocate forcibly removing them from their homeland for the benefit of the settlers.[169]

Lehi used a grenade to kill a sergeant on the first day of April, 1944, but succeeded only in wounding two constables on April 5. Shoot-outs with police continued, and an assassination attempt on two British constables at the Northern Police Station in Tel Aviv on April 9 failed despite the use of both firearms and explosives. Of several further assassination attempts against police in Tel Aviv on April 10, one was successful.[170]

Zionism's "blood ownership" of Jews made Palestine's Jewish civil servants "traitors" by definition, and so in May, Lehi distributed pamphlets that included a Black List of Jewish policemen. One on the list was assassinated on May 10 with gunshots and a bomb. Mortars and "rearguard action" were used against the Police Fort on 17 May, and that evening "some 40 armed Jews from the coastal area" attempted to hijack the broadcasting station in Ramallah and ambush the police. The attackers shot up the control desk and two aerials

April-July 1944

after unsuccessfully questioning the station operator in Hebrew, but the attack was disrupted by the chance appearance of a Palestinian taxi that ran their blockade.[171]

That evening, about thirty Jews in khaki shirts and shorts used boards studded with nails to incapacitate a taxi with three Palestinians, then ignited explosives under it, knocking the car off the road. The Palestinians survived the blast, but the Jews fired on them as they fled, hitting two. Some hours later, at about 2:30 A.M. on May 18, a police patrol was attacked northeast of Lydda. When police returned the fire and damaged the assailants' truck, the six attackers slipped into the darkness. Shortly afterwards, two more trucks came from the same direction, and (apparently seeing that the first group had met resistance) about eighteen men and women ran from it. In the trucks the police found gelignite and boards studded with nails, as had been used earlier to disable the Palestinian taxi. The trucks had been stolen (their owners attacked and bound) and fitted with false plates.

During the night of July 13-14, the District Police Headquarters and Land Registry Offices were attacked with gelignite bombs, grenades, tommy guns, and automatic pistols, killing two Palestinians and critically wounding a Jewish constable. Militants dressed as police shot the guards as others in plain clothes carried in the explosives. The Irgun "boastfully claimed" responsibility. The next day (July 15), militants hijacked an explosives truck and murdered a constable. More bombings followed on July 28.[172]

"It cannot be denied," the Commissioner's Offices in Jaffa reported that month, "that the recent outrage of the Irgun Zvai Leumi has increased their reputation enormously amongst Jewish youth," and further successes would "considerably enlarge their field for recruits." The Chief Secretary in Jerusalem, similarly, reported that a large segment of the settlements' youth "looks upon these terrorists as the *Kanaim* [holy warriors] of modern times." Palestinians continued to die in Zionist attacks, and this "has inevitably increased Arab hostility towards everything Jewish."[173]

Setbacks to the Nazi armies during the summer of 1944 caused some concern that Zionism would suffer a setback as well.

"In political circles," the Chief Secretary in Jerusalem wrote, "there appears to be some tendency to fear that Nazi oppression will end before it has been possible to obtain permission for large numbers of Jewish refugees to enter Palestine on that account." Similarly, MacMichael reported that Agency leaders were trying to "utilize all remaining vacancies" of the White Paper's 75,000 permits quickly, in order to create an immigration crisis "while the refugee problem is still acute."

Ben-Gurion as well appeared to be addressing the Nazi setbacks when, lecturing in Tel Aviv on April 2, he warned that the defeat of the Axis would not end the threat against Jews—indeed the Allied victory would make matters *worse*, bringing "mounting anti-Semitism" and "many other countries" ready to enact "Hitler's solution."[174]

Ben-Gurion's biggest success of the summer of 1944 was Churchill's creation of the Jewish Brigade, under pressure from the United States but against the overwhelming advice of Churchill's own military. The alleged rationale for an all-Jewish army was that it would afford Jews dignity in the fight against the Nazis.[175]

British generals, however, argued that a segregated brigade was strategically inefficient and only exacerbated the struggle against the Axis. Jews, they noted, already served in the British military along with everyone else. They argued that Zionists demanded a Jews-only army for two reasons unrelated to the Nazis: one, to claim after the war that the segregated Jewish army had been a *de facto* acknowledgment of Jewish "nationality" (and thus of a "Jewish state" in Palestine); and two, to send back to Palestine a professionally trained Zionist army to achieve its political objectives by force.[176]

Those objectives, a Memorandum to the War Cabinet outlined, were a state based on ethnic supremacy :

> It is clear from both the public and private utterances of the Zionist leaders that ... they do not want a joint Jew and Arab state. They want a purely Jewish state, and they are determined to get it, by any means in their power. That is the motive underlying the agitation for a Jewish army ... [The Palestinians] will have no share in the government

of the country—that will be reserved entirely for Jews. We must face the fact that this is their conception, and that they will accept no other.[177]

That state's eventual expansion into Lebanon and Syria was already being pursued. An emissary of the Jewish National Fund was sent that summer to the Lebanese and Syrian governments "for extensions of the Fund's activities to those territories," as MacMichael put it. As the Brigade was being finalized, Ben-Gurion boasted to the Agency that they would take Palestine by force of arms and "if the country be too small, we shall expand its boundaries."

The *NY Times* as well argued that the Brigade was a ploy to claim statehood, and criticized US politicians who pressured Britain to accept it. Sixty-two US rabbis signed a press statement condemning the idea of a segregated Brigade, saying it would "add to the unhappy plight of our stricken people." Writing eloquently against the Brigade, Morris Cohen, Professor Emeritus of Philosophy at City College, described as anti-Semitic the "contention that the Jews are a foreign national group everywhere except in Palestine," and warned that "the complete moral bankruptcy of racialist nationalism [referring to Zionism] has been made obvious by Nazi Germany."[178]

When on August 8, Palestine's High Commissioner Harold MacMichael left Jerusalem for Jaffa, his vehicle was escorted by police fore and aft. At a sharp bend on a cliff the little entourage was ambushed with US grenades and gunfire by about twelve Lehi members disguised as a surveying party. The driver was shot in the neck and lost control of the vehicle, but an officer next to him grabbed the wheel and directed the car to a bank. Another passenger was shot in the lungs, while MacMichael received minor bullet wounds. Police followed the assailants to Givat Shaul settlement, where they were blocked from apprehending them, just as they had been blocked from apprehending Lehi members said to be hiding near a settlement at Beit Dajan three days earlier.[179]

Aug-Sept 1944

Attempts by the police to pursue terrorists in the settlements had created such "severe disorders" by 1943 that MacMichael himself, though considered a hardliner, decreed that no further searches of

Jewish settlements would be made, for fear of all-out rebellion. When this latest and most brazen assassination attempt led the British to put renewed pressure on the Jewish Agency for cooperation, it agreed only to ask for "volunteers" to help the British. With the Yishuv making "open and almost boastful pronouncements regarding the achievement of maximum Zionist aims in Palestine," the Palestinians, MacMichael observed, "are showing increased concern at the audacity and strength of the Jewish terrorist organization, which they fear will ultimately be used against themselves."[180]

Coordinated attacks on August 22 against the Jaffa Divisional Police Headquarters and two Police Stations on the Jaffa - Tel Aviv border took two officers' lives. After mining and booby-trapping approach roads and rail crossings to kill or delay first responders, three separate parties, each about a dozen men, attacked with bombs, grenades, and sub machine guns. On September 27, one person was killed in an attack on the Eastern Police Station, and ten were injured when their truck was blown up by a land mine. Four police stations—Haifa, Qalqilya, Beit Dajan (Beth Dagon), and Qataa (Qatara)—were attacked the next day, "planned and executed by a force estimated to have been at least 150 strong and armed with bombs and automatic weapons". Four Palestinians were murdered in the attacks. Lehi assassinated Police superintendent J.T. Wilkin in Jerusalem on September 29.[181]

A £P100,000 Irgun theft of textiles on October 6 was used in part to finance a bunker for the terror group's commander, future Prime Minister Menachem Begin, whom the Haifa police chief described as "a ruthless thug who made Al Capone look like a novice." In the background to the attacks against governmental and civilian authorities, Palestinians continued to be attacked by "bands of Jewish youth" on the seashore, and Tel Aviv was "buzzing with a rumor that His Majesty's Government is going to bring in partition."[182]

The British, indeed, after abandoning Partition as unworkable several years earlier, had decided upon it as their escape plan by early 1944 but withheld the news because it could not spare the troops to handle the violent reaction it expected. They were keenly aware that the "extremists dominating the [Jewish] Agency" would resist Partition "with the forces at their disposal—forces which past experience and recent intelligence (on the HAGANA) has shown to be both fanatical and well disciplined."[183]

The relentlessly messianic Weizmann condemned the rumors of Partition with the lament that "Pharaoh once offered us to make bricks without straw"—the word "us" ensuring that twentieth-century European Jewry had been plucked out of the Old Testament and left the page about the Pharaoh dog-eared. It was however the British on the ground who proved to be the prophets, worrying that Partition would cause the "extremist Jewish element" to "raise the excuse of Arab outrages" in order to steal whatever portion of the land is allotted to the Palestinians.[184]

Relentless Jewish terrorism, a British report from October lamented, is the "sabotage of the general effort of the United Nations* in their life-and-death struggle against the worst enemy that Jewry has ever known." In print and over the airwaves, the British beseeched the Jewish settlers to cooperate for the sake of defeating the Nazi menace.

> Palestine ... has enjoyed five years of virtual immunity from the horrors of war ... Palestine has however been the scene of a series of outrageous crimes of violence by Jewish terrorists, acting with the deliberate intention of bringing about by force developments favourable to the realization of political aims ... These events are proceeding side by side with the bitterest phase of the critical fighting between the United Nations and Nazi Germany.[185]

Yet the British on the ground reported increasing "numbers of Jewish young men and women who are becoming infected with the gangster virus [providing] recruits for the terrorist organisation" in order to force the "maximalist aims [of] a Jewish state covering all Palestine and ultimately Trans-Jordan." Youth are nurtured by the

> propagandist nature of much teaching in Jewish schools, the Youth Movement (unpleasantly reminiscent of the Hitler Youth), and the totalitarian organisation and regimentation of the Yishuv by the agency of the

---

* "United Nations" here refers to the Allied Nations, not the UN, which was established in late 1945.

Histadruth, etc. These things constitute the negation of free thought and speech.[186]

The Palestinians, meanwhile, "are losing their lives, here and there, in small numbers, at Jewish hands in the course of terrorist operations." As reported by the Jerusalem District Commissioner's Office in October,

> The killing of Arabs by Jewish terrorists, and the distribution of Arabic copies of notices by the Irgun Zvai Leumi threatening that the hands of any Arabs raised against the Jewish [Zionist] cause would be cut off is creating an atmosphere of tension and hatred comparable with that of [the Palestinian uprising of] 1938-39.[187]

The Irgun posted pamphlets in principal Arab towns announcing that it was the Palestinians' "new government," and warning in what the British described as "offensive terms" that they must not interfere with its operations. Yet British officials continued to comment on the Palestinians' failure to respond in kind. As the Chief Secretary of Lydda District reported,

It is noticeable that the continuance of Jewish terrorist outrages has not so far provoked the Arabs to retaliation…[188]

When the moment was right, the War Office predicted, the settlers would increase their anti-Arab violence to elicit a reprisal, which they would frame as an attack. There was evidence that

> whatever course the Zionist leaders may adopt, they will deliberately provoke Arab reaction to it, in order to increase the justification for the use of force in 'self-defence'.[189]

Two days after a Palestinian policeman from Gaza was murdered, "a party of about sixty Jews from a neighbouring settlement chose to pay a visit to Gaza and parade through the streets," yet the Palestinians resisted the taunt. Their restraint, the British observed, was largely due to their awareness that they would "be playing into the hands of Jewish propagandists." Similar remarks came independently from the Chief Secretary in Jerusalem in October: "not even the deeds and propaganda of Jewish terrorism" have driven the Palestinians to respond in kind.[190]

Jews with political sense "draw a parallel" between Zionist militancy and "the rise of Nazism, and express the fear that the groups are gaining an increasing number of adherents amongst the youth." Jewish terrorism "is becoming so much a part of the everyday life of Palestine that the average Jew is showing little interest so long as he is left undisturbed himself." The British continued to fear that forceful attempts to stop the terrorism would unleash retaliation from "Zionist circles both within and without Palestine."[191]

Along with the escalation in terrorism was an escalation in Jewish "hiking parties." Twenty-eight "hikers" from the Emek settlements scouting the lands east of Jenin were stopped on October 23, followed five days later by two more parties totalling thirty "hikers." More "hiking" teams were recorded by the Commissioner's Offices in Nablus, which noted their cameras and anti-personnel grenades. Arab Legion* soldiers arrested yet more "hikers" in Galilee District but, as described by the Galilee District Commissioner, the soldiers diffused the incident by "entertaining the hikers to dinner and immediately releasing the insolent Jews on arrival at the camp."[192]

November 6 brought the first Zionist assassination outside of Palestine. As Lord Moyne, the British Minister of State in the Middle East, returned home in Cairo at 1:10 in the afternoon, two Lehi operatives jumped out from hiding. "Don't move," one demanded in what Capt. Andrew Hughes-Onslow, who had exited the Packard saloon car, described as "English, without any noticeable trace of accent." One thrust the barrel of his gun into the open window and shot Moyne three times, firing "separately and slowly." The driver, who had gone to open the car door for Moyne, lay dying on the ground. The killers escaped on bicycle as per their plan but were spotted by a policeman on motorcycle. Both were captured.[193]

Nov 1944

Moyne, heir to the brewing firm Guinness, was a target because of his criticism of political Zionism. Two years before his assassination, he succinctly pinpointed the Palestine problem in the House of Lords :

---

* The Arab Legion was an army formed and led by the British in 1920 to defend the Transjordan region occupied by Britain after World War I. It played an important role in the fight against the Axis powers in World War II under John Bagot Glubb, who commanded the Legion from 1939 to 1956, when it became the Jordanian army.

> The Zionist claim has raised two burning issues: firstly, the demand for large-scale immigration into an already overcrowded country, and, secondly, racial domination by these newcomers over the original inhabitants.

To charges of anti-Semitism and innuendos of Nazism, Moyne replied that

> If a comparison is to be made with the Nazis it is surely those who wish to force an imported regime upon the Arab population ... [the] proposal that Arabs should be subjugated by force to a Jewish regime is inconsistent with the Atlantic Charter, and that ought to be told to America.[194]

Moyne's anti-Zionist views were one of three reasons Lehi gave for his execution. The gang also wanted to demonstrate its policy of personal terror as a warning to others, and to use a high-profile assassination to promote its demands on the global stage. A massive media effort by American Zionists to depict the assassins as "martyrs" and grant them a reprieve failed, even after garnering support from US politicians and figures as public as Arturo Toscanini. The two were tried and hanged.[195]

Under international pressure after Moyne's murder, the Jewish Agency pursued non-Hagana terrorists in a period commonly remembered as "the season." The Hagana employed "unconventional attempts to extract information" from Irgun members (though Moyne's assassins were Lehi), and the British saw the cooperation as "largely political," an opportunity to eliminate "persons obnoxious to the Agency on party grounds." As MI5 put it, the Agency fought terror "when it suited their political book."

In the wake of the assassination, Rabbi Fishman (Yehuda Leib Maimon), future Israeli MP, persevered in the view that "under no circumstances should we permit co-operation with the Government" in fighting terrorism, and Yitzhak Gruenbaum, who previously argued against rescue and who would become first Interior Minister of Israel, described Moyne's assassins as "nothing less than national partisans." Palestine's chief Ashkenazi Rabbi Herzog declared that handing over terror suspects to the authorities was against Biblical

Law. Publicly, Ben-Gurion and Weizmann expressed outrage at Moyne's assassination, but the Israeli state would soon hail both assassins as "heroic freedom fighters." In 1975 the assassins' bodies were laid in state in the Jerusalem Hall of Heroism, and in 1982 Israel issued postal stamps honoring them.[196]

Jerusalem, as seen from the north. Early twentieth century.
On negative: " Jerusalem of the North, Nablous [Nablus] Road".

Part II
The Fall—and Rise—of Fascism

4

Allied Victory, 1945

> Jewish leaders decried, sneered and then attacked me as if I were a traitor ... I was openly accused of furthering this plan of freer immigration in order to undermine political Zionism.
> —Morris Ernst, aide to President Franklin Delano Roosevelt, upon provisional success in opening the US' and several other nations' doors to a half million DPs in early 1944.[197]

"The Christian world," Lord Moyne's successor, James Grigg, said in early 1945, "will not stand for the development of a regular Nazi type of gangsterism which has caused so much terror and destruction in Palestine." But as Germany's surrender seemed more and more imminent, the Zionist press continued to hail Moyne's assassins as "martyrs," and Palestine's "Nazi type of gangsterism" intensified.[198]

President Roosevelt died on April 12, 1945. "From the purely Zionist point of view they [Zionist leaders] are not seriously perturbed," the British observed, "as they feel that their influence in the U.S.A. is sufficiently strong to keep the new president [Harry Truman] on the right lines." A malleable, "naive diplomat," as Sharett put it, Truman assumed the presidency at a critical time, the eve of the Allied victory.

Ben-Gurion had long argued that Zionism should "exploit the confusion and war weariness of the post war period" to achieve its political objectives. He cited the occupation of Vilna by the Poles after World War I as a precedent for the tactic, and stressed that their goal in Palestine will only be achieved by force. Aware of the danger of a V-Day coup, Britain's War Cabinet agreed to give the Mandatory government as much forewarning of the V-Day announcement as possible: forty-eight hours' warning was requested, and half that was hoped for.

"We must consolidate every one of our existing positions," Ben-Gurion argued in preparation. "Every area of land already in our possession must be settled immediately ... we must bring in immigrants from all possible countries by every means," the emphasis being human facts on the ground, not saving Jews.[199]

The Irgun and Lehi had similar plans to exploit the post-war exhaustion. The Irgun's US operations were being monitored by a British informant code-named Y 32, who trusted only a certain Catling, a member of the Palestine Police, to confide his identity (he was ex-Irgun member Jankelis Chilevicius). Catling went to the US to get Y 32's report in person. Meeting in New York on the first day of October (1944), Y 32 told Catling that the Irgun "has plans far advanced for a full-scale Jewish up-rising in Palestine, scheduled to begin some two or three months after Germany is defeated." Palestine would be "denuded of British troops, and a fair number of Jewish [Brigade] troops [would be] back in Palestine." The Irgun and Lehi would seize key positions: the Ramallah Broadcasting Station, Jerusalem General Post Office, Secretariat, and the government offices in Jerusalem, Haifa, and Tel Aviv. "Should troops be used against them," he reported of the Irgun's thinking, "the propaganda value of a wail that British soldiers were killing Jews in their own homeland would turn world opinion in their favour." More worryingly, Y 32 told Catling that "Jews in the armed forces are heavily involved"—that there are Zionist plants in the British military.

Independent confirmation of a post-war blitz came from a Cairo prison cell six months later (April 1945) when Yacov Meridor, a former Irgun commander, boasted to a prison warden that he "must be in Palestine by V-Day" to take part in the plan, because "it will be the greatest day in Palestine's history."[200]

Thus when in the early afternoon of May 7, the BBC broadcast announcing the unconditional surrender of Germany was heard in Haifa, Palestine entered a new dynamic. Bands of Jewish youth celebrated the two mornings following the Allied victory by parading through the Wadi Salib Arab quarter in Haifa with Zionist flags, taunting the Palestinians until being stopped by the police. Coordinated mortar attacks the Irgun had planned for the night of May 13 were foiled, but not its campaign of telegraph pole bombings: fifty-seven were hit on May 14-15. A malfunction largely spared the telegraph route north of Hadera: only six of the many bombs ignited. On May 16, militants bombed the Lydda Police Station and Tel Aviv Police post, and tried to bomb PMF Camp Sarona but the device exploded outside. Two more mortar bombs missed the Jaffa police station, and more than 200 telegraph poles were found rigged with explosives, most near Lydda. The communications blitz continued with the destruction of lines on the Tel Aviv - Jerusalem road on May 17, the Haifa-Lydda road on May 18, near Givat Shaul and Mikve-Israel on May 21, and the sabotage of government lines on May 22. The next day bombs severed oil pipelines belonging to the Iraq Petroleum Company in two places near Indur in Galilee District, and the pipelines were bombed again on May 25 near Haifa. Police in Sarona were attacked on May 26, and mortars loaded with incendiary projectiles were discovered in a nearby orange grove. There was, however, a noteworthy act of resistance: on 13 May a truck containing four mortars, detonators, gelignite, and "73 anti personnel blast" was apprehended by members of the Kfar Hassidim orthodox settlement near Haifa and turned over to police. Meanwhile, reconnaissance "hiking parties'" discovered in the Nablus area "provoked comment but no incidents" among the Palestinians.[201]

When Sharett was again pressed by the British for cooperation against terrorism, he now "admitted that the majority of the [Jewish] community was not necessarily so opposed to these activities as to make them willing to assist in their suppression." The relationships among the three major terror organizations was fluid; Teddy Kollek

May 1945

(sometimes known as "Scorpion"), an occasional informant and future mayor of Jerusalem, reported that summer that although neither the Irgun nor Lehi "was willing to lose its identity" to the Hagana, they all cooperated.

Kollek confirmed British suspicions that the Zionist establishment's disavowal of terror was choreographed: according to Kollek, the Hagana and Irgun would agree on a particular terror attack, the Irgun would carry it out, and the Jewish Agency would then publicly condemn it. As a defense summary put it, "the Hagana will have a lot of its dirty work done for it, without carrying any responsibility."[202]

A bridge on the Bejaz line was blown up on June 12. More Irgun pamphlet bombs exploded, but a mortar attack, apparently intended to destroy the government printing press in Jerusalem, was thwarted. The next day the British, following a tip said to come from the Jewish Agency, discovered a loaded triple mortar battery behind the YMCA at Jerusalem, "aligned in the direction of the King David building, the saluting base area for the King's birthday parade."[203]

On Juy 13, "a lorry containing 500 lbs of high explosives intended for use in a quarry was ambushed in daylight by ten armed Jews near Petah Tiqva." Constable Wilde, escorting the truck, was murdered, and the explosives vanished, raising the suspicion that Temporary Additional Constables (TAC) were themselves Irgun or "had been squared by them." When police dogs followed the scent to the orange groves of Givat Hash Shelosha settlement near Petah Tiqva, the settlers refused to cooperate, at which the British authorities ordered the police to call off the search because "any attempt to search the Jewish settlement would lead to severe disorder."[204]

Two of the policemen nevertheless continued to hunt for their colleague's murderers and the stolen explosives, but were again stopped by their superiors. In frustration, the policemen wrote an impassioned letter to the British government recounting the inexplicable end of their investigation. "Two of the under-signed," the letter summarized, "were in the search which, after discovering ample evidence, was called off, for no accountable reason, when on the point of discovering more, and better, evidence." Several policemen reported this calling-off of the pursuit of Jewish terrorists, and many complained bitterly of the

> June-Aug 1945

severe restrictions placed on their right to defend themselves. The same two reasons prevailed: British fear of an insurrection from the Yishuv if the terrorists were pursued into the settlements, and fear of handing Zionists a propaganda windfall in the United States.[205]

Lehi joined forces with the Irgun on July 23 to bomb the railway bridge on the Haifa-Cairo line near Yavne. The collaboration continued two days later when the combined terror groups blew up a five-span girder bridge on four stone piers on the main Kantara-Lydda line near Yibna, between Gaza and Lydda. Police dogs traced the scent to three Jewish colonies, but the settlers remained mute. Another government vehicle carrying explosives vanished to an Irgun hijacking the next day.[206]

In the US, the Irgun's Bergson Group had so woven itself into American life that on the first day of August a retiring US Senator, Guy Gillette, became the new president of the terror organization's American League for a Free Palestine, and chief political adviser to its so-called Hebrew Committee of National Liberation. In Palestine, "a large party of armed Jews," numbering "between 30 and 90, including several women," attacked an explosives store on August 13, stealing 450 lbs of gelignite, fuses, and detonators. Joseph Davidescu, formerly with military intelligence, was assassinated on August 22.[207]

Reconnaissance "hiking" missions, which the British now recognized as "foreshadowing further infiltration and settlement," intensified. "Apprehension has been aroused," a September report from Nablus states, "by the activities of large Jewish walking parties ... It is popularly believed that the role of these parties is to 'spy out the land'." While Nablus was reporting this reconnaissance in the north, the District Commissioner's Office in Gaza reported more "hiking parties" in the south and cited them as "the chief reason" for the heightening anti-Jewish feeling in the Gaza area, which had been "comparatively mild."[208*]

After a failed robbery of the Palestine Discount Bank in Tel Aviv on September 2 by "a party of Jews" (Irgun), British officials, nervous

Sept 1945

---

* This report from the Gaza District Commissioner refers to "a separate report [that] has been submitted to you on the subject" of the hikers, but which the author has not been able to locate.

over rumors that terror attacks were planned for mid-September, arranged another meeting with Teddy Kollek. "Despite the lull at the present time," Kollek told them, "the N.M.O. [Irgun] particularly were very active indeed ... generally putting their house in order." Among their to-do list was enlarging their dwindling stockpile of explosives, explaining the recent rash of explosives thefts. The Irgun and Lehi were currently collaborating and "were feverishly training new recruits, particularly in such fine arts as shadowing." The Irgun was also busy perfecting its new 40 kilo (88 lbs) mortar known as "V.3.," with a longer and more accurate range, planting them in pre-arranged positions to be used at later dates. Due to political deliberations in London, the Irgun and Lehi were likely to engage only in robbery during the coming few weeks—"pedal slowly," Kollek said, was the Jewish Agency's orders to them.[209]

Kollek's information was largely corroborated by Irgun documents seized five months later, on February 28, 1946, during a British raid on 45 Zichron Moshe Street (Jerusalem). One document codified an Irgun-Lehi agreement to carry out attacks in Palestine "or outside, if necessary," and celebrates their first joint operation, the destruction of the bridge at Yibna (presumably the July 23 sabotage), "the results of which have been described by news agencies and broadcasting systems throughout the world as an attack on one of the most vital roadways of British imperialism by units of the National Military Organisation [Irgun] and Stern Group [Lehi] under their respective commanders."[210]

Five pamphlet bombs "of a larger size than hitherto exploded in various parts of Jerusalem" on September 15, injuring nine people (all Jewish). This was likely the Irgun, whose operatives also shot dead a constable in an attempted robbery that day. Four days later, militants blew up a bridge and bombed an armored car escorting diamonds. A constable was shot dead outside the Tel Aviv Post Office on September 28.[211]

September's most disturbing news came with the British intercept of a message sent by Moshe Sneh, head of the Hagana, to the Jewish Agency's London office, that again proved the Agency's hand in terror. The message spoke of causing a "serious incident" that would be merely a warning of "much more serious incidents" to come if the

British failed to heed the Zionists' demands, incidents that would "threaten the safety of all British interests in the country."²¹²

"Immigration from all sources by all means" was the unanimous battle cry at a mass meeting at the Jewish Centre on October 8 in which once-moderate factions now demanded the immediate creation of a Jewish state in all of Palestine. Thus the Jewish Agency was all the more furious when the next day Hebrew University president Judah Magnes lambasted the "growing trend towards totalitarianism amongst the Jews." He railed against the pressure, "particularly in America, to yield to Zionist totalitarianism which seeks to subject to its discipline the entire Jewish people." In response, the Agency smeared Magnes with a Nazi allusion, saying his words were akin to "praising the Germans at the time of Dunkirk."²¹³

Oct 1945

The night of Magnes' speech, Palmach operatives broke into the Athlit Clearance Camp, where immigrants were held pending immigration permits. After murdering a constable, they raided the depot, bound and gagged eleven new immigrants, and freed the rest. One of the gagged victims—a Christian woman—was dead, suffocated. These eleven had "presumably refused to participate in the escape," the British report read, whereas the Hagana's Sneh put the number they'd tied up at thirteen and dismissed them as "illegal immigrants" (apparently meaning that the other ten or twelve were also Christian). The victims were smeared as Magnus had been, Sneh charging that they "had maintained contact with the Nazis."

The hunt for those responsible followed the usual patterns. When police tried to enforce a road check in the area, they were ambushed "by Jews armed with rifles, sub-machine guns and grenades," killing a constable on the spot and seriously wounding another. In the hills about seven hours later, a police detachment detained nine suspects en route to Meshek Yajour, but while their identities were being established, a "party of 100 Jewish men, armed with pick halves, arrived on the scene" from that Jewish colony and forced the police, who had been forbidden from using firearms, to free the suspects. At about the same time, police pursuing terror suspects in the Montefiore quarter of Tel Aviv (not related to the Athlit incident) "were attacked by a mob of 150-200 Jews who threw stones" and blocked them, while more settlers were bused in from nearby quarters to stop the police from taking away three suspects. In a message to a contact in London, Sneh described the Athlit attack as a "great success!"[214]

The Irgun raided an army camp October 11, seizing hundreds of rifles, guns, grenades, and ammunition. On October 16, "at about 10:30 A.M. a number of unknown Jews attempted to hold up an Army truck at the Salameh railway crossing," apparently having learned that the truck carried £14,000 in solders' pay. A second Irgun attempt further up the road left one casualty, a fourteen-year-old Palestinian bystander. Down south, a large number of "hiking parties" were operating in the Beersheba region (Negev), and in London the secretary-general of the Arab League received a "final summons" from "the Messiah" (probably Lehi) threatening "[w]oe to all Arabdom" should he in any way question the "return" of the "Israelites."

Meanwhile in Palestine the High Commissioner, Viscount Gort, gathered three of the Zionist leaders and "solemnly" warned them to end the terror. The three appeared little impressed, replying only that they would take their instructions from their superiors (then) in London.[215]

Gort, a veteran of both world wars, turned to a Mr. Newton, a Hebrew-speaking former resident of the settlements, for insight into the quagmire in Palestine. "Violence and intransigent nationalism," Newton testified, "was fostered by the Jewish educational system," and "the incitement and hysteria fostered systematically among the Jewish youth in Palestine. This education and political propaganda has produced youths and girls who were ready to use murder for their political ends."[216]

Thus a prerequisite for peace in Palestine, Newton said, would be "the re-education of the Jewish youth." As for the Palestinians, they "did not wish for violence and indeed it was only the intense Zionist propaganda" that led them to "a renewed interest in politics," with "a growing number of young [Palestinian] men who were interested in social and economic matters and were more up-to-date in their ideas" than the established figures from old prominent Arab families.

Europe's persecuted Jews were "being used as a political weapon to gain control of Palestine," and any "declaration of a policy unfavourable to extreme Zionism" would be met with terror. Jews "who were against political extremism ... were exposed to intimidation [and] had no political influence." Independently, a British report that month noted an example of such "intimidation": an American Jew in Nathanya named Cliansky was ostracized, both his sons were fired from their jobs, and he was evicted from his synagogue to shouts of "he is defiled."

This push to extremism was hardening with the end of the war. "Until recently," the Jaffa District Commissioner noted in October, Jews "deprecated the resort to force" of the terrorists, while refusing any assistance to stop it. Now, however, "it is no exaggeration to say that the whole of the Jewish urban community is in sympathy with the saboteurs."[217]

The Jewish Agency itself was the ringleader of the next blitz, "a series of concerted attacks" during the night of October 31 – November 1 that "was made by armed Jews on Palestine railway system, culminating with a full-scale attack on the railway station and goods yard at Lydda" in which several people were killed. Intercepted telegrams show that the Agency enlisted the collaboration of both the Irgun and Lehi. Railway tracks were severed in 242 places, and police naval vessels were bombed. The country-wide sabotage, the Hagana's Kol Israel announced, "serves as a warning to the Government of the White Paper."

Nov 1945

In the morning, the police discovered a bomb that had failed to explode in the night's carnage, raising hope that police dogs could follow the scent to the terrorists' hideout—which they did. The dogs led a small patrol under a Mr. Gould to Ramat Hak Kovesh settlement, but when they were sighted the school bells rang and "a large part of the population turned out at the gate to bar his progress." Gould explained that they were interested only in apprehending a suspect in the night's attacks, and that "it was wrong of them to harbor a terrorist". As he spoke, the crowd of settlers began threatening him with stones, fresh supplies of which were brought to the scene in boxes, and soon "considerable parties" of reinforcements, principally from Kefar Sava settlement, began arriving "on foot and in transport of all kinds." The police patrol left without daring to challenge the settlers.

This vast-scale sabotage of the railways, and its civilian dead, "failed to elicit even the usual formal expression of deprecation" from Zionist leaders. Instead, the "dominant note was satisfaction at the display of organisation and the strength of the Yishuv's armed forces"—this reference to the three terror gangs as the "Yishuv's armed forces" an early acknowledgment that they would coalesce into a state army. The *Palestine Post*, forerunner of the *Jerusalem Post*, pointed to the attacks "as evidence that Palestine Jewry had gone over to the offensive."

Kol Israel radio railed against the Arabs, "ignorant people [who] have done a great deal of harm to themselves in trying to stand in our way." Meanwhile, preparations to remove those 'ignorant people' continued: the British confiscated documents from an Egged bus that contained detailed surveillance about Palestinian villages, clearly the fruit of the "hiking" parties.[218]

In London on November 2, British Foreign Secretary Ernest Bevin met with Weizmann and Sharett and pressed them about the attacks. Weizmann blamed the British, saying that their delay in announcing a lifting of immigration quotas had "encouraged the spark which had set off the charge." Bevin countered that "every one of these outrages had been carefully planned and kept secret so that they should operate simultaneously." Internal Hagana documents reveal the Jewish Agency's actual attitude: these bragged that the "500 explosions" of the single night of October 31 had stopped railway traffic "from the Syrian frontier to Gaza, from Haifa to Samakh, from Lydda to Jerusalem … The activities have made a great impression on the country. The authorities are bewildered."[219]

The Palestinians' reaction to the violence and taunting, as recorded in a mid-November report to the British Minister in Beirut, continued to be "general dissatisfaction but NO disposition to violence" [capitalization original].

The Middle East's indigenous Jews remained distrustful of Zionism: Jewish citizens of the Levant states, the report states, are "apprehensive of Zionism and show solidarity with local Arab population." Most tellingly, the region's native Jews "regret [the] inclusion of pro-Zionist America in Enquiry Commission," the Anglo-American Commission of Inquiry, newly-formed to advance a solution to the Palestine question.[220]

Politicians of that "pro-Zionist America" were now demanding that Britain admit an additional 100,000 Jews into Palestine immediately—an electioneering gimmick, charged Bevin. "Any other alternative to relieve suffering unless it was founded upon Palestine policy alone," he complained, "was rejected by the United States Government and by the Jews."

But Bevin's most scandalous charge was that American support for Zionism was largely fuelled by anti-Semitism. The fear of Jews turning up on New York's shores, he claimed, was the reality behind much of the US support for a "Jewish State" in Palestine. The remark elicited venomous outrage, with Senator Robert Wagner accusing Bevin of anti-Semitism for his "echo from Nazi dogma [which] will not be excused or forgotten."

Bevin had however merely pulled the veil off an indispensable part of the Jewish Agency's method: two days earlier, future prime minister Sharett had again assured the Jewish Agency Executive that the Americans could be relied on to support a Zionist state because of the "American fear" of Jews "opening the gates of New York." As the British Embassy in Washington put it, "the average citizen does not want them in the United States, and salves his conscious by advocating their admittance to Palestine."[221]

All Jewish boys and girls aged 17-18 were to do Hagana "national service" with no exceptions—so ordered the Agency in a notice in the *Palestine Post* on November 6. Eight and nine days later, the district offices in Tel Aviv were attacked for the third time in five years, destroying two floors, along with many of their documents. A curfew imposed in the wake of the attacks proved impossible to maintain: cars were overturned, a military truck set afire and burned out, part of a railway line torn up, Arab buses stoned, and several buildings wrecked and looted. The Post Office's interior was partially destroyed, but the crowd's attempt to burn it down failed. When the police, under heavy stoning by a crowd of about 5,000, attempted to charge the crowd with batons, the crowd advanced against them instead and the police had to retreat. Emergency crews attempting to reach the burning District Offices were also stoned, while Hagana leader Sneh, addressing a large crowd in Jerusalem, baited the Palestinians. The army camp at Rosh-HaAyin was raided on November 22.[222]

On the night of November 24-25, "Jews opened fire with automatic weapons, rifles and hand grenades" at Sidna Ali coast guard station. Three of four bombs exploded, seriously damaging the building. Similarly, the coast guard stations at Givat Olga "was surrounded by Jews who opened fire with automatic weapons and grenades," who then "succeeded in placing gelignite charges against building which wrecked it." Once again, the settlers stopped the police from any investigation—but this time the police persevered, and "large crowds [of] Jews ... poured in from surrounding country" on buses to block them. Still the authorities did not give up, now forcing their way into Rishpon settlement with tear gas, guns, and batons. There they discovered a man badly injured by a grenade, presumably one of the attackers, along with 175 lbs of the explosive ammonal, twenty sticks of gelignite, grenades, military uniforms, and clothes stained with sea water.

As the British had long feared, the Jewish Agency turned the capture of the terrorists into a public relations fiasco. It announced that "British troops and police forcibly entered three peaceful labor agricultural settlements [and] wantonly beat hundreds men and women ... without any reason ... intimidating the Jews of Palestine into submission." Pieces appeared in the US media alleging, in messianic melodrama, British atrocities against (as one such article put it) the "Children of Israel."[223]

In what must have seemed to the British a consummate irony, the Jewish Agency now sought to force Britain to yield to its demands by holding it hostage to the debilitating debt it incurred fighting the Nazis—a debt that only a loan from the US could relieve, but that Zionist pressure in the US could block. An informant code-named Circus was present at a mid-December secret meeting of the Jewish Agency Executive, at which Ben-Gurion stressed that "our activities should be directed from Washington and not from London."

Dec 1945

The United States was the key to their plans, and "Jewish influence in America is powerful and able to cause damage to the interests of Great Britain," with the post-war loan the recurring threat.

Anti-Semitism remained an important aspect of the strategy: "if they do not wish an influx of European Jews as immigrants to the United States," Ben-Gurion assured the Executive, "they would be well advised to support the Zionist claim to Palestine." Zionism's need to assure perpetual anti-Semitism did not go unrecognized, for example being satirized by the cartoonist David Low, whose output condemned fascism in its various incarnations.[224]

Opposition to Reconstruction continued, lest conditions in Europe "be improved sufficiently to induce Jews to resume residence there" rather than emigrate to Palestine. To counter that "threat" of European improvement, Circus reported that the Agency "decided to increase propaganda measures among Jews in Camps and other countries in Europe." Emissaries were being sent from Jerusalem, London, and New York with the goal that "85% of the Jews in Europe [i.e., not limited to DPs] can be persuaded" to emigrate to Palestine.

Corroborating this, former settlement member Newton testified that Zionist leaders are

> exploiting the situation of the Jews in Europe ... counting on the natural humanitarian feelings of England and America to further their schemes. They were not interested in Jewish rehabilitation in Europe. They were afraid that with the improvement of conditions in Europe the pressure on Palestine would subside.

Circus confirmed the core Zionist strategy that any "differentiation made between the problem of the Jew and that of Political Zionism" had to be stopped—and so when in a public speech on November 13, Bevin distinguished between Jews and Zionists, the fallout was again swift and vicious. A world-wide smear campaign ensued, and Bevin became an assassination target.[225]

As the British observed Christmas on December 25, the Irgun raided the army camp at Beth-Naballa. This attack failed in its goal, the "requisition of weapons," but the setback lasted only two days. December 27, indeed, proved to be a prelude to what was to come in 1946, the year that marked Britain's effective loss of control of Palestine to the Zionist militias.

A "serious Jewish terrorist attack" began at 7:15 that evening, when Police Headquarters Jerusalem was "attacked by armed Jews" in a "savage and ruthless" manner that "will be viewed with horror by all the civilized nations of the world." After "Jews armed with automatic weapons and explosives" killed two police and blew open the door to a building opposite Police Headquarters in order to gain access to its balcony, "other Jews laid explosives at one corner of the Police Offices" under cover of fire from the balcony and blew it up, burying ten people under the rubble. Five were still alive when pulled out.

A policeman named Flanagan was on his way to the hospital in answer to an emergency call to donate blood when he learned of the ongoing attack and, rushing to assist, was murdered by the militants, as was a Constable Hyde as he passed near Zion Cinema, and a policeman Nicholson.[226]

About two minutes after the Jerusalem attack began, District Police Headquarters in Jaffa was "heavily attacked by armed Jews in the Jaffa/Tel-Aviv Road"—the first of coordinated attacks on two police stations and two military barracks intended to prevent reinforcements from reaching the scene. A Palestinian telephone operator was killed in the attack, which wrecked the ground, first floor, and telephone exchange. About three minutes after the Jaffa attack began, "the Jews cut through the wire fence" of the R.E.M.E. Depot at Levant Fair in Tel Aviv, and "murdered in cold blood an unarmed British soldier L/Cpl. R. Symons. The Jews then lobbed a grenade through the window of a room in which a number of men were asleep." Ten people were killed in the day's carnage, and eleven wounded. "The attacks," an Irgun *Proclamation* announced, "were carried out with zeal and heroism by all the fighters according to predetermined plan."[227]

When the British made fresh appeals to the Jewish Agency to help stop the terror, Ben-Gurion and Sharett "disassociated themselves from the murderous attacks" but reiterated that the terrorism would not stop as long as Britain stood in the way of Zionist nationalist ambitions. Sharett went so far as to state this publicly, telling reporters that "any appeals to Jews to obey the law would fall on deaf ears" unless Zionist demands were met.

Hoping the gesture would serve as an olive branch and encourage cooperation, the British authorized another 1,500 more Jewish immigrants a month (the White Paper's quota was exhausted in December). But this overture, an "open breach" of the White Paper to appease the Jewish Agency, was without effect. "Minor" incidents continued, such as a random attack on New Year's Eve against two Britons that left one with a concussion and loss of memory.

The year-end news that Transjordan was granted independence elicited a dual reaction: publicly, Zionist leaders like Sharett condemned Jordanian independence, claiming that the land had been promised to them as part of the "Jewish state"; but privately, Zionist planners calculated that it could be a lucky turn of events, because it would be much easier for them "to infiltrate into a weak but independent Arab State" (as British sources put it) than wrest Transjordan from British control. In anticipation of future claims on Jordan, Jewish Agency propaganda began referring to Palestine as "Western Palestine," and Hagana Commander Sneh made clear in an interview for the *New York Post* that he spoke of "both banks of the Jordan." Year-end rumors of Partition within "Western Palestine" (i.e., Palestine) received the same split reaction: publicly, they were condemned, but pragmatists "would even welcome partition," since Partition would mean statehood, and statehood would enable "infiltration and expansion."[228]

For the militias, none of this was happening fast enough. Hagana chief Sneh warned Sharett that they were "anxious for action" and that the Agency's laxness had already led to the defection of 250 Palmach members to the Irgun. According to Circus, Ben-Gurion reaffirmed the core unity of purpose, reassuring the Jewish Agency Executive that he "would never agree to Agency assistance to the Administration and police in stopping Irgun activities."[229]

Documents seized from Sneh's flat show that the Agency did more than cooperate with the Irgun: it actually helped finance the terror gang. Jewish Agency treasurer Eliezer Kaplan is the likely author of this penciled comment to Sneh :

But if they really do free us from all expenditure on illegal immigration it will enable us to increase the allocation to the Irgun.[230]

Another document, a four-page plan of action clipped to a letter to Ben-Gurion and copied to Sneh, stressed that the "final solution" in Palestine will be determined by "the relative forces on the spot," not by Partition. The point is then restated more bluntly, "seizing control of the country by force of arms." Conscription into the Yishuv's military "will be backed when necessary by physical force," and the Agency's rule over Jews would be absolute, with a supreme body that "can impose on any [Jewish] person, group, or enterprise any duty or prohibition it finds necessary." Its powers over Jews would extend "beyond the 'legal' boundaries."[231]

Railway bombing, 1946. Photograph captioned 'Demolished Rail Car'.

5

Race for Fanaticism, 1946

> [We] live here like the Moranos once lived in Spain!
> —*Jewish survivor, 1945, describing life for non-Zionist Jews in the Zionist-controlled DP camps.**²³²

"**P**owers beyond the legal boundaries" certainly characterized the events of 1946, the year that Zionist leaders and terror organizations exploited the long-awaited post-war opportunity that was now theirs for the taking. As the world picked up the pieces from this global cataclysm, the once-only opportunity it presented Zionism brought heightened campaigns of terror to Palestine, the first Zionist bombings in Europe, new efforts to preserve Jewish "racial purity," accelerated recruitment into the militias, tightened repression of the Yishuv's actions and thoughts, and new methods of violence against the war's Jewish survivors.

Europe's Jewish survivors presented a threat to Zionism should they wish to emigrate anywhere other than to Palestine or opt to remain in their own countries—which "under no circumstances," Sharett lectured

---

* *Moranos* [Marranos] refers to Jews who were forced to pretend conversion to Christianity in Spain at the close of the fifteenth century, and so observed their true beliefs in secret.

to the Jewish Agency Executive, should be permitted. An Intelligence Summary from April of 1945 quotes Eliyahu Dobkin, then head of the Jewish Agency's Immigration Department, as saying that terrorist methods would be used to force European Jews to move to Palestine after the war, and to prevent Jews in Palestine from leaving. "We should not treat this danger lightly," Ben-Gurion said of the "danger" that the war's Jewish survivors would not want to go to Palestine.[233]

This, however, was indeed the case—the best estimate available is that after the war, only fifteen percent would willingly have gone to Palestine despite years of the Zionists' propaganda efforts. To address this "problem," a triple campaign was waged: the forceful isolation and coercion of the survivors themselves, the sabotage of international safe haven for them, and the kidnapping of Jewish orphans.[234]

Influencing Jewish survivors required that they first be segregated from other DPs. The Truman Administration acquiesced to Zionists' demands that this be done, despite misgivings among many that it echoed Nazi behavior. Even the staunchly pro-Zionist Churchill was uncomfortable with the forced segregation: he wrote to Truman that the Control Commission "have endeavored to avoid treating people on a racial basis," noting that "people from almost every race in Europe" had been shipped to the concentration camps, and that "there appears to have been very little difference in the amount of torture" they endured. But with these people now segregated by virtue of their Jewish "nationality," "relief" workers from the Jewish Agency could now set about indoctrinating them, or forcing them, into the Zionist cause.

The Irgun as well was active in the camps—MI5 reported "ample evidence of the existence of Revisionist and Irgun cells in Displaced Persons camps in both the British and American Zones" in Europe. The terror groups' influence would become more visible with the bombings by Jewish DPs of European trains and hotels in 1947.[235]

Many Jewish DPs were not convinced by the Zionists' indoctrination, and so where persuasion failed, the DPs were shunned, ostracized, their rations reduced, and in some cases subjected to violence. When for example a Jewish survivor in the Bergen-Belsen DP camp began to voice the suggestion that all countries, not just

Palestine, be open to them, she was physically attacked and "dragged down the steps." Men who refused to join the militias were sometimes beaten. DPs were trained to organize mass aliyah, and—an urgent task in late 1945—to give fanatical *only-to-Palestine* statements to the Anglo-American Commission of Inquiry.[236]

Thus when in early 1946 the AACI visited the Jewish DP camps, they were greeted by prominently displayed Zionist flags and notices reading *Our answer to the Anglo-American Commission—Palestine or death*. "Everywhere," the Committee reported, "Jews shouted or chanted, '[t]o Palestine, to Palestine'," and threatened "waves of suicide" if denied this. Its findings were extraordinary: in a complete reversal, now ninety to one hundred percent of the DPs insisted that they must go only to Palestine. When asked what alternatives to Palestine they might consider, they repeated *en masse* that their only alternative would be mass suicide. When the option of the United States, the historically favored destination, was raised, the DPs refused, saying that they would not be safe in the United States. Publicly, the Committee claimed that they had no idea "how the Jews in the camps had got this idea."[237]

However, if the Committee was shocked by the DPs' fanaticism, the Committee's American members had nonetheless gotten the answer they had come to hear. When Britain first approached the US about such a Commission to find solutions to the crisis, the US

> agreed in principle to the formation of a joint Committee, but wished to shift the emphasis in its terms of reference from the general problem of Jewish displaced persons to the particular question of their entry into Palestine, and indeed tried to eliminate any reference to countries of possible settlement other than Palestine.[238]

By late 1946, MI5 reported that "para-military training in Jewish camps appears to be an everyday occurrence," and Bergen-Belsen, a DP camp "of some 11,000 Jews," had become "a semi-autonomous state" that defied the Allied authority. Some survivors escaped the camps and settled in Europe, heightening Jewish Agency fears that peace was damaging the Zionist project.[239]

Orphans of Jewish background adopted by European families were another crack in the Zionist narrative. For Yitzhak HaLevi Herzog, Ashkenazi Chief Rabbi of Palestine since 1937, the "solution" to these children was to kidnap them. Thousands of Jewish children were forcibly removed from the adoptive families that had saved them when their parents perished years earlier, the kidnappings sometimes assisted by armed Jewish Brigade soldiers.[240]

Rabbi Herzog praised the "rescue" of the children and in 1946 made a six-month tour of Europe to track them down. Ten thousand children was the number he cited as his goal for the kidnapping trip, but upon reaching Europe he confronted fierce resistance by local Jewish organizations. The *Œuvre de Secours aux Enfants* (OSE), for example, had a list of 600 Jewish children growing up in Christian homes, but the relief organization was not interested in making the children orphans for a second time. Herzog lambasted OSE for doing "nothing ... to take the children away" and used his power to circumvent them. He succeeded in removing 250 children from their homes.[241]

Next, finding himself up against a French resistance, Herzog "met the Prime Minister of France from whom [he] demanded promulgation of a law which would oblige every family to declare the particulars of the children it houses" in order to forcibly expose those children who were Jewish so they could be taken away—quite a Kafkaesque twist on Passover for these children who had just been spared the Nazis. He however "had to satisfy [him]self for the time being with 1,000-1,500 children" taken from their homes and put in a Talmudic school until they "can be transferred to Palestine."[242]

Switzerland as well proved difficult for Rabbi Herzog because of the influence of what he called Jewish "assimilants," particularly a Mr. Bloch who was Chairman of the Jewish Community. Herzog prevailed, Bloch was forced to resign, and Herzog "then approached Government circles" to extricate 600 children from their adoptive homes. He worried, however, that "Swiss Jews cannot be relied on" to perform the kidnappings, and so suggested that "a special committee be sent from the Yishuv" (i.e., from Palestine) to insure that the children are taken away.[243]

In Belgium, Rabbi Herzog again faced the obstacle of a "Jewish committee ... composed mainly of assimilants." The Committee knew of 400 families who had adopted Jewish orphans, but it was not interested in his demands to "rescue" them, and so Herzog went to the Prime Minister, the Crown Prince, the Catholic Cardinal, and the Minister for Justice, and won legal backing to force them to hand over the list of children. When the horrified Jewish committee still refused to divulge the information, Herzog had "considerable pressure" put on the committee, after which it "supplied me with names but withheld addresses." He appealed to the authorities for "full legal assistance" to force the Jewish committee to divulge the addresses so the children could be removed from their homes and shipped to Palestine.[244]

In Holland, the situation was particularly frustrating for Herzog, because "during the war, the Dutch treated the Jews very well." It is too upsetting to remove the children, the Dutch told him, as "attachments have been formed between them and the families." Herzog nonetheless appealed to the government for "the necessary legislation" to force the children from their families.

Poland was more of the same. Herzog left Poland frustrated that he could only "rescue" half of what he believed to be the country's 4,000 Jewish orphans. Great Britain was worse still: the rabbi failed "to win over the Jews there in support of my work," because the "assimilants there do not show much understanding." Jews, he warned in summary, "must not be exposed to the tactics of non-Zionist Jewry."[245]

In Herzog's view, these Jewish "assimilants" were condemning the children to a fate more terrible than death. For a Jew to be raised as a Christian, he said in justification for his kidnappings, is "much worse than physical murder." Yet even Herzog's extremism fails to explain what was actually taking place, because at the same time Herzog was "rescuing" Jewish orphans from their (non-Jewish) families, Zionist leaders were sabotaging *Jewish* adoptive homes for young Jewish survivors, for the single reason that those homes were not in Palestine.

In August 1945, Jewish activists in Britain asked their government to allow one thousand Jewish child survivors still without homes to emigrate to England. Among the organizers were those who had run the *Kindertransport* in 1939 that had saved the lives of many Jewish children. Britain agreed, and the first three hundred children were flown to England, where they were received by members of Jewish youth movements, teachers, and nurses knowledgeable about refugee issues. They were united with their adoptive families and received excellent attention from the local Jewish community, enjoying frequent visits by community leaders and rabbis.[246]

But when word of the "transport" reached Zionist leaders, they forcibly stopped it, and the remaining 700 child survivors were left to remain in the orphanages, on display to garner world pity for opening the gates to Palestine until they could be shipped there as facts-on-the-ground. Even as doctors reported the desperate condition of the camps, and the shortage of food, heat, and medical attention, Ben-Gurion sanctioned the use of force to stop the evacuations to Jewish homes in Britain. The actual driving force was not saving Jewish children from a Christian home "much worse than physical murder," as Rabbi Herzog explained it, but gathering ethnically-correct human fodder for the settler nation. A similar rescue program was sabotaged in France.[247]

Some of the children were in their mid-teens and, fully understanding what was happening, wrote letters to the Zionist leaders who had taken control of their lives. The teenagers explained that they had lost any hope that their parents were alive, that they had been offered new lives in England and the opportunity to study in London, and asked that they not be blocked from this new life—but to no avail. As further insurance, Jewish children were forbidden from seeking out family members who survived the war, for fear that ties in Europe might be reestablished.[248]

What might have been the most important resettlement program of the entire post-war period was sabotaged by Zionist leaders in the United States. When President Roosevelt proposed his plan "for the easy migration of the 500,000 beaten people of Europe" to his friend Morris Ernst, co-founder of what would become the American Civil Liberties Union, he explained that if Britain would open her doors, he could get the US to do the same. Ernst went to

London on Roosevelt's behalf in February of 1944, when the second Blitz hit. The British accepted Roosevelt's proposal, agreeing to provide for 150,000 refugees if the US would reciprocate. Roosevelt was excited: "150,000 to England—150,000 to match that in the United States—pick up 200,000 or 300,000 elsewhere [in the Americas and Australia], and we can start with half a million of these oppressed people."[249]

The rescue programme was dead within a week. "The dominant vocal Jewish [Zionist] leadership of America won't stand for it," Roosevelt told Ernst, after making a sarcastic quip about Stephen Wise. Ernst, bewildered, began to lobby influential Zionist friends on behalf of freer immigration, but facing an "often fanatically emotional vested interest in putting over the Palestinian movement," he was "thrown out of parlors" and accused of treason.[250]

This "passive" violence against Jewish survivors persisted despite being exposed in media as influential as the *New York Times*. "The unfortunate Jews of Europe's D.P. Camps," its publisher Sulzberger complained publicly and in print in 1946,

> are helpless hostages for whom [Israeli] statehood has been made the only ransom ... Admitting that the Jews of Europe have suffered beyond expression, why in God's name should the fate of all these unhappy people be subordinated to the single cry of statehood?[251]

When an explosion on New Year's day of 1946 brought the police to 84 Dizengoff Street in Tel Aviv, it proved to be an accidental blast from Lehi explosives, exposing their hideout in the cellar of the building. There the British found a small arsenal that included revolvers, grenades, bombs, "a very considerable quantity of chemicals and laboratory equipment, Army, Police, and RAF uniforms."

Jan 1946

More interesting, however, were the documents found there. Some suggested imminent targets: there was a plan and photographs of the court in Jerusalem, of the Jerusalem railway station, and the government printing press. Other papers showed that Lehi nurtured contacts (involuntary informants) with police, government officials, and watchmen, while agents (active informants) were sought among soldiers, seamen, technical specialists, radio and telephone operators, and factory owners. Lehi activities outside Palestine were pursued through foreign Jews and agents sent abroad. Training and meetings took place at synagogues, schools, stores, flats, factories, workshops, offices, orange groves, and packing sheds. Lehi assassinated the officer who filed the report about the find.[252]

The Yishuv's Recruiting Centre made a New Year's announcement calling on "all girls and boys born in 1928" to report. Five hundred new recruits had joined this "Jewish Brigade Group" the previous month (December 1945), and another two to three hundred would be added shortly. The main Jewish Brigade was the subject of news from Europe: it was believed "not unconnected" with "the recent seizure of 40 tons of [Allied] arms in the S. of France." The Brigade was increasingly a problem in Palestine as well: "the evidence is clear," British Commander in Chief Sir Bernard Paget reported, that Jewish (ex-Brigade?) soldiers in the British forces were "a menace to security" to the extent of murdering fellow soldiers and police, confirming Y 32's warnings. Since there was no way to distinguish Zionist plants from Jewish soldiers, Paget pushed to have all Jews released from service "as early as possible."[253]

On the second day of 1946, pamphlet bombs exploded in Tel Aviv and Haifa announcing that the attacks six days earlier, December 27, had been a joint Irgun-Lehi operation. But the militias were running short of cash, and so January 12 was devoted to fund-raising. At 10:10 that morning, the Irgun—aided, according to Circus, by the Palmach—blew up the Haifa-Jerusalem passenger train as it passed about two miles north of Hadera, the blasts overturning "engines, coaches, and the majority of the wagons." As the crippled train reeled to a halt, "fire was opened at the train from both sides by party of some 70 Jews, including women, armed with rifles and Tommy guns." The militants had learned that the train carried £P 35,000 in railroad staff salaries, and the train's guards, even "after extricating themselves from the wreckage," could not prevent the robbery by such a large armed mob. Pepper was used to obscure the scent of their escape, causing investigators to lose the trail half-way between the station and Hadera. ("Am concerned," Sir Alan Cunningham, who had assumed the position of High Commissioner after Lord

Gort, wrote in an understated cypher telegram, "at news that such a large sum of Government money has fallen into the hands of the terrorists.") Meanwhile in Jaffa, the Irgun's armed robbery of the Arab gold exchange of £P 6,000 brought its one-day bounty to £P 41,000.[254]

At about 8:00 P.M. on January 19, an employee at the Jerusalem Electric Corp called the Power Station to report that the padlock and chain to the Sub-Power Station in Musrara Quarter had been cut through. Shortly he "was held up by an armed Jew [who] ordered him to leave the premises," and the plant was bombed by "five Jews [including a girl]." Next, radios went dead as Jerusalem's Palestine Broadcasting Service was knocked out by four explosions. While this attack was in progress,

> other parties of armed Jews, including girls, were taking up positions in St. Paul's Road, Queen Melisande's Way and adjoining small streets ... three or four Jews [were] lying in the road manning a Bren gun ... About eight girls were crouching against a wall [with arms, and] the Jews were wearing battle-dress and steel helmets, some of the girls blue shirts and khaki shorts.[255]

After the Bren gun party opened fire on a military patrol, "a confused period followed" with explosions from grenades, incendiary bottles, and mines, the shrapnel causing injuries far from the blasts. Roaming militants shot the Deputy Superintendent of Police in both legs on St. Paul's Road; one leg had to be amputated. Two groups of assailants, one about fifteen strong, the other about eight, slipped in and out of alleys. It was about 9:30 when the Assistant Superintendent of Police attempted to neutralize one of the mines, but it was booby trapped: the explosion killed him and injured another. When the military came out in force, roaming gang members turned to sniper fire from streets and rooftops, shooting dead a student at the Middle East Centre of Arab Studies, and hijacking a taxi, shooting the driver in the head. The Irgun and Lehi jointly claimed responsibility for the evening of terror.[256]

British anxiety over their inability to distinguish Zionist plants among Jewish personnel took a turn for the worse when the Givat Olga Coastguard Station blew up on the night of January 20-21.

There had been no attack—rather, the "workmen" who had rebuilt the structure after its bombing two months earlier (November) were Palmach and had incorporated the new bomb into the reconstruction. As recorded by Cunningham, the explosives were "planted in the building with the assistance of Jewish workmen engaged in repairing the damage caused in the previous attack by armed Jews." The new blast demolished the tower and injured seventeen people, at least one of whom died of his wounds.

The radar station at Mount Carmel was also attacked that day but, in the Hagana's words, "the activity failed. The members were not taken out." Firing caps used in the failed Haifa bombing were "of local manufacture and defective," the British found, and a booby trap on the device was defeated. Hagana Commander Sneh sent a letter to British headquarters congratulating the soldier who had outwitted the device's tamper-proofing.

January closed with a small success and a major fiasco that would have been comical if fiction. In a fund-raiser attributed to Lehi or the Irgun, on January 25 "twenty armed Jews" stole (P?)£6000 of an unusual bartering commodity: yarn. Three days later, seventeen Irgun members commandeered forty machine guns and more than five hundred Sten guns in a raid on the RAF base in Akir—but then their stolen truck sank in newly-ploughed ground during the retreat and had to be abandoned. They escaped by jeep.[257]

The trio of militias remained active in February. The Irgun raided the RAF base in Tel Aviv on February 3 and the Hagana attacked the Safed police station and its sentry on February 5. In a hit on the military camp at Agrobank on February 6, Lehi murdered three (Jewish) civilians and two servicemen, including a doctor, and left several wounded. As was their habit, the militants mined the approach road to blow up anyone coming to the victims' aid. Some of the stolen arms were used by the Irgun in an attack on a railway workshop in Haifa on the evening of June 17, testifying to the current cooperation between the gangs. Indeed, in its newsletter *Herut*, the Irgun praised "this glorious week" of "united action of all three organisations [Irgun, Lehi, Hagana]" and "the support of the entire, united Jewish youth."[258]

Haifa's Superintendent of Police at the time was Raymond Cafferata, who seventeen years earlier had helped protect victims of Hebron's 1929 anti-Jewish riot but whom the gangs had since accused of cruelty in his treatment of Jewish terror suspects. As a vehicle escorting Cafferata passed on Mt. Carmel Road just outside Haifa at about 8:25 on the morning of February 15, both Lehi and Irgun assassins were in position waiting for him. A truck blocked the road as he approached, and "Cafferata was about to slow down when his British police escort noticed tommygun concealed under raincoat of Jew nearby," as a telegram from Cunningham read. Cafferata's driver successfully accelerated around the truck. Another truck appeared and chased after him, "firing heavily," but the police engaged the truck and Cafferata escaped. The hunted Superintendent returned to England, where Irgun assassins allegedly tried, but failed, to find him.

Several high British public figures were joining the Lehi-Irgun assassination lists, with Foreign Secretary Bevin still a particular target, the murder to be carried out in England by operatives connected with a Revisionist newspaper printed in Manchester, or during the Foreign Secretary's visit to Egypt. Assassination specialist Lehi was recruiting "recently arrived refugees some of whom fought in Poland and demobilized soldiers of British and Polish armies."[259]

Another Lehi hideout was discovered on February 18 in a penthouse at No. 3 Hashomer Street in Tel Aviv. Among the articles found there were a "U.S.A. type transmitter" set to the frequency normally used by Lehi, "U.S.A. type earphones," and "U.S.A. type speech amplifiers." Two days later, as the appearance of more "hikers" unnerved the Arab Legion, the R.A.F. radar station at Haifa was bombed by the Palmach, exactly a month after the previous attack. Several people were severely wounded in the extensively damaged facility. The Palmach was active again the following evening, bombing police stations at Shafa Amr, Kefar Vitkin, and Sarona, leaving four women and one child in shock amidst the wreckage. Electricity to the entire town of Jenin was sabotaged the following afternoon (February 22) in preparation for an attack on the village's police station, but the station had a generator and the attack failed.

Forty to fifty thousand settlers and Jewish Agency officials turned out in Tel Aviv on February 24 to honor four Palmach militants killed in attacks a few days earlier. Among the crowd were several high Jewish Agency officials, including Ben-Gurion himself, who (as British records put it) did not "normally care to associate themselves publicly with terrorist activities." The dead were buried as "national" heroes.[260]

"It is the extremist tail that wags the dog," as the High Commissioner put it. The Jewish Agency, through its constant propaganda, "have so inflamed Jewish young men and women that terrorist organizations have received a fillip both in recruits and sympathy." In a situation to be mirrored by the future Israeli state, the Agency created such hysteria among the settlements that it forfeited even the option of moderating terrorism, instead "being forced to greater lengths of extremism" by its own hyperbole.[261]

In the United States in the last week of February, Zionist organizations announced an extraordinary initiative: they would "recruit young American Jews as emigrants to Palestine," using the available British permits intended for European Jewish DPs. The project had the "full support" of the Zionist Organization of America (ZOA) and leaders such as Abba Silver. What this meant was that every American Jew sent to be a settler in Palestine deprived a European Jewish DP of that opportunity, what the same organizations claimed was his or her only hope of survival. Some of the US citizens emigrating to Palestine would soon bomb the *Empire Lifeguard* (pages 215-216, below).[262]

About fifty Irgun members, "dressed in Battle Dress or as Arabs" attacked three RAF airfields on February 25: Lydda, Petahtikvah, & Qastina. British records say that sixteen aircraft were destroyed and five damaged beyond repair, but the Irgun dismissed these figures, claiming that it destroyed "25 four-engine heavy bombers and a number of fighter planes." One of the leaders of the attack, Dov Cohen, was in the British Commandos.

When two days later an assault on the Arab Legion Camp at Jebel Canaan was repelled, the attackers were traced to Birya Settlement. Aside from the expected stockpile of weapons and explosives, in Birya the British found a cache of documents that were "full details of Arab villages, giving the population, water supply and the number of stock carried," including numerous sketches, maps, and notes about reservoirs, water wells, bridges, police stations, telegraph poles, the height of fences, and topographical information. Not coincidentally, these were accompanied by a "diary of hiking trips." The diary covered the period of March 4 through April 19 of the previous year (1945), during which eleven of these reconnaissance "hikes" were conducted by this one settlement. The teams averaged five members selected from a pool of nine. Other papers detailed the security and secrecy measures of this group, which described itself as "an integral part of the Alef," an Irgun-Hagana alliance.[263]

An uneven moderation in the violence came with the presence of the Anglo-American Committee. The first major attack of March, however, was another vindication of the military's warnings that they had trained the Jewish Brigade only to return to Palestine as conquerors. At Sarafand Military Camp on March 6, Jewish Brigade soldiers "located inside the camp facilitated the entry" of fourteen armed Jews disguised as airborne troops. They seriously wounded a female welfare worker and, according to the Irgun, took British officers and soldiers captive. Two days later, a Jewish (Brigade?) corporal was caught harboring two Irgun operatives and transporting a cache of gelignite, demolition charges, detonators, automatics, stens, and suits of battle dress. Several attempted attacks on March 25 were foiled: the bombing of the bridge on the border of Jaffa and Tel Aviv, an attack on the railway bridge near Rehovot Railway Station, and the bombing of an electric transformer. Road mines and road blocks had been set to delay emergency vehicles' access to Tel Aviv had the attacks succeeded. Three more incidents continued after midnight, the last by "4 Jews disguised as Arabs on the sea shore at Bat Yen, south of Jaffa."[264]

The relative lull that was observed for the Anglo-American Committee's presence lasted for four days after the Committee left Palestine, until the evening of the fifth day, April 2, when widespread sabotage again crippled the railway infrastructure. Block houses and bridges between Yibna and Arab Shukreir were attacked, the line was bombed on either side of the Yibna Railway Station,

> March-April 1946

"and bridges there and at Arab Shukreir were seriously damaged." Tracks leading to the station were mined, local telephone lines cut, policemen injured, patrols blown up, the Na'aman bridge near Acre demolished, and the railway stations at Yavne and Ashdod hit. Trains were "attacked and burnt out by Jews" with five people injured (one seriously), and railway lines were cut in several places near Mishmar Hayam Colony. At Na'Amin Bridge south of Acre, Jews dressed as Arabs held up a police guard while about 20 armed Jews blew up the bridge. Just after 10:00 that night, the militants attacked the Isdud Railway Station between Majdal and Yibna, murdering a policeman and bombing a railway engine. Further attacks were thwarted on April 3 when the British tracked "some thirty armed Jews" south of Bat Yam at about 8:30 in the morning, some disguised as Arabs, and three hours later another group of about thirty was discovered by air reconnaissance. Among the weapons they carried were Bren, Sten, and Tommy guns, and "48 locally manufactured grenades." The Hagana attacked the Haifa-Lydda train on April 5 and stole 6,000 rounds of cannon shell.[265]

Just after midday on April 13, "six men in the uniform of the Jewish Brigade, using W.D. vehicle," robbed the Army Convalescent Depot at Nathanya. About forty minutes later, "between ten and fifteen armed Jews disguised as Italian 'collaborators'" attacked the Army Leave Camp in Nathanya (a separate report read "20 men in Italian P.O.W. uniforms"). All were Irgun. To make good their escape, they bombed the bridge between Nathanya and Kfar Vitkin on their exit, the blast injuring the crew of a police car. One of the attackers was apprehended near the bridge with an anti-personnel bomb.[266]

When a "British sergeant" in battle dress appeared at the Ramat Gab (Gan) police station on April 23, he had important news to report: "Arabs" had been caught stealing from the nearby military establishment. "British soldiers" then appeared at the police station with the "Arab prisoners." Once inside, "sergeant," "soldiers," and "Arabs" proved to be an Irgun Trojan Horse. As they seized the building, the (Jewish) wireless operator managed to slip into the wireless room and bolt the door. The attackers blew open the door and stopped the wireless set, but too late—the distress message had already been understood and military and police reinforcements soon approached. In their escape the attackers murdered a Palestinian TAC, wounded two other constables, and made off with an assortment of weapons and seven thousand rounds of ammunition. Simultaneously (and perhaps as a diversionary tactic) the Irgun attacked the Tel Aviv Railway Station. Four bombs exploded and rocked the waiting room, but then "one Jewish terrorist was injured while igniting bombs and captured."[267]

At about 8:45 on the night of April 25, Irgun operatives threw an anti-personnel bomb into the Airborne's Division's car park in Tel Aviv, and as it exploded, a group of 20-30 "armed Jews in civilian clothes" murdered "anyone they saw," under cover by heavy fire from accomplices in adjoining houses. After killing the sentry, they entered the park, "shone torches on the occupants asleep in the tents and killed them out of hand," and finished by killing two more people in the car park. Two signals from militants planted in nearby houses appear to have been the order to withdraw and confirmation of success: a bugle sounding twice, and a light flashing on and off three times in an upper window. As usual, the Irgun had mined all approaches, which "seriously hampered the bringing of medical assistance to the casualties." Irgun notices posted in the morning read: "With their aims achieved our people withdrew with their arms and booty ... All our fighters returned to base safety. Fatal casualties were inflicted on the Enemy." For the British, it was "a premeditated and vicious attack obviously designed to cause the maximum casualties." Sniper fire and vehicle bombings continued.[268]

British nerves were rattled by a near-disaster on May Day of 1946 when explosives were discovered on the HMS *Chevron*, rigged to blow up by the ship's magazine. "The ship was carrying thirteen Jewish naval ratings [non-commissioned sailors] from Alexandria to Haifa for discharge," a telegram from Cunningham read, and when they were found onshore one had a detonator sewn into his clothing, and others had explosives similarly concealed. (Seven months later, HMS *Chevron* would rescue about 800 Jewish immigrants shipwrecked on the small Greek island of Syrna.)[269]

May 1946

Newly intercepted messages demonstrated once again the Jewish Agency's collaboration with the Irgun—indeed that Ben-Gurion himself sometimes wielded the baton on its podium. One intercept about "the Jewish Agency and 241* policy" stated that

> 241 and the N.M.O. [Irgun] have worked out special plans for actions against Military installations in the Emek Israel, Galilee and the Sharon. These plans will be put into effect on receipt of instructions from BEN GURION in America.²⁷⁰

Another intercepted telegram, from Sneh to a "Daniel" in London, read: "Please pass on to Ben Gurion the text of the broadcast of Kol Israel [Hagana] sent herewith; with a note that the broadcast was made at the request of Shertok [Sharett]."²⁷¹

For the British, the intercepts provided

> irrefutable evidence of the complicity of the Jewish Agency in terrorism ... [Ben Gurion, Sharett, Sneh, Joseph, and others], under the cover of their positions in the Jewish Agency, have been for long engaged in directing, planning and organising sabotage of all kinds throughout the country and also in directing [broadcasts which] praised the terrorist acts of sabotage and murder in the highest terms and have poured forth a stream of perverted propaganda of a standard imitated from NAZI GERMANY. It is further revealed that, under the direction of those high officials, the HAGANA and PALMACH have assisted the STERN and the N.M.O. [in their attacks].²⁷²

Some British members of the Anglo-American Committee now proposed abolishing the Jewish Agency because of its direct involvement with terrorism. When word of this leaked out, Weizmann warned of the consequences with more apocalyptic theater: abolishing the Agency would mean the destruction of the "Third Temple" and the last hope of Jews "throughout the world."²⁷³

Although the British continued to fear that taking stronger action against the terror would (as they put it) "alienate the Americans," they condensed the various evidence they had compiled against the Jewish Agency into a booklet in order to justify raids on its offices

---

* '241' referred to the number of alleged terrorists held under emergency regulations.

and settlements. A "jumble of alleged telegrams" is how the Agency dismissed it when the Colonial Office printed this *Palestine Statement of Information Relating to Acts of Violence* two months later, in July.274

Seemingly meaningless attacks against civilians were, the British surmised, youthful recruits getting hands-on practice. On May 14 ten armed settlers held up a café in Petah Tiqva to steal a jeep, but being unable to start it, they set it ablaze, while four others stole a jeep in nearby Tel Aviv by shooting the driver in the leg. The pros were back the next day, stealing 100,000 small-arms ammunition from a special RAF train en route from Acre to Wadi Sarar (Nahal Sorek). An armed bank robbery in Nablus on May 20 was, the British suspected, the work of the Irgun, and Irgun records confirm this. Mortar fire targeted a police post in Nathanya two days later.275

On June 6 Lehi militants freed an imprisoned colleague as he was being escorted to a clinic for medical attention, wounding two sergeants, one seriously. The patient was no ordinary Lehi operative, but Israel Eldad, a key assassin who in two years would be party to the murder of Count Bernadotte. Today, the Israeli colony of Israel Eldad, near Herodion in the (Palestinian) West Bank, is named in his honor.

June 1946

The pace increased on June 10 with attacks on three passenger trains. In all three, "armed Jews, disguised as Arabs, [were] distributed along the train with about 1 or 2 in each coach." At about 6:30 that Monday evening, a train coming from Jerusalem to Jaffa was stopped at a predetermined spot, about 3.8 km (2.4 miles) from the Tel Aviv station, by one of the "passengers" pulling the communication cord. In coordination, thirty armed Jews—twenty-five men and five women—converged on the train, forced everyone off, and blew it up, completely gutting five coaches and wounding a TAC.

Roughly simultaneous with that attack, a train bound for Jerusalem from Lydda was stopped when a girl pulled the communication cord and people on the line were seen waving a red flag. About fifteen more militants met the scene by truck, drenched the five coaches in petrol and set them ablaze, completely destroying them.

An hour after these two attacks began, roughly 7:30, a train travelling between Lydda and Haifa was also stopped by a "passenger" pulling the communication cord. One (real) passenger described the attacking party as consisting of "four men and four girls, all below the age of 25, the girls approx 16 years." An explosive charge was pulled out of a luncheon basket and detonated in the locomotive, but the militants then left, probably unnerved by the more exposed location and fear that word of the first two bombings had already spread.[276]

When early the next morning a Palestinian railway employee discovered an explosive charge of about 50-60 lbs on the line southwest of Lydda, he followed the device's electric cable to a nearby orange grove, surprising its three authors, Irgun or Stern militants dressed as "Arabs." The bomb would have blown up the night train from Kantara, which was due to pass the spot a half hour later.

More explosives rigged on the main line near Hadera went undetected and exploded, severing the track. In Tel Aviv, an explosion led to the discovery of sixty-four homemade bombs at 57 Mizrahi 'B' St., most primed and packed in cases. An assassination attempt against the District Officer in Haifa on June 14 left him seriously injured, and that evening a bomb thrown into Cafe Central in the Arab market area left two casualties.[277]

Paralyzing attacks hit roads and rail bridges at or near the Palestine frontiers during the night of June 16-17. The worst hit was the Yarmuk bridge on the Hijaz railway between el Hamme and Samakh, which was irreparable, with reconstruction estimated at more than a year. As Cunningham reported it to Secretary of State for the Colonies G.H. Hall,

> It is composed of three spans, the center one being fifty metres in length passing over a deep gorge. The tops of the two pillars supporting the girders were blown up in such a way that the center span collapsed completely to the bottom of the gorge...

The same night, "the railway bridge at Az Zib, north of Acre, was blown up by a large party of Jews," but one powerful charge apparently ignited prematurely, as "the body of one of the attackers and the remains of a considerable number of others were found near the bridge." Six haversacks filled with gelignite were discovered on a road bridge nearby. The main bridge at Wadi Gaza was also hit, but being of ferro-concrete construction it did not collapse and was repairable. Nearby Bedouin were attacked by the saboteurs.[278]

Road bridges fared no better. The Allenby Bridge "was blown up after a determined attack lasting about forty minutes by a party of some twenty armed Jews," and the nearby frontier control building was bombed. The pier on the Palestinian side of the Jordan was destroyed, and "as a result of the demolition of the pier," the Palestinian end of the bridge's center span "weighing approximately 200 tons is now resting on the river bank." Police dogs trailed the Allenby Bridge attackers to Kivutsat Ha Hugim Jewish settlement, but the soldiers were blocked from apprehending them by settlers, both men and women, "lying down on the ground with legs arms interlocked," and by women attacking the soldiers with sticks.

Bombs sent the Palestinian end of the bridge at Jisr Sheik Hussein collapsing into the river, destroying the entire structure. At Jisr Banat Yacoub (Northern Frontier), the bridge on Damascus Road was bombed, crumbling into the river "so badly twisted and bent that it must be regarded as a total wreck." A bomb disposal officer of the Royal Engineers attempted to save the bridge at Jisr Damiya near Jiftli, but the bomb exploded as he struggled to disarm it, killing him and wrecking the bridge as its authors intended.

The nocturnal blitz continued with the bombings of the bridge and culvert on the road north of Metulla, and the road bridge at Wadi Gaza. Finally, in order to cripple relief efforts, the militants accompanied their night of region-wide destruction with a series of diversionary bombings.

This blitz bore all the hallmarks of the Irgun or an Irgun-Lehi collaboration—but it proved to be the handiwork of the Jewish Agency's Hagana. According to Weizmann, Sharett had the Hagana carry out the attacks to give the British a "kick in the pants" while he, Weizmann, continued to reassure the British that "a Jewish Palestine" is "the surest of all available bulwarks for British power in this part of the world."[279]

Two journalists sympathetic to the Jewish Agency—one named Simon who worked for United Press, the other identified only as Gottgetreu (presumably Erich Gottgetreu, Associated Press)—had tickets to attend a concert of the Palestine Orchestra (forerunner of the Israel Philharmonic) on the night of June 17. Neither went: when the day came, someone at the Agency "suggested" to both that it was a good evening to stay home. At about 9:30, as the concert progressed without them, about thirty militants used grenades and automatic fire to break into the Palestine Railways workshops at Haifa Bay and set bombs. "After several loud explosions ... searchlights from Mount Carmel went into action and night planes were sent out to investigate ... Explosions continued till late night" and the fires raged until sunrise. Vital railway machinery was destroyed, crippling railway maintenance and thus making subsequent terror attacks on the railways all the more serious. The approach to the workshop was mined to target first responders, and so the Haifa Municipal fire engine that rushed to the scene was blown up, leaving several firemen injured in the wrecked vehicle. Further incidents of sniper, grenade attacks, and bombings dotted the evening.

The next day, the Hagana extolled the latest attacks, boasting on Kol Israel (radio) that the government was no longer in control in any part of Palestine: the militias wreaked havoc even "in the purely Arab parts of the country" and fully to the borders. Obviously, the Jewish Agency knew in advance that it was a good night for two journalists to stay home.[280]

That afternoon (June 18) at 1:20 PM, "twelve Jews armed with tommy-guns" drove up in four taxis and two light trucks to the Officers' Club in Tel Aviv's Hotel Hayarkon. After cutting the telephone lines and suspending traffic, they "went round the dining room inspecting shoulder tabs" and seized five senior officers. Two who attempted to resist were struck on the head with lead piping. At about 3:15, "armed Jews drove up in a taxi" and tried to abduct two more officers, but settled for shooting them in the legs when they successfully resisted. An eighth officer was abducted in Jerusalem; he managed to slip his bonds and escape from the house on Moshe Street where he was being held.

When word of the kidnappings reached London, military officials argued that talks with the Jewish Agency about raising the immigration quota should be suspended pending their release, but government officials, in deference to the United States, refused. The saga ended on July 4 when the three remaining kidnapped men were chloroformed, put in a coffin-esque wooden box, and dumped on the corner of Shedal and Rothschild Street in front of "hundreds of passers-by," none of whom, the British complained, "apparently considered the occasion worthy of note, and no information was obtained from them."

In the evening on the day of the kidnappings (June 18), a train driver came across red flags on the tracks near Kafar Jindis, two miles north of Lydda. The driver, savvy to this Irgun ruse, kept going as a bomb blew up under the train and Irgun fighters fired on it from the sides.[281]

Sharett exuded confidence when he addressed an extraordinary session of the Jewish Agency Executive the next day. Their political influence in the US, he assured the members, will "suffice to compel the President to act energetically and quickly" for the Zionists, and the US knows that "the threats of the Arabs are worthless and that their military potential is nil … We shall exploit to the maximum the American pressure on the British government," emphasizing the US' "pre-election period" and "Great Britain's dependence on the U.S.A." for its post-war loan. Sharett continued to speak of Europe's Jewish DPs as Agency property: they must be permitted no future other than Palestine.[282]

A new terror organization began appearing about this time, Otsray Ha Magifa—literally "the stoppers of the epidemic," this "epidemic" being friendships between Jews and non-Jews and the threat to the "purity" of "Jewish blood" such friendships posed. The terror group seriously wounded a recalcitrant Jewish girl with acid, leaving her blind in one eye.[283]

Another diamond heist on June 26 by "some 30-40 Jews" (probably Irgun) raised speculation that these robberies were sometimes pulled off as insurance scams in (probably involuntary) collusion with the owners, who would buy back their merchandise with the insurance money. The British, meanwhile, had new indications of the Agency's surveillance abilities: they intercepted a letter, dated June 27, from the Jewish Agency in Washington to Eliezer Kaplan in London, containing details of a private meeting of the Anglo-American

Committee three days earlier.[284]

Both the Irgun and Lehi were active in Italy. A weekly periodical, *La Risposta* ("the response"), began publishing in Florence under the Irgun emblem, advocating terror and the establishment of a "Jewish government" outside of Palestine. The editor, Corrado Tedeschi, had worked for the Psychological Warfare Branch and published a translation of a violent Irgun pamphlet that originated in the US. On June 22, the English-language *Rome Daily American* carried an interview with a Lehi member who "threatened the British Ambassador in Italy and various other Government officials with assassination when their activities became inconvenient to the Jewish cause, and described in highly coloured detail the training given in Rome to Jewish terrorists."[285]

To the north, Irgun recruitment was accelerating in what the British described as the terror gang's "considerable activity" among Jewish DPs in the US Zone of Austria. Polyglot Irgun leaflets encouraged Jewish youth to "join the Crusade for a great and independent Palestine." In Salzburg-Parsch, a DP camp was now named "New Palestine" and organized into Zionist nationalist associations. As reported in the intelligence summary *Mitropa*,

> Those in the Badgestein [Bad Gastein] contain a core of fanatical Palestinian nationalists who are organised into units of the Irgun Zvai Leumi. These Jewish fanatics are a constant security problem.[286]

At Pocking, in the US Zone of Germany, a similar but smaller group of about 250 members carried out regular drills with the objective of reaching Palestine by any means necessary. The streets of Prague were plastered with Irgun posters enlisting support for the "Jewish struggle in Palestine," concluding with "Glory to Russia, America and Czechoslovakia," the last of these a major arms conduit for the coming Israeli state.[287]

Telephone lines throughout much of Palestine went dead at 3:45 on the morning of June 29. A massive blitz to nip terrorism, code-named Operation Agatha, had begun. The British considered Agatha "a declaration of war against the Jewish extremist elements" and extraordinary efforts had been made to keep it secret: US President Truman was notified only seven hours before it began, a timing that would marginally satisfy diplomacy while "ensuring that the message does not arrive in the White House until it is too late for leakage to be of any consequence." But despite the extreme precautions, "a large degree of surprise has been lost" due to "a leakage through military channels of part of the original plan." That leakage included "the black list of names of those to be detained" which, to the Brits' palpable unease, was reproduced and "plastered all over the walls of Tel Aviv." Should the document "find its way to America," the British worried, it might have "the most unfortunate results for us."[288]

Moshe Sneh, for one, had been tipped off and slipped away, and when British soldiers seized the Jewish Agency offices, it was "apparent that a number of documents had recently been removed from safes." Nonetheless, the documents still there made "clear that the Agency ran an elaborate espionage organization" and that "the Jewish Agency offices were the center of a vast organization for the theft of Top Secret diplomatic, military and police documents," including police personnel and Weekly Intelligence Summaries. Six secret reports from British intelligence organizations were found, as well as a note to Ben-Gurion that read: "Attached herewith a report from American Intelligence. It is interesting because it reveals the opinion of the State Department." Jewish Agency possession of these US documents likely explains why the Agency's US representative, Stephen Wise, had begun pressuring Truman to dissociate US policy from his own State Department, which the US President did—dismissing the "rumors" that Wise raised, and "loyally and wholeheartedly" assuring him about his support for "Jewish immigration into Palestine."[289]

Officially, Agatha "did not specifically include a search for arms," any such search being "purely incidental." Whether this was indeed the case, or whether it was to protect informants and minimize the risk that targeted settlements would get advance warning, one settlement, Mesheq Yagur, was searched. Three major and about thirty smaller caches were uncovered, despite the elaborate methods devised to conceal them. Of the major cache,

Operation Agatha, Mesheq Yagur, June 29, 1946. A soldier poses by a children's see-saw whose fulcrum is the ventilation shaft of a large underground armory.

The ventilator shaft of the store was identical with the central prop of the childrens see-saw. Entrance into one of these store rooms was effected after a paving stone with a small trolley beneath it had first been lowered by a worm and wheel and then pushed aside along a ramp.

The smaller caches "were skillfully hidden" as well,

> their entrances being disguised beneath paving stones, or rubbish, or behind sliding panels in rooms. Two were found in the cow shed, one in the nursery and several built into the masonry of culverts.

The weaponry found "were most diverse in type, varying from German 80 mm mortars to Polish detonators, and grenades concealed in beer cans". Much was from Britain and the US, and many were of unknown origin, lacking any of the usual identifying markers, apparently "made in PALESTINE or by private contract in some other country" by makers "anxious to hide their identity." Some probably found their way to

Palestine via the many thefts by Zionist gangs from US arms supplies in Europe; it was known, for example, that ex- Jewish Brigade personnel had concealed "huge quantities of war materials" in hut partitions and elsewhere in a shipment from a US army camp to Palestine.[290]

The Hagana suspected that the discovery of arms in Mesheq Yagur was not luck, and suspicion turned to two Jews, Freund and Papanek. Papanek was a Czech who had lived in Yagur settlement before the war, and then returned to fight in the Czechoslovak army, despite pressure from the Jewish Agency not to do so. After being discharged he moved to Haifa, where he shared a residence with Freund.

Papanek was visiting friends in Yagur when the British raided the settlement, and the (apparently coincidental) timing made the Hagana believe he had tipped them off. On July 3, Hagana operatives chloroformed and abducted them both, then chloroformed and moved them again the next day. Freund was released a week later, but Papanek was tortured, beaten, and burned on various parts of his body, including his penis, in order to elicit his "confession." He was found guilty of "high treason" by the Hagana "tribunal" or "High Court of the Underground Movement." His luck changed suddenly: en route to his execution, his captors came to a military check point and had to hide him, at which he escaped. The British safely repatriated him to Czechoslovakia, while Kol Israel announced that a "Jewish people's court" had banished him.[291]

> July 1946

The terror gangs reacted to Agatha with a spectacular sneer of British impotence. The British were still assessing the results when, on July 22, Irgun terrorists under the helm of Menachem Begin blew up a wing of Jerusalem's King David Hotel. Executed with the approval and cooperation of the Hagana, the attack was timed for when "the maximum number of people were in the building," as a British report gloomily observed. It was "mass murder," wrote Cunningham, "obliterating a complete cross-section of the public service": the ninety-one dead included forty-one Palestinians (the British themselves using the word "Palestinians" rather than "Arabs"), twenty-eight British, seventeen Jews, two Armenians, one Russian, and one Egyptian. Sixty-nine people were injured.

The bombing of the King David Hotel. July 22, 1946.

The meticulously planned operation began when Irgun operatives disguised as "Arabs" removed the reception clerk as other Irgun "Arabs" rounded up the remaining hotel employees in the basement. "Milk cans" filled with 500 lbs of high explosives were delivered to the hotel basement through the passage to *La Regence* Restaurant and placed directly under the café, timed to explode at about half past noon, the lunch hour. Security quickly became aware of the intruders, and might have found the bombs in time to evacuate—but other Irgun operatives, also dressed as "Arabs," launched a diversionary bombing between the hotel and the YMCA (which an Irgun *Communique* later called a "warning bomb"), then fled in a saloon car.

At 11:00 that night, the Hagana issued a General Order enacting various measures to protect those responsible for the massacre. False names should be used and no identity cards produced; suspects should not sleep at their own address; special armed squads should return to their settlements until things calm; and should the British find an arms cache, an attack was to be launched at least one kilometer (0.6 mile) from the scene (apparently meaning a diversionary attack).

According to what the British called a "reliable report," representatives of the Irgun, Lehi, and Hagana had met the previous day, July 21, in the Sderoet Chen area of Tel Aviv to plan the bombing. Menachem Begin, Nathan Friedman-Yellin, Moshe Sneh, and Itzhak Ish-Shadeh (Feldman) were present. To decide which of the three gangs would carry it out, they allegedly drew straws.

The day after this best-known terror attack from the Mandate period, "[Jewish] youths plastered all walls and shops in Tel Aviv" with broadsides extolling the bombing. Over the next ten days, however, the event "prompted a number of people in this country to provide the authorities with information regarding possible terrorists in Palestine."[292]

Notwithstanding the story of drawing straws, four years later Begin allegedly told the Knesset that Ben-Gurion himself ordered the King David bombing, but he "had been asked by him to let [the Irgun] bear the consequences of the crime in the eyes of the world in order to exculpate the Jewish Agency." This is supported by internal Jewish Agency documents that show that Moshe Sneh knew of the King David attack beforehand, but that the "Jewish Resistance Movement" (Hagana and Jewish Agency) could deny knowledge of it; and by the Hagana's "General Order" to protect the bombers.[293]

Following the international condemnation, on July 24 the Irgun issued a statement blaming the British for the King David attack, expressing its regret that there were Jews among the dead, and claiming that it had made phone calls to the hotel giving warning to evacuate. British documents at the time categorically deny that the hotel had received any such call in time to evacuate, and this is supported by the author's interview with a survivor of the blast. The Irgun's claim is also at odds with their having timed the bomb for when the area was most populated.

But regardless of any merit of the alleged calls as a moral defense, it is not plausible that anyone, even the operators receiving such calls, would then wait inside the building to get blown up. The British, to be sure, were keenly aware of the hotel's value as a political target: security precautions at the building, according to a document dated exactly seven months before the bombing, "are all that can be taken without declaring open war and going into a state of siege." Nor were Irgun "warnings" credible: the terror organization made fake bomb scares as a tactic of disruption.[294]

The King David bombing endures as the iconic terror attack of the Mandate years, and history books cite it as the most deadly. This is of course false. The 1940 bombing of the *Patria* was three times deadlier, killing about 267 people, and the two atrocities are identical in the claim that no one was 'supposed' to die. Of those in which the killing was the acknowledged purpose, at least one of the Irgun's bombing of Palestinian markets killed more (July 6, 1938, about 120), and the Zionist armies' coming slaughter of villages such as Deir Yassin would also kill more people than the King David attack. Why, then, the status of the King David attack as the defining image of pre-state terror? The answer would seem to lie in the adaptability of this bombing to the Zionist narrative: unlike the more deadly terror attacks, the building itself can be explained as a military target, since it housed the seat of the British colonial administration.[295]

"We will continue to go our way," the *Voice of Fighting Zion* announced after the King David bombing, "the way of sufferings, the path of war." The Hebrew daily, *Davar*, stated that not only would the attack "not alter ... the political struggle of Zionism," but this struggle for "the secret plans of Zionism" will be "even more terrible and bitter." In its newsletter *Herut*, the Irgun referred to their terror campaign as the "third world war." For the Palestinians, the bombing reaffirmed the fear that (in the words of a British report) the "Government could not protect Arab lives and property from Jewish terrorists."

In comic irony, Brig. Iltyd Clayton joked that the way Zionists are extolling terrorism, we might one day even see Menachem Begin head the Zionist Organisation—scarcely imagining that Begin would become Prime Minister of the Israeli state and be accorded the Nobel Peace Prize. "Will nothing," this veteran of both World Wars wrote,

> ever convince people at home that in dealing with political Zionism we are dealing with something based on sentiment, on lust for power and I believe hatred for the West, and that it is fundamentally unjust........[296]

The King David outrage prompted another massive anti-terror operation, this one code-named Shark. On the morning of July 30, twenty thousand troops, mainly from the 6th Airborne, cordoned off Tel Aviv and screened 100,000 residents with instructions to "watch particularly for:- (a) Bogus women. (b) Bogus sick." Over the next four days, the Operation led to the discovery of five arms caches. Tel Aviv's Great Synagogue, 110 Allenby Street, proved to be the hiding spot for a large weapons cache, counterfeiting equipment, and according to some reports, $1,000,000 in counterfeit Government bonds. Another large weapons cache was discovered behind a hollow wall in the washroom of a technical school.

The Irgun, and to a lesser extent Lehi, continued to enlarge their ranks with defectors from the Hagana. Three reasons for disaffection were cited: anger at the Hagana's betrayal of some Irgun agents to the British (this "betrayal" on competitive rather than moralistic grounds, according to Kollek); anger at lax security that had allowed the British to seize documents and "acquire a great deal of information on the organisation"; and "disgust at [Jewish] Agency denials of association with HAGANA and all it has accomplished." The Irgun had won considerable clout, claiming for example that Britain's commuting of two terrorists' death sentences and other concessions were "done with the sole purpose to calm American opposition [fostered by the Irgun's US branch] against the American loan to Britain." To stem the exodus to its rivals, the Hagana promised "stronger activity in the future."[297]

August began with the bombing of rail tracks near Petah Tiqva. On the second day of the month, the people of Salzburg, Austria, woke up to a city "plastered with posters in ten languages" encouraging young Jews to enlist in the Irgun and go to Palestine, what the British called the continuing "deliberate and highly organised plan" to force the creation of a Zionist state by exploiting "the sufferings of unfortunate people."

Aug 1946

> Herded into over-crowded and unseaworthy ships, with insufficient food and in conditions of the utmost privation and squalor, they are brought across the Mediterranean inspired by a conviction, which has been instilled into them, that this is their only road to safety.[298]

Instilling that "conviction" required the terror of a war that never ended, whose only relief would be a Zionist state of (literally, geographically) Biblical proportions. Thus in London that month, *The Jewish Struggle* published a cartoon showing the British 6th Airborne sending emaciated Jews into a gas chamber, and Prime Minister Attlee and Bevin gleefully destroying Jews' last hope of survival by symbolically taking a scissor (i.e., Partition) to a map of Palestine and Transjordan (page 158).[299]

When a Red Cross ambulance arrived at the Government Hospital in Jaffa on August 11, five hospital orderlies—or so they were dressed—emerged and asked for the ward where two injured Irgun members were recovering. The sentry became suspicious and called for reinforcements. A gun battle ensued, but the five imposters escaped in their stolen ambulance.

A change in British policy on August 13 threw new fuel into the terrorists' fire. Until then, illegal immigrants were not denied landing in Palestine, but were held in the Athlit Clearance Camp until they could be released under the current quota (in excess of the White Paper) of 1500 per month. Since this policy effectively presumed unlimited Zionist immigration, it was seen as prejudicial to a decision on the future of Palestine, and so the new policy required that the immigrants be taken to DP facilities on Cyprus pending that decision. Exceptions were made for the sick, children, and pregnant women.

Relatively minor terror *du jour* punctuated the month. Among several incidents on August 16, Lehi bombed a Tel Aviv flour mill because its owner refused demands for 'contributions'. On August 21, three Hagana swimmers placed bombs on the vessel *Empire Rival* in Haifa harbour, blowing a hole in it eight by three feet. At 20:00 Palestine time on August 29, Britain announced the commutation of death sentences for eighteen Lehi terrorists, following repeated intelligence warnings of a surge in terror and assassinations should the sentences be carried out. August also brought calls for a "Jewish" atomic fission facility in Palestine.[300]

In September in the United States, Peter Bergson produced Ben Hecht's play *A Flag is Born*. With a cast that included Marlon Brando and Paul Muni, the play raised money for the Irgun, whose terror it romanticized. In a brilliant stroke of marketing savvy and irony, Bergson wooed American progressives to his ethnic supremacist cause by refusing to perform in segregated (black/white) venues. Hebrew University president Judah Magnes, who was in the US, assailed the play's glorification of Jewish violence; in response, Hecht ridiculed "Jews in fancy dress with frightened brains."

Sept 1946

Bevin now called for a London Conference between Arab and Zionist leaders to discuss Palestine's future. Arab states agreed to attend, but Palestinian representatives did not—they maintained their right to self-determination and thus saw nothing to discuss. The Jewish Agency refused to attend because Britain would neither accept preconditions nor state its proposals in advance. "If, for instance," Bevin wrote, "it leaked out that we were willing to consider partition"—a word that had become synonymous with Zionist statehood—"the Jews, having got us to that point, would, I am certain, change their tactics and put pressure on the United States for the whole of Palestine."

Among the Jewish Agency's preconditions for attendance was global control of Jews: it demanded the power to control which Jews, worldwide and regardless of nationality, could attend. When challenged on this point at a press interview, Golda Meir (then Meyerson) pursued non-sequiturs and finished by stating that the Jewish Agency was the "spokesman for Jewry." Other preconditions set by the Agency appeared to Prime Minister Attlee to be "an obvious manoeuvre to put the Arabs in the wrong and to avoid a position where the Jews would have to come out for partition"— this reflecting a tactic proposed by Ben-Gurion in which Partition would be exploited but never advocated (see *Outline of Zionist Policy*, pages 237-238, below). Thus, representatives of Arab states were the only attendees to this London Conference. Palestinians boycotted it peacefully; Zionists boycotted it with fury.[301]

"This is our protest against the London Conference," the Irgun scowled in a type-written statement taking its share of credit for a three-day bombing blitz that began on September 8—a "Day of Bomb Outrages in Palestine, Terrorism on Eve of Conference in London," as the *Times* headline read. After blowing up some bridges, the militants bombed a signal box near Haifa, wrecking the building and killing a Palestinian child nearby. Bombings of the railway system continued throughout the night. Communication lines between Palestine and Transjordan were blown up; a bomb at a railway bridge near Haifa exploded as attempts were made to remove another bomb; a level crossing near Haifa Oil Refineries was bombed; three oil pipelines were cut and oil set ablaze; the Lydda-Jerusalem railway line was bombed between Bittir and Jerusalem; and the main Haifa-Kantara line was destroyed in several places in a series of bombings. Six explosions near Tarshiha (Acre) incapacitated the Haifa-Beirut line, while more bombs discovered there and on the Lydda - Tel Aviv line were discovered and detonated, sparing lives if not the infrastructure they rigged. The British continually hunted for more bombs, averting further attacks.[302]

"Sergeant Killed by Jews" is how the *Times* headlined Lehi's assassination in Haifa on the morning of September 9 of a Sergeant T. G. Martin, in retaliation for having captured Yitzhak Shamir of the terror gang's high command (The future two-time Prime Minister of Israel had camouflaged himself as a bearded orthodox rabbi).

That evening, "Jews dressed as soldiers" drove in two taxis to the Food Control Office, and after killing the guard were engaged by the local Haifa security officer, Major Desmond Doran, who was on his balcony where he had been dining with his wife. The militants—all Lehi—demolished Doran's house with a mine, burying the couple and at least one other person under the rubble. Doran survived briefly. The cornucopia of bombings continued, targeting communications, transportation, anyone maintaining public order, and relief workers: an ambulance assisting the wounded was blown up north of Hadera.[303]

When a jeep patrol sent to investigate explosions at Caesarea, Tulkarm, and Petah Tiqva was halted by mines, it was a trap: a sergeant exited the vehicle to investigate and was shot dead. Fifteen minutes later, two bombs were thrown at a jeep passing Ramat Hadar. Numerous roads south of Rehovot were mined; an officer and soldier were injured near Kefar Vitkin; charges were found on the railway between Lydda & Kafr Jinnes, and explosions rocked "Cheloucheevs" (Chelouche) on Petah Tiqva Road. A trolley carrying civilians near Ras El Ain was bombed and blown off the tracks, and a railway was blown up in the Hadera-Zichron-Binyamina area. Civilian trains near Battir and near Qalqilya were targeted with bombs, as was a railway by a culvert near Rehovoth. The Greek monastery in the outskirts of Jerusalem was the site of a shoot-out between the militants and police. Eight thousand British troops were sent to Tel Aviv and nearby Ramat Gen, but what Cunningham called the "outrages by Jewish terrorists" continued.

Irgun boasts of its anti-Conference terror occupied its September 11 broadcast of *Voice of Fighting Zion*, while Lehi used its *Bulletins* to catalogue its own contributions. The tallies followed the expected divisions of the two terror gangs' philosophies: the Irgun had carried out the bulk of the mass destruction, while Lehi had focussed on narrower targets and assassinations.

The Irgun hit the Ottoman Banks in Jaffa and Tel Aviv on September 13, killing two people during a diversionary attack on Central Police Station in Jaffa. Arriving in jeeps at the main thoroughfare of Bustrus Street in Jaffa, the militants threw petrol cans which hit pedestrians as they burst into flames. Simultaneously, another group attacked the police station at the other end of the Street, and a third group attacked the Ottoman Bank. A broadcast by Kol Israel announced that the attacks were a joint Irgun-Lehi undertaking, and in London *The Jewish Struggle* reported that the organizations had "raided banks in various towns in Palestine," and killed four Arabs. An attempt to bomb the railway near Qalqilya was thwarted on September 18, but the next day militants enriched themselves with "a daring daylight robbery" (as the British recorded it) of an entire conference of Diamond Exporters in Tel Aviv.[304]

At ten minutes to one o'clock on the afternoon of September 20, the Eastern Railway Station in Haifa was bombed, wrecking much of the station, as well as railway cars and nearby shops. Three days later an oil train on the Haifa-Kantara line north of Hadera was ambushed, bombed, and attacked with automatic fire. "One third of the train was derailed by remotely controlled charges of high explosive ... the attackers opened fire on the train guards and attempted to ignite the oil with incendiary bullets." A guard was killed in an attack on a bridge on the Lydda-Jaffa branch, and on September 27 "a mob of about 400 Jews" stoned a Palestinian bus in Jaffa.

Dogs, already used for tracking, were now proving their ability to find hidden objects that their handlers' metal detectors did not. The trained dogs indicated a "find" by scratching the dirt and then sitting or lying down on the suspect area, and if accurate were rewarded with meat. At Ruhama, a dog named Dumbo found a hidden wireless transmitter, and a dog named Rex sensed something strange at Dorot. Digging out the area indicated by Rex, the British discovered a wooden trap door three and a half feet underground, concealing a large cache of light and heavy machine guns, machine Carbines, mortars, and sundry other military equipment. Dumbo and Rex got meat.

Acting on a tip, the British scoured Haifa harbour on September 29 and found "an ingenious contrivance" of arm and springs that would have held its 50 lbs of explosives firmly against the side of a ship refuelling at the jetty at Haifa Oil dock. Its likely intended targets were British destroyers refuelling there. As with the attempted destruction of the HMS *Chevron* four months earlier, the explosives were positioned to ignite the vessel's ammunition magazine. When on Haifa – Tel Aviv Road the next evening a jeep was hit by a small mine, the driver was able to keep the vehicle moving as the bombers jumped out from hiding and showered it with gunfire, causing only minor injury. Later that evening, militants drew up in a car alongside a British officer on motorcycle and shot him dead with automatic fire.[305]

A new plan to end the carnage, and the Mandate, was proposed in late September by a committee represented by seven Arab states, the Arab League, and the British government. It outlined a democratic Palestine with a government made up of Jews and Arabs of all religions, with both Arabs and Jews free to become head of state. Its authors were confident that the plan was consistent with international principles of self-determination. Lest the US be unaware of it, Bevin personally handed US Secretary of State Byrnes "the proposals for a democratic State as set out by the Arabs." But Zionists rejected the plan outright, adamant they would accept nothing less than a "Jewish state" in all of historic Palestine.[306]

Musa Bey Alami, who after the 1948 expulsions would work with Palestinian refugees to make the desert in the Jericho area bloom, visited Bevin in late 1946. Bevin described him as "frank and honest and extremely helpful." He blamed Zionism and the Balfour Declaration for destroying centuries of peaceful coexistence among the region's Jews, Christians, and Muslims, but stressed that there was no point looking back. The settlers were a reality and Palestinians wanted to live at peace with them—but as equals. Rather, "this movement into Palestine was a spear-head," and Partition merely a tactic.[307]

Zionist "persecution of Jews" and "intimidation is complete"—so warned "a Jew before an audience at a dominion club" and noted in War Office records. Zionism's course, he continued, "is potentially disastrous to Jewry and to the peace of the world as a whole." Like other witnesses, he compares the Hagana's conscription of teenagers to Hitler's Youth Movement.

> Every boy of 16 years of age must join the Hagana. If he declines, his life at school is made unbearable and professional training and openings are withheld from him. If parents object, they are encouraged to deceive them in secret obedience to the 'call.' Even children 10 years old are enrolled in political parties—and this, eighteen months after we all believed we had destroyed Hitlerism for all time.[308]

Speaking "from first hand knowledge," even Orthodox Rabbis fear for their jobs and their lives, should they speak out. It is fundamentally "difficult to reconcile the pleas" to force open Palestine's door when safe haven elsewhere is thwarted by the Zionists. Zionism was never predicated "on the sufferings of our people," but on political objectives. As one example of how the DPs are made "propaganda pawns of Zionist Power Politics," the speaker mentions the case of Australia.

> No greater betrayal of the tortured Jews of Europe is it possible to imagine than the refusal by the Political

Zionists of Australia to accept the generous offer of the Australian government to open its shores.[309]

"Despair," a British report agreed, was exploited "to swamp the country [Palestine] with a Jewish majority." Any relief for the suffering of Jewish DPs, other than Palestine, was shunned. Stories of British atrocities, "so distorted as to be unrecognisable," were circulated to empower US leverage against Britain. There were in fact "large numbers of Jewish refugees in Europe [who] are seeking to emigrate to other parts of the world where living conditions are surer and more attractive than Palestine," British intelligence reported separately in September, and so "to combat this 'regrettable' trend," propaganda and "a species of blackmail" are waged "to keep the flame of zionism alive." Through "the exploitation of human misery and despair ... the Jewish remnants are being actively incited to embark on stinking unseaworthy hulks" in a promise that the Zionists cannot keep.[310]

On the last evening of September, a jeep returning to Tel Litwinsky from Nathanya was ambushed with a molotov cocktail and sprayed with automatic fire, hitting a girl in her back. Near Peta Tiqva, a man from the First Parachute Brigade was gunned down from a passing car. Then a new tactic appeared, probably the work of Lehi: a sign was placed on the side of the road bearing the word "mines," next to six dummy mines made of shoe boxes. When a vehicle stopped at the sight of the warning, it was ambushed and the occupant murdered. The British interpreted the "shoe box" murder as confirmation of reports (and, soon, Lehi broadsides) that Lehi was widening its tactic of personal terror to "less important" and random victims.[311]

Oct 1946

Indeed, October heralded a heightened Lehi campaign of assassination favoring off-duty personnel. On October 1 it assassinated a senior NCO of the Airborne Division, and tried but failed to kill the occupants of a jeep on the Haifa - Tel Aviv road. In Tel Aviv the next day, the Irgun blew up the house of a (Jewish) woman who refused to finance them. On October 6, two British RAF personnel who had just arrived in Palestine that day were gunned down with automatic weapons, leaving one dead on the spot and the other in critical condition. The method was Lehi's signature: the operatives shot their victims in the back and instantly disappeared "into a conveniently placed Jewish quarter," as the British put it. The heightened assassination campaign was accompanied by "a steady stream of road mining," causing more deaths.

The British did not keep record of the ongoing attacks by Jewish settlers against Palestinians, except occasionally to confirm that they continued. An attack that evening (October 6) in which "an Arab was stabbed in the back by Jewish youths on the Tel Aviv sea front," was described by a British Intelligence Summary as being "typical of many that have occurred" against Arabs by Jews.[312]

Two days later (8th), Palestine saw renewed "widespread road and rail mining operations ... by Jewish terrorists". In one incident, the worst was averted: although a bomb exploded as a train passed about 30 miles south of Haifa on the Haifa-Kantara line, that bomb was merely the detonation charge for a much larger bomb that failed to explode. The road to the Government House in Jerusalem was mined, a Palestinian civilian was hit by a land mine in the Sheikh Jarrah quarter on the Mount Scopus Road, and a Palestinian car was bombed in Tel Aviv.

A "prepared charge of considerable size" was electrically detonated on the Jerusalem-Jaffa Road, blowing up a truck and killing two of its five occupants immediately, severely wounding the others. The attackers then waited on the side for the first responder, which was a policeman: they killed him as well, and then disappeared into Givat Shaul settlement. Three more roads were mined, causing at least one more casualty, another Palestinian civilian. People were maimed by mines between Jaffa and Beit Dajan, and more mines were discovered on the roads between Petah Tiqva and Wilhelma (now Bnei Atarot), between Tel Aviv and Petah Tiqva, and east of Kirbot-Beit—"main traffic arteries mined throughout the country," as the Irgun described its day's accomplishments. Lehi claimed responsibility for a series of attacks on October 9 in which it paralysed major roads with mines, attacked a train on the Haifa-Kantara line, and exploded a bomb on the Jerusalem-Jaffa road, killing two and injuring six.[313]

"A large gang of armed Jews raided a Military Training Depot" at about 1:00 AM on October 11, stealing various guns, grenades, and bayonets, along with three trucks. October 12 brought an unsuccessful grenade attack and October 13 the successful robbery of the wages of the workers of the Yahalom Diamond Company, whose owner had refused to pay Lehi "subscriptions." The terror gang mined roads "in many sectors" on October 14, and wrecked a police truck, injuring its passengers. When the Pal Central-Haifa line went dead that night, the break was traced to Yarkona, where "about 8 Jews" were preparing to attach a bomb to the end of the cable by way of a pull ignitor, to kill the repairmen sent to fix it.

Lehi was more successful two days later, on October 16. After sabotaging the main telegraph cable between Haifa and Tel Aviv, it booby-trapped the cable with mines which exploded when the repairmen arrived. Anyone who helped keep Palestine a functioning society now had to fear. When the next day Inspector Bruce, condemned by a "Hagana court," was assassinated on Jaffa Road in Jerusalem, "none of the Jewish occupants of the street" who witnessed it, the British complained, "will throw any light on the matter."

Extensive mining of the roads during the night of October 17-18 left the British uncertain as to whether the Irgun or Lehi was responsible. Although road mining was typically Irgun, the night's array of bombs seemed calculated specifically to kill, and only secondarily to wreak wider havoc. Their suspicion is borne out in Lehi records that cite road-mining in four regions, and an attack on an army motor transport. Lehi was widening its scope.

The same militia blew up an army jeep (Lehi described it as a truck) near Rishonlezion on October 20, choosing a site near Beit Dajan between an ice factory and a cold storage building. Inside the vehicle, which was "reduced to a mangled wreck," the two occupants were found alive, "severely injured" with serious burns and multiple abrasions. "Minor" incidents continued, such as the severing again of the Haifa - Tel Aviv cable. The next day, the militants attacked a train near Jerusalem, destroying "two heavy mountain wagons," attacked an army truck near Haifa, and blew up a jeep near Rishon Le Zion, seriously injuring two.

Bombs derailed a train on the Jerusalem-Lydda line on October 22, an army truck was attacked near Haifa on October 23, and three checking posts were bombed in Jerusalem on October 24, killing two and injuring eleven. A bridge near Hadera was bombed, and the Jerusalem-Beirut and Jerusalem-Cairo cables were cut. Lehi buried several bombs during the day in various key locations, but the British, suspicious that multiple assassinations were planned, made last-moment changes in personnel's locations. The worst attack in store for the evening was averted when a "diabolical" shrapnel bomb "of formidable dimensions" failed to explode.[314]

Alarmed by rumors of Partition, the Jewish Agency expedited the establishment of new outposts in the Negev and southern Palestine, and the Hula area in the north, in order to secure regions that it predicted would lie on the Palestinian side. As Cunningham put it, the Agency was planting "further Jewish outposts in an area at present unlikely to be allotted to them in any scheme of partition," regardless of cost; for example spending some £30,000 to lay a 25-30 km (15.5-18.6 miles) water pipeline to establish two new outposts deep in a region it was confident would be on the Palestinian side of Partition.

The spectre of Partition led former US Senator Guy Gillette, now in his second year in the employ of the Irgun's US operation, to place large messianic advertisements in the press directed at the recently formed United Nations. The "fate of the Hebrew," the notices read, "has long been the barometer of civilization," the "oldest unfinished business in history." The only way to "finish history's business" was to hand Palestine over to the Zionists.[315]

When the ZOA held its annual convention on October 26, President Abba Silver categorically condemned any discussion of Partition—*Silver demands all of Palestine*, as the *NY Times* headline put it—and he demanded an "aggressive and militant line of action" to get all of it. Silver stressed "that the Zionist movement must stand on the proposition that it is not an immigration or a refugee movement but a movement to rebuild the Jewish state for the Jewish nation"—hence American Zionists' enthusiasm for awarding Americans immigration permits intended for European DPs. Healthy Americans made better colonizers than the downtrodden survivors of the war.[316]

158 | STATE OF TERROR

> FROM DAN UNTO BEER-SHEVA AND FROM GILEAD UNTO THE SEA—IT WAS OURS AND IT WILL BE

Foreign Secretary Ernest Bevin (left) and Prime Minister Clement Attlee "partition" Palestine into two with scissors, thus giving the Zionists less than all of Palestine and Transjordan as they demanded. On the left, the war is not over, and the British are the Nazis: Britain's 6th Airborne send Jews to a gas chamber. London, *The Jewish Struggle*, August 1946.

Lehi killed two soldiers on October 29 in an attack on a truck near Wilhelma, east of Tel Aviv, what is now just northeast of Ben-Gurion Airport. The Irgun was active as well: its bombers blew up vehicles on the Haifa-Jaffa road, then escaped to the settler colony of Gan Hayim, while others blew up a Palestinian civilian truck and a British military vehicle in the Sheikh Jarrah area of Jerusalem, killing two immediately and leaving four in serious condition, then disappeared in the direction of nearby Jewish quarters.

Zionist bombings made their European debut on the night of October 30 with the bombing of the British Embassy in Rome. This, however, was merely the postscript to a busy day in Palestine. It began at 5:45 in the morning when "Zionist extremists" (as the *NY Times* referred to them) blew up a truck in Jerusalem, killing two soldiers and injuring seventeen, four seriously. The blast was so strong that it set fire to the truck behind it, destroying its cargo of blankets and bedding, plunged a truck over an embankment, and overturned a (civilian) Palestinian truck bringing grapes to the city market. One of the victims was hurled thirty yards (Lehi boasted of a similar attack on 27 October, but this is probably a mis-dating). Elsewhere, the Haifa-Lydda train was derailed, a truck was "ensnared by a wire mesh across the road," a jeep was blown up causing two casualties, and a truck was destroyed by an electrically detonated mine, killing two. A large cache whose explosives paraphernalia included detonators for acid bombs, was discovered at Givat Shaul in a shack near a biscuit factory.[317]

At about three o'clock that afternoon (October 30), a green taxi pulled up to the Jerusalem railway station. A girl exited the taxi carrying three suitcases loaded with high explosives, walked into the booking hall, and abandoned the suitcases. As she ran back, she shot at a Palestinian civilian who had become suspicious and tried to stop her. Once in the taxi, her accomplices fired at the station precinct as it sped off.

A police sergeant dragged one suitcase outside and destroyed it by detonating it with a revolver. He returned to repeat the procedure on the other two, but the next one exploded, killing him and destroying the waiting room, station master's office, booking office, and military transport office.

There are two curious footnotes to this attack. The *Palestine Post* printed a Hagana claim that it had sent a member to remove the explosives, but that he was too late and was killed in the crossfire between the police and the taxi gang. But the Hagana knew that such suitcases were booby-trapped, and only the Palestinian bystander is mentioned in other reports. The other enigma is that the British captured four of the attackers, while a fifth, known as Yanai (but whose actual name was Hans Reinhold), disappeared. The Irgun suspected that he was an informer, and the following May its operatives tracked down the man they believed to be Yanai in Belgium and tried, unsuccessfully, to assassinate him.[318]

So end the daylight hours of October 30. That night, October 30-31, four months after Zionist gangs used the Italian media to threaten attacks on its soil, the Irgun destroyed the British Embassy in Rome with suitcase bombs detonated by timer. The explosion shattered windows throughout a wide area and severely damaged a school run by nuns across the street. Reports conflict regarding the several casualties, but one man who happened to be passing the building when the bombs detonated was "so badly hurt that it has been impossible to question him." With no immediate claim of responsibility, the media suspected Communists as well as Zionists, and the Communist Party in turn blamed Fascists. Four days later (November 4), several American correspondents in Rome received a "Communiqué the Supreme Command of the I.Z.L. [Irgun] in Eretz Israel" taking credit for bombing of the Embassy.

> [We] will continue to fight the British enslavers, the attack against the British Embassy in Rome is the opening of the military campaign of the Jews in the diaspora ... May God be our aid I.Z.L. published in the Diaspora 2nd November 1946.[319]

Jewish refugee centers in southern Italy were, according to the British, "exceptionally well-organised strongholds of extreme Zionism." Four UNRRA (United Nations Relief and Rehabilitation Administration) camps in the heel of Italy were "an extreme Zionist enclave on Italian territory ... believed to be full of hidden arms," but the Italian authorities "are not unnaturally afraid of the political consequences of provoking a row with UNRRA." The Anglo-American Committee became aware of the camps' radicalization when it visited them the previous February—indeed certain members woke up to slashed tires. The Rome bombing forced authorities "to bring under proper control the camp and admin. machinery," which was suspected of financing terror by selling UNRRA rations on the black market. As always, the British worried about upsetting the Americans, "since otherwise we may have them, as well as the Jewish terrorists, against us." Both the British and the Italians avoided searching the Jewish camps for fear of violent resistance and the exploitation of it to the US audience.[320]

Seven weeks after the bombing, the Italian press reported what the British called an "officially inspired" statement on the Embassy bombing: several "foreign Jews" from the DP camps, including one from the camp in nearby Ostia, had set up a bogus correspondence bureau in an office near the Embassy. Then "about twenty persons came from Palestine with precise instructions how to carry it out, the written order being hidden in the sole of a shoe." After the attack, the Irgun office moved elsewhere with all its equipment, but the police were able to seize two suitcases full of documents and propaganda, which included instructions for the use of explosives written in German and translated into Hebrew. What is certain, however, is that the principal suspects escaped, apart from one who was killed by Italian police in the attempt.[321]

Five years later, the Israeli state lobbied Britain to pressure Italy not to pursue the terrorists, claiming that doing so would "evoke memories of past bitterness." The result was a token trial *in absentia* of eight suspects, all living in Israel. On April 17, 1952 the Rome court sentenced ringleader Moishe Deitel to sixteen months' imprisonment, and seven other bombers to a maximum of eight months, these nominal sentences then forgiven. As the *Daily Express* summarized it,

> Light sentences, automatically wiped out by amnesties, were imposed today on eight Jews accused of blowing up the British Embassy in Rome in November 1946. None of the eight appeared, and it was said that they were living in Israel.[322]

It is about the time of the Rome bombing, October-November of 1946, that the British began systematically undercounting casualties in terror attacks—or so Lehi claimed. "The enemy has <u>for the first time</u>," their *L.H.I. Bulletin* bragged, "been issuing fake lists of casualties. We know for certain that on several occasions the casualties suffered by the British were higher than those 'officially' disclosed." Meanwhile in London, *The Jewish Struggle* mocked Yehudi Menuhin and Bronislaw Huberman for performing in Royal Albert Hall, comparing them to the *Moshke* who danced and sang for his oppressors in seventeenth century Poland. The juxtaposition of the two famous violinists was curious: ten years earlier, Huberman had founded the Palestine Orchestra; and Menuhin was the son of Moshe Menuhin, who after attending Yeshivas in Jerusalem and the ultra-nationalistic Gymnasia Herzlia in Tel Aviv became an articulate and impassioned critic of Zionism.[323]

Threats of Zionist terrorism on Britain's home soil date back at least to early 1944 (Irgun) and 1945 (Lehi). Even the ardently pro-Zionist Winston Churchill incurred Lehi's wrath by condemning its assassination of Lord Moyne, and so was cited as a target by May 1945. That fall, reports warned that both Lehi and the Irgun would try to infiltrate Britain by posing as merchant seamen and service personnel in ships reaching British ports from the eastern Mediterranean. More warnings of maritime infiltration followed quickly: the British learned that agents for Swedish and Norwegian vessels in the Greek port of Piraeus were willing to arrange passage for individuals as crew members, and Zionist terrorists would exploit this to enter Britain. January of 1946 brought the first confirmation of specific Lehi plans to assassinate Bevin, and the roster of targets widened in February.

In August, intelligence reported that five Irgun/Lehi cells would go to London if the death sentences of eighteen Lehi operatives were confirmed, contributing to the commutation of their sentences on the eve of the London Conference. Several British officials, including Colonial Secretary Arthur Creech Jones, received death-threat letters dated from Barcelona but postmarked from Lisbon, claiming to be from Lehi. Most threatened that the "execution" of the "stinking British pigs" will "soon take place by silent and new means." Meanwhile, in what the British called "one more victory for the pressure groups," the US granted Moshe Sneh an entry visa, and so he and Ben-Gurion reportedly left France for New York in an American aircraft on August 28.[324]

In the hours after the Rome attack (October 31), a truck was blown up two miles south of Petah Tiqva, killing two and seriously injuring two. Another truck tripped and detonated a road mine near Ir Ganim Colony (Haifa), and a police mobile patrol was attacked north of Tel Aviv. On November 1, a mine was detonated under a goods train on the Haifa-Kantara Line between Hadera and Binyamina, damaging a bridge along with the train. Nonetheless the British, ever fearful of violent backlash from the settlements, initiated what the *Times* called an "official policy of turning the other cheek."

An attempt to sabotage an oil pipeline near Kishon Bridge at Haifa on November 2 was foiled—the bomb was discovered strapped to the pipeline, removed, and detonated. Near Jaffa, a truck was blown up and burnt out, injuring ten, three seriously. Electrically detonated explosives hit a culvert, a truck was ensnared and forced off the road by a wire mesh stretched across the road north of Petah

Tiqva, a road bridge was blown up on the main Haifa - Tel Aviv Road near Telmond, and vehicles were attacked near Hadera and in Jerusalem. In the north, the new anti-Partition settlement planned for Hula was founded.[325]

Jews continue their terrorist activity, the Jaffa-based *Falastin* reported the next day, as militants blew up a train on the Haifa-Kantara line south of Qalqilya, killed two Palestinians, injured eleven soldiers, and blew up a train on the Lydda - Tel Aviv branch line near Battir village. When the Jerusalem-Beirut telegraph cable was sabotaged again, engineers were unable to locate the underground break; fully eight kilometres of the cable had to be replaced.

Militants bombed oil train no. 57 on the Haifa-Kantara line near Qalqilya on November 5, and then attacked the train and the railway blockhouse. A car was blown up on Beit Dajan Rishon le Zion Road, the railway was bombed near Kiryat Haim, two mines were electrically detonated under a train on the Haifa-Kantara line, and telephone wires were cut again. A military train travelling on the Haifa-Kantara line was mined by the Irgun on November 6, and Lehi bombed the Cairo-Haifa train on November 7, derailing two coaches, then bombed the tracks at both Neane and Sht Ha Tiqva on November 8.[326]

More sophisticated railway bombs were making their debut. In a November radio broadcast, the Irgun claimed credit for the devices' increasing sophistication, their "military experts" having developed a new type of railway mine that cannot be dismantled and is capable of paralyzing any railway system. According to the broadcast, the device automatically regulates itself to destroy both heavy and light trains. The newer devices could be completely buried and were better booby-trapped to kill anyone who might discover them. They worked as planned: two people were killed and several injured when the first one was uncovered.[327]

Nerves were given a reprieve by what a Captain in Airborne Field Security described as "an amusing anti-climax" regarding a Palestinian man whose house lay within what had become a Divisional Training Centre. He was "long-established" and the British were loath to evict him. Enjoying the rare opportunity to relax security and trust a civilian, they simply gave him a key to the military gate and made it his responsibility "for seeing that it is secured" when he returned home every day from his field, which lay outside the camp.[328]

In the morning of November 9, police received an anonymous phone tip about a hidden arms cache in an abandoned house. Four officers were sent to investigate. Shortly after entering, the booby-trapped house blew up, killing all four men—what Lehi explained as its retribution for the police "tracing Hebrew arms." Keeping to its Biblical pretence, the terror gang dated its report the Hebrew month of *Tishrey*.

The El Ain railway station was the principal target the next day. Four Jews dressed as police entered the station and planted suitcase bombs in the station master's office while they held the station master at gunpoint, then left. One Palestinian was killed and several people injured in the attempt to remove the bombs, and the station was completely demolished. The Jerusalem-Beirut telegraph cables were cut again, and 80 meters (262 ft.) of rail were destroyed on the Haifa-Lydda Line.[329]

Terrorists Say 'Nothing Can Stop Us' screamed the headlines of London's *Daily Herald* on November 11, as their war to bring Palestine to its knees forged ahead. The railway station at Rosh Ha'Ayin was destroyed, the railway line near Qalqilya was bombed, two coaches were sabotaged near Tel Aviv, telegraph lines were hit, and a railway trolley was attacked near Jerusalem. In England, Scotland Yard locked its gates as Parliament opened with "detectives on the watch for [Jewish] terrorists who might have smuggled themselves into the country mixed with Remembrance Day crowds in Whitehall." A primary suspect was a 32 year old woman who was said to be "the fiancée of a prominent member" of the Irgun. According to news reports, she entered on a British passport but, according to Lehi, a fake one: Lehi's *L.H.I.-Bulletin* of December 1946 claimed the passport used by "Mr. Irgun's fiancée" had been "issued by the L.H.I. [Lehi] passport department."[330]

The British media's nervous coverage of the Zionist terror threat was treated by the militias as proof of their success. Adding to British unease was the continuing "security problem presented by the presence of suspect Jewish terrorists in His Majesty's Forces."[331]

Lehi, describing "England in Terror," claimed responsibility for two attempted bombings of the Colonial Office, and seemed to suggest—enigmatically—that "Jews" had attempted to poison water wells in London, as if to bring to life the medieval anti-Semitic lie. The cause of the panic in London, its November *Bulletin* said, "was certainly not the fear of poisoned wells, though Jews were involved in this affair." Lehi, however, was probably referring to the intended poisoning of German water supplies by the *Nakam*, a terror group composed in part of Jewish Brigade soldiers. Nakam allegedly planted operatives in the water filtration plants of five cities—Munich, Berlin, Weimar, Nuremberg, and Hamburg—ready to poison the water for the indiscriminate murder of Germans on a massive scale. The delivery of the poison was foiled, though Nakam killed a few hundred German detainees by having an operative secure employment at the bakery that supplied their bread, then lacing it with arsenic.[332]

Railway terrorism had become so epidemic in Palestine that trains were limited to daylight hours and preceded by a special armored car. Days began with a "dawn patrol which daily combs railway lines for bombs," as the Associated Press explained the job known as the "suicide patrol." Those assigned to the task not only risked happening upon booby-trapped bombs, but also being targeted by the bombers themselves. At five o'clock in the morning of November 13, six people—four Palestinians and two British—were murdered in an Irgun ambush of such a railway patrol looking for mines. Later that day a fireman and policeman were injured when a locomotive and three wagons were hit by electrically detonated mines, and an electrically controlled bomb was detonated on St. George's Road in Jerusalem, injuring ten policemen, three seriously. Lehi was busy as well, assassinating two policemen in the course of the day. On the October 15, bombers used a remote-controlled mine in a culvert to blow up a trolley patrolling the line at kilo 44 on the Haifa-Lydda Line near Benyamina. Three of the several victims suffered serious injuries.

In the United States, the Political Action Committee for Palestine —formed the previous February by a soon-to-be-infamous Rabbi Baruch Korff—more than rivalled Bergson's media rhetoric. Britain, one of Korff's newspaper ads said, was not merely as bad as the Nazis:

it was worse. Britain was running "concentration camps" for Jews that "are even worse than the Nazi German concentration holes ... where millions went to their deaths." No one could "remain Christians" and "accept" the "torture, suffering and murder of 6,000,000 Jewish men, women and children," the wording nearly suggesting that the Holocaust was ongoing and being conducted from London.

Like Bergson, Korff seduced bigots with the lure of fewer Jews, and threatened everyone else with being smeared as anti-Semitic or un-Christian. Korff then went further: Christians had to fear not just for their reputations, but for their very lives, because Britain is "a malignant cancer from which no people eventually will be safe." But whichever lure applied, there was a solution: pressure the US government to cancel its post-war loan to Britain unless it cedes to Zionist demands.[333]

November 17's violence began at 5:20 in the morning, when a worker discovered a bomb on the Haifa-Kantara line near Kafr Sirkin. His attempt to protect the morning's first train was an Irgun death sentence: the booby-trap's anti-lifting device killed him and injured another man. Another mine was discovered fifty-five minutes later (6:15) on the narrow gauge track near Haifa. A half hour after that, a mine exploded under a train on the Haifa-Kantara line between Rehovoth and Yibna. But in what the British describe as "a most astonishing incident," it was faulty and did not blow up until under the seventeenth waggon of the thirty-one waggon train. Probably in fear of the traditional militia attack coordinated with the bomb, the driver continued on, the fifteen derailed waggons destroying a mile of track as they were dragged along. A fourth bomb was found on the Jaffa-Lydda branch outside Tel Aviv. The worst attack of the day came in the evening, when bombers blew up three civilian vehicles and one British vehicle on the Haifa-Jaffa road. Three policemen in their twenties and one RAF sergeant, returning from the cinema, were killed instantly, and six people wounded. The bomb was so large that, according to *Falastin*, the explosion "was heard to resound in Jaffa and Tel Aviv."

Safety workers who discovered a bomb the next day (November 18) on the Haifa-Kantara line were surely aware of the militants' predilection for booby-traps, but the device still outwitted them. Four were killed and six injured, one blinded in both eyes. The use of multiple, hidden anti-tamper triggers on a single device, the British were learning, was among the Irgun's new fetishes. As the day wore on, a pressure mine on the Lydda-Rehovot line derailed a train and injured the driver, a mine was detonated under a train on Lydda-Jaffa branch, and a rail trolley that was checking for bombs was blown up. Further bombings were spoiled when militants were discovered laying road mines near Givat Shaul.[334]

"A complete shut-down of railway traffic" hit Palestine—so boasted the Irgun of the day's sabotage on November 19. One person was killed and four injured, one seriously, while attempting to neutralize a bomb at Kfar Sirkin, a constable was murdered in Tel Aviv, a mine was detonated under a train on the Haifa-Kantara line, and more mines were discovered on the same line, as well as on tracks near Benyamina and near Battir. An attempt to blow up a police car failed, and in Jerusalem a land mine shattered windows without known casualties. Cunningham decried "the continuance of terrorism with its almost daily toll of lives," while a small group of enraged British policemen lost all discipline and rampaged Tel Aviv, resulting in an anti-British feast in the media.[335]

The Income Tax office in Jerusalem was blown up and destroyed by the Irgun on November 20, killing a (Jewish) policeman and wounding ten people. At 8:00 that evening, two "juveniles, riding bicycles" shot and gravely wounded 22-year-old Shimon Azzulai as he was walking with his wife and their baby, in what was judged a political crime: he was in possession of a British passport and was contemplating leaving for London in a week. Constable Moshe Ben Bezalel was assassinated on November 21 for refusing to cooperate with Lehi, and a railway track was sabotaged on the Jaffa-Lydda line. A curious, uncorroborated message from the Hagana that day claimed that a large mine had been planted on Manilah Road in Jerusalem in an attempt to blow up government offices, but it "dispatched squads who dismantled and removed the mine without being observed." Fifteen metres of track were blown up at Sht Ha Tiqua on November 23, and a military vehicle was attacked near

Beitdajan on November 25. On November 30, roads were mined in several parts of Jerusalem and a police billet in Mustashfa was hit by bombs, gunfire, and grenades. "Jerusalem rocked by bombs, gunfire in revived terror," the *New York Times* headline said. "Jews are attacking Jews," the *Times* reported.[336]

"This is murder and nothing else," a mother wrote to the government on the first of December after her son was killed, one of the many letters that reached members of Parliament from parents, spouses, and siblings protesting their loved ones' murder at the hands of the Zionists.

> What right have our Sons, who went bravely to fight for their Country, having been taken from their studies, their homes, and everything that was dear to them, and suffered without complaint, be murdered now in such a cause…[337]

The Jews in Palestine "hate our men," wrote another, less eloquently.

> We must get these terrorists under control … Will you please get our youth out of Palestine before they all get blown to smithereenes.[338]

When the Council of Christians and Jews met in London in early December, it adopted a resolution condemning "Jewish terrorism," and the Archbishop of Canterbury levelled blame at the United States: "I do not think that we can possibly feel that from across the Atlantic there has been much to help the relieving of this situation." Cunningham, similarly, complained of the militants' increasing confidence deriving from the "effective pressure which Zionists in America are in a position to exert on American Administration…"[339]

In an effort to protect people from the bombs, the British prepared a restricted pamphlet that gave "a brief summary of present-day methods employed by Jewish Terrorists with mines and booby traps." Various devices that had been recovered intact were dissected and analyzed, and methods of booby-trapping them described and illustrated. The book warned, however, that every device encountered must be treated anew. "Take nothing for granted … Having discovered one means of firing, look for a second—and a third; they are seldom used singly," this doubling and tripling of firing mechanisms having caused the death of many relief workers.[340]

Lehi started off this last month of 1946 by mining the roads using rivet-filled devices. Rocks and broken glass were sometimes scattered over the ground above the bomb in order to increase the effect. All four people in a jeep were killed in a bombing near Seven Sisters Road at 11:45 on the morning of December 2, and at least two more people were killed and three seriously wounded in continuing attacks over December 2-3. The bombs were placed on, or dug into, the camel track by the edge of the road, with the detonating wire tailed off into the nearby terrain. On December 3, after a gang member was injured in a thwarted attempt to steal funds from the Polish Refugees Committee, his accomplices brought him to (and held up) the hospital for an operation and then took him away.[341]

Two or three hours after leaving a Tel Aviv repair shop on the morning of December 5, a three-ton truck appeared at Sarafand Camp, driven by a tall, fair-skinned Jew, who produced identification and a work ticket. He spent a couple of minutes working inside the truck, then "tinkered with the engine," told the sentry he was going to the NAAFI,* and left. The blast from the explosive-laden vehicle killed two people on the spot and wounded twenty-eight, including five civilians, demolishing nearby medical and operational buildings.

A grenade and firearms attack on the Mustashfa police station seriously wounded a constable, and the GOC's residence was attacked with grenades, but bombers' carelessness averted what could have been the worst attack of the day. "A terrorist motor convoy ... consisting of a truck with over 400 lbs of explosives and two taxis in line astern" was proceeding down Street of the Prophets in Jerusalem for an attack on Air Headquarters. The militants in the second taxi were about to lay mines by the Police Billet as a diversionary attack when they ran over a traffic island, detonating the mines they were transporting and killing two of the bombers. Aware that the explosion had likely alerted the British, the other militants stopped, booby-trapped their vehicles, and fled. The British, indeed quick to the scene, assumed that any attempt to disarm the vehicles would be a suicide task. They had no choice but to explode the rigged vehicles (two taxis and a

---

* The Navy, Army, and Air Force Institute was a canteen service for the British.

truck) where they were, causing considerable damage to nearby Palestinian houses.

A few days after the failed attack on Air Headquarters, three Halifax aircraft left the airfield and risked dangerous weather conditions to drop food, clothing, and medicine to illegal Jewish immigrants shipwrecked off the island of Syrina. In gratitude, the Jewish Agency gave the Flight Commander three crates of beer, but the gratitude was short-lived: although Britain brought the injured, women, and children to Palestine independent of quota, it brought the uninjured men to Cyprus, for which the Agency warned of retaliatory terror attacks.[342]

December brought a lull in significant bombing of the railways—the result of a business deal the Irgun and Lehi struck with Jewish citrus interests that needed the trains at this point in the harvest cycle. Both gangs issued pamphlets assuring the public that the attacks on the railways would resume once the citrus season ended.

High-profile attacks on the British also entered a brief, relative lull with the opening of the Zionist Conference in Basle on December 9. The terror groups were not, however, inactive. "During the lull," British intelligence reported, "the Jews have turned their attention to Arabs and to unpopular Jews." Two days after the Conference began, in the village of Salame—a village that would be levelled and erased by the Zionist armies in a year and a quarter—a Hagana gang kidnapped two Palestinian children and shot the mukhtar who tried to help them. *Palestine Arabs Schedule General Strike As Protest Against Zionists' Terrorism*, the *NY Times* headline read, as Palestinians organized non-violent resistance that the War Office described as "orderly." Cunningham as well remarked on the Palestinians' restraint, but worried that "further Jewish provocation" would risk "isolated acts of retaliation."[343]

Not coincidentally, a "well-informed Jewish contact" told the British that Zionist leaders were spreading the propaganda that "the only real solution to the "Arab" problem in Palestine" (to which was inserted "[sic]"), is a transfer of 'Arabs' out of Palestine, and a transfer of Middle Eastern and North African Jews into Palestine.[344]

Zionist violence against "uncooperative" Jews continued, with four attempted assassinations of Jewish civilians by the Zionist gangs recorded within a ten-day period in December. Three were over refusal to fund the Irgun: one on December 6, another two days later when Selig Kunin of Nathanya found an explosive charge fixed to the exhaust manifold of his truck, and a third on December 18 when a Mr. Jacobson of the Rehovot area went to drive his new American car and saw a bomb with a burning fuse under it.

A fourth incident suggests that Zionism's anti-Jewish violence was under-reported, as fear kept victims from coming forward. Hayim Klear, a resident of Nathanya, had publicly denounced "terrorist methods and policy," and so on the evening of December 8, his car was blown up. But after an initial report to the police, something reversed Mr. Klear's attitude: he suddenly refused to speak about the matter and moved to "an unknown address in Tel Aviv." The bombing was now officially reported as an "accident." In another instance, one Yerovcham Wardiman, a prosperous cinema owner, "departed hastily for the USA." after refusing the Irgun's extortion. As a local informant remarked, Zionist terrorism was a "profession" devoid of any alleged "ideal."[345]

December 24 brought the end of the Basle Conference, and of the lull in violence. When in Rehovoth that evening, "a gang of approx 80 young Jews, under control of a leader," went on a rampage against uniformed personnel, the Jewish Special Police made no attempt to stop them. Then a "gang of 10 Jewish youths" set upon four soldiers, but were stopped by the Palestine Policemen. The following day, Christmas, militants blew up a truck, killing two people and injuring twenty. Another Irgun(?) diamond factory robbery followed on December 26, and an attack on the Divisional Police Headquarters in Rehovot on December 30.

Jews are not Zulus, Lehi railed in a crop of new pamphlets that appeared in the last week of December accusing the British of treating Jews like "natives"—a complaint shared across the Zionist spectrum, from this most fanatical of terror gangs to the 'moderate' Weizmann. The present occasion was Britain's flogging of a teenager convicted in the deadly bank robbery spree of September 13.

In retribution, four British army personnel were kidnapped and flogged on December 29: one abducted from Rishon Cafe (Cafe Theresa in Rishon LeZion), one from Hotel Metropole (Nathanya), two from Hotel Armon (Tel Aviv).

"Palestine's regime of terror," the *NY Times* reported of the coordinated abductions, now "threatens to assume increasingly serious proportions."[346]

Two men who survived a road mine pose for
a photograph by their mangled vehicle. (c1946)

6

"A Besieged Garrison," 1947

> In the long run no Zionists in Palestine will be satisfied with the territorial arrangements of the partition settlement. [They] will continue to wage a strong propaganda campaign in the US and in Europe [and] the demand for more territory will be made as Jewish immigration floods the Jewish sector. —*Secret report by the CIA, November 28, 1947, the day before the UN passed the Partition Resolution.*[347]

And so began the fateful year of 1947, heralding an "even greater reluctance than formerly" of the Jewish Agency to cooperate against terror, and an increase in the scope and number of attacks. Many ex-Brigade members returned to Palestine and joined the militias, some having engaged in assassinations in Europe, others having assisted in the kidnapping of Jewish orphans from their adoptive homes. Still others were in the United States, "endeavouring to influence U.S. public opinion, through Veterans' Organizations and through individuals." The flow of money from the US continued, and when the British again used diplomatic channels to ask that Irgun fund-raising be stopped, leaked word of these overtures was publicized as "British pressure" against Jewish "philanthropic organizations."

The American Council for Judaism, meanwhile, warned of the consequences of Americans being "drawn into supporting directly or indirectly a racial-nationalist Jewish state in Palestine," contrary to the high principles which Americans espouse. It predicted that the "self-imposed ghetto" that Zionists sought, "using a gun and forcing themselves into another land," will cause terrible harm to Jews.[348]

"Recruits for the Irgun," British intelligence reported, "are said to be coming in fast," as students became captive audiences to Irgun coercion "after the silencing of the teacher by overpowering him or by other means." Among the terror gang's newer recruiting methods was to "borrow" the projection room of movie theaters: cinema-goers found their films interrupted by Irgun propaganda.[349]

In a massive assault on January 2, terrorists used flame throwers against people, buildings, and vehicles in Jerusalem, in Galilee, and in Tel Aviv, where Jewish Settlement Police were discovered to be working with the Irgun. According to the British,

> At 1800 hours on 2 Jan the Jewish ghaffirs [corporal rank] at the gate of CITRUS HOUSE [which housed British military headquarters] told the sentry that they were being relieved. This was NOT in fact true, but they then disappeared, and nine minutes later three Jews, carrying flame-throwers, and armed, two with TSMGs and one with a pistol, opened fire...[350]

Some of the choreographed attacks on Citrus House proved too ambitious: under cover of fire from a neighbouring building, "flame-throwers [reached] the northern perimeter wire" of the building, while a coordinated "stream of oil was directed towards the vehicle park" to be ignited by the flame throwers, but they failed. The *NY Times* reported that "forty or more terrorists on the roof of a building opposite Citrus House" opened fire on the House's third floor with machine guns and small arms, "but this was the wrong floor and they merely hit the kitchen help." At least one of the day's wounded soon died. Among those less seriously wounded was a "Jewish NAAFI girl," one Rosa Hirsch of Tel Aviv, who when hit imprudently exclaimed: "My husband told me not to go to Citrus House to-night." Her husband had already slipped away when police went to question him.[351]

In Jerusalem, grenade attacks against the Syrian Orphanage and the RAF Unit failed to cause serious damage, though the Orphanage would be less fortunate in two months' time. Grenades were thrown at a military billet and into the Air Ministry Works Dep't Yard, and a road mine was planted in the Sheikh Jarrah area. In Hadera, the R.E.M.E. Camp was attacked, seriously wounding a Palestinian, the Fire Brigade was attacked, and two jeeps blown up. A Bren gun carrier was destroyed by a road mine near Haifa, killing one person and wounding four. Near Kiryat Haim colony, a military camp was attacked with bombs and automatic weapons. A taxi was blown up by a mine on the Haifa - Tel Aviv Road, and another mine targeted two Sixth Airborne Division vehicles. In Tel Aviv, a police billet and military post were attacked with mortar bombs and automatic fire, wounding four, one seriously. Several explosions rocked the city's streets, and a police armoured car was blown up, injuring two.[352]

A new type of shrapnel mine was used "most effectively" in the day's attacks, probably as a trial run, because "it is customary for the terrorists to try out new equipment before putting it into mass production." The Irgun was producing this newer, more lethal device in two sizes, one with eighteen pounds of explosives and eighteen pounds of scrap metal, the other with twenty-four pounds of explosive and twenty-two pounds of scrap metal. Designed for use against people and communications, it presages the deadly *flechette* (dart) bombs that Israel uses today. That evening (January 2), one such mine blew up between two jeeps.[353]

Early the next morning, another of the new shrapnel mines hit a vehicle near Petah Tiqva, and a third targeted (but missed) a "civilian lorry near the cold storage depot" between Rishon and Beit Dajan, the site of three previous attacks. At 7:20 that morning, yet another of the new mines blew up a jeep, putting three people in the hospital. The next day (January 4) a military police truck was blown up on the Jerusalem - Bethlehem Road, and two people were injured when a mine blew up a truck in Haifa.[354]

Mines failed twice to cause injury on the morning of January 5—against a mail van at 5:15, and against a civilian bus three hours later—but the day's "success" was the Hagana's dynamiting of three (apparently randomly chosen) houses in the village of Safed, north of the Sea of Galilee. Fourteen Palestinians were killed. On January 6, the Irgun attacked the railway station at Hadera and blew up a military vehicle on the Lydda - Petah Tiqva Road near Petah Tiqva.[355]

In Italy, the Irgun threatened to "attack nerve centers" unless the Italian government helped enforce Zionist demands, and on January 10 pamphlet bombs exploded in eight major Italian cities, though these were amateurish in production and most of the pamphlets were destroyed in the explosions. Two men planting the bombs in Milan and Padua were caught; both were from the Zionist-run DP camps. A series of Irgun bomb threats against US and British interests in Italy caused havoc, but none materialized.[356]

As the Zionist Organization of America allocated $800,000 for a new propaganda campaign, Ben-Gurion returned to Palestine from a "peace mission" to Europe. In a goal-setting broadcast from Tel Aviv on January 11, he made no reference whatsoever to the problem of terrorism. Lehi, meanwhile, held up the owner of a Chevrolet utility vehicle and drove off with it—in itself not an usual occurrence, and indeed taxi drivers appear to have had to accept 'lending' their vehicles to terrorists as a requirement of their job—but such hijackings often portended an attack.

The next day, Sunday, January 12, the vehicle, now explosive-laden, was driven to the District Police Headquarters in Haifa. The driver ran away, guards saw the fuse, but time was too short—the vehicle exploded as they were evacuating the area. Two British and two Palestinians were killed immediately, and among the sixty-two wounded were two in critical and several in serious condition. As Lehi claimed credit and bragged that "there were no casualties among our men," gang members murdered a railway guard near Haifa. When the next day the British again confronted Ben-Gurion about the continuing terror and the Agency's complicity, he gave a new reply: if the Agency used "physical force" to stop the terror, he said, it "would result in Jewish leaders being killed by themselves."[357]

Those leaders were expanding their intelligence-gathering antennae. Beyond the extensive network of well-placed informants and wiretapping, establishments patronized by British soldiers and police were used (and even designed) as fruitful eavesdropping operations, and Jewish sex workers were exploited to garner particularly confidential indiscretions from the right customers. When the British found that "some Jewesses ... employed as business bait by the manager of the Armon Hotel in Nahariya" were "remarkably well-versed" in sensitive intelligence, pressure was applied to have them removed from the hotel employ. This proved futile: the women continued in the espionage trade without the convenience of the hotel because, as the British would learn, the gangs left them no choice (pages 229-230, below).[358]

"Jewish terrorists struck again tonight," the *Daily Telegraph* reported on January 26, "when they broke into the home of Mr. H. E. Collins, a British banker, beat him insensible, chloroformed him and carried him off in a sack." He was, in fact, in the flat of a (Jewish) friend on Mamillah Road in Jerusalem, who could not summon the police until she was released by the abductors about forty minutes later, at 5:50 PM. British media, though well aware that civilians were targeted if they played any role in maintaining a functioning Palestinian society, were struck by the terrorists' choice of Collins because he was an official in a bank owned and operated by British Jews.

The most brazen kidnapping came the next day, January 27, when Judge Ralph Windham was abducted right from his court room in Tel Aviv by eight armed Irgun operatives, four of whom were listening to the proceedings inside the court. Telephone communications had been severed, and all other offices in the building were held under the gun. It is at this point that British officials publicly acknowledged that no one in Palestine was safe against Zionist terror, and that British women, children, and non-essential civilian personnel must be evacuated. Three days later, High Commissioner Cunningham ordered this evacuation.

The Irgun confirmed that they held the two high profile figures as hostages to force Britain to stay the execution of terrorist Dov Gruner, scheduled for January 28—a strangely Machiavellian demand on the Irgun's part, given that Gruner would ultimately refuse a life-saving appeal that the British wanted to give, and that this "suicide" was allegedly at the Irgun's instructions.[359]

"Palestine Jews Given Ultimatum" (*Daily Telegraph*) and "Ultimatum Gives Jews 48 Hours to Free Britons" (*News Chronicle*) were typical of British headlines as the fate of the hostages remained unknown. But it was the militants' ultimatum, not Britain's, that decided the issue: the British stayed Gruner's execution, and the two hostages were freed. The government led the media to believe that Gruner had appealed to the Privy Council, but he had not.

Judge Windham had been kept in an outhouse and given a copy of Arthur Koestler's newly-published Zionist novel, *Thieves in the Night*. In contrast to Collins, he was not gratuitously maltreated. When Collins regained consciousness from the chloroform, he found himself bound, blindfolded, gagged, and covered by a sack, being frogmarched over rough terrain to a cave with a mud floor and water that dripped continuously overhead. His burns from the chloroform were so severe that it was impossible for him to eat. An Irgun doctor tried to stitch his head wound, but his captors' treatment continued to be what he described as "brutal and coarse." If Gruner were hanged, his captors explained, so would he.

After the stay of Gruner's execution, Collins was forced to sign a statement saying that he had been well treated. He was then blindfolded and led over stones and ditches for about a half hour and abandoned. Collins never recovered; he died from the chloroform.

The British combed two suburbs of Jerusalem in an attempt to find the kidnappers, alleged to be members of a "Black A Squad," but the Jewish Agency denounced the search, saying it "alters the situation beyond all expectation."[360]

When on the day of the would-be execution, the House of Commons listened to Arthur Creech Jones explain why Britain was powerless against the kidnappings, they were listening to someone who had been imprisoned as a conscientious objector during the First World War and had directed a rescue of hundreds of Jews from Czechoslovakia after the Munich Agreement was signed. Jones told the House of Commons that

> The suppression of terrorism demands the active participation of the whole Jewish community and also direct cooperation by the Jewish Agency, which I regret has not been forthcoming.[361]

Schools remained the prime venue for the Irgun's recruitment of youths between the ages of fifteen and nineteen, with teachers powerless to protect their students. Behind closed doors, the Va'ad Leumi spoke of the terror groups' "domination and coercion, intimidation and threats, the extortion of money and use of force against teachers and pupils, policemen, drivers and others," yet like the Jewish Agency, refused to challenge it. JNC chairman David Remez, future Knesset member, acknowledged that they

> compel Jews to join them and help them against their conscience. People are compelled to subscribe money and assistance against their will ... Pupils in the schools and youth movements are also compelled by beating and threats to join these organizations. Headmasters and teachers are also similarly constrained."[362]

With all evidence demonstrating that the Jewish Agency was complicit in the terror, the British decided to call its bluff: they challenged the Agency to live up to its claim to be the nascent government of a coming civilized nation. On February 3 they "invited the Jewish Agency and the Va'ad Leumi to call upon the Jewish community for their assistance in bringing to justice the members of the terrorist groups who had been guilty of murder and other crimes over a considerable period." Such, the British pointed out, would be the behavior "of any civilised state." The Agency's response was that to do so would be "contrary to Jewish political interests."[363]

Ben-Gurion, meeting with the British Lord Chancellor, repeated that there would be no cooperation in stopping the terrorism unless Britain acceded to the Jewish Agency's demands; the same condition was voiced at plenum meetings of the Va'ad Leumi. On the other side of the Atlantic, the Archbishop of New York wrote of the

> deep and growing indignation over the treacherous and cruel outrages [and] world-wide Jewish propaganda. Justifiable anger is felt not only against the actual terrorists,

but also against the reckless and unscrupulous support which they receive from Jews in the United States and elsewhere."[364]

The Archbishop then repeated the obvious question that the British had pressed: how will the Jewish Agency, failing to control terrorism now, control it in a Jewish State? With the memory of the Hagana's massacre of fourteen Palestinians in Safed still fresh (January 5), the diplomatic correspondent of the *Daily Telegraph* summed up the situation thus:

> The inflation of Jewish claims from a modest spiritual home to a Jewish state, which they were seeking to enforce by terrorism, had driven the Arabs to the point of exasperation.[365]

The *Times*, reflecting not just Palestinian fears but what was to many self-evident from the Agency's behavior, put it this way: statehood would "give Jews a bridgehead capable of indefinite expansion."[366]

The next move in this "indefinite expansion" came on February 7 when hundreds of Hagana militiamen "roared south in a truck convoy today and founded three new Jewish settlements near the Egyptian border" in anticipation of Partition. In "Samaria" (the British report using the Biblical name, now part of the West Bank), more "hikers" continued their intelligence-gathering in preparation for the final showdown everyone assumed was imminent. Expansion into Lebanon remained a goal as well: Uriel Heyd, a Jewish Agency official then in London with Kollek, discussed with fellow official Eliahu Epstein (Eilat)—who in a year would become Israel's first US ambassador—the goal of absorbing "the Lebanon" into Israel.[367]

When the illegal immigrant ship *Merica*, said to have been financed by the Irgun's "Bergson Boys" in the US, reached Haifa on February 9, "it was noticed," the British commented, "that a large number of the passengers, both male and female, had worked themselves into a state of hysteria, and were obviously playing to the gallery of numerous press reporters." The passengers, all of whom "were in a disgusting state of filth and squalor," attacked the British with broken bottles and tins, injuring several soldiers. But according to what Airborne Field Security judged a "reliable source" (British internal reports do appear to have been candid about source integrity), "a reasonable state of hygiene was maintained" during the voyage. However, about a day before reaching land, "orders were given to convert the ship into a veritable pig-sty" for propaganda value. The report tallied with others received about the camps in Cypress.

Most of the wartime immigration voyages were nightmarish and had no need to feign misery. But a separate report states that "there is ample proof" that after a voyage of strict discipline and cleanliness, "an atmosphere of poverty, misery and filth is encouraged" for the final two days before interception or beaching. Nowhere in British records is the plight of European DPs trivialized; but the British began making a distinction between desperate victims of war exploited as pawns by the Zionists, and the Jewish Agency's preferred immigrants, healthy colonizers. There is "a considerable discrepancy between the picture painted" by the Agency's propaganda of the weak, desperate survivor arriving in its vessels, and the Europeans and Americans it often selects instead, the young and healthy who "will make ideal colonizers" or fanatical members of the militias. The passengers of its overcrowded vessels serve to confuse "the two entirely different issues of displaced persons in Europe, and the Jewish population of Palestine."[368]

On the night of February 11—one day shy of a similar attack by Lehi in 1944—the Irgun used Molotov cocktails to burn down two youth clubs of the Hashomer Hatzair. This and other incidents, Air Headquarters Levant reported, "confirm the belief that the active intervention by Jews to wipe out terrorism must inevitably involve civil war."

On February 13, as Dov Gruner's sister arrived in Palestine in a failed attempt to persuade her brother to sign the appeal to the Privy Council that would save his life, explosions in Haifa port sunk two vessels. The next day, it was the Hagana that claimed responsibility, and over the next several months its public brand became indistinguishable from the Irgun's.

In Jerusalem on February 18, Lehi blew up a truck by a remote control mine near the Jerusalem Zoo, injuring five, two seriously, and a similar device blew up another vehicle on the Haifa-Jaffa Road opposite Gan Hayim Colony. These mines probably evaded detection by being disguised as kilo stones (distance markers), as the following day (February 19), two mines disguised as such were discovered on the main Gaza-Rehovot Road, attached to electric detonating sets in a nearby orange grove.

More mines exploded in Haifa outside the Moriah Cinema, two army trucks on Mount Carmel were bombed, the airfield at Ein Shemer was attacked by mortar and arms fire, and oil pipelines near Afula (Haifa) were sabotaged—though the British were grateful that the "Afula sabotage cell" appeared to be poorly trained and its botched job did not cause a serious loss of oil. Shoddy work had also minimized the damage to the airfield: "not one of the Irgun's major technical achievements," the British reported upon examining some mortars found fixed on the airfield. A female Irgun member with what was described as an American accent telephoned correspondents to claim credit on behalf of the organization. Continuing sabotage of the pipelines strained oil supplies, with some "leaks" only later discovered to have been caused by explosives.

The last day of February heralded a bloody March, with the bombing of the Haifa Shipping Agency on the third floor of Barclays Bank, leaving two dead and seven seriously injured, some with fractured skulls. "The incident was carried out by two Jews dressed in khaki uniform, carrying army packs, who walked into the building in a leisurely manner, talking to each other." Both of the dead were Jewish, leading Lehi to publish the fabrication that two "Hebrew clerks" had been forced "by the enemy officers" to remove the bomb.[369]

At 10:45 that morning, the illegal immigrant ship *Ulua* ran aground at Ras El Kurum. Less than two hours later, before any announcement of the inelegant landing had been made, the British were perplexed to see printed posters rallying the Yishuv to action against the British for having imprisoned all 1,350 of the *Ulua's* passengers who, the posters said, had jumped into the water after the vessel beached at Bat Gallim. As it turned out, the plan was indeed for the ship to beach at Bat Gallim, but a miscalculation had brought it to Ras El Kurum, where the prepared script of "hundreds of refugees jumping into the water" did not take place. Prepared posters had been disseminated at the agreed hour, before the mishap was known. The British, suspicious of a curiously well-informed *Hamashkif* reporter, offered to bring her to the scene, but gave her no details. "Tears came into her eyes" when she realized that they were not heading to Bat Gallim. Among the *Ulua's* "European refugees" were settlers from the United States.[370]

Irgun broadsides now threatened worldwide "hell" until its demands were met, and civil administration in Palestine, British officials admitted in private, was "a besieged garrison." For the first day of March, that "hell" began at 3:20 in the afternoon when the Goldschmidt Officers' Club in Jerusalem was bombed in a well-planned attack, killing fourteen people immediately, of whom ten were civilians, and injuring sixteen. As the militants ploughed their truck through the building entrance, one exited the vehicle under the cover of automatic fire from five locations: two points in the Yeshurum Synagogue, the Jewish Agency grounds, Pikovsky's printing press, and an unidentified point. He planted a phosphorus bomb while others threw a suitcase through a side window and planted more bombs against the building. The terrorists escaped as a big explosion "destroyed the South end of the building, which collapsed burying a number of occupants."[371]

March 1947

At 6:45 that evening, "six armed Jews" laid explosives at the naval car park in Haifa, wrecking fourteen vehicles. Two minutes after that attack began, a road mine exploded under two vehicles at Khirbet Beit Lid, and at 7:00 a truck was hit by a land mine at Kiriat Haim on the Haifa-Acre Road. Both caused injuries but no deaths. Ten minutes after the hour, eight mortar shells were fired into a military camp near Khirbet Beit Lid, killing one and injuring three. After a half hour reprieve, at 7:45 another land mine exploded on the Haifa-Jaffa Road near Petah Tikva, followed fifteen minutes later by three separate attacks. Old stock appears to have been used up on an attack on a truck at Kiryat Motzkin—it was, as the British put it, "of the pre-shrapnel period types," and caused no serious injury.

Several people witnessed a jeep get blown up by a shrapnel mine disguised as kilo stone in Haifa that day (March 1). The bombed vehicle continued down the road with its dead driver, hit a pile of stones, turned a complete somersault, burst into flames and was completely gutted. Three of the occupants were dead; one appears to have survived with serious injuries. Of the eye-witnesses, two were a Jewish couple who "were sweeping up broken glass quite calmly" when 317 Airborne Field Security reached the scene about two minutes later, but "as usual, neither had seen anything." Another was a Palestinian, who supplied a description of the assailants to police. But there were other eye-witnesses unknown to the British at the time: "a party of young Jews" including a woman who, some months later, was with a man in 317 Airborne. The woman

> told a member of this section that she had witnessed [the bombing of the jeep on 1 March], and volunteered information, whilst in an intimate mood, which exactly confirmed the description of the operators which had been obtained [from the Palestinian man] ... [W]hen the saboteur ran past within a few feet in HERZLIYA Street, she said "Look, he's the one that did it." "Shut up," said her escort, "and mind your own business." The party then walked into a nearby cafe, as they had originally intended to do, while the bodies of the British soldiers were lying, as yet undiscovered, by the side of MOUNTAIN Road.

In other attacks on the first of March, a vehicle was blown up on the main road between Rehovot and Rishon Lezion (8:35), another was blown up by a land mine on the Haifa-Jaffa Road, killing two people (11:15), and bombs were thrown at the Rehovot Police Stations. An attempt to bomb the military camp at Hadera using a mortar hidden in an orange grove failed—the first bomb exploded in the barrel. At a quarter to midnight a scout car was blown up by a land mine on Rehovot Gaza Road, adding three more dead and one more seriously wounded to the day's tally. Twenty-three people died and twenty-five injured in the day's terror attacks. Thirteen of the casualties were civilians.[372]

The next day (March 2), as martial law was declared in parts of Palestine, a "Bedford 3 tonner" was blown up by an electrically detonated mine at a roundabout near Hadera. The chaos continued on March 3-4, as nine people—five British and four Palestinians—were injured, five critically, in continuing Zionist attacks. Three men were seriously hurt when their army truck was blown up near Rishon le Zion, and civilian workers were hurt when their truck was hit by an electrically detonated mine near Ramle. A canteen at a military camp in Haifa was hit by grenades thrown from a stolen taxi, a camp near Hadera was hit by automatic and small arms fire, and "armed Jews" raided the booking office of Orion Cinema in Jerusalem.

On March 5, pedestrians were injured by grenades thrown at a CMP vehicle and into a Jerusalem street, and five people were wounded in an attack on a military camp on Hadera - Givat Olga Road. A civilian vehicle going between Rishon and Le Zion was blown up by a road mine, killing one person and injuring another. "An unknown Jew" placed a russet-brown suitcase in Haifa's Municipal Assessment Office, which then blew up—"as suitcases are wont to do in Palestine," the Security officer added wryly. Five soldiers were wounded the next day in an attack on a military camp on Hadera-Givat Olga Road. Two grenades that were thrown into a car park but failed to explode were analyzed: they contained American TNT and rivets.[373]

In the US that month, full-page ads by the United Zionists-Revisionists of America, based at 55 West 42nd Street in New York, pushed for a boycott of Britain to stop what it called the British "war of extermination on the Jewish people," waged by the "successors of Hitler's extermination campaign against Jewry." Meanwhile in Britain, authorities monitoring domestic Zionist terror suspects were getting increasingly nervous about impending attacks in London, but the suspects' careful language left little to act upon. What, for example, to make of a suspected terror cell's tapped telephone conversations of February 21, involving the transportation of some object to Britain by small plane? And that "even then, we have to carry it around ... have to bring it from the landing spot" and wait for a reply from Palestine "as to whether they want it done?"[374]

The concern was vindicated when on 7 March a bomb exploded at the Colonial Club and Colonial Welfare Department, 6 St. Martin's Place, causing "considerable structural damage" and injuring several people. That evening, an unnamed man from France left his hotel near Victoria Station with a case and visited Abraham Abrahams, co-editor of the New Zionist party organ the *Jewish Standard*, in his private flat. Shortly before midnight, British surveillance recorded a conversation between Abrahams and his wife in which he skirted around explaining to her why he must keep the visitor's case, pending his return. Yes, it has a false bottom, he conceded, but only "some papers from abroad" were hidden there.[375]

"Circumstantial accounts" of how the Colonial House bombing was accomplished came a few days later in France, when Lehi claimed responsibility. Robert Misrahi—who was a protégé of the anti-colonialist, but ironically pro-Zionist Jean-Paul Sartre—allegedly wore a coat with explosives sewn inside it. Lehi explosives artist Yaacov Eliav (Levstein), who was perhaps responsible for the development of the letter bomb used in a wave of Zionist attempts on public figures, probably made the device.[376]

Lehi bombing of a civilian car (foreground) and police car (background, left). Photo stamped 6th Airborne Div. May 1947.

In Palestine the day London's Colonial Club was bombed, a military staff car on tow on the Haifa-Jaffa Road near Hadera was blown up, injuring two. The next day (March 8), a military camp in Haifa and a police camp at Sarona were both hit with grenades, injuring those inside. Coldstream Guards in Tel Aviv were attacked by heavy small arms fire, killing one guardsman, two armored cars were blown up, and two policeman in civilian clothes were shot, killing one immediately. Grenades thrown at a patrol in Jerusalem seriously injured three people, and heavy small arms fire hit Police Headquarters in Jaffa. Attacks continued into March 9 as one person was killed and six injured when a camp near Hadera was hit with automatic fire and bombs. A police truck was attacked near Khirbet Beit Lyd, and telephone lines in Haifa and Upper Galilee were sabotaged.[377]

"The whole Zionist community is allied in spirit with the terrorists," the *NY Times* reported on March 9. "A prominent Zionist official privately acknowledged," the reporter continued, "that Irgun Zvai Leumi, with its bombs and guns, and not the Jewish Agency, was dictating the policy of Palestine Jewry, [and] once their deeds are done the terrorists melt back into the population. They are not betrayed to the authorities." What the *NY Times* reporter did not know was that the British, noting the correlation between the terror tactics of the Zionists and those of the defeated Axis powers, now sought the help of "a small number of Officers who have both technical and psychological knowledge of terrorism, having themselves been engaged in similar operations on what may be termed the terrorist side in countries occupied by the enemy in the late war."[378]

The Syrian orphanage in Jerusalem was the target of a grisly attack on March 12. Early that morning, Zionist terrorists blasted a hole through the orphanage's twelve-foot wall and then made a diversionary attack while bringing in three fused sacks of gelignite. When the first sack detonated it "rocked every building in the vast Orphanage [and] threw many of the boys from their beds." The blast "was followed by the sickening sound of falling masonry as a large part of the interior of the building collapsed, burying the occupants beneath the dust and debris. Many were injured and one person succumbed to his injuries almost immediately." The full intended carnage was averted: one armed and uninjured British official chased the bombers and prevented them from detonating the other two sacks of gelignite.[379]

The same day (March 12), a military camp near Karkur was attacked with grenades and fire arms, an Arab truck was targeted with a mine on Gaza Road near Rishon LeZion, a WD vehicle was blown up by road mine near Saron, and vehicles were attacked near Tulkarm and on Haifa-Jaffa Road.

Whatever deal the Irgun and Lehi had struck with Jewish citrus growers to spare the railroads from terrorism for the growing season, was now over. On March 13 terrorists used an electrically detonated mine to blow up a goods train south of Jerusalem, near Beit Safafa, killing its Palestinian engineer and injuring its Palestinian fireman. North of Lydda, bombers hid near the scene as they watched their five contact mines blow up an oil train, knocking nineteen of the train's cars off the tracks and destroying 500 yards of track, then jumped out from hiding and sprayed the train with gunfire for fifteen minutes. In Tel Aviv, the Toelet Ashrai Bank was robbed, presumably for arms money.

On March 14, a branch of the main crude oil line running from the Iraq Petroleum Company's fields to the Haifa oil docks was bombed by four Irgun operatives. "The choice of targets," the British noted, "and the placing of the charges shows a fair theoretical knowledge on the part of the saboteurs." Near Beer Yaacov, two mines were detonated under a freight train on the Lydda-Gaza line. The Officers Club and a food depot in Hadera were demolished by the Irgun on March 15.[380]

The Irgun's savvy choice of pipeline targets continued on March 16 with the bombing of the IPC (Iraq Petroleum Company) crude oil feed near Kfar Hussedini (Haifa), causing considerable loss of oil. Its attacks on the British continued with the bombing of a military vehicle, leaving four casualties. Another incident that day was not routine: the bombing of the Jewish Agency press room and tourist agency on Jerusalem's Ben Yehuda Street. No group appears to have taken credit for the Agency bombing, but the Irgun blamed the "Nazi-British Rule." Perhaps not coincidentally, two days later and at the safe distance of a thousand miles, a "representative of Jewish Agency in Romania" called on the British Consulate "to read out a statement he had been instructed to make by the Jewish Agency

Palestine" expressing "sincere condolences" to the families of its terror victims—a statement perhaps originally scheduled to have been made on Ben Yehuda Street?

A jeep was hit by a mine in Tiberias that day (March 18), while a second mine was amateurishly prepared and failed to explode. The British, indeed, noted a trend of shoddy work among the Irgun, which they attributed to their arrests of many of the gang's better operatives, leaving some jobs to the inexperienced.[381]

One constable was killed and six injured on March 19 when a bomb was thrown at police and soldiers near Zichron Yanqov Police Station in Haifa. At 2:45 the next morning, a remotely detonated bomb missed its targets, a sergeant and three constables. "Six armed Jews" held up and robbed the Palestine Discount Bank on March 24, "apparently assisted by members of gang already in the building." When three days later, "a grenade was thrown by Jews at the car of a party of police," the police managed to throw the grenade out of the car, but the explosion injured two pedestrians. The attackers turned to gunfire and a flash bomb, injuring a constable.

The next day (March 28), at about 9:05 in the morning, "five Jewish youths dressed as Arabs" drove a truck to the Acre Bay area. Three got out and walked to "a carefully reconnoitered point," where seven oil feed pipes ran together above ground. They laid explosives under each. The blast came about ten minutes later, igniting oil and benzine, and about fifteen minutes after that the heat of the fires caused two further explosions. Meanwhile in Tel Aviv, "six Jewish youths armed with sticks" killed a police corporal.[382]

There was one new, incongruous target that day: in Kiriat Haim (Haifa area), the water supply line valve and inspection chamber were bombed. But the sabotage of the water supply line proved to be a botched mission, more evidence of the Irgun's current shortage of decent help. Six days later, at two-thirty in the morning on April 3, "a party of Jews entered a house at Kiryat Haim near Haifa and beat up a Jewish civilian," and in the course of the day as many as sixteen more Jews "were similarly beaten up," three so seriously that they were hospitalized. Pressing them for an explanation, the British learned that the Irgun had sent them to sabotage an oil pipeline, but they blew up the water main by mistake. The beatings were punishment, and the day they were beaten up, new operatives did the job correctly, sabotaging oil pipelines near Kfar-Hassidim.[383]

An officer and police inspector were gunned down on horseback on March 29. Both died. Militants attacked a WD vehicle near Ramleh that day, and Lehi sabotaged oil pipelines near Afula and near Haifa.

The most catastrophic attack ever to hit Palestine's oil pipelines came two days later, on the last day of March, with the bombing of the Shell-Mex oil tanks. The blasts rocked the entire Haifa coastal area, destroying about 20,000 tons of oil, disrupting oil supplies and causing huge fires that raged for three weeks and devastated a quarter-mile of Mediterranean waterfront. Lehi again took credit, noting in its *L.H.I.-Bulletin No. 5* that its fighters had successfully penetrated the heavily guarded zone "and returned safely to their bases, without loss." No longer just the assassination virtuosi, Lehi now fully rivaled—and outdid—the Irgun and Hagana in the field of mass destruction.

That day, the illegal immigrant ship *San Filipo* reached Palestine. This vessel was so dangerously unseaworthy that the British had already rescued a third of its passengers during its voyage. Spinning these latest settlers' arrival in bluntly messianic terms, the Jewish Agency called the *San Filipo* passengers "Palestinian subjects returning home." They "had owned Palestine for thousands of years."[384]

With one hundred thousand British troops in Palestine impotent against Zionist terror, public servants and victims' families continued to write to the government in despair. One former constable's letter typifies the exasperation of those charged with maintaining public safety:

> We keep hearing the postponement of [convicted Jewish terrorists'] execution ... Did we do that with the Arab? No, his house was burned, Arabs were hanged by the dozen [but] there seems to be a feeling that we are afraid of the Jews. It is a well known fact that you will <u>never</u> get any co-operation from the Jewish people in your efforts [to stop terrorism] ... we accuse you of [not carrying out your duty and] being influenced by American and Jewish propaganda.[385] (underline original)

Creech Jones replied.

> First there are very considerable differences between the Arab disturbances of 1937-1939 and the Jewish terrorist organizations of to-day. The Arab insurgents were loosely-knit bands of guerillas operating in the country districts whereas Irgun Zvai Leumi and the Stern Gang, the terrorists active today, are secret societies of well-trained saboteurs, some thousands strong, buried in the heart of an urban population.[386]

Jones and other witnesses stated that Arab communities offered assistance in fighting terrorism, which is borne out in British records from the time. "During the Arab disturbances," as Jones explained, "the Police and the Army did enjoy this co-operation to some extent, and were able to track down the guilty parties." In contrast, Jewish community institutions made the decision "to withhold all aid in this matter [and] the Security Forces have been confronted by the stolid refusal of the Jewish civilians to give what information they may possess ... the Jewish Institutions have maintained their attitude of non-co-operation."[387]

"It is a situation," Cunningham wrote from Jerusalem, "in which a policeman is shot [by a Jewish terrorist] and lies wounded in the street beside a bus queue, no member of which will lift a finger to help him." Those who do not understand why one hundred thousand soldiers are powerless against the terror, forget that "the use of military force is an aid of a still functioning civil power."

> The placing of explosives against the walls of a building under covering fire [a tactic of Zionist gangs] was a method successfully used by the Germans in 1940 against the strongest fortifications in Europe ... The chances of its succeeding are plainly improved where, as in Palestine, the law-abiding members of the community for purely political reasons have combined in deciding not to distinguish themselves from the members of the attacking forces, who thus emerge from within a civilian population at any moment with full initiative and every operational advantage.[388]

April 1947

April brought what should have been very good news for Jewish DPs, when US Bill H.R.2910 was introduced in Washington DC.

The bill was to provide immigration to the United States for 400,000 displaced persons from Germany, Austria, and Italy over a four-year period, as non-quota immigrants. The State Department supported the admission of Jewish DPs, and the bill was championed by the (non-Zionist) American Council for Judaism. Yet none of the famously proactive, vocal Zionist organizations demonstrated any support for the bill, and it died.[389]

On the first day of the month, as fires raged along the Haifa coast from Lehi's attacks on the oil supplies, two Jewish militants entered a railway control box near Nahariya (Galilee), murdered the sapper and stole weapons. Four constables escaped attempted assassinations that day, while another civilian was murdered in the course of a botched assassination of a sergeant. In Cyprus the next day, the Palyam, the sea force of the Hagana's Palmach, bombed the British freighter *SS Ocean Vigour*.

"In broad daylight, and in full view of the local Jews," militants set up an explosive device on the corner of Mountain Road in Haifa on 3 April. They blew up a ration truck, seriously injuring two, the attack "calmly witnessed by a number of local Jews taking breakfast in flats overlooking the scene."[390]

Domestically, British intelligence had long been concerned about the radicalizing of Jewish youth at the hands of the Revisionist organization Betar and its North London premises. This "militant Jewish Youth Movement," as Percy Sillitoe, then Director General of MI5 described it, "bears a striking resemblance both in general structure and character to the Hitler Youth Movement." Children under ten were in a section called Shoalim (MI5 spellings), those aged ten to sixteen in Betar Zeirar, and sixteen to twenty-three in Dargat Halegion.

Among Betar's protégés was the Irgun terrorist Dov Gruner, whose execution the British continually delayed in fear of the repercussions. When Gruner's execution was stayed in late January, Churchill knew that it was not, as the media had been told, because Gruner had appealed, but to win the release of the Irgun's hostages, H. E. Collins and Judge Windham. ("Is it not a very serious thing," he asked Arthur Creech Jones, "to turn aside from the normal process of justice because of threats of murder by terrorists launched against hostages who they have taken?") By April, however, the British ran out of ways to avoid handing the Irgun a martyr. He was an engineered martyr: the militia, led by Begin, saw that Gruner would be more powerful for the settler state if executed, and so it convinced him not to cooperate with the reprieves that would spare him, to ensure that he is put to death—which, on April 16, he was.[391]

His impending "martyrdom" caused heightened security when on April 11 Gilberte Elizabeth Lazarus (aka Betty Knut), the young but battle-seasoned granddaughter of the composer Alexander Scriabin, reached England. Immigration believed her story: she had come to visit one Chun Chan Yeng at Trinity College whom she had met in France. Four days later, feigning the need for the loo, she got past the guards at the Colonial Office with a substantial bomb concealed in her coat, and deposited it in the lavatory, wrapped in copies of the *Evening Standard* and *Daily Telegraph* ("firmly right-wing," a Scotland Yard investigator mused). As she left, a cleaning woman named Lizzie Hart saw the package and did exactly the wrong thing: she began removing the wrapping paper. The next instant, however, passed without catastrophe. The bomb was not booby-trapped and, as Scotland Yard later explained, "one of the hands of the watch was pressed too close against the face—and the watch stopped before it reached zero hour. Otherwise it would have blown the sort of hole in the Colonial Office" that crippled the King David Hotel, though this was surely an exaggeration. Curiously, the watch bore a fingerprint on record with the British, that of Lehi bigwig Eliav, leading to the (unlikely) theory that the bomb was a taunt, intended to fail. Its tolamite bore the trade mark of the explosives factory of St. Martin de Crau, France, and would later match explosives discovered in the Paris residence of Rabbi Baruch Korff after a thwarted aerial attack on London.[392]

"The bomb planted by our fighters in the British Colonial Office in London was perchance discovered before it exploded," Lehi conceded in the June issue of its *L.H.I.-Bulletin*. They had, nonetheless, "penetrated into the heart of the Empire," and the chief of Scotland Yard was unable to keep his public promise to "arrest within 48 hours" the female terrorist. Lazarus had, indeed, slipped back to France.

Fruitless (diversionary?) leads led the British nowhere: "A Polish Jew named Beffinger" was the source of a tip communicated to the British in Djibouti by the firm Gellatly Hankey, suggesting that an American Jew named Rispi or Skripski, travelling on a Dominican Republic passport with Manchuria shown as the place of birth, was behind the attempted bombing. As Britain hunted for the terrorist, bomb and death threats continued to rattle its Embassies and Consulates throughout the world—in Chicago, Athens, Bogota, Buenos Aires, Santiago, and Tunis.[393]

In Palestine in mid-April, as the last fires from the March 31 Shell-Mex attack were extinguished, road themselves were set afire: the Irgun doused mined roads with gasoline and ignited them at the presence of a mobile patrol. "Minor" or failed terror incidents became so numerous as to merit only the most cursory mention in British records, such as a bomb that was discovered and diffused at Jerusalem's Eden Cinema on April 16.

Two days later (April 18), "eight Jews drove up in a truck" to No. 61 Field Dressing Station and its two prominent Red Cross flags. They "shot the British sentry dead and laid explosive charges" at the Nathanya-area facility, blowing up the medical inspection room adjoining a ward of sick people. The Irgun claimed responsibility.

In Tel Aviv, militants assassinated a policeman using firearms and a bomb, killing a civilian as well. Military despatch riders in Haifa were targeted from a saloon car on Herzl Street, and others were targeted on King George Avenue. The Irgun claims it mined a train near Rehovot that day, and random military personnel were the targets of sniping from a commandeered taxi in Haifa on April 19.

On April 20, an Arab Legion truck was blown up by a land mine on Acre Haifa Road near Kiryat Motskin. A Red Cross depot was bombed, injuring many people, and two road mines were uncovered in Haifa, one with a considerable amount of Italian explosives, partly buried in a heap of asphalt. At Ramat Zev, a land mine blew up a Sherwood Foresters truck, injuring four, and in Jerusalem another "kilo stone" mine was exposed. The day's most serious attack was at the Camp Cinema at Nathanya Convalescent Depot, where a bomb was thrown into the cinema just as the audience of about 200 was leaving. Four people were injured, one seriously, though this was probably a disappointing tally for the bomber, given his target. The next day (April 21) a military truck was blown up by a mine on the Khirbet Beit Lid Haifa Road.[394]

April 22 brought minor failures for the militants. Police found and freed a taxi driver, a truck driver, and one other person kidnapped in Tel Aviv. In Jerusalem a hand grenade thrown at a military vehicle missed it target, as did a land mine in Haifa targeting an army car. An attempted bombing of Sarafand Camp was also thwarted.[395]

These disappointments were however dwarfed by the day's great success: the bombing of the Cairo-Haifa train, killing eight people on the spot and leaving six wounded, three seriously.

The next morning, a furious High Commissioner Cunningham called in Ben-Gurion. After the Jewish Agency leader professed his condemnation of the attack but refused the General's plea for cooperation, Cunningham asked if his refusal was especially strange given that the UN was currently reviewing the Palestine situation. Ben-Gurion replied with "a flood of polemics" and told Cunningham that the British "were still bound to interpret the Mandate as the Jews see it." Meanwhile, two more trucks were blown up that day on the Lydda - Petah Tiqva Road, with four casualties, the assailants reinforcing the blasts with automatic weapons.[396]

The attacks raised new questions in Parliament about protecting the railways against Jewish terrorism. Counter-terrorism measures already in place before April 22 included "frequent examination of lines, patrols, guards and restriction of traffic to hours of daylight. In addition, curfew prohibiting all movement outside built-up areas is imposed as the situation demands." It was conceded, however, that the terrorists' "use of remote-control electronically detonated mines makes it most difficult to take effective precautions against sabotage."[397]

April 24 brought scattered bombings and two odd incidents. In one, five armed Jews entered a Tel Aviv hotel "and inquired whether any Britishers were present." A British businessman guest was abducted, and then released "on finding that he was a Jew." In Haifa, a certain house had been booby-trapped with the (apparent) intention of killing the policemen who would be summoned to investigate—a well-proven Lehi technique. But the plan went afoul when a Hagana member, obviously unaware, entered the house and was blown up instead. The next morning (April 25) at about 8:55, a Post and Telegraph vehicle was stopped by a Jew dressed as a Palestinian constable, at which eight militants appeared and abducted the driver and a postal employee. They were taken to the Benei Braq area, held under guard, and later abandoned, still bound.[398]

While British records do not make the connection, it was probably this vehicle that Lehi used for a brazen attack on Sarona camp that began an hour and twenty minutes later, at about 10:15, when two of its operatives dressed as employees entered Sarona in such a vehicle. The guards were at first suspicious but found nothing irregular, and the men's passes appeared to be in order. These "workers" parked the van between two buildings containing the Telephone Exchange Office and Company Office, then returned to the gate carrying a ladder and wire, saying they needed to repair the telephone cable outside the perimeter. The explosion followed quickly upon their exit, shaking the camp and destroying both offices. According to the British, five people were killed and sixty injured, some seriously, but Lehi scoffed at these figures. The dead, it countered, numbered "much more than the number officially disclosed," and added that before "our fighters all returned safety to their bases," they rigged more heavy charges of explosives.[399]

In Haifa that day, a bombing was averted when the device triggered while the operative was carrying it, killing him. Another attack failed in Jerusalem, when the bomber was caught depositing a mine in a tree. The usual sorts of "minor" incidents continued: hand grenades thrown at vehicles, hijacked taxis, and the like. On April 26, A.E. Conquest, chief of the CID in Haifa, was assassinated by Lehi.

The next morning, three separate attacks occurred within a twenty-two minute period. The first came at 10:30, when a remote-controlled explosive device was triggered under a goods train on the Lydda-Jaffa line near Tel Aviv. Fifteen minutes later, another goods train was targeted on the Haifa-Kantara Line near Benyamina, and at eight minutes to eleven in the morning, the Ramleh railway station was blown up and completely destroyed. The day after that a grenade was thrown at a CMP vehicle in Jerusalem, injuring a civilian. On April 30, a large land mine found buried on Jaffa Road in the outskirts of Jerusalem was safely dismantled; it consisted of two four-gallon petro cans containing a large quantity of explosives and rivets.[400]

May's routine terror was overshadowed by the successful defeat of security at the Acre Prison on May 4. The operation began when "a party of armed Jews, some of whom were wearing British military uniforms," entered the Acre market in British military transport. Explosions and gun fire broke out immediately in various localities, with four huge blasts near the old Turkish baths abutting the prison. This attack was more than a blow to British security; it deepened the soul-searching in London because it advertised just how little control Britain actually retained in Palestine. Three days later, officials were groping to explain to the House of Commons and the British public how such a heavily fortified facility "can apparently be attacked with impunity."[401]

May 1947

Indeed High Commissioner Cunningham's dispatch about the attack was, ultimately, an admission that "the civil and military authorities are quite unable to put down [Jewish] terrorism." Yet as outraged as the government was, it feared that publishing Cunningham's report might cause repercussions, "especially in the American press," because it necessarily addressed "the general political background in Palestine which is, in effect, a most severe castigation of the Jewish community and its leaders."[402]

On the same day as the prison break, military camps were attacked, mines were laid on roads over a large area, and a truck was blown up near Kiryat Haim. On May 8, the shops of five Jewish merchants who refused to fund the Irgun were gutted with incendiary bombs. Four days later, on May 12, two constables were murdered and a workmen's train was sabotaged. Calls for a Palestinian resistance to the ever-increasing Zionist terrorism were heard, and even talk of an "Arab awakening," but the Palestinians, British intelligence observed, "appear no keener to disturb the peace than hitherto."

In the New York suburb of Lake Success, the fledgling United Nations grappled with the Palestine debacle. Representatives of the Arab League objected to the "Zionist plea to the United Nations to base a solution for the Palestine controversy on the homelessness of Europe's displaced Jews" (May 9), while the Irgun filed a claim to turn all of Palestine and Transjordan over to them for a Jewish state (May 14). As they did, they bombed a cinema at Sarafand camp and a railway line north of Hadera, but also had two failures: their attempted bombings of a military court in Jerusalem and of a railway line west of Hadera.[403]

A mine discovered on May 15 on the Haifa-Beirut line near Acre exploded while being dismantled, killing two officers and injuring three, one seriously. Near Rehovot a goods train was blown up. Passengers, both Arabs and Jews, were the targets of an attempted train bombing near Bat Gallim, as they were employees of an army depot in the vicinity of Haifa. The bomb was positioned to send the train crashing down an embankment, but the alert driver saw something irregular ahead and stopped the train before triggering it. A mine on the Lydda-Jerusalem branch was also discovered in time, and the mining of a railway line near Tel Aviv failed. The next day a constable was killed and three people injured by a remote controlled shrapnel bomb in Haifa.[404]

Even Irgun-seasoned readers of the *New York Herald-Tribune* and the *New York Post* were likely taken aback by May's full-page appeals to finance terror in Palestine. The ads, in the form of an open letter to the Palestinian terrorists by the playwright Ben Hecht, abandoned any pretence of "military" targets, celebrating even the bombing of trains. In what would otherwise be seen as vile anti-Semitism, he states that US Jews take joy at the terror—all except for the "rich Jews," whom he ridicules.

> Every time you blow up a British arsenal, or wreck a British jail, or send a British railroad train sky high, or rob a British bank, or let go with your guns and bombs at the British betrayers and invaders of your homeland, the Jews of America make a little holiday in their hearts … Brave friends, I can imagine you wondering, "If the Jews

of America are behind us why don't they help us with their support and money?" It so happens that a certain small percentage of the Jews of America are not behind you yet ... Unfortunately, this small percentage includes practically all the rich Jews of America...[405]

While Hecht's call to terror was supported by the popular columnist Walter Winchell, the British once again lodged protests with the US for allowing such ads, and indeed for not even revoking the terror group's tax-exempt status. Truman's mystifying response to the terror fund-raising on his soil was that it was better not to "inflame the passions" in Palestine, while the relevant government agencies replied that even revoking the tax-exempt status "would stir up more trouble than it would be worth."[406]

A New York City government worker reported that "higher ups" in the city's government "frequently stretched" regulations on behalf of Revisionist causes, otherwise strictly enforced. When a new front, the Palestine Relief Committee, began sending large sums of money to Palestine, the nature of its remittances to Palestine "raised eyebrows" even within New York Mayor William O'Dwyer's particularly pro-Zionist (indeed pro-Irgun) City Hall. Nonetheless, the city's accountant was told not to record the identity of the money's recipient in Palestine "for obvious reasons," and the Committee's purpose was officially recorded as "the dissemination of public information for Palestine."[407]

There was a spurt of resistance that appeared in Palestine at this time from a Jewish organization called the Anti-Terror League. It accused the militants of "using the same methods" as the Nazis, and "will therefore cause to the Jews the same fate like the Nazis did suffer." The British, probably correctly, believed its members to be from the socialist Hashomer Hatzair. The League appears to have been very short-lived and had no identifiable influence, an obscure footnote.[408]

A failed attempt to kill four police in a CID car on the morning of May 20 was followed by a more successful raid that evening. At 8:15, "a number of armed Jews entered an Arab café and searched the occupants. On leaving they placed a mine in the building and fired a number of shots killing one Arab" and wounding the rest, three seriously. The military destroyed the bomb *in situ*, completely wrecking the Palestinian café. At about 9:00 PM, roughly forty-five minutes after the café attack began, about twenty-five "armed Jews entered Arab Sarwarkeh Encampment near Petah Tiqva and opened fire on the inhabitants, killing one Arab" and planting a land mine as they left. The long-ubiquitous bombings of vehicles continued, such as a convoy targeted in Tel Aviv by a remote controlled device.

It was in Paris two days later (May 22) that the arrest of five young Lehi members brought a new clue to the bombing of the Colonial Office in London on April 11. One of the five, Jacques Martinski, had bomb-making materials believed to be related to that attack.[409]

Two train stations and two railway lines were bombed on May 27: Ramle Station (which was destroyed), a station near Zichron Yaacov, the Haifa-Kantara line near Benyamina, and the Lydda-Jaffa line near Tel Aviv. The next day, an attack on the IPC oil dock and office in the Haifa port area was substantially thwarted, with only slight injuries to a police sergeant and a burst 10-inch water pipe. The Air Ministry Works Dept compound in Jerusalem was bombed on June 3. On June 4, a train on the Haifa-Kantara line was blown up north of Benyamina, and a train on the Lydda-Jaffa line was bombed. The day after that, both the Athlit Railway station and an oil pipeline northeast of Jalama were bombed.[410]

In Europe, the Zionists' battle for Jewish DPs continued. Hagana envoys, using relief work as a cover, accelerated their campaign to persuade "these uprooted individuals that their only hope for a decent future is to turn Zionist," in the words of British intelligence. Among those resisting the Zionists was the Bucharest-based Jewish Democratic Front, which claimed that Zionist envoys convinced Jewish families to sell their worldly possessions in order to leave, only to find they are penniless and abandoned in neighbouring countries. A May telegram from the Foreign Office described the situation as

> a racket largely organised and financed by Zionists in the United States, themselves in no personal danger, who are persuading the Displaced Persons of Europe by false promises to sell all their property and belongings and embark in search of a "land flowing with milk and honey," whereas

June 1947

in fact they will be herded in over-crowded, unseaworthy vessels without regard to conditions or safety of life.[411]

The Hagana quoted a figure of $200 as the cost of "transporting one refugee across the Mediterranean" to Palestine, of which $40 was getting the person overland through Germany, $10 was bribes, and $150 was everything else: loss of ship, indemnity, and insurance. The finances and accounting were dense, with several people investing and no paper trail. In but one example of these opaque dealings, a Greek national who was "a procurer of women in Alexandria" backed such a settler voyage by paying harbour dues owed in Britain by a Swedish shipping company (The "definition of a Zionist," Air Headquarters Levant quipped, is "a Jew who pays another Jew to send a third Jew to Palestine).

The Agency's campaign to displace North African Jews, begun at least as early as January 1943 (pages 80 & 170, above), was bearing fruit: a Hagana-sponsored ship arrived in Palestine carrying not European DPs, but North African Jews. The British also received intelligence that a vessel with European immigrants would arrive "for the benefit of the Fact Finding Commission (UNSCOP) and the 60 odd journalists who will accompany it"—what would prove to be the *Exodus*.[412]

In France, explosives guru Yaacov Eliav and the energetic Gilberte Lazarus set out on a new mission, this time in Brussels. Their luck, however, ran out at the Belgian border on June 2, where suspicious officials pulled them aside and found fourteen sticks of explosives "secreted on the person of the woman" (in her girdle). Under her suitcase's false bottom were detonators, pencil batteries, and six letter bombs "identical with those dispatched to Britain from Turin," corroborating British suspicions that the letter bombs mailed from Italy originated in France. Eliav was carrying more of the batteries, but allegedly managed to dispose of a watch that would have proven incriminating for its similarity to the watch used in the failed Colonial Office bomb that bore his fingerprint.[413]

The ranks among the terror gangs ran the gamut from their self-serving, opportunistic leaders to the traumatized survivors of the war who were their easy prey. In her young teens, from 1940-44, Gilberte Lazarus fought in the French resistance under the name

Betty Knut, and was wounded by a land mine. About a year before her arrest, she received an anonymous phone call to meet in the *Café de la Paix* in Paris concerning a so-called "Jewish resistance" organization—Lehi. Under the gang's grooming, battlefields blurred; enemies blurred; the war had not ended. Well seasoned in the tasks requested of her, she was given rendezvous points and descriptions of contacts—sometimes a man, other times a woman—and instructions to transport a case. Usually she did not know its contents. Her capture, interrogation by the Belgian police, and year in juvenile prison, appear to have begun a reckoning, as if finally she might leave the war behind.

The *Exodus* affair helped turn public sympathy in her favor—as it would for vastly less sympathetic characters like Rabbi Korff. In 1951, Lazarus moved to Beersheba and opened its first nightclub, "The Last Chance." Whether she intended the name as a reference to the city's southern location, and/or to her final hope for a normal life, it would also prove unintendedly autobiographical. Fourteen years later, Gilberte Lazarus died of a heart attack at the age of 37.[414]

Two days after Lazarus and Eliav were arrested at the Belgian border, on June 4, an envelope bearing Italian stamps reached the home of Harold MacMichael, the retired High Commissioner who had returned to England nearly three years earlier. He began to open it, but stopped short upon seeing two pieces of cardboard between which were "a quantity of material with the appearance of toffee" and wires. MacMichael was certainly experienced enough to realize, in that instant, that he was fortunate to still be alive: carbon paper often obscured the interior, and unfolding the plain white paper surrounding it might have already completed the circuit to the detonator.

His was one of several Zionist letter bombs that reached various British officials in England in early June, among them Ernest Bevin and future Prime Minister Anthony Eden. A bomb intended for MP Arthur Greenwood was misdirected and reached a different Arthur Greenwood, the owner of a laundry in Gypsy Hill (The laundry owner proved savvier than some MPs, and alerted the police). One MP's secretary began opening an envelope for her boss, but sensed heat and thrust it into a pail of water kept handy for the event.[415]

The inside of a Lehi letter bomb, with explosive sac and detonators. Batteries have been removed. Mailed to London, 1947–1948.

Winston Churchill was among the intended victims of a new rash of more potent letter bombs that began arriving on June 7, twenty of which originated from Turin. Other recipients included the Admiral of the Fleet Lord Fraser and the Postmaster General. One reaching Nairobi was caught in time and analyzed: it was similar to those sent from Italy, consisting of slabs of gelignite sandwiched between two pieces of cardboard, with detonating wires fastened by small nuts.[416]

President Truman, whose pro-Zionist influence would prove decisive in Palestine's future, also received letter bombs that summer. When one senior mail room worker was called back from vacation because of a backlog resulting from the Palestine question, it was not from volume, but because some letters reaching the president's mail room "had obviously been intended to kill."[417]

In response to a British request, the UN appointed the United Nations Special Committee on Palestine (UNSCOP) to examine the debacle in Palestine and make recommendations for a solution—or more accurately, a means to a British exit. Unknown to the

Committee, the Jewish Agency prepared for its arrival in Palestine with an elaborate spy ring, manuscript records of which were found among other Hagana papers uncovered by the British in Jerusalem on 3 August. Some of the words used were euphemisms, such as the word "hotel" which the British believed to mean the Jewish Agency, but these appeared not to be deliberate code.

The ring comprised three networks, a "drivers network," "waiters network," and "theater network." Five spies were needed for the drivers network, but a sixth was recruited just to displace a Committee driver who happened to be Palestinian. The other five drivers "supplied information daily on the movements of the Committee members their meetings etc.," the manuscript notes read in translation, but "to our regret the drivers had not too much understanding [i.e., English?] and therefore they did not utilize fully their special position." Further limiting their effectiveness, most of the cars had a glass partition between driver and passengers, making listening difficult. One driver spy, however, accompanied a Committee member on a likely fruitful trip to Beirut. The "waiters network," similarly, "operated for the purpose of tracing the meetings of the Committee's members with various persons."

By far the most productive, however, was the all-female "theater" segment of the spy ring. "Through full cooperation of the general labor exchange [Histadrut?] we were able to engage 5 house attendants at Kadima Building."* Just what these "theater" girl spies did while serving the (all-male) UNSCOP members is not elaborated, but two qualifications were cited: they had to be educated and, most importantly, they had to be "daring." Finding suitable candidates was difficult:

> The time allowed for procuring these girls was very short—we succeeded in pushing in three suitable girls and two others on recommendations by close persons— but they proved insufficiently daring and their educational standards was much less than that of the first three.

---

* Beit Kadima was a building complex in Jerusalem built by the British two years earlier for the families of British officers, but which was used to house the entire UNSCOP Committee while it was in Palestine.

The three better-educated and "sufficiently daring" girls

> proved their great importance. They brought considerable and first rate material. Through them we received among other things Bancz's letters and reports, Sir Abdur's and Sandstrom's questions as [and?] also Hood's telegram to his government.* The three girls showed great devotion, understanding and a great deal of risk which must be recorded.

Although the two "insufficiently daring" girls were less productive, they "did not prove an obstruction and their material was emptied and brought by the first three." After the mission, the Agency faced "the lack of an expert stitching group [?] of Secondary and high education which knows the English language thoroughly." The "machinery staff" pitched in for the stitching, but "it was only after the completion of the examinations at the University that we succeeded in recruiting a number of female students for this work."[418]

UNSCOP held its first public hearing in Jerusalem on June 17. This was the committee that would decide Palestine's fate, yet most of its members were, according to the *NY Times* reporter Elbert Clifton Daniel (who would later marry President Truman's daughter) "obviously unaware of some of the simplest facts about the country [Palestine]" and were "groping for information." Jewish Agency officials like Sharett were there to supply that "information" to UNSCOP, and its liaison officers maintained a close association with the Committee throughout its visit.

As would happen at the UN in November, only India's Sir Abdur Rahman attempted substantive debate, which Sharett "sidestepped," to use the *NY Times'* word. Seated around a horseshoe-shaped mahogany table in the auditorium of the Jerusalem YMCA, Sharett stated bluntly that the Jewish Agency would never accept equality ("unity") with the Palestinians, justifying the discrimination to UNSCOP with the argument that "Palestine owes its existence to the fact that it is the birthplace of the Jewish people." Denying the

---

* Bancz = ?; Sir Abdur Rahman, representative from India; Justice Emil Sandström, representative from Sweden; J. D. L. Hood, representative from Australia.

ethnic cleansing that he thought his audience, or at least his British audience, feared was soon to come, he claimed that "not one single Arab village has disappeared from the map of Palestine" due to the Zionists—the qualification of "map" a curious one, though non-Jewish villages would soon be erased from the map as well as the land.

Carter Davidson, another American journalist in Palestine covering the Committee's visit, was approached in secret by a man bringing a message from Irgun Commander Menachem Begin: Begin wanted to arrange a clandestine meeting with Committee members. Davidson conveyed the request to Committee chairman Sandström; Sandström agreed. On June 24 Davidson and three Committee members, Mr. Sandström, Dr. Victor Hoo, and Dr. Ralph Bunche, "went for a stroll" and met a pre-arranged taxi. They were driven to a darkened street and left there. Then "a pretty girl approached, mentioned the pre-arranged password and took us on a circuitous walk" to a second taxi that drove them for fifteen minutes through an unlighted route to the meeting place with Begin and two of his aides.

"The peace of the world," Begin vowed to the UNSCOP representatives, will be threatened if Partition is approved and "the Hebrew homeland" not returned in its entirety to "its rightful owners." Lest there be any doubt as to what this "homeland" encompassed, it is "the territory which stretches between the Mediterranean and the desert East of the Jordan and from Dan to Beersheva."

Why not simple democracy in Palestine? the Committee asked. Yes, Begin agreed, but three thousand years ago the land had a "Jewish State," and so Jewish blood, worldwide, now constituted the citizenry of Palestine. All Jews, worldwide, were its electorate. What if, despite his methodology, Jews worldwide still did not vote as he wished? Begin replied by enlarging the dimensions of his Jewish "electorate" from the geographic to the temporal: Such a vote would be illegitimate, because the Jewish "nation" belongs equally to Jews of all generations to come, and therefore no majority of "this generation of Jewish people" mattered if it voted contrary to Zionist interests.

The meeting with this most wanted of terrorists was kept out of the Committee's report and not acknowledged until Davidson revealed it in the *NY Times* a month later. A formal transcript of it was produced by the Jewish Legion, but the first transcript was type-written by the "Diaspora Headquarters of the Irgun Zvai LEUMI by Authority of the High Command in Eretz Israel" of the "Irgun-Unscop Conference," the fourteen pages apparently posted to the British from London.[419]

UNSCOP's presence brought only a partial lull in Zionist violence. On June 3, an RAF office on the grounds of the Italian Hospital was bombed, and two trains were mined on June 4. Both the Athlit Railway Station and the IPC pipeline in the Haifa area were bombed on June 5, causing extensive damage in the former and the loss of 800 tons of crude oil in the latter.[420]

On June 9 at about 5:00 PM, the telephone line at Gal Gil swimming pool at Rammat Gan went dead. Seven "Jews armed with T.S.M.G.S. and revolvers" entered and abducted a sergeant and constable. As they threw two smoke bombs to hide their escape, one witness saw "ten men and one girl" pull the captives into a (stolen) truck. The Hagana issued a statement ordering the Yishuv not to give information about the kidnappings to the British, but rather to "the Yishuv's Security Institutions." At noon the next day, the British cordoned off Qiryat Shaul settlement and recovered the two men, whose captors had told them that their fate was dependent on the outcome of ongoing trials of accused Irgun members. Among the weaponry uncovered were a Thompson submachine gun and "U.S.A. pattern grenades." The terror gangs attacked the Reuters office in Tel Aviv on June 12, and that evening staged bombings as warnings to uncooperative Jews, one a wine merchant, the other the owner of an ironmonger shop who was accused of buying milk from Palestinians.

The Irgun, meanwhile, had been busy boring a tunnel to Army HQ in Tel Aviv's Citrus House from the basement of a neighbouring building. Citrus House had long been in the Irgun's cross-hairs, and the 250-300 foot tunnel would have given them a deadly advantage. As was their practice, the gang booby-trapped their handiwork to kill any unwary snooper, and so when at about 11:00 on the morning of June 18 a Hagana operative, Zeev Weber, came across the tunnel, a bomb detonated, killing him. The explosion was heard outside and alerted the British. The Jewish Agency made great play out of their fallen hero saving British lives, and though "saving British lives" was the inadvertent consequence of Hagana snooping to "prevent a major incident during the U.N.S.C.O.P. visit," it was nonetheless true. British representatives attended the funeral in respect.[421]

On June 22, an Assistant Superintendent of Police was knocked unconscious with an iron pipe in Jerusalem's Jordan Book Shop by "four men and a girl," but the attackers fled when a nearby merchant raised the alarm. That evening a small bomb blew up in a porch of the English Girls School on Shabatai Levy Street in Haifa, intended to deter Jewish mothers from sending their daughters to a "foreign" school. A Sten gun and ammunitions factory discovered on June 20 proved to be "one of a chain of such factories" maintained by the Hagana. Two days later, an attempt to kidnap the Frontier Control officer in Jerusalem was foiled.

On the evening of June 24, a small explosion was heard in the garden of a house near the Salvia Hotel opposite the Jerusalem Military Courts. The British, well aware of the terrorists' penchant for baiting police into a booby-trapped house, did not enter until daylight. Their suspicion of being lured into a death trap was vindicated: inside they found a mattress, but rather than disturb the mattress, they attached a rope and pulled it from a safe distance outside. The explosion demolished the entire wall. A drawer of a table was also booby-trapped.[422]

On June 25, militants burst into the Jerusalem flat of an UNSCOP liaison officer and struck him on the head with a pipe. He resisted his attackers' attempts to chloroform him long enough to run outside and signal a passing military vehicle, foiling the abduction, though the assailants shot the driver as they fled. Meanwhile in Devon, Britain, the theft of explosives from two quarries heightened terrorism concerns. Wiretaps strongly suggested that the explosives were now destined for terror in Britain in the Zionist cause.[423]

Four soldiers were gunned down in two separate attacks on Saturday, June 28. Lehi attackers used a taxi ("borrowed in the usual manner") to drive by the Astoria Restaurant on Haletz Street in Haifa and spray it with automatic fire, killing an officer and wounding two. The restaurant was known to be crowded with British officers on

Saturday evenings, and the "Jewish proprietress [was] well known for her reasonable outlook" on the Palestine issue. On the Allenby Road in Tel Aviv, four British officers were gunned down from behind, the signature Lehi method. One survived. Bombs exploded in Jerusalem behind the Vienna Café, and on June 29 soldiers were attacked while bathing near Hertzliya, two presumed not to have recovered from their wounds.

Increasingly convinced of Irgun boasts of undefeatable booby-trapping, a bomb discovered on the tracks between Kafrsanir and Athlit was destroyed *in situ*, destroying sixty yards of track. Lehi, in the meantime, added an imaginative twist to booby-trapping: it began distributing pamphlets and banners that exploded if burned.[424]

The Irgun's infiltration into European DP camps made Europe a new front in the terror. In May and again in June, Zionist-mentored DPs attempted to bomb trains on the main railway line between Berlin and Hanover, but the explosives were discovered before their intended deadly disasters. The first traceable clues as to the source of the bombs came with an attempt on the Hanover-Hamburg express train on June 28. The bomb was typical: thirty kilograms (66 lbs) of gelignite of the type used for quarrying, with an electrical detonator. Part of the paper used as wrapping in the device had Hebrew printing, which was traced to a publication called *Unsere Stimme* ("Our Voice") from Belsen Camp. This and other bits of paper wrapping placed the source of the explosives to a quarry at Bochum in the Ruhr, where the foreman's records, combined with separate investigations in Hanover, led to the arrests of four individuals, two in the vicinity and two in Munich. "Although the terrorists were reluctant to give information," one of them later confirmed that the Irgun's European operation was headquartered in Paris, "with subordinate headquarters in Munich, the whole being supported by the United Zionist Revisionist Organisation."[425]

The first week of July was "marked by a number of assassinations and attempted assassinations of British soldiers," Lehi's retaliation for the disappearance (and alleged murder) of sixteen-year-old member Alexander Rubowitz by Major Roy Farran on May 6 (although Farran was cleared of involvement, Lehi continued to believe, possibly

July 1947

correctly, that he was guilty). But it was July 18-19 that brought Palestine to the headlines, when the overburdened vessel *President Warfield* reached Haifa brimming with 4,515 Jewish DPs, unwitting actors on a grand stage that stretched from Germany to the Promised Land and with an audience as large as the world. Choreographed for the global media and timed for UNSCOP's visit, the vessel itself became the stage prop—its sponsors renamed it the *Exodus* for the obvious Biblical iconography, and Ben-Gurion extolled its passengers as even more heroic than the Jews who had rebelled and died in the ghettos of Europe. Yet Britain, as the story was spun, refused to allow these desperate survivors of fascism to disembark in their promised land, their only hope of survival. Britain found itself in its worst public relations catastrophe of the entire Mandate.

The British were not taken by surprise; but having to choose between Zionists' "unscrupulous attempt to exploit the sufferings of unfortunate people, in order to create a situation prejudicial to a final settlement," or "unleashing a storm of atrocity propaganda," it chose the latter.[426]

Ben-Gurion called the *Exodus* affair an "enormous, awesomely great spectacle," with *spectacle* the revealing word. He cried out against Britain's having "forcibly returned" Holocaust survivors "to the land of the Nazis." But this was a lie: it was he and other Zionist leaders who forced the survivors back to Germany. The Jewish Agency Executive sabotaged efforts to get the passengers true safe-haven elsewhere, such as in Denmark; and but for the Jewish Agency, the Exodus passengers could at least have disembarked in southern France. As described by Professor Idith Zertal, these survivors of the Holocaust were for that moment

> Zionism's trump card, and the greater their suffering, the greater their political and media effectiveness. Not only did the Zionist leadership make no effort to spare the refugees the appalling return to Germany; it actually took distinct steps toward preventing any solution other than Germany.[427]

Once the curtain fell on the Final Act of the *Exodus* show, its human cargo were quickly forgotten by Ben-Gurion. "It's over, finished," he quipped impatiently to an inquiry about them because, in the bitter words of one of the ex-*Exodus* passengers, "we are no longer a sensation." In the years to come, Israel simultaneously exploited the Holocaust to shield the state against criticism of its own racial-nationalist policies and expansionism, while treating the survivors "with condescension ... as second class citizens," as one put it. The state would systematically steal German reparation money intended for survivors who continued to live in poverty, and Ben-Gurion would frame them for atrocities he knew to have been committed by his military, in order to insulate the state (e.g., page 309, below).[428]

The *Exodus* passengers were split among three vessels for the return to Europe. A British officer from the 6th Airborne accompanied the passengers on one, the *Runnymede Park*, and wrote a first-hand account of the voyage and the control of the DPs by the onboard Zionist officials. "By no possible stretch of the imagination could they [the DPs] be called Zionists," but Palestine was the only choice they were offered in the Zionist-controlled camps. "They had all been told what to say" and would "repeat whatever political mumbo-jumbo" was required. They survived at sea at the mercy of "quite a little Nazi organization - complete with muscle-men, group 'führers,' and capped by Hitler himself, or so we called" the *Exodus* leader Mordechai Rosman. The DPs lived in terror of the "organization." For example, "an old woman, her face lined with suffering," who though "as hard as nails ... came one morning in terror of her life" when she was accused by the onboard regime of "co-operating"—that "cooperation" being her service to the ship's (British-run) hospital. "Jabbering with fear," she said that "if she was still working at 11 o'clock she would be put to death." The British would protect her? No, the British "do not understand"; they might protect her during the voyage, but if she continued to help in the hospital, the regime "will kill me afterwards." She passed the remainder of the voyage in silence and seclusion.

When the three vessels carrying the ex-*Exodus* DPs reached Port de Bouc in southern France, all were free to disembark rather than continue to Germany. The *Exodus* script, however, required the imagery of the DPs being "forcibly" returned to Germany, and so "persistent

Zionist threats and propaganda," as an official communiqué reported it (and as an announcement from the Hagana itself confirmed), were used to be sure the DPs did not disembark in France.

In response, the British "set up a secret disembarkation center in the [ship's] hospital" to smuggle out any *Exodus* DPs at Port de Bouc willing to risk the Jewish Agency's wrath and "being torn to pieces in the holds" for endangering the *Exodus* narrative. One couple who escaped the *Ocean Vigour* in this manner naively returned to retrieve some belongings, "unaware that their secret had leaked out. They were set upon and would undoubtedly have been killed by the thugs detailed for the job" had eleven men not raced to their rescue. These eleven "were attacked with tins of bully and broken-off bottles" but extracted the unconscious victims from the Agency thugs. Both survived. Fearing that the incident would prove difficult to explain if the press learned of it, the Agency concocted the story that the two were Gestapo agents, taken aboard to bring them to justice.

Meanwhile, the British once again called the Jewish Agency's bluff. They appealed to Golda Meir (Meyerson) to spare the DPs from the horrific return to Germany: Why not send an Agency representative to Port du Bouc to remind the DPs that they are free to disembark there? That they need not return to Germany? Meir scoffed at the suggestion. "No Jew," she said as if it were a reply, "could contemplate advising another Jew to proceed anywhere but Palestine."[429]

On the evening of July 11, two sergeants in civilian clothes, Mervyn Paice and Clifford Martin, met at the café Pinati in Nathanya with a friend, Aharon Weinberg, sat at a table near the orchestra and (as a British report put it) "consumed a quantity of beer." Conversation was, according to Weinberg, of a general nature, and the attitude of the other patrons was "mutely hostile." After leaving the café at about half past midnight, Weinberg decided to accompany the two non-commissioned officers as far as his home. Walking along Herbert Samuel Street near the café Rimon, "a dark saloon car passed and stopped in front of them, and some six Jews, armed with sub-machine guns and pistols, alighted." All three were abducted, blindfolded, and chloroformed. Weinberg was later abandoned in an orange grove, hands and feet bound. An intensive search for the two sergeants was stymied by false leads and (apparently deliberate) misinformation. Their fate remained unknown for three weeks.[430]

Two trucks carrying military personnel on Tiqva-Lydda Road were targeted on July 16 with electrically detonated mines, killing one and injuring three, one seriously. On the Haifa - Tel Aviv Road north of Petah Tiqva, an electrically detonated mine struck a jeep, injuring four. A mine exploded in Jerusalem, injuring eight, and an electrically detonated mine hit a staff car on Haifa-Jaffa Road.

Near Kfar Bilu (Rehovoth) on July 18, a truck was blown up by an electrically detonated mine, killing a sergeant and injuring three others. Jerusalem was hit by scattered attacks by grenade, incendiary bomb, and automatic fire, wounding three, one (a civilian) seriously. Two constables in plain clothes were assassinated by Lehi the next day in Haifa, shot in the back as usual; a civilian was also killed. A truck was blown up in Jerusalem, wounding five civilians and three military personnel, and incendiary bombs were thrown at vehicles.[431]

When a bomb thrown at a British Constable in a main thoroughfare failed to explode, the Constable attempted to make an arrest, but then a "hostile crowd" assaulted the officer and made good the suspect's escape. "July," British records lament, "has given no further hope for belief in the cooperation of the Yishuv to help restore order in the country."[432]

In London that same day—July 19—British fears of continuing domestic Jewish terrorism heightened. Harry Isaac Presman, "prominent in Jewish circles in North London," owned two cars which he had kept in adjacent lock-up garages on Fairholt Road until two weeks earlier, July 6, when he told his chauffeur that one of the garages had been rented, and so one vehicle would now be kept at new premises he had acquired at the rear of Church Street.

The next day (July 7), Presman phoned Leo Bella, whom the British believed to be a "controlling figure" behind the plans for domestic terror attacks. The British were listening: Presman wanted to get back into the garage because "I had to leave some things in there, some of my chauffeur's things, and as he is rather nosey I would like to have those things removed." Twelve days passed without the chauffeur needing access to the garage. But on July 19, wanting to wash both cars, he needed box-ends that had formerly been kept there. He went to the garage door and found that although the padlock was locked, it had not been put through both ends of the hardware. Opening the door, instead of box-ends he faced twenty-four hand grenades and twenty-three detonators. He alerted a mounted policeman. Although a stash of Irgun literature awaited the police in Presman's flat, Presman claimed ignorance: the garage was being rented from him.[433]

Efforts turned to the figures British intelligence had already been following, in particular Leo Bella, Boris Senior, Abraham Abrahams, Chonel Poniemunski, Paul Homesky, Eric Prinz, Moyses Kaplan, Cyril Ross, and the South African Revisionist Israel Lifshitz. These men clearly assumed that they might be trailed and wiretapped, and behaved accordingly, speaking in what appeared to be plain language code. Poniemunski, suspected in the quarry theft of June 25, seemed to be toying with the police "to make them look foolish." He traveled frequently, but searches of his baggage yielded nothing damning—"about 10 small tins of surplus American contraceptives" on one inspection.

The morning after the garage hideout was exposed, Bella called Senior at the Waldorf Hotel and in what British eavesdroppers described as nervous, disguised language, told him that "something had happened." Then Bella, who owned an Auster aircraft and had been taking flying lessons, called his instructor in Cambridge, asked if it was good weather for flying, was told "yes," but then said he would not have his lesson today. British intelligence were aware that Senior, in the course of flights between England and France, was making unreported 'emergency landings' in fields to collect or drop off unknown items. Bella was now very anxious that he deliver something to him at 11:30 the next morning (July 21), and this had something, unspoken, to do with the Auster.[434]

July 20 brought more railway bombings and attacks by mortar, mines, and firearms. By 9:00 AM, five separated instances of bomb-rigged tracks had been discovered by the "suicide patrols." At noon, a bomb detonated in front of a goods train on the

Haifa-Kantara line. An hour later, an electrically detonated mine on the Jaffa-Haifa Road north of Hadera killed one person and seriously injured two more. A constable on duty at Mustashfa billet was shot from the roof of a neighbouring house. Two police were shot in the back by three young Lehi militants as they walked down Hehalutz Street in Haifa. Both died on the spot.

It was in Haifa as well that the next day's attacks began, when at 1:30 in the morning "Jews armed with machine guns and grenades" attacked a radar station, and two hours later "armed Jews" bombed a wireless transmitter, destroying it, and mined nearby roads. A jeep was blown up by an electrically detonated mine, killing one (Jewish) boy and injuring six. A Palestinian civilian was seriously injured by a mine, and roads were extensively mined, one bomb exploding on the Haifa-Jaffa road near Hadera. IPC pipelines near Affuleh and near Kfar Yehoshua (Haifa) were bombed, but another bomb in Haifa was discovered in time and destroyed. The next day (July 22) a military truck was hit by an electrically detonated mine, grenades were thrown at a Palestinian civilian truck, and shots were fired at an RAF vehicle, injuring two, one a civilian. A fire bomb was thrown at an RAF vehicle in Jerusalem, two civilians were burned by a fire bomb intended for a police car, and the Mustashfa Police Billet & Station was attacked. British records detail numerous further, daily attacks by sniper fire, bombs, mines, and hand grenades that failed to cause major injury but maintained the state of pervasive fear without relief.[435]

A particularly revealing terror attack—one that involved elaborate, costly, months-long preparation, served no possible or intended benefit, and risked the lives of hundreds of Jewish refugees—was the Jewish Agency's bombing of the British vessel *Empire Lifeguard* on July 23. The *Empire Lifeguard* was doing precisely what the Zionists wanted: bringing Jewish refugees (and some American colonists taking the place of the intended DPs) to Palestine for permanent settlement. There was nothing to be gained, not even the fanatical alleged justification of the *Patria* bombing. Yet to taunt the British, the Agency risked the lives of all aboard to the accuracy of a detonator timer, the fickleness of the seas, and unpredictable maritime delays.

The bombing was carried out by Zionist settlers from the United States in collaboration with the Hagana, using British entry permits intended for European DPs. The American "immigrants" had begun their voyage from Miami in another vessel, the *Hatikvah*, and boarded the *Empire Lifeguard* in Cyprus along with the war's DPs who were held there awaiting their turn for emigration to Palestine. The conspiracy required several people to smuggle aboard the large amount of explosives required, hiding the material in bags in the small of their backs, in shaving cream tubes, in a nurse's handbag, and even in a handicapped person's wheelchair. Hagana operatives in Cyprus taught one of the American settlers how to make the bomb. He is said to have concealed the pencil-shaped detonator in his anus.

The Hagana also taught the bomber to booby-trap the detonating timer so that no one would be able to thwart it once set—including him. If the acid ate through the delaying switch quicker than estimated, or if the vessel's arrival were delayed more than briefly, it would have become a suicide bombing. This, indeed, nearly happened: the vessel was stopped outside of Haifa for a medical check, its human cargo confined above the device, its British captain unaware that they sat on a floating bomb.

The bomb exploded as the passengers were disembarking. It blasted a hole in the hull six by three feet and ignited a raging fire in the engine room that took fire fighters both inside and outside the vessel to extinguish. Cunningham reported "believed no loss of life" in a preliminary report filed a few hours after the blast, while other sources (including Zionist) state that sixty-five people were killed and forty wounded. Regardless of the figures, the bombing was terror for its own sake. The Agency gambled the lives of hundreds of refugees and their crew for a jeer devoid of purpose.[436]

British efforts to evacuate and care for the *Empire Lifeguard* immigrants were complicated by the militants' sniper fire, fire bombings, and road mining around Palestine. As the vessel sat crippled on the bottom of Haifa's twenty-foot deep inner harbor, a military truck was mined in Haifa, killing one and seriously injuring three, and another truck was blown up near Rehovoth, injuring nine, of whom two succumbed to their wounds. A school compound in

Haifa used by the military was bombed, injuring one; a car park in Haifa was bombed, injuring three, and an ambulance was blown up by a mine on Haifa-Jaffa Road near Khirbet Beit Lidd, killing two and injuring two seriously. After the railway near Gaza was bombed, the British found an array of land mines, grenades, explosives, mortar bombs, and detonating sets left behind by the bombers that suggested that far more ambitious sabotage plans had been stymied.

July 24 brought three more bombings, one causing extensive damage to the Haifa-Kantara line near Zichron Yeaqov, as well as another Irgun or Lehi diamond heist, and an unsuccessful attack on an officers' mess. But it was the sum of the "minor" incidents, too numerous to catalogue individually, that now formed what Airborne security descrbed as an "all out effort on the part of the Jews to cooperate in creating a wave of terror."[437]

That "wave of terror" hit Germany the next day, July 26, when "Irgun in the Diaspora" attacked a British train in Hanover. Although the British described the train as military, the Irgun appears to have assumed it was civilian, as it boasted that with their attack on the Hanover train they forced the British to "protect their civilian" installations worldwide.

The increased focus on civilian targets was apparent in Palestine that same day: two repairmen were killed, and eight injured, when they tried to repair a cable the militants had sabotaged and booby-trapped to target any workers sent to fix it. "New measures are being adopted by the saboteurs," the War Office observed, "namely that of attempts against the lives of repair parties by the concealment of booby traps and mines."[438]

Still the same day, arson attacks targeted the identity card office in Tel Aviv and a wooden railway bridge—that wooden bridge itself a temporary replacement for the original bridge that was destroyed in a previous terror spree. An attempt to blow up the Haifa-Kantara train near Ness Tsiyona was foiled.

Two people were injured on July 27, one seriously, in the contact mine bombing of a military trolley on the Lydda-Jaffa line. When a rail worker discovered a mine on the line south of Hadera, the bombers were watching and attacked him. In Jerusalem a military convoy was attacked by grenades and gunfire, injuring two, one seriously. A time bomb filled with rivets exploded in the open air cinema at Tel Litwinsky on July 28, leaving eight casualties. Bombers targeted two vehicles by electrically detonating a mine on Gaza Road near Kfar Bilu, a grenade was thrown at W.D. vehicle in Jerusalem, and a police car was attacked by a mine and gunfire. The next day, a check-post at the Acre roundabout on the Haifa-Acre road was bombed and destroyed, a police car was targeted by grenade, and a mine blew up a considerable length of track on the Haifa-Kantara line near Athlit. Two people were killed and thirty injured on July 30 by an electrically detonated mine near Hadera. A bomb in the Romema Quarter of Jerusalem was successfully neutralized.[439]

It was in Jaffa that afternoon, July 30, that District Police Headquarters received an anonymous phone call about the two sergeants kidnapped on the evening of July 11. Police had already followed several tips without result, but the caller specified a precise map reference where their bodies would be found. At 7:40 the next morning, the last day of July, members of a Nathanya Jewish Settlement Police Patrol reported that two bodies had been seen hanging from trees in a government eucalyptus grove at Umm Uleiqa.

At 9:00 the British found the corpses of the two young men, aged twenty and twenty-one, as promised. (Police surmised that the terrorists' original intent was to hang the bodies in public display, but that this proved too risky.) The police assumed that the Irgun had mined the area, and used mine detectors before approaching the hanging bodies, but failed to consider that the militants might have booby-trapped the bodies themselves. When an Army Captain tried to free the first victim from its noose, the corpse blew up in his face.[440]

The discovery of the hangings was but the beginning of the troubles of July 31. Jewish mobs in Tel Aviv ransacked the Barclays Bank, the Post Office, and the Income Tax Office. An RAF vehicle was overturned and set afire by the crowd, a police car was stopped and stoned, a RASC driver was dragged from his vehicle by a mob who set fire to the vehicle and then prevented the Fire Brigade from extinguishing it—this last fracas on the Tel Aviv street named for Balfour. In Jerusalem, the Military Billet and Defence Post were attacked with automatic fire and bombs. A mine was electrically detonated under a train between

Zikron Yaacov and Ben Yemdina, derailing the engine and wagon and damaging 50 meters (164 ft.) of track. Mines were discovered on the Jaffa-Lydda line and on the Haifa - Tel Aviv road.

Although the sergeants' murders were statistically unremarkable in Palestine's daily tally, the shocking method and the symbolism were seized upon by bigots as "vindication." That evening in Tel Aviv, vigilantes in the British military and police went berserk, murdering five people, and in England, news of the sergeants' executions ignited a five-day rampage. British Jews were assaulted, their windows smashed, and swastikas painted on Jewish businesses.

The British anti-Jewish pogrom is but one illustration of Zionism's self-fulfilling and self-perpetuating cycle of anti-Semitism. If one accepts Zionism's claim that it is inseparable from Jews and Judaism, then its crimes are Jewry's crimes, thus "justifying" and perpetually regenerating the very anti-Semitism that Zionism depends upon.

In print as well, the battles of anti-Semitism continued alongside those of radical Zionism. *The Jewish Struggle* extolled Zionist terror and threatened that "every community in the diaspora [will become] a centre of revolt." British authorities were even more concerned by a neo-Nazi paper, *The Protestant Vanguard*, and back in March of 1945 Parliament had held debates on the wisdom of forcibly suppressing it. Its publisher insisted on "the absolute right of any Briton to be anti-Jewish if he wants to be," and suggested to unhappy government officials they purchase from him *Protocols of the Elders of Zion* and other hate literature. In the United States, the terror gangs' fund raising for the "liberation" of "Eretz Israel" continued, while the anti-Semitic periodical *Christian Patriots* attributed all wars since the French Revolution to a Jewish conspiracy. If on the surface the neo-Nazism of *The Protestant Vanguard* and the violent Zionism of *The Jewish Struggle* appear to be polar extremes, some people continued to understand both as forms of anti-Semitism.[441]

Aug 1947

On August 2 the Irgun exploded pamphlet bombs in Petah Tiqva, injuring four people, and attacked a military patrol and the RAF Club in Jerusalem. The next day a bridge on the Haifa Kantara line near Rehovot was bombed, killing one Palestinian and injuring another. In Europe that night (August 3), the Irgun bombed Vienna's

Sacher Hotel by two suitcase bombs planted in the coal cellar. In Tel Aviv the next day a bank cashier, a Sephardic Jew, was killed in an armed robbery of a Barclay's Bank by "seven Jews and one Jewess [Hagana], all armed." A check post in Jerusalem was mined, but the device was discovered and destroyed.[442]

Two armed men speaking Hebrew walked into the Department of Labour in Jerusalem the following day (August 5), deposited a bomb, and left. After the building was evacuated, employees described the position of the bomb to police. Four police entered the building, located the bomb and, tragically, tried to remove it. The explosion killed three on the spot. The fourth was seriously injured, and the building was heavily damaged. Two days later (August 7) a mine on the Haifa-Kantara line between Ras El Ain and Qalqilya derailed nineteen oil wagons, and an electrically detonated mine near Hadera injured four in a military staff car. In the outskirts of Jerusalem, a grenade was used in an attempted assassination of the Bethlehem District Officer, two mines were discovered on the road near Petah Tikva, and near Gaza a length of the railway was blown up.[443]

One of the terror gangs' favorite devices, disguising themselves as "Arabs," had been overused. As recorded by British officials that day,

> Arab Guards on the Ajami Police Station, Jaffa, challenged a man dressed as an Arab and leading a camel. The man ran away and was captured with the assistance of the public. He was found to be a Yemenite Jew and to be carrying a haversack containing a grenade and detonating device. In panniers on the camel were found two mines.[444]

Eight Jews (Irgun?) with automatic weapons robbed the Hasharon Cooperative Bank in Ramatgan on August 8. The Cairo-Haifa train was bombed by the Irgun the next day, killing the engineer, a Jew from Tel Aviv, and leaving two passengers critically injured. This attack was unusual in that it occurred on a plain with little place to hide, and two of the three bombers, aged fifteen and nineteen, were caught. The third escaped by spraying the scene with machine gun fire.[445]

On August 10, on the outskirts north of Tel Aviv near an Arab village, the Hawari café, a "Jewish owned cafe in which an Arab has an interest" was attacked with automatic weapons and hand grenades. Four Jews and one Palestinian were killed on the spot, and eight people were injured, three seriously. The British never determined who the five attackers were—did the Zionists target it because its Jewish owner worked with an Arab? Or did Arabs attack it because it was Jewish owned? Each side blamed the other, and in the "numerous stabbing, stoning, shooting and arson incidents" springing from the dispute, nine people were killed, four Jews, four Palestinians, and one of unknown identity. Forty-eight Palestinians and twenty-three Jews were injured.

In Jerusalem on the day of the café attack, a tip warned of a bomb planted inside the Income Tax Office; it was evacuated in time before the device detonated. In Haifa, an attack was averted by a terrorist's carelessness: Lehi militants were driving a taxi they had stolen when one of their bombs accidentally exploded. All three were found nearby with various injuries, one with a hand blown off. In Gaza, a military vehicle was attacked between Nuseirat and Julis.[446]

The bombing of the Naim Railway Line south of Gaza on August 11 was one success among a handful of failures. A bank robbery in Jerusalem (presumably for arms) was foiled, as was an attack on a Haifa post office with a rivet bomb. The next day police and military repelled an attacker at the Police Headquarters in Jerusalem, a phosphorus bomb was discovered on Ben Yehuda Street in Jerusalem, and a land mine on Jerusalem-Beit-Hakerem Road was found and safely detonated.[447]

High in the Austrian Alps that night, August 12,* a Medloc train left the station at Mallnitz with 130 men and 40 women aboard, plus a crew of about five, heading toward Spittal. The train proceeded at slow speed up a considerable gradient, and about twenty minutes out of Mallnitz it exited a mountain tunnel onto a steep trestle. As it did, a bomb exploded underneath it—but what would have been the most dramatic Zionist terror attack on the railways, failed.

---

* Irgun records in Kister cite two Irgun attacks on trains in Europe in mid-August of 1947, neither corresponding to this attack whose time and place are well documented. One is on August 13 "near Linz," which is roughly 200 km (124 miles) from the Mallnitz attack. The second is recorded as August 14 and simply "in Austria". The author has not been able to corroborate these attacks. (Kister, *Irgun*, 194 & 275)

"I was flung to the floor of the compartment," a passenger recalled,

> and from that position the coach appeared to travel some distance in a series of bumps until finally coming to a standstill. On regaining my feet I found the coach considerably listed but I made my way along the corridor to the coach door, and avoiding the electric wires which hung over the coach, ascended to the track.[448]

Medloc train after the Irgun's unsuccessful attempt to blow it off the trestle into the ravine on the evening of August 12, 1947.

The attack was designed to be catastrophic—the bombers' choice of this remote mountain pass was intended to plunge the train to the abyss below, sending its 175 passengers, including Allied troops and civilians of the Allied Commission for Austria, to their deaths. But the main explosive failed, and the initial charge exploded under the baggage van instead of under the engine, and so failed to knock the train off the trestle. However disappointed, the Irgun distributed handbills in the Jewish DP camps in the Salzburg area claiming responsibility.

Four DPs were arrested for the attack, three from the US Zone, one from the British. The first to be caught, a seventeen-year-old member of the DP camp police who lived in the Bad Adelschloss Hotel in Bad Gastein (US Zone), confessed to being the lookout. Bad Gastein had become so infamous as a stronghold of fanatical Zionism that Major General Harry Collins, commander of the US Zone in Austria, had months earlier forbidden British civilians from going there.[449]

Two and a half hours after the train bombing, a "Red Devil" type bomb exploded outside the office of the Camp Commandant 138 BDE at Velden, Austria. A bomb threat followed on August 15, causing the evacuation of the Hotel Sacher, the hotel that had been bombed twelve days earlier. A spate of bomb threats followed on August 19: against the United States Legation in Vienna, the Minister's residence, a power plant in the American zone, a "moving picture house" in the British zone, the plant where the British German-language newspaper was published, and once again the Hotel Sacher.[450]

Anti-terror policies were reassessed in the wake of the Medloc attack. The first on a list of eight recommendations was to "Get Austrians to move Jews to a camp as far as possible from our L of C" [Lines of Communications]. Another was a change in the twenty-minute rule for when a pilot engine (used to check for bombs) should precede the train, as this effectively told terrorists when the train would be coming. These pilot trains were an unrecognized drain on the Allies caused by the terror threat: each day they consumed about twenty-five tons of coal.[451]

US and British military personnel in Europe faced constant risk from DPs conditioned in the Zionist-run camps. Lucius D. Clay, commander in chief of US Forces in Europe and military governor of the US Zone in Germany, stressed the seriousness of this violence against Allied soldiers to members of UNSCOP when he met with them in Berlin on August 13, the day after the Mallnitz bombing about 550 km (341 miles) to the south. General Clay told the delegation that the Jewish DPs from eastern Europe should be sent to Palestine quickly—because US personnel had been beaten, robbed, and killed by them, and that as a result of their "violent, asocial, and criminal behavior," anti-Semitism was growing sharply in US military units in the US Zones of Austria and Germany. Clay feared "severe spontaneous reactions on the part of other soldiers" if the situation were to continue, and his claims were emphatically reinforced by the Deputy British Military Governor, Sir Brian Robertson.

The Jewish Agency was well aware of the violence it had nurtured in the DP camps. Eliezer Kaplan, treasurer of the Jewish Agency, told Mapai (Workers' party) leaders the previous October that he had been "reliably informed" that US military reports submitted to Truman were "very pessimistic" about disturbances in the Zionist camps, and that the US feared having to use force to quell them.[452]

Near Petah Tiqva the day after the Medloc attack (August 13), two Jews shot a Palestinian dead from passing cars and left his body on the roadside. The next day, a Palestinian watchman at a factory in Ramat Gan was abducted by Jews who stabbed him to death and threw his body into an orange grove.[453]

Some British officials now proposed boycotting the Jewish citrus crop pending Agency cooperation against terror, but this was shelved on four counts: British business interests, especially as much of the payment for the crops had been made in advance; the difficulty in determining the origin of the fruit; the fear that the action would backfire and be met with increased terrorism; and the surety that a boycott would play into the propaganda campaigns in the US.[454]

Two more Palestinian watchmen were stabbed to death by a gang of Jews near Jaffa on August 15. One was thirteen years old. In Jaffa, three Jews vandalized a Palestinian shop and poured paraffin over its contents, but local (Jewish) residents intervened and stopped them from setting the shop ablaze. A bomb exploded under a goods train near Hadera, and Jews attacked a Palestinian on the Jaffa-Jerusalem Road, burning out his car.[455]

The bloodiest attack of the day was near Petah Tikvah, where "a party of 30-35 Jews in khaki shirts and shorts and armed with automatic weapons approached an Arab owned building in an orange grove near Petah Tikvah," as a British official recorded it. "As the Jews approached, they split up, several entering the building, and all firing indiscriminately." Four Palestinians were shot dead, and then "the building was almost completely demolished by an explosion, probably electrically detonated. 3 males and 4 females are believed to be buried in the debris." The dead bodies pulled out of the rubble confirmed the figure: five children and their parents, and one further victim murdered outside pushed the total dead to twelve. The Hagana claimed responsibility. Two days later, a gang of Jews seized a Palestinian man in a café in Tel Aviv near the Jaffa border, dragged him to an alley and stabbed him to death.[456]

The summer of 1947 thus marks the beginning of the final phase of the Zionist project, the phase that remains ongoing these seven decades later. Britain had given the enterprise recognition and autonomy, had defended it from the indigenous resistance, and had now served as the colonial oppressor against which Zionism postured itself as a native liberation movement. Although the UN vote had yet to take place, there was little question that the Mandate would soon end. Britain was reduced to a defeated co-conspirator now wanting only to extricate itself as quickly as possible. No matter what form the UN decision might take, the Palestinians themselves now remained as the final "problem."

The coming reckoning also meant that the Irgun and Lehi found themselves in competition with the Hagana for international respectability as a path to power. The result was that both the Irgun and Lehi seized upon Hagana slaughter of Palestinians to posture themselves as the principled alternatives. Even as the Palestinians were increasingly all three militias' targets of choice, Lehi and the Irgun distributed pamphlets condemning the Hagana for murdering Arab "women and children who are beyond any political controversy," and denouncing as "traitors" any Jew who harmed any Arab. The Hagana, similarly, accused the Irgun of needing a new *raison d'etre* now that a Zionist state appeared imminent, and assigned about a hundred members to "beat up in public known [Irgun] extortionists." Sharett went to the United States and told the media that the Jewish Agency was "trying to organize a campaign of enlightenment among Jews to open their eyes to the freak charlatan aspect" of Bergson (the Irgun's US branch). Among the layers of this power play was the rivalry between Ben-Gurion and Begin, which would culminate with Ben-Gurion's burning of Begin's *Altalena* and its arms shipment in June, 1948, which Ben-Gurion would cleverly wield under the guise of principle.[457]

Near Jerusalem on August 16, militants exploded a time bomb in a games room at Tel Litwinsky, injuring six. Less dramatically but more significantly, Palestinians threw stones at a Jewish bus near Haifa, and the next day Palestinians fired three shots at a Jewish bus on the Jerusalem-Jaffa Road—early evidence that the Palestinians' nearly decade-long refusal to reward Zionist terror was beginning to wear. Another Palestinian was attacked on the Tel Aviv sea front, and more clashes followed on August 18-19. On August 20 a Jewish café owner was assaulted by six Jews because he employed Palestinians.

When a Hagana arms cache was discovered in a Jewish school that day, the Agency spun the embarrassment by announcing that they had "so hoped [to use] these particular arms" to fight terrorism. Jewish snipers fired from rooftops at police cars, and a mine (Irgun?) on the railway line near Gaza was discovered and diffused. On August 21 a road mine near Nathanya injured two, one seriously. Just before midnight on August 26 three Jews in Samaria District were injured when they challenged Lehi militants who had entered the village to distribute pamphlets. Lehi continued its threats against Jewish civil servants, and when a member of the gang was caught with a phosphorus bomb after a foiled raid on a Jerusalem bank that month, he was identified as the son of an Assistant Superintendent of Police.[458]

One of the more bizarre terror projects came to the fore in September of 1947. Rabbi Baruch Korff, a US citizen, had been raising money to enact, in his words, "the greatest exodus since Pharaoh" by his organization, the Political Action Committee for Palestine. According to the Committee's money-raising ads in the New York Post in March, DC4 aircraft would make four round trips daily from "a certain port in Europe," bringing Jewish women and children who would be "directed to secretly designated makeshift landing fields in Palestine, whilst able-bodied men would be unloaded by parachute" to assist them. In a June interview in the

New York Sun, Korff gave a variation: he was going to drop Jews by parachute to Middle East waterways, where they would be picked up by waiting PT boats and smuggled into Palestine.

The money, in truth, was financing (to quote British intelligence) a "project for an air-raid on London" from France, "in the course of which leaflets were to be dropped in the name of the Stern Gang, together with high explosive bombs." For the task he hired an American pilot, Reginald Gilbert, but this was a bad choice: Gilbert informed the French authorities, and when he and Korff, accompanied by Judith Rosenberger (who some sources say slipped into Belgium when Eliav and Lazarus were caught) reached the Toussus-le-Noble airfield, they were apprehended. To the backdrop of *Exodus* sympathy, Korff was treated leniently and soon released. He later came to the limelight as a vociferous defender of Richard Nixon in the midst of the Watergate scandal.[459]

Korff's may not have been the last London terror attack to be foiled. One agent working for Special Branch, Glasgow, learned of "Jews [in Britain who] are anxious to have the 'stuff' as soon as possible," preferably TNT, otherwise gelignite, to use "as a counter demonstration to what may happen in Palestine," probably meaning the UN decision. At 3:30 in the afternoon on September 3, a parcel slipped off a conveyor belt at the SW District Post Office and exploded, injuring two postal employees. What appeared to be part of a watch was found in the debris.[460]

Sept-Oct 1947

When on September 9, the three vessels carrying the ex-*Exodus* passengers reached Hamburg, one of the DPs (or one of their minders) affixed a bomb to his ship, the *Empire Rival*, that would have torn a six-foot hole in its hull. It was discovered and removed, breaking about a dozen windows in nearby buildings when it exploded outside. The following day at Haifa, where the *Exodus* DPs had been refused entry, four bombs exploded at the heavily-guarded Consolidated Refineries. Evidence suggested that Jewish employees had facilitated the attack from the inside. Meanwhile, a terror group called Lameri, said by British military headquarters to be "the extremist group of Hagana," distributed pamphlets claiming that "the Arabs" were preparing a revolt, likely to begin in October.

On September 26, three constables transferring money from the Barclay's Bank in Tel Aviv to the Treasury in Jerusalem were murdered by ten or more Lehi members, netting the gang £150,000. Two more police were murdered in the chase. The Irgun continued its pastime of holding up cinemas to project its propaganda onto the screen for the edification of the audience, to the accompaniment of "patriotic" Irgun songs played from records.[461]

"An Arab constable at the front door blew his whistle, and the next moment he was blown to bits," the *NY Times* reported about a gruesome attack on District Police Headquarters in Haifa three days later, September 29, when the Irgun tried out a new massive tar barrel bomb which it said was "catapulted by a special mechanism from a lorry." Timed for the first day of the Feast of the Tabernacle, the explosion killed twelve people, both police and civilians, and injured fifty-four, thirteen seriously. Six of the dead were Palestinians, one a woman.

> Some of the small detachment of men on duty at the front door and in the orderly room were torn to pieces … Scarcely any structure in the immediate neighborhood escaped damage, [and] part of bodies were blown fifty yards across the Kings Way.[462]

"The general reaction" of the Jewish settlements to the massacre, according to a military report, "was one of admiration for the way the outrage was implemented and very little sympathy was reserved for the dead and wounded."

The more routine attacks continued. That same day, an explosion hit the rear of the Immigration Office in Jerusalem, and a rivet-type mine was detonated under a jeep on the Lydda - Petah Tiqva Road, injuring two. The bombers hid nearby and fired on those who came to investigate. On September 30, "Jewish thugs"—the terminology part of military officials' new tact to deny them any glamor associated with "terrorist"—exploded a mine beneath the Cairo-Haifa train, south of Haifa. A truck carrying ice was blown up in Rehovot on October 1, and the day after that a Parachute Brigade truck was mined about a mile north of Hadera.[463]

At about 10:15 on the night of October 6, between fifteen and twenty militants approached two Palestinian tents, spread out into a semi-circle around them, and indiscriminately opened fire into the tents with 160 rounds—a prelude to the three-pronged assault, known as Plan Dalet, that would depopulate Palestinian villages in a few months' time. Neighbouring Palestinians fled for safety, but the attackers killed two more in their escape.

Despite the increasing anti-Palestinian violence, the arrival of October failed to usher in the prophesised Palestinian revolt. Disappointment among Zionist leaders, whose plans to conquer Palestine in the name of self-defense required an "Arab threat," was sufficiently visible that it was noted in a British military report for the fortnight ending October 10:

> The Jews continue to exhibit signs of anxiety because the lack of [Palestinian] disturbances shows unexpected control by the Arab leaders over the masses.

Whether or not "the Jews" were correct in attributing "the lack of disturbances" to "Arab leaders," the Palestinians were not responding to the violence. There was, in fact, a Palestinian "disturbance" that month, but not directed against Jews. In what the British military described as "a token of disgust" at US behavior at the UN, an "Arab Committee of Struggle" claimed responsibility for a bomb that caused minor damage to the American Consulate on October 13—a one-off with no follow-up.

The Irgun tried a new ploy on October 18, probably inspired by Lehi's invention of explosive-laden pamphlets: it now displayed banners in Tel Aviv and Jerusalem rigged with explosives intended to blow up the worker sent to remove them. In a further sign of the coming reckoning, on October 23-25 the Irgun and Lehi met outside of Tel Aviv to agree on joint tactics to fight Partition.[464]

Jewish sex workers continued to be exploited as an espionage network, but in November, at great risk, one testified to the British. She and her colleagues did not cooperate willingly. They would be confronted by men identifying themselves as "Stern Gang Intelligence," though the British believed they were not Lehi, but were using the Lehi brand because it was even more frightening than "Hagana" or "Irgun." The Jewish state, the women were assured, was

Nov 1947

imminent. Upon its founding they would be tried for "sleeping with the enemy," convicted, and executed—if not simply assassinated, "shot out of hand for collaboration with the enemy." "Stern Gang Intelligence" was however giving them the opportunity to save their necks by cooperating now, since they "have continual access to a large number of slightly inebriated and highly repressed officers and men," and thus to their information and their thoughts.

"As can be imagined," the British realized, "the average night club hostess, cafe girl or prostitute falls readily and is able to furnish the organisation with an astonishing amount of personal and official information concerning the activities of British army personnel." Any one woman would mingle among different cliques of men, since they "work at one place or another according to the amount of custom they bring to the management." The operation was so large and well organized that they were supplied with copies of a printed questionnaire to be filled out after each patron.

The form pressed the indentured spies to extract the expected military and personal information, and to use their conversation to identify any British who betrayed any sympathy with the cause and might be recruitable. The women were instructed to "exploit your activities to the full" to garner all information possible, and to "comply strictly with instructions." This information was to be clear, concise, and clinical. They were also encouraged to offer any comments and opinions that might prove insightful, but these were to be strictly separated into the "special remarks column." Every ten days, "Stern Gang Intelligence" would visit the women and collect their forms.[465]

November also brought a bold announcement from the Jewish Agency: it was forming an elite "Mishmar Force" to stamp out terrorism. However suspect the opportunistic timing, just as the UN was about to decide Palestine's future, the British nonetheless removed police and troops from the area in order not to interfere with this anti-terror "Force," which the Agency said would be established within ten days. No such force was ever established.[466]

Police remained targets even in the lead-up to the United Nations vote. A Jewish police corporal was assassinated at his home in Jerusalem on November 3, and a constable was seriously wounded at the city's Northern Police Station. In Tel Aviv, two police were shot from behind, left on the ground and ignored by the passing Tel Aviv public until the arrival of a British patrol twenty-five minutes later. Both died. After two suspects in a separate incident were brought to the Apak Police Station, "about ten Jews armed with pistols and sub-machine guns" overpowered the station and released their comrades. On November 12, five CID personnel in Cafe Haas in Haifa were sprayed with bullets from a Thomson sub-machine gun, killing one and critically wounding three.

A tip that day led the British to a Lehi "criminal school" in a house in the Ra'anana area. The British burst in and "took the 'thugs' completely by surprise" despite heavily armed sentries in a nearby orange grove. Lehi "men and girls jumped from the windows and doors," attacking with a variety of firearms, grenades, and bombs, but were overpowered. Among the Lehi trainees were "children of tender years," some of whom died in the battle.

On November 13, three grenades were thrown into Cafe Ritz on King George's Avenue, killing two and wounding twenty-five, five seriously. Two constables were targeted, one assassinated on the spot and the other critically wounded. The deadliest attack of the day was in Haifa, where four British civilians were murdered as they left the Armon cinema. They were oil workers and thus targets: three were employees of Shell Oil and the fourth worked for Socony (now Mobil).

Two soldiers walking in Colony Square in Tel Aviv, and two constables walking on Jaffa Road in Jerusalem, were murdered on November 14. Throughout Britain that day, Town Clerks received Irgun leaflets posted from Tel Aviv warning that any interference in the Irgun's plans, whether by the British or the Arabs, would bring a campaign of terror to British shores. Meanwhile, the "Hebrew Legion" was formed in Britain, a group that MI3 (a defunct division of the British Directorate of Military Intelligence) described as "the Jewish equivalent of the Mosleyite toughs," a reference to the British racial supremacist and Nazi sympathizer. The Legion was an extension of the American Hebrew Committee of National Liberation.

The immigrant ship *Aliyah* beached in the early morning hours of November 16, transporting the Agency's favored settlers: not the downtrodden of Europe, but "some three hundred carefully selected young Jews, earmarked and trained for service with HAGANA."

At 4:30 in the morning on November 20, "a party of about 6 armed Jews entered an Arab house at Ra'anana" and executed what the British called five "quite harmless Arabs" who Lehi had falsely accused of being British informants. Four died on the spot, and a fifth later succumbed to his wounds. This time, some Palestinians retaliated, injuring five people in a Jewish bus.[467]

The big news for Palestine came on November 29.

Irgun broadside condemning Partition, summer of 1947.

Part III
"Only a Beachhead"

7

Partition, the "temporary expedient," 1947–1948

[Americans do not realize] the extent to which partition was refused acceptance as a final settlement by the Zionists in Palestine, [nor the conviction among Zionists that] they cannot be satisfied with Palestine alone, that they must not only have all of Palestine, but Trans-Jordan, part of Syria and Lebanon, parts of Iraq and parts of Egypt as well. —*Kermit Roosevelt, Jr. (grandson of Theodore), addressing the National War College in Washington, 1948.*[468]

On November 29, 1947, the United Nations General Assembly, honoring the principles emblazoned in its Charter, defeated Resolution 181, which would have denied Palestine self-determination—or so history would have read, had the Truman Administration not secured a delay in the vote in order to use, in the words of Under Secretary of State Sumner Welles, "every form of pressure, direct and indirect," to "make sure that the necessary majority" would be secured. Only once the two-thirds majority was assured did the US allow the vote to proceed. Non-binding General Assembly Resolution 181 passed, recommending the division of Palestine into two proto-countries, the larger for the minority Jewish population, the smaller for the majority Palestinians, principally Muslims and

Christians. A small, central region encompassing Jerusalem and Bethlehem would remain an international zone administered by the UN. Alexander Cadogan, a British statesman remembered for his opposition to appeasement of the Nazis, described Resolution 181 as "so manifestly unjust to the Arabs," that it is difficult to see how "we could reconcile it with our conscience."[469]

Partition—and thus Israeli statehood—was a capitulation to Zionist terrorism. UNSCOP had also proposed a single, federated state for Palestine, which the Palestinians would have accepted despite concerns that, as recorded in British Cabinet papers, it did not "altogether close the door to eventual partition." The Zionists, "on the other hand," would have begun "an intensification of Jewish terrorism" at such a decision, making the single state "not capable of being enforced."

The disproportionately large land area awarded the new state was also driven by the fear of Zionist violence. Those deciding Palestine's future assumed that the new Israeli state would disregard the Partition, and so they hoped that by giving it more land up front, its aggression might be delayed. Israel's "desire for expansion"

> might develop earlier if the Jewish State occupied a smaller area and would be felt more strongly if the Jews were dissatisfied with the frontiers.[470]

This appeasement, however, failed to postpone Israel's "desire for expansion" beyond Partition.

What Cunningham described as "hysterical celebrations of victory" in the settlements following the passage of Resolution 181 were not about having won a Zionist state in more than half of Palestine. The celebrations were, rather, because 181 was "a preliminary step to a Jewish state in the fullest extent of its historical [Biblical] bounds." The Yishuv envisioned "the present state only as a welcome forerunner of greater things ... [they] are still not satisfied with its size [and] hanker after the whole." Vowing to fight to undo the "injustice," Meir Grossman, president of the United Zionists and Revisionists of America, expressed his "deep sorrow" that the UN had decided "to reduce the Jewish national territory from 44,000 to 5,500 square miles"—the larger figure based on Zionist claims to much of the Levant, not just Palestine.

The various Hebrew media varied in tact, but their message was consistent: "The youth of the Yishuv," as the newspaper *Haboker* put it, "must bury deep in their hearts the fact that the frontiers have not been fixed for all eternity." This was the ever-present subtext as "vast crowds of rejoicing Jews swarmed the streets," in the words of British intelligence, "dancing and singing ... as though they had won a war—the scenes in Jerusalem were reminiscent of VE Day, and continued with staggering endurance for almost two whole days."[471]

When Partition was first seriously proposed a decade earlier, in 1937, Ben-Gurion assured the Zionist Executive that "in the wake of the establishment of the state, we will abolish partition and expand to the whole of Palestine." He wrote to his son that

> The decisive question is: Does the establishment of a Jewish state [in only part of Palestine] advance or retard the conversion of this country into a Jewish country? My assumption ... is that a Jewish state on only part of the land [i.e., Partition] is not the end but the beginning ... Our ability to penetrate the country will increase if we have a state.*

Adolf Eichmann, visiting the Zionist settlements in October of that year, heard much the same from his host, the Hagana's Feivel Polkes: Once a state was secured, "then the borders may be pushed outward according to one's wishes".[472]

When in late 1941 Ben-Gurion left London for the United States, the British secretly searched his luggage and found a document entitled *Outline of Zionist Policy*, Ben-Gurion's blueprints for the future. In it he described how Partition would be passively exploited: it would be "an irreparable mistake" to *suggest* Partition, he wrote, but rather, statehood should be extracted from the *offer* of Partition. That state must then be enlarged at least to the Jordan River, and into Transjordan if possible.

---

* The accuracy of passages from this widely-quoted letter has been contested by the Zionist watchdog CAMERA. In response, the editors of the JPS undertook a fresh, critical translation of the full original letter, and it is from that translation that this extract is quoted. See "JPS Responds to CAMERA's Call for Accuracy: Ben-Gurion and the Arab Transfer," in *Journal of Palestine Studies*, Vol. XLI, No. 2 (Winter 2012), 245–250.

Perhaps most revealing, Ben-Gurion refers to Palestinians by the extraordinary phrase "Arabs who happen to be in Palestine"—ethnic "purity" was clearly on his to-do list.[473]

By 1944, opposition to Partition had "hardened throughout all shades of Jewish opinion," as the Chief Secretary in Jerusalem put it, and in December of that year the Inner Zionist Council and *Assefat Hanivcharim* (Yishuv Elected Assembly) passed resolutions that placed "special emphasis on the rejection of partition."[474]

"Can we really believe," the British Secretary of State for Foreign Affairs asked rhetorically,

> more particularly after reading the newest memorandum of the Jewish Agency, that the Zionists ... will accept as final the frontiers as proposed? ... It seems inevitable that [they] would fill their State up far beyond its capacity and so prove their need for more living space."[475]

One month before the UN vote, the *Jewish Standard* published a full-page disavowal of Partition. "Whatever might be signed or pledged by the few Zionist spokesmen at the United Nations," the *Standard* argued, would still be subject to the resolute opposition to Partition and the "struggle for the integrity of Eretz Israel" in all of historic Palestine. The "power and passion opposed to Partition" represent a force of Jewish public opinion "of uncompromising resolve."[476]

In London, *The Jewish Struggle* equated Partition with the final genocide of the Jewish "race." In Palestine, *Voice of Fighting Zion* denounced Partition with virulent broadcasts, and Tel Aviv mayor Israel Rokach headed a movement dedicated to fighting Partition. In the US, the ZOA railed against the Jewish Agency for so much as discussing Partition. Privately, however, even the Irgun and Lehi agreed with Ben-Gurion's pragmatism: Partition meant statehood, and statehood was the weapon to conquer the rest.[477]

One month before the UN approved Partition, the CIA warned that an Israeli state would never abide by Partition, indeed that not even "the more conservative" Zionists would honor Partition. "Moderate" Zionists would gradually take over all of Palestine west of the Jordan River, while the less moderate would fight to take over Jordan as well, along with parts of Syria and Egypt.[478]

Arab representatives at the UN believed the rightfulness of their case to be self-evident, stressing that they were neither asking for favors nor basing their claim on anyone's promises. Their right to independence rested, rather, on the

> high principles which [after the First World War] were to govern the organization of international relations and serve as the basis of the structure of modern civilization [and] the rejection of all ideas of conquest and recognition of the right of self-determination.

Kermit Roosevelt (Jr.) agreed, testifying to the National War College that "most of the Arab arguments for their case in Palestine are taken from American and democratic thought." Ben-Gurion, however, asserted that such principles were trumped by Jewish exceptionalism. It did not matter, he told the UN, that their alleged ancestors had left Palestine "a considerable time ago," because "we did not give it up," the preposterousness of his *we* passing unchallenged. To Arab negotiators, the claim seemed so fantastic as to scarcely need rebuttal:

> What should then be said when an effort is made to set the clock of history back by twenty centuries in an attempt to give away a country on the ground of a transitory historic association?

Similarly, when Ben-Gurion repeated the argument that Jews would bring Arabs a more advanced civilization, Palestinian representatives could only say the obvious:

> Even if the premises on which this argument rests were true, [it would be] an immoral argument [which would] justify any aggression by the more advanced nations against the less advanced.

Roosevelt said much the same:

> If you are looking to determine the rights to a land on the basis of who could most efficiently develop that land, then you are going to have a pretty disastrous series of world shifts and revolutions. And if that was our theory, then on what grounds did we, for instance, oppose the Nazis?

Nor, Roosevelt lectured, was the premise true. The Palestinians had been removed from the land by settlers receiving vast outside financial backing with no expectation of having to repay it.

Aside from UNSCOP's Sir Abdur Rahman, Ben-Gurion encountered little critical debate at the hearings. When Ben-Gurion stonewalled Rahman's questions with non-sequiturs about British atrocities, Sir Abdur stood fast, telling him: "We will not finish for two months if you go on in that way. I do not mind if we take two months or two years." But Ben-Gurion continued his oratorical obstructions until the compliant Chairman simply changed topics.

The Jewish Agency leader told the Committee that "the relations of the Jews of this country cannot be judged by a rule applied to other countries," and accused any who disagreed with him of Nazism. "There is only one reason that the people here say 'No, we will not let those Jews come back'," Ben-Gurion charged, and to identify that "one reason," he segued to the Nazis and murdered Jews. His messianic 'come back' left unchallenged, he said that "Jewish right" to Palestine has existed for 3,500 years.[479]

The day before the UN Partition vote, the CIA reinforced earlier warnings :

> Even the more conservative Zionists will hope to obtain the whole of the Nejeb [sic], Western Galilee, the city of Jerusalem, and eventually all of Palestine. The extremists demand not only all of Palestine but Transjordan as well. They have stated that they will refuse to recognize the validity of any Jewish government which will settle for anything less, and will probably undertake aggressive action to achieve their ends.[480]

Upon the passage of Resolution 181, "young Jewish volunteers with money boxes swarmed through the streets of Haifa ... blackmailing the public into buying rapidly produced [Zionist] flags for large sums of money." In a second wave of this campaign, names were taken of those few who refused.

Meanwhile at the UN, Arab representatives—whose request to have the legality of Partition reviewed by the International Court of Justice had already been denied—took advantage of a twenty-four hour reprieve granted them to put forth a conciliatory alternative. They proposed, in vain, a single democratic nation with what the *Times* described as "a constitution similar to that of the United States."[481]

<small>Dec 1947</small>

Scattered ethnic violence marked the first several days after the UN vote. There were bombings of Palestinian homes, cafes, bus queues, and a cinema, and there was more of the anti-Jewish violence that had begun to resurface by mid-August when the UNSCOP recommendations were formalized. Most Palestinians, however, appear to have resigned themselves to the new dynamics, and wanted simply to get on with their lives. Cunningham described "the initial Arab outbreaks" as "spontaneous and unorganized ... more demonstrations of displeasure at the UN decision than determined attacks on Jews."

The Arabs' main weapons, Cunningham pointed out, were "sticks and stones," and the unrest would likely have subsided had it not been that the settlers ratcheted up the provocation. Until then, "the Arab Higher Committee as a whole, and the Mufti in particular," wanted non-violent resistance—boycott—and "were not in favour of serious outbreaks." The British military cited several cases "of Mukhtars of Arab villages visiting the adjacent Jewish settlements and insisting that they want to remain on friendly terms with their Jewish neighbours."[482]

Palestinian anti-British violence, which had ceased by 1939, did resurface on a small scale, though the British security forces reported that it "should not be considered ... part of a deliberate plan, and in many cases the Mukhtars have apologized profusely for damage and casualties ... the Arabs as a whole are loath to start hostilities."

Peaceful Palestinian protest also marked the aftermath of the Partition vote. On December 5, about 1,300 Palestinians in Gaza—Muslims and Christians, men and women—carried banners that read "Down with Truman and Down with Partition." Near Khan Yunis, 3,000-4,000 Palestinians demonstrated for four hours and then sent a delegation to speak to the police. A thousand Palestinians walked in peaceful procession in Kefar Saba against Partition.[483]

The Jewish Agency's defiance of Resolution 181 was visible within a week of the vote, with its decision that "a number of 'national institutions', including the Chief Rabbinate," would not be within the borders it had agreed to, but illegally in Jerusalem, in the UN-administered international zone.

Intelligence reports in mid-December betray how soon after the Partition vote the British themselves acknowledged the UN's promise of a Palestinian state to be fraudulent. One secret report warned of "the illegal appropriation of land in PALESTINE by the Jews in order to est[ablish] new settlements" on land designated for Palestine. Another British report, a scant two weeks after Resolution 181, stated outright that the promised Palestinian state would never be, that "it does not appear that Arab Palestine will be an entity." The British were already aware that Ben-Gurion was collaborating with "an Arab ruler," King Abdullah of Jordan.

Anti-Palestinian attacks intensified. On December 12 Jews (Irgun?) bombed a Palestinian bus in Haifa, killing four, and in Jaffa the Irgun threw a bomb into a Palestinian café, killing an eleven-year-old child and wounding three other children under twelve. Jerusalem was the scene of similar attacks, where "four Jewish youths hurled six grenades into two Arab taxicab offices, one cafe and the street outside." That evening, "Jews disguised as policemen and soldiers raided the Arab village of Shefat" on the outskirts of Jerusalem, bombing two houses. The next day (December 13) "4 truck loads of Jews" attacked Al Yehudia, killing six Palestinians on the spot and wounding several. Three days later, two sergeants walking in Zion Square (Jerusalem) were shot by Lehi; both died.

On December 18, Palmach militants under Yigal Allon, future IDF general and Israeli statesman, attacked what was widely considered a most beautiful Palestinian village, the mixed Christian-Muslim village of Khisas, situated on a terrace overlooking Lake Hula. The onslaught began at about 9 PM, when two carloads of Hagana men drove through this northern village, blowing up houses along with their sleeping occupants, "burying the victims in the wreckage where their bodies were found only today by police searches," as the *NY Times* reported the next day. Fifteen Palestinians, five of them children, lay dead.

The Hagana justified the attack as defensive, a reprisal raid—a claim dismissed outright by the British military, as "the villagers did not use any firearms to defend themselves, and as far as is known, the village is not in possession of any." The British were correct: Zionist archives state that the massacre was undertaken by Allon for "experience." Khisas was only partially depopulated by the Zionist armies' 1948 purge, but on June 5 of the following year, three weeks after Israel's admittance to the UN, the IDF forced the remaining Khisas villagers onto trucks and dumped them in the wilderness.

With these post-181 attacks, the Jewish Agency and Hagana no longer feigned abhorrence of terror, now boasting in Irgun-Lehi fashion that civilian casualties had been much higher than the British acknowledged. When shortly after midnight on the morning of December 20 the Hagana launched a new attack, this time on the Palestinian village of Qazaza, the Hagana claimed it had killed more than the one person reported. Terror gang rivalry had, indeed, become a race for fanaticism, and so when the group Americans for Haganah held a rally in New York's Manhattan Center on December 23, it was disrupted by protestors accusing the militia of "appeasement."

On Christmas eve, four British soldiers leaving a café in Tel Aviv were attacked by the militants, leaving two dead and two wounded. The day after Christmas, an English driver was shot dead at the English Girls High School in Haifa, a half year after a bomb exploded at the "foreign" English Girls School; and Ben-Gurion assigned the Hagana a "major offensive" to "greatly reduce the percentage of Arabs in the population of the new state."[484]

"The Jewish Agency's Hagana," Cunningham reported by telegram that month, has been

> responsible for severe attacks on Arab villages, which have caused considerable loss of life (including women and children) and damage to property. Hagana members have, also, turned their weapons on British Police and troops attempting to restore order. Jewish terrorists have been responsible for unprovoked attacks on both Arabs and British Police and soldiers, yet, while ostensibly condemning such attacks, it is known that the Jewish Agency is cooperating with the terrorist leaders…[485]

Lehi as well was becoming even more radicalized now that Palestine's opportunity-filled plunge into post-Mandate anarchy was dawning. In the words of a member of the 6th Airborne, the terror gang was making

> particularly bestial attacks on Arab villages, in which they showed not the slightest discrimination for women and children, whom they killed as opportunity offered.[486]

With this slaughter came the heightened need for the dehumanization of the victims. A cartoon by the noted graphic artist Arthur Szyk, for example, depicted stupid, thuggish, swastika-flaunting "Arabs" opposing precisely what the Palestinians had sought all along—freedom and democracy.[487]

Cartoon reinforcing the dehumanization of the Palestinians as the Zionist forces' ethnic cleansing was underway. By the well-known artist, book illustrator, and political caricaturist Arthur Szyk, in *The Legionaire*, "Voice of the Hebrew Legion," London, February 13, 1948.

The decisive campaign to jump-start an ethnic civil war came in the form of three Irgun-Hagana "flying bomb" attacks during the last two weeks of 1947. The first "flying bomb" hit the Damascus Gate on December 13, killing seven Palestinians and wounding fifty-four, and a deadlier attack hit the Damascus Gate on December 29. As the *NY Times* reported this second attack, "a bomb thrown by the Jewish terrorist organization Irgun Zvai Leumi from a speeding taxi today killed eleven Arabs and two British policemen and wounded at least thirty-two Arabs by the Jerusalem Damascus Gate," many of them women and children. More of the wounded died soon afterwards.[488]

The Palestinian reaction to the Damascus Gate massacres was to set up road blocks at the old city under the supervision of the British, which was "recognized by the Government as a reasonable measure of self-defence on the part of the Arabs having regard to the indiscriminate outrages carried by the Irgun Zvei Leumi"—but the Jewish Agency seized on this defense against the attacks to claim that "1,800 members of their community inside the Old City were besieged, starved, and about to be massacred." On December 29, as militants killed a soldier at Tel Litwinsky Camp, the Irgun launched a seaborne attack on Jaffa.[489]

"Provocation by the Jews" against the Palestinians, a British military report ending January 1 stated, "has continued during the past two weeks on an almost unprecedented scale," and although there was no Palestinian retaliation ("cycle") to the two Damascus Gate atrocities, such was tragically not the case in Haifa, where a third "flying bomb" attack can be seen as a penultimate spark that ignited the Jewish-Arab "civil war." Haifa, as the Hashomer Hatzair noted, had been quiet until December 30, the day after the second Damascus Gate attack, when the Irgun launched this third "flying bomb" attack against about one hundred Palestinian workers outside the city's oil refinery, killing six immediately and wounding about forty, many seriously. The purpose of the terror attack was the same as the others—to "provoke reprisals," as the Hashomer Hatzair stated bluntly—which this time it did, quickly and indiscriminately against the refinery's Jewish employees, forty-one of whom died in the anti-Jewish rampage.[490]

On two separate occasions, individual Jews risked warning specific Britons that they were marked for assassination and must leave, but otherwise the assassination of public workers continued. Two constables, nineteen and twenty years old, were killed in Mahan Yehuda market by an electrically detonated mine on December 30. The Irgun murdered a policeman outside Fink's Restaurant in Jerusalem on New Year's Eve, and four British men who went together to Tel Aviv on New Year's Eve were later found, shot, in their crashed jeep. The four had entered the Park Hotel on Hayarkon Street when the first was shot, and when the other three tried to rush him to the hospital, two more, including the driver, were shot.

It was the Hagana that made New Year's Eve decisive, the beginning of the so-called "civil war" and the ethnic cleansing of Palestine. As the New Year struck and the corks popped in Tel Aviv, the Jewish Agency's militia massacred sixty Palestinians in Belad esh Sheikh, including many women and children, and attacked the Wadi Rushmiyya neighborhood of Haifa, expelling non-Jews and blowing up their houses. According to Ilan Pappé, the Zionists conducted these two attacks in part to test the British reaction—and that reaction, to the Jewish Agency's satisfaction, was to "look the other way."

Both Jaffa and Jerusalem were targets on the first day of 1948. The Qatamon Quarter of Jerusalem was bombed by "approx 30 armed Jews, who placed charges and threw grenades," while the Irgun sped through Jaffa and fired at Palestinians sitting outside a café. The gang murdered two café-goers and wounded nine before crashing through a road block and vanishing into Tel Aviv. The same day a "small party of Jews" placed a bomb inside a block of flats in the rear of Jaffa's Shell petrol station, demolishing a block of Palestinian flats.[491]

Claims that the United States was a major source for the bombs wreaking havoc in Palestine were vindicated on January 3. As crates bound for the Jewish settlements in Palestine were being loaded onto the freighter *Executer* at the docks at New Jersey that day, one marked "Used Industrial Machinery Parts" fell, breaking open and revealing its true contents: Cyclonite. There were twenty-five more crates like it. As described by the British military,

> The total consignment consisted of 65,000 lbs of Cyclonite TNT ... in the warehouses from which the original consignment had come they [the police] found 5,200 combat knives, pig metal and machinery suitable for the production of arms ... On the following Thursday and Friday, 110 tons of Cyclonite, also allegedly destined for the Jewish State, was confiscated in the New York counties of Ulster and Monmouth.[492]

The journalist Sam Pope Brewer—whose then-wife would run off with double-agent Kim Philby, son of John Philby who had tried with Weizmann to "purchase" Palestine—reported that because of the rising anti-Arab terror in Jaffa, road blocks had been set up at all the approaches to the city "for the special purpose of intercepting possible [Jewish] terrorists." On January 4, however, two men "dressed as Arabs" driving a truck loaded with oranges did not arouse suspicion as they entered Jaffa and headed down the street leading to the port. The "Arabs" turned their truck into an alley between the Barclay's Bank and the Arab National Committee Building, parked, and were driven away in a waiting car. Bombs hidden within the orange crates detonated quickly, completely destroying the "Old Serrai" in Clock Tower Square and "shook the city and smashed doors more than a mile away." Fourteen people were known dead right away, and about a hundred wounded, with twelve more bodies pulled from the rubble as relief efforts continued through the evening. The terror worked: "The local people," Brewer reported, "shaken by this outrage, are shooting at anybody with a suspicious appearance."

Lehi claimed responsibility for the bombing, but it was the Hagana that blew up the Semiramis Hotel in Qatamon the next day, January 5, killing twenty-six people, most from two Christian families, wounding scores, and indiscriminately blowing up private houses as they retreated. Among the dead was Manuel Allende Salazar y Travesedo, the Spanish vice-consul. The attackers, all wearing European clothes, first threw a grenade into the building as a diversion, then used the ensuing confusion to set the bomb, which exploded about a minute later.

Through a night of icy, torrential rains, British soldiers combed the ruins looking for survivors. The next morning, a young woman named Hala Sakakini recalled that

> All day long you could see people carrying their belongings and moving from their houses to safer ones in Qatamon or to another quarter altogether. They reminded us of pictures we used to see of European refugees during the war. People were simply panic-stricken.[493]

On January 7, a final survivor was extracted from the rubble, trapped for thirty-six hours next to the body of her fifteen-year-old son. British officials angrily confronted the Jewish Agency, impressing upon them that the Arabs had never organized an attack against any building containing women and children, in contrast to the Hagana and the other Jewish terror groups. The British knew the hotel and dismissed as "without foundation" the Agency's claim that the hotel was a base for Arab militants. Zionist militias nonetheless pushed on, bombing fourteen more buildings until, as recalled by the Palestinian scholar and eye-witness Sami Hadawi, "5,000 Zionist 'fedayeen' made their last assault and occupied the quarter." All non-Jews were forced to evacuate.[494]

Another "flying bomb" hit on January 7. Using a Jewish Settlement Police armoured vehicle, five Jews threw a parcel bomb packed with rivets as they sped past the Jaffa Gate. Fifteen Palestinians were killed on the spot, and forty Palestinians and British injured, some of whom are presumed to have died from their wounds. According to witnesses, the attackers then turned onto Mamillah Road and threw a second bomb while travelling at high speed. Now pursued by police, the car, "having apparently also caught the blast of the exploding bomb, came to a standstill against the wall of the Moslem cemetery." Inside were thirteen grenades still to be used.[495]

In response to the emerging ethnic cleansing, Alexander Cadogan testified to the United Nations that

> the Jewish story that the Arabs are the attackers and the Jews the attacked is not tenable…[496]

Renewed fears of Zionist terror in Europe further strained Allied resources. On January 6, the Counterintelligence Corps of the US Army warned the British of another Zionist attack on a Medloc train in Austria, to "wreak vengeance" for the imprisonment of a Jewish terrorist. Although additional precautions had already been enacted after the near-catastrophe of August 1947—three or four empty coaches or fully fitted freight wagons now ran attached to the pilot engine on the Vienna sleeper train and a few other at-risk lines—the alert was met with heightened monitoring at both ends of the tunnel.

Barely a month had passed since the Truman Administration shoved through the Partition vote when it was overcome with buyer's remorse. Secretly, it proposed to Britain that the US would announce a change of heart if they, Britain, would cancel its planned evacuation and remain in Palestine as caretaker until after the US presidential election in November. British officials scoffed at the suggestion and US irresponsibility: Full-page Irgun ads in the US were predicting that Britain would not keep its word, Palestine had already fallen into chaos, and the UN could not afford to appear indecisive on this early important mission, as such wavering had fatally weakened the League of Nations.

Two months after the vote, the Administration's conundrum became public: on January 27 the *NY Times*' James Reston reported the "conviction, widely held at the State and Defense Departments, that President Truman's decision to support the partition of Palestine was influenced by the political strength of pro-Zionist organizations in key political centers of this country." Reston's sources predicted that Israel would not stop at its borders, but instead "once the Jewish independent state is established," it would seek US support for its "external policies." Meanwhile, Britain sold the Jewish Agency twenty-one Auster aircraft.[497]

In early February, the Truman Administration tried another tactic to turn back the clock and undo Resolution 181. Secretary of Defense Robert Lovett told the British that the US had "developed doubts" as to the "constitutional validity" of Partition, and "made it pretty plain that [the] United States government were now having second

Feb 1948

thoughts on the whole matter." But his proposal that a Special Assembly be held to reconsider Partition "filled everyone here with horror" because US "vacillations" were discrediting the UN.[498]

At the United Nations, the Jewish Agency distributed a *Memorandum on Acts of Arab Aggression* and beseeched the international community to intervene on its behalf against the alleged aggression. There were, to be sure, no Arab armies in Palestine, and there would not be for another three and a half months, after much of the Palestinian side of Partition was already occupied by the Zionist armies. Small "Arab Guerilla Bands" (as Cunningham called them) that had tried to check Zionist advances had quickly been defeated, and instead "provided them [Zionists] with the excuse that they are merely defending themselves against Arab aggression."

Nonetheless the *Memorandum*, dated February 2, charged that the Arab League was engaged in "a campaign of threats, incitement and propaganda"; that "direct acts of aggression" had been "recently organised and sponsored by the governments of Syria and Lebanon against the Jewish population of Palestine"; and, essentially a repeat of the first, that "threats and preparations for aggression in Palestine" were "being made by all or several governments represented in the Arab League." Using Biblical arithmetic, the memorandum charged that the area allotted to the Zionists (56.5% of Palestine) was a mere one-eighth of what had been "promised" them, seven-eighths forfeited to placate the Arabs.[499]

"De-Arabising" Jerusalem was a priority for Ben-Gurion in order to resist Resolution 181's internationalization of the holy city, and so on February 5 he ordered the Hagana to expel non-Jews from parts of Jerusalem and replace them with Jews. Those Jews who wanted no part of the population transfer were intimidated and, if that failed, forcibly loaded onto trucks and transferred. The work was swift: two days later, he congratulated the Mapai Council on the areas that were now "one hundred percent Jews," claiming that he had effectively returned the city to late Biblical times.[500]

It is at this point, still more than three months before the end of the Mandate, that both the British and the Americans knew with certainty (if they ever believed otherwise) that the Palestinians would not get the state they were promised. British documents acknowledge the deal that the Zionists were striking with Jordan's King Abdullah, and rather than any objection to this abrogation of Resolution 181 and the betrayal of the Palestinians, the US administration was "happy" with it, and the British saw "certain advantages" in it for themselves.

Key to the documents' meaning is that they refer to Abdullah's portion of the spoils not as the Palestinian side of the Partition, but as "the area of Palestine not under the control of the Jewish State." In other words, both the Partition itself, and the promise of a Palestinian state on one side of it, were a charade. Two years later a secret British report reaffirmed this: in early 1948 it had been "assumed that Jordan would absorb the eastern part of Arab Palestine"—no Palestinian state. Meanwhile, new CIA assessments during February and March reaffirmed its earlier warnings: the Zionists will ignore Resolution 181 and try to "set up a Jewish state in all of Palestine and Transjordan."[501]

Since the end of World War II, many Jews resident in Palestine had been trying to leave for their homes in Europe, or for new homes in the United States or Australia, subject to "various forms of pressure" (as the Foreign Office put it) by the Zionists to remain in Palestine. Britain's imminent departure now made the Jewish Agency tighten its "ownership" of Jews, announcing that it controlled "the exit of all Jewish persons between the ages of 17 and 40" regardless of their nationality. It claimed the right to conscript people by virtue of being Jewish, including US citizens; this finally prompted a protest from the United States. Travel and ticket agencies, public places, and venues such as movie theaters, were monitored to catch "deserters." When the Hagana discovered that one Jewish family's eldest son was no longer in Palestine, it confiscated their house. Another Jewish family's son had gone to England; the Hagana took control of their house, forced the family to pay $4,000 (about $40,000 in 2015 dollars), and gave them six weeks to get the son back in Palestine, else an additional $8,000 and other penalties would be imposed.

In late February, about two hundred US citizens tried to board a ship in Haifa to begin their voyage home, but since they were Jews the Hagana invaded the pier and began throwing their passports into the sea until British marines stopped them. The Hagana, meanwhile, set up recruiting centers in cities like Leeds, Manchester, Liverpool, Glasgow, and London. One was secretly established in London's Marks & Spencer.[502]

On February 22, explosions rocked Jerusalem's Ben Yehuda Street in one of the era's most iconic attacks against Jews. The atrocity was accompanied by the distribution of a broadside from "The British League Palestine Branch," with language strikingly reminiscent of London's neo-Nazi *Protestant Vanguard*. British officials privately expressed suspicion that the bomber was a certain renegade Briton known to them.[503]

Lehi bombed the Cairo-Haifa train near Rehovot on February 29, killing twenty-four people (apparently Palestinian civilians) immediately, and injuring sixty-one, six of whom soon succumbed to their wounds. The Salam Building was Lehi's next target: fourteen Palestinians were killed when the militia blew it up on March 3.[504]

> March 1948

Targeting the British, who were eager to be free of Palestine, served no further tactical purpose by late 1947; yet it continued, terror without an apparent object. After the militants bombed the Park Hotel in Vienna on March 19, murdered eight more British personnel in Palestine, and widened their reach to target Britons recovering in hospitals, the Jewish Agency grew concerned that the British "might even ultimately be driven to side with the Arabs in repulsing Jewish attacks." The Agency kept control by deflecting "Jewish resentment" against the British to a so-called "Farran Group" within the British forces, alleged vigilantes led by the hated Major Farran.[505]

In response to the Jewish Agency's February memorandum claiming Arab aggression, the Arab delegation to the UN distributed its own *Black Paper of the Jewish Agency and Zionist Terrorism*. It claimed that the Jewish Agency and the terror gangs worked together, and warned of their "totalitarian" methods.

> The Zionists have purposely and deliberately aggravated the [European Jewish] refugees' problem. They have exploited the miseries of the refugees to win world sympathy for Zionism [and have even formed] kidnapping rings for abducting children and taking them to Palestine.

The memorandum described the methods by which Zionists indoctrinate Jewish youth, methods that "have molded a generation of Jewish fanatics," and how the Zionist terror organizations "rob, terrorize, blackmail and murder Jews."

That much had all been amply documented by the British. However the memorandum went further, charging that the Zionists have "set up laboratories for bacteriological warfare." This, too, was proven correct: Ben-Gurion's laboratory, the so-called "Science Corps of the Hagana," enabled his armies to infect Palestinian villages' wells with typhoid and dysentery in order "to make sure the Arabs couldn't return to make a fresh life for themselves in these villages," as Naeim Giladi, a participant in the biological attacks, would later explain it.

In early May, the Hagana injected typhoid into the aqueduct supplying water to the "Capri" spring that served Acre, causing an epidemic that expedited the ethnic cleansing and expropriation of this city that lay on the Palestinian side of the Partition. Vaccine was in short supply, and by early May the disease had spread to neighboring villages.

A then-secret telegram from Cunningham adds a rather mysterious layer to the question of *why* the typhoid vaccine was in short supply. In it, Cunningham complains of "the dilatory and even obstructive attitude by the Jewish bacteriologist" in obtaining the vaccine to contain the outbreak.

Whether the bacteriologist was a Hagana plant or acting on personal initiative, the biological warfare against Acre "worked so well," former gang member Giladi wrote, "that they sent a Haganah division dressed as Arabs into Gaza" to launch a similar biological attack there. Indeed on May 27, two Hagana operatives—now soldiers of the two-week old Israeli state—were caught putting two cans of bacteria, typhoid and dysentery, into Gaza's wells.[506]

The "Jewish Army," with the Hagana at its core, was according to British intelligence "based on the German organization in the years 1935-36." Described by the CIA as "a ready-made army for a Jewish state in Palestine," at the time of the Partition vote the CIA estimated Hagana membership at 70,000-90,000, with the ability to mobilize 200,000 soldiers and enough modern weapons to arm all of them. Fully 5,000 were permanently mobilized commando troops (the Palmach). The Irgun and Lehi were estimated at 8,000 and 500 members respectively. Both the Hagana and the Irgun had excellent intelligence, the latter having exceptional secrecy because of its cell-based structure. New recruits (including from the US and UK), Jewish DPs from Europe, and about 5,000 soldiers from the Jewish Brigade completed the army.[507]

Yerachmiel Kahanovitch, a machine-gunner in the Hagana's elite Palmach unit, described ethnic cleansing missions conducted in early 1948, months before Arab troops entered Palestine.

> We cleared one [Palestinian] village after another and expelled—expelled them, they fled to the Sea of Galilee ... we shot, we threw a grenade here and there

and fired on them as they fled on boats. With Ben-Gurion's knowledge, Palmach Commander Allon instructed them to use axes rather than bullets when possible "so that they won't hear it" at the British police station. Their orders were to "leave no trace."

> Yes, you march up to a village, you expel it, you gather round to have a bite to eat, and go on to the next village.[508]

Corroborating survivors' accounts, Kahanovitch testified that the Palmach killed anyone hiding in mosques or churches. Anti-tank weapons (PIATs) were used to exterminate those taking refuge inside a cave mosque :

> Let me tell you what it does—you make it like it was a beautiful painting by an artist. You think. He makes a hole about this big and inside everybody's crushed on the walls from the pressure it makes inside.[509]

Anyone attempting to escape was slaughtered. How many people were killed with one blast? "Plenty. [It was now] an empty hall [with] everyone on the walls." After Ben-Gurion gave the order to expel the survivors, it looked like "our [Jewish] refugees walking, from Germany." Palestinian refugees were killed for sport, since watching them on their forced march was boring ... There was a cow there that ran off and this guy tried to chase it and I shot them both.[510]

He spoke of Arabs caught pretending to be Jews in order to stay safe, a twist on the *Marranos* of post-1492 Spain. Some were executed, such as one doctor who "we thought this was a Jew, a Russian who came here, an idealist" who they then discovered not to be Jewish. When another non-Jewish doctor was exposed, they cut off his testicles. The ex-Palmach soldier alluded to further atrocities that he would not cite on the record.[511]

Rape was a systemic weapon in Israel's 1948 ethnic cleansing of Palestine. The Israeli historian Benny Morris documented twelve cases of the rape of Palestinian girls by the IDF in 1948, but warned that these were "just the tip of the iceberg." Even if the girls survived—the soldiers sometimes murdered them, as well as their fathers or brothers—few cases were reported, yet those that reached Ben-Gurion's notice were numerous enough to warrant mention in his diary every few days.[512]

It had been four years since President Roosevelt's plan to provide international safe-haven for European Jews was thwarted by American Zionists (pages 124-125, above). Roosevelt's emissary for the plan, Morris Ernst, had however not given up. He now proposed a new plan to offer Europe's remaining Jewish DPs (a number he put at a quarter million) safe haven in various countries, and met with Bevin on April 9 to discuss it. Ernst told Bevin that both he and Roosevelt had always felt that the cause of the Palestine problem was Zionists' refusal to allow "the settlement of the Jewish problem as a whole." Bevin "reminded him that that was the very argument I had advanced to President Truman, Mr. Byrnes and the United States Administration." Ernst confirmed this. Bevin continued:

April 1948

> I asked him [Ernst] the reason why I could get no response, and he said that it was really the question of the Jewish Agency. In their inner councils they had always held the view that if they allowed any diversion of Jews from Palestine and their settlement elsewhere, their attempts to raise money and to carry on their campaign from Palestine would be seriously affected. That was the truth of the matter.[513]

As Ernst and Bevin spoke in London on April 9, about 3600 km (2237 miles) away, the Irgun, in coordination with the Hagana, wiped out the Palestinian village of Deir Yassin. Deir Yassin was not the first Palestinian village to be depopulated by the Zionist armies, and was certainly not the last; but the terror inflicted on Deir Yassin took on iconic significance because of its high visibility in the Jerusalem environs and the presence of witnesses. The Irgun boasted, surely accurately, that the terror it instilled hastened the evacuation of other Palestinian villages.[514]

As described by British intelligence, Deir Yassin was wiped out

> accompanied by every circumstance of savagery. Women and children were stripped, lined up, photographed and then slaughtered ...

Those taken prisoner suffered "incredible bestialities." An early eyewitness was the head of the International Red Cross Delegation in Palestine, Jacques de Reynier. Arriving in the village, he described the Irgun soldiers :

> All of them were young, some even adolescents, men and women, armed to the teeth: revolvers, machine-guns, hand grenades, and also cutlasses in their hands, most of them still blood-stained. A beautiful young girl, with criminal eyes, showed me hers still dripping with blood; she displayed it like a trophy.

Forcing his way into some of the houses,

> Here the 'cleaning up' had been done with machine-guns, then hand grenades. It had been finished off with knives, anyone could see that ... I heard something like a sigh. I looked everywhere, turned over all the bodies, and eventually found a little foot, still warm. It was a little girl of ten, mutilated by a hand grenade, but still alive ... everywhere it was the same horrible sight ... there had been 400 people in this village; about fifty of them had escaped and were still alive. All the rest had been deliberately massacred in cold blood for, as I observed for myself, this gang [the Irgun] was admirably disciplined and only acted under orders.

As described by a Palmach member, the survivors,

> some twenty-five men ... were loaded into a freight truck and led in a 'victory parade,' like a Roman triumph, through the Mahaneh Yahudah and Zikhron Yosef quarters [of Jerusalem, then] taken to a stone quarry between Giv'at Shaul and Deir Yasin and shot in cold blood.

Israel's official Holocaust memorial, Yad va-Shem, borders the ashes of Deir Yassin.

Three days after the massacre, on April 12, the Hagana formally took the Irgun into its fold. Chief Rabbi Herzog—the same who conducted a massive kidnapping ring of Jewish orphans two years earlier—was credited with brokering the marriage.[515]

The US Administration's fudging about Partition brought pro-Zionist protests and impassioned speeches by political leaders. Reconstruction in Europe still condemned as an obstacle to Zionism, Congressmen were rallied with the cry that they could not be both pro-Marshall (European Recovery Program, or Marshall Plan) and pro-Israel. In mid-April, the US was still prodding the UK to delay its departure from Palestine, but the British replied that it would be they who would die in the ensuing terror as a result of the US having bulldozed through the UN "a plan which represented the extreme demands" of the Zionists.

Bevin, in obvious exasperation, summarised the entire debacle thus:

> If [the Jews] could be brought to see that the principle of one man one vote applied in Palestine to Arabs and Jews alike as much as anywhere else our difficulties might be solved.[516]

But Truman renewed his support for Partition having, according to US sources cited in British documents, "been persuaded that he must do obeisance, until election time, to the fund-raising powers of the Jewish community." In the early 1950s it would be revealed that Truman's "obeisance" extended to interfering in the judicial process when Israeli agents were accused (and convicted) of violating the Neutrality Acts.[517]

The Hagana, over which Ben-Gurion was effectively the Commander in Chief, was producing mortars they called the Davika, containing 60 pounds of explosives that it catapulted about 300 yards, and "barrel-bombs" filled with explosives, shrapnel, glass, and nails, designed to cause maximum casualties, and terror, in Palestinian villages. Another Hagana method was to place explosives around houses at night as people slept, drenching wooden parts in petrol, then igniting it by gunfire from a distance.

Fear—psychological terror—was another potent weapon in the ethnic cleansing of Palestine. "Horror recordings" blared through loudspeakers warning those who remained that they would suffer the fate of Deir Yassin. Rumors of plagues were given credence by the Hagana's poisoning of wells, and a whispering campaign warned that the Zionist armies were preparing to use the atomic bomb on Arab villages.*

On April 21 the Zionist armies began a final, precipitous ethnic cleansing of Haifa. Cunningham reported by telegram that heavy fighting began about midday, with

> Jewish attacks on Arab outposts at Burj Hill and Prophets Steps and telephone exchange successful by night. Khoury House, Headquarters Palestine Railways, on fire and gutted with all records. Jewish forces have captured Salameh Building and positions Station Street - Burj Hill and are now closing in on Khamra Square. Fire in port caused by mortaring has been extinguished. Heavy firing continues with mortaring of Suq [market] area which is reported deserted.[518]

As the Zionist militias literally pushed the Palestinians into the sea, some 3600 km away in London, the US ambassador told Bevin

---

* The Zionist narrative alleges that Arab authorities told the Palestinians, by radio broadcast and/or loudspeaker, to vacate the land, that the Palestinians "obeyed," and thus forfeited any right to return. Such claims are irrelevant. All people have the unqualified right to leave their homes during a conflict (or indeed during peace), no matter who told them what—one need merely apply this claim to any other people or place to expose how ludicrous it is. Further, the allegations themselves are untrue. The historical record shows that Arab leaders beseeched the population *not* to leave. In particular, a report by the then Greek Archbishop in Galilee was used by the Israelis in books and in testimony to the UN to claim that the Palestinians were given evacuation orders (if that mattered). But the Archbishop himself has put on record that his words meant something very different—indeed antithetical—to what he called the "concoctions and falsifications" of the Israeli "propagandists." See, e.g., Erskine B. Childers' "The Wordless Wish: From Citizens to Refugees," in Abu-Lughod, *Transformation*.

that the "Jewish attitude" was "[w]hy should they cease hostilities when they had so many trained men and munitions, and were in a position to win, with their goal [land beyond Partition] in sight?" British landing craft, meanwhile, evacuated the Palestinian survivors to Acre.[519]

The ambassador met with Prime Minister Attlee and his Foreign Minister on April 28, two weeks before the Israeli declaration of statehood. There was no disagreement among them that the aggression was coming from the Zionists ("the Jews"), and that no defensive action had been taken by Palestinians. Yet

> United States policy was to allow no Arab country to help their fellow Arabs anywhere, but for the U.S. to assist the Jews to crush the Arabs within Palestine and to allow the slaughter to go on, and then to ask the British Government to restrain [Jordan's] Abdullah [who had merely dug trenches on his own territory but taken no action].

The Jews had disregarded all the appeals that had been made to them by the United Nations, the US Ambassador was reminded, and now threatened to attack Jerusalem. The US Ambassador nonetheless stood by the Zionist position and warned that "if Great Britain maintained her present attitude [critical of the Zionists], the repercussions might be very serious"—presumably the ever-present threat of pulling the US' post-war loan.[520]

The militias attacked Saint Simeon Monastery and the Katamon area of Jerusalem on the night of April 29-30, and just before 7:00 in the evening on April 30 "two ambulances clearly marked with the Red Cross and proceeding to evacuate wounded from the area [were] heavily fired upon"—a scene to be repeated in modern times in Israel's attacks on Lebanon and Gaza. During the next few days, the British tried, but failed, to counter an Irgun offensive against the population of Jaffa.

"It should be made clear," Cunningham reported,

> that I.Z.L. [Irgun] attack with mortars was indiscriminate and designed to create panic amongst civilian inhabitants. It was not a Military operation.[521]

The British identified the mortars being used by the Jews as their own—"British of Eley make"—a detail they noted to counter any claims that shells fired in Jerusalem from Nebi Samwil (which the Palmach was trying to capture) could be by Arabs because the devices were of British manufacture.

The scene in Jaffa was a repeat of Haifa: Zionist forces surrounded the Palestinians on three sides—the fourth being the sea—and the British, unable to stop them, rescued by landing craft those whom they could. The Irgun hoisted the Star of David over the town and handed control over to the Hagana, and thus the Jewish Agency, which vowed not to "give an inch" on this city that lay on the Palestinian side of Partition. The British, increasingly overwhelmed, considered cutting the Mandate short and evacuating before the announced date of 15 May. A half century later, the Israeli Ministry of Defence published a book that justified the ethnic cleansing of Jaffa by calling it "a festering cancer in the middle of the Jewish population."[522]

When Cunningham saw that the media were reporting the Zionist's brutal ethnic cleansing as "Jewish military successes," he sent an angry telegram to British and US contacts. These "successes," he wrote, are in truth

> operations based on the mortaring of terrified women and children.

The Yishuv was well aware and approving of what was being done on their behalf. There prevailed "among the Jews themselves a spirit of arrogance," as they boasted of their ability to dictate the fate of the Palestinians. "Jewish broadcasts," Cunningham added, probably referring to the Hagana's Kol Israel, "both in content and in manner of delivery, are remarkably like those of Nazi Germany." A week later he wrote that

> The Jews are still jubilant and still busy [with] their campaign of calculated aggression coupled with brutality…[523]

A British intelligence briefing, meanwhile, reported that

> the internal machinery of the Jewish State is now almost completely organised and includes staff for press censorship

and all the equipment of a totalitarian regime, including
a Custodian of Enemy Property to handle Arab lands.[524]

Thus Israel's confiscation of lands by ethnicity ("enemy") was built into the machinery of the new state at its birth. As for the Jewish settlers, the intelligence report paints imagery of a population gone berserk:

> In the Yishuv itself persecution of Christian Jews [converts] and others who offend against national discipline has shown a marked increase and in some cases has reached mediaeval standards.[525]

A series of anti-British and anti-Arab bomb scares disrupted New York and London in the months leading to Israeli statehood. A bomb was discovered in the Arab Office in Chelsea (London) on January 21, and on February 23 a larger device with "Jewish markings" was planted in a building partly occupied by the Colonial Office, fifty yards from Big Ben.[526]

A bomb scare closed London's Victoria Station on the evening of March 7. Ten days later, a New York bound British airliner received a radio message claiming that a bomb had been planted aboard it; among its passengers was the Assistant Secretary to the Foreign Office. As the pilot made an emergency U-turn to London, New York's Empire State Building received its third bomb threat when a woman called from the Gedney exchange (Brooklyn) and said that the building "is going to be blown up." The floors scoured by the police included the British Consulate General. At least five bomb threats were made to Arab offices during May, including the Syrian and Egyptian delegations to the UN, the Consul General of Lebanon, the Iraq Consulate, and the manager of the Arabic language newspaper *Al-Hoda*.[527]

The real bombs struck without warning. On the morning of May 3, Rex Farran, a draughtsman in the West Midlands, received a volume of Shakespeare addressed to "R Farran." He opened it, and a moment later he was dead. The parcel—a gift from Lehi—was presumed to have been intended for his brother, the infamous Roy Farran who had been found not guilty in the disappearance of a teenage Lehi recruit. Years later, Lehi members claimed that the innocent Rex was indeed

May 1948

the target, that the "mistake" was a more torturous way of punishing Roy. Given Lehi's use of the initial "R," and that it could have known that Roy was not then present, this is plausible.[528]

The day that Rex Farran was killed, twelve days before the end of the Mandate, an internal US State Department memorandum stated that

> the Jews will be the actual aggressors against the Arabs. However, the Jews will claim that they are merely defending [themselves]. In the event of such Arab outside aid the Jews will come running to the Security Council with the claim that their state is the object of armed aggression and will use every means to obscure the fact that it is their own armed aggression against the Arabs inside which is the cause of Arab counter-attack.[529]

The CIA issued a new warning regarding domestic security: Zionist operatives were impersonating both US military and American Airlines personnel, and this, along with their clandestine air transport operations and international network of "bought" officials, constituted a threat to the security of the United States.[530]

Since US citizens serving in the Zionist militias were breaking US law as it then stood, some senators were pushing through a bill to make serving in this foreign army legal. More remarkably, in early May the Irgun's American League for a Free Palestine brought together senators from both major parties in an attempt to sponsor a six-point initiative. Its goal was unprecedented: blanket US recognition of Israeli sovereignty over any lands its militias could seize beyond Partition, even before the state existed.[531]

In London on the morning of May 11, Lieut. Gen. Sir Evelyn Barker received a cylinder of the type used for posting magazines, mailed locally. The wife of this former military commander in Palestine, and her maid, were both alert enough to notice an unconvincing W.H. Smith label, and what seemed excessive postage. She began to unwrap the package, revealing a rolled copy of the American magazine *News Review*, but stopped at the smell of an odour resembling disinfectant and the sight of wires and black tape. This was not the first assassination attempt against Barker: Ezer Weizmann, a former RAF pilot and nephew of Chaim Weizmann (and like his uncle a future president of Israel) had already tried to assassinate him by mining the walkway to his house.

A new spate of letter bombs targeted British officials that spring. Among the recipients were Winston Churchill, the Lord Speaker, Ernest Bevin, Philip Noel-Baker, Oliver Stanley, Admiral Lord Fraser, and Anthony Eden. Eden carried his around in his briefcase for a full day thinking it was a Whitehall circular he could open later. A police alert reached him in time.[532]

The newer letter bombs were designed to explode in water in order to defeat the standard method of rendering them inert. Many now contained a packet of the poison sodium cyanide to assure death from an otherwise non-fatal wound. The main explosives sac of the letter bomb sent to Winston Churchill was removed and detonated under controlled conditions; "it badly bent a ¼ [¾?] inch steel plate."* Specialists determined that the detonators in the devices mailed from Italy in 1947-1948 were of US manufacture, among them Dupont, "enormous quantities" of which had been left behind in Italy by the Allied troops. Malfunctions, usually weakened batteries or broken contacts, had kept some from exploding. This rash of anti-British terror continued to be violence for its own sake. With the British evacuation set, Zionist political ambitions had nothing to gain from British targets.[533]

On May 14, 1948, in the final hours of the Mandate, the Palestinians of Haifa who had fled to Acre now faced the Zionist armies again as the Hagana overran this key city that, unlike Haifa, lay on the Palestinian side of Partition.† The Irgun, in concert, captured five more northern villages that were supposed to be in the Palestinian state. Even as the Declaration establishing the state

---

* In TNA, EF 5/12, "Statement of Dr. Watts" says "it badly bent a ¾ inch steel plate," whereas another document ("Letter Bombs," June 16, 1947), cites a ¼ inch plate.

† A public release by Britain had mistakenly reported the figure of 35,000 Arabs in Haifa. In private, officials acknowledged that this was about half the correct number of about 70,000 Arab Christians and Muslims, but debated the risk of correcting it and drawing attention to the error, since "considerable damage may be done in the Middle East if any such obvious error on the part of our Information Service were exploited." See, among others, TNA, CO 537/3860, red "65," "63," letter from M.P. Preston dated May 6, letter from W.B. Osborne dated May 1.

of Israel that night failed to acknowledge any national border (it defined Israel geographically as the Biblical *Eretz-Israel*), the US Administration jumped on board with *de facto* recognition just after midnight, quickly followed by Iran (though it had voted against Partition). Russia jumped the queue to become the first nation to accord Israel *de jure* recognition on May 17.

President Truman's speedy recognition of Israel, Lehi bragged in a radio broadcast of June 3, was not "out of conviction," but because he "needed the Jewish vote"—though demographically, the "Jewish vote" could hardly explain Truman's acquiescence to the Zionists. Morris Ernst, who had earned the wrath of American Zionists for his efforts to open US doors to Jewish immigration, and who described himself as "opposed to any joinder of religion and state, or race and state," was surprised to find himself propositioned "to act in behalf of the Jewish State."[534]

In mid-June, the Foreign Office impressed upon Washington the necessity of establishing permanent borders, else "with the aid of American dollars," Israel would in due course "burst out of its frontiers and attempt to enlarge itself." The summer also brought renewed warnings from the CIA of "increased Israeli intransigence" and the "growing feeling of self-sufficiency and confidence on the part of the Israeli[s] which portends willingness to take matters into their own hands without being bound by the UN." The new state already regarded the United Nations as a nuisance, "deterring Israel from expanding" beyond its boundaries, whereas "the Arab states," the CIA reported, "appear to have been fairly conscientious in cooperating with the mediator and the UN."[535]

The post-Mandate campaign against Britain continued. In early June, now a few weeks after Britain had abdicated rule and effectively evacuated, a newly-invigorated campaign against Britain was launched in the US by the "Sons of Liberty Boycott Committee," which named itself after a group from the American Revolution. Operating out of 106 West 70th Street, it financed full-page ads in New York that denounced Britain's (allegedly ongoing) "invasion of Israel." All good Americans, it said, will join the boycott of Britain, so that when London sees the resulting "red ink," this "nation of merchants and bookkeepers" (the categorization strangely one of Jewish stereotypes) will be made to stop "destroying Israel." The calls for boycott were taken seriously enough to worry the cigarette giant Philip Morris when it realized that some people perceived it as British (which it was until 1919). The company published a full-page ad assuring the public that Philip Morris was American, and reproduced a letter from the "Sons of Liberty" confirming that it was not a target of the boycott.[536]

Britain normally bought about nine million cases of citrus fruit from Palestine each year, half from Palestinian and half from Jewish growers. But so precipitously had the militias stolen Palestinian farmers' land, orchards, and equipment, that nearly all Palestinian citrus production had been commandeered, leading some officials to consider alternative sources rather than purchase stolen goods.[537]

In London, the bomb sent to Evelyn Barker had led authorities to monitor the actions of one Monte Harris, a resident of 14 Gravel Lane in East London who was associated with the Hebrew Legion (Irgun) and ran a grocery shop that he had inherited from his father. Suspicions were reinforced when on August 15 thick blue smoke filled the interior of his flat, forcing Harris to keep his door open to let it clear, and to invent an explanation to a concerned passer-by. Still the police monitored without interfering, until on August 28 they arrested him, preventing "a wave of incendiarism and sabotage in England," including plans to bomb army vehicles. Others with similar ideas were not caught: fires on two troopships that left Southampton about this time were believed to have been caused by parcel bombs set by Zionist extremists within Britain.[538]

British intelligence was also tracking Cyril Ross, Managing Director of the lucrative Oxford Street furrier Swears & Wells, who was thought to have been head of the Jewish Agency's spy network in the UK. The British believed that Israel now had informants "in every [UK] Government department of importance" as well as "contacts in the U.S. Embassy in London, who provided him [Ross] with U.S. secret reports."[539]

The UN named Folke Bernadotte, a Swedish diplomat who had secured the release of 30,000 Jews from German death camps, to

> Aug-Sept 1948

mediate the chaos in Palestine. Although the principled Bernadotte believed an Arab-Jewish union to be the best solution, the US Administration turned against the idea "due to violent American-Zionist opposition in the midst of a presidential election campaign," according to a 1949 report by the National War College that was declassified after the 1967 war.[540]

Bernadotte set about devising a second plan. Regarding the Palestinians who had been ethnically cleansed, he argued that

> It would be an offence against the principles of elemental justice if these innocent victims of the conflict were denied the right to return to their homes while Jewish immigrants flow into Palestine…

Bernadotte made no secret of his intention to recommend the demilitarization of Jerusalem as per Resolution 181, and this in particular led to new threats of terrorism in Europe by both the Irgun and Lehi in early August, and to thinly-veiled Lehi threats against Bernadotte's life:

> We hereby warn the United Nations observers, Bernadotte's generals and all officials and soldiery who may be sent here to demilitarize Jerusalem and set up a non-Jewish administration—it cannot and will not be.[541]

On September 17, the day after Bernadotte finished his plan for Palestinian-Israeli peace, Lehi made good its pledge: Using the name "Fatherland Front," it assassinated both Bernadotte and a UN observer, with the knowledge and tacit blessing of the Israeli military.

While publicly lamenting the Mediator's murder, the Israeli government thwarted any investigation of the crime. This most notorious of Zionist assassinations occurred on a busy road, yet Israel did not cordon off the scene until more than twenty-four hours later, did not examine Bernadotte's car until after it was repaired, and did not question witnesses. Lehi suspects appeared unconcerned about being arrested, then turned their "prison" into a co-ed celebratory party scene, complete with beer and freedom to visit the local café if they so chose.

The assassins' care-free willingness to be rounded up is an

early example of the profound change that Zionist statehood had brought. They knew that their fate would not be that of Lord Moyne's murderers. All were soon freed even as they refused to renounce terror, and it was left to the Swedish government to investigate the crime. As Cyril Marriott, British consul-general remarked, Israeli leaders freed them not just because in truth they welcomed the crime, "but also of their fear for their own skins and of the recognition that they would not have been able to keep them prisoners." Bernadotte's new plan was to have remained secret until being submitted to the General Assembly, but when he was murdered, Ben-Gurion had already secured a copy through an American contact.[542]

Nathan Yellin-Mor, whose previous infamy rested with his overtures to the Nazis and his involvement in Lord Moyne's murder, ascended to the Knesset. Seven years later, assassination architect Yitzhak Shamir joined the Mossad and would eventually be elected Prime Minister of Israel—twice.[543]

Six days after Bernadotte's assassination, September 23, an Arab Airways *Rapide* passenger plane departed Beirut for Amman following its customary path. A bit more than half way through the flight, that path brought it to the eastern (Syrian) shore of Lake Tiberias, whose coastline the *Rapide*'s pilot, S. G. Nowers, followed south. Roughly half-way down the lake, as the plane began to veer slightly east in its path to Amman, it briefly entered Israeli-held territory on which sat the settlement of Ein Gev—a distant outpost founded in 1937 when the Peel Commission presented a partition proposal that placed the area in the Palestinian state. As it did, an Israeli fighter plane attacked the crimson passenger plane.

Nowers dived to 5,000 feet in an effort to escape the attack as he diverted to the nearest Jordanian airspace and tried to make an emergency landing in a field. The Israeli pilot followed the little *Rapide* and attacked twice more, killing three people, including two correspondents, John Nixon of the BBC and David Woodford of the *Daily Telegraph*. Among the three burned survivors was Dr. Ovid Sellers, Director of the American School of Archaeology in Jerusalem. Israel justified its downing of the unarmed passenger plane on the grounds that it had entered its airspace; yet Israel had been making daily armed incursions over Jordan with impunity, and continued to do so into the 1950s. Two years later, Israel forced down another Arab Airways passenger *Rapide* as it flew over the Negev en route to Egypt.

Like the fate of Bernadotte's assassins, the lack of any meaningful response to Israel's deadly downing of an unarmed passenger plane over other people's territory is an early example of the extraordinary power of statehood—had the same incident occurred five months earlier, it would have elicited world outrage as an unprovoked act of international terrorism.[544]

The stories of two Palestinian villages, Deir Yassin and Al-Dawayima (or Dawaymeh), provide a "before" and "after" to illustrate the power of statehood over perception. In the body of world opinion, the extinction of Deir Yassin on April 9, five weeks before statehood, was terrorism, indeed it quickly became iconic of racist savagery. However, the bloodier massacre five and a half months *after* statehood, on October 28 in the village of Al-Dawayima—a village that Israeli intelligence considered "very friendly"—is remembered as a military operation, when it is remembered at all. By that time there had, indeed, been "a number of incidents like Deir Yassin," as Yigael Yadin, IDF head of operations put it; but Zionism now spoke the newspeak of nation-states.[545]

Whereas it was the Irgun—acknowledged to be a terror organization—that ravaged Deir Yassin, it was Israel's 89th Battalion—the military of a sovereign state—that massacred Al-Dawayima. The soldiers approached the village on three sides (Plan Dalet), and "jumped out of the armoured cars and spread through the streets of the village firing promiscuously at anything they saw," as a survivor testified. In the words of one of the soldiers, his Battalion began shooting from the rooftops and

> we saw Arabs running about in the alleyways [below]. We opened fire on them ... From our high position we saw a vast plain stretching eastward ... covered by thousands of fleeing Arabs ... [Our] machine guns began to chatter and the flight [of the refugees] turned into a rout.[546]

Oct 1948

Acting under orders, the soldiers forced many of the people into houses and then blew them up. Of those who escaped, some took refuge in the mosque, others hid in a nearby cave. The next day, the bodies of men, women, and children littered the streets. Sixty people who had taken refuge in the mosque lay dead. Eighty-five men, women, and children who had hidden in the cave had all been butchered. The hundreds murdered included 175 women and children. A soldier who participated in the attack testified that

> The children they [the Israeli soldiers] killed by breaking their heads with sticks. There was not a house without dead ... One soldier boasted that he had raped a woman and then shot her. One woman, with a newborn baby in her arms, was employed to clean the courtyard where the soldiers ate. [Then] they shot her and her baby.[547]

Scores of villages both within Israel and beyond the Partition suffered similar fates. The following day, October 29, the village of Safsaf, in the Galilee region, was the first to be levelled in so-called Operation Hiram. Although Israeli records remain classified, an officer stated that the inhabitants had "raised the white flag" as the IDF attacked with two platoons of armoured cars and a tank company from the 7th Brigade. Fifty-two men were tied and shot dead, several women—including a fourteen-year-old girl—were raped and slain, left lying in a thicket, "among them a woman clutching her dead child." The people of two more villages, Ilabun and Faradia, "greeted the soldiers with white flags," upon which the soldiers "opened fire and after thirty people had been killed they started moving the rest on foot." Again in the village of Salha, the people raised a white flag but "there was a real massacre" of sixty to seventy people.[548]

The United States remained an important destination for Zionist—now Israeli—officials. Massive arms and other military equipment continued to flow illegally from the US to Israel, often by way of bribed Latin American dictatorships. Teddy Kollek was there toward the end of 1948; the British Intelligence Service believed that he was purchasing tanks and radar equipment, and establishing an espionage network. Sneh, former head of the Hagana, went to

Nov-Dec 1948

the United States in October and appealed to the public to stop the Bernadotte plan, claiming it would "rob the Jewish State of the possibility of existence." Most publicly, Begin—who laid blame for Bernadotte's murder with the United Nations for failing to give all of Palestine and Transjordan to the Zionists in 1947, therefore creating Lehi's need to do away with him—went to the US in November to garner support for the takeover of what remained of Palestine.[549]

Begin was received with great pomp in New York, a lavish motorcade escorting him through the garment district of Manhattan to an official welcome at City Hall. Mayor O'Dwyer joked about his being wanted as a terrorist, saying that in New York City the Police Department were singing for him. Begin railed against the assassinated Bernadotte for attempting to limit Israel's expansionism, railed against Albert Einstein for being among twenty-one academics accusing him of "openly preach[ing] the doctrine of the Fascist state," and accused the American Council for Judaism of anti-Semitism for its criticism of him. To cheering New York crowds, Begin openly preached violence to seize yet more territory:

> The fight is not yet over, and not yet has the aim of victory been achieved. We shall continue the fight ... until the whole of [Biblical] Israel is liberated and the whole of our people are back in the country.

At New York's Diplomat Hotel, Begin spread the same message to two hundred youths aged ten to twenty-three years, all members of the militaristic youth group Brith Trumpeldor, standing in uniform at attention. He addressed a crowd in Carnegie Hall to the accompaniment of a small protest outside; his presence was also condemned by such religious leaders as Reverend Henry Sloan Coffin, Father John La Farge, and Rabbi Lazaron. When the issue of Deir Yassin was raised, Begin countered that the villagers themselves were to blame, because when the Irgun invaded, they resisted (an explanation still used by the Israeli state).

As he spoke, the British Consulate-General in Jerusalem was reporting, wryly, that "the Arabs left in Palestine are having a very poor deal ... Arabs left in the Jewish State have been dispossessed of their property, and many of the villages have been wantonly blown up or destroyed after being looted by the Jews." Israel attributed the destruction to "hostilities," but "this explanation is obviously untrue," the Consulate-General wrote. International observers on the scene from the Red Cross and elsewhere "have fully confirmed this wanton destruction by the Jews of Arab property."550

While Begin was still in New York, Ben-Gurion announced as policy what had always been the reality: that Israel would not abide by Resolution 181. Stopping off in Paris, Begin sought support to "finish the struggle for the liberation of all of Palestine," and back in Israel he rallied the public for an "undivided Fatherland." By campaigning for the conquest of the rest of Palestine, Begin quickly won fourteen seats in the Knesset for his new Herut Party in the nation's first elections. He denounced any "alignment with the United Nations" and warned of new terror should Jerusalem remain an international zone.551

A Security Council resolution to halt Egyptian-Israeli hostilities in the Negev was accepted by Egyptian government, but (as recorded in Cabinet papers) "the Jewish authorities, so far from complying with them, retained their new positions and launched a second offensive against the Egyptians on December 22"; and in the north, refused to vacate Lebanese territory. Yet "despite the clear refusal of the Jewish authorities to comply," the Security Council "failed to act as required." Israel's impunity, the British said, was a result of the "reluctance of the United States Government to be associated with any measures which could be regarded as hostile" to Israel, and of the Israeli representative's success in confusing the public by deliberately mixing up two separate UN resolutions.552

The Acting Mediator reported to the Security Council that Israel alone was to blame for the fighting in the south. There had been no acts of provocation on the Egyptian side, and Israel "entirely prevented the United Nations staff from observing the operations in southern Palestine. This was the culmination of the obstructive attitude" by Israel. Reports received on December 29 alleged that Israeli troops had invaded Gaza, but the UN could not confirm them because Israel blocked its observers, and so Britain sent a reconnaissance flight on December 30 which found that Israeli forces were about twenty miles inside Gaza; further reports confirmed this.

The US and the UN were aware of the British reconnaissance flights and concurred with the need for accurate information about Israeli aggression. "Fresh incursion in strength" by Israeli troops was sighted on January 6, and so the next morning Britain sent four Spitfire aircraft to investigate and photograph. Israel responded by shooting down all four of the British aircraft over Egyptian territory. Three pilots survived by parachuting and were assisted by Bedouin, but two of them were then seized by the Israelis. The fourth pilot, according to a Bedouin eye-witness, was machine-gunned while parachuting. Britain sent four more Spitfires, now escorted by fifteen Tempest aircraft, to learn the fate of the others. They ventured as far as Rafah. As they turned back, they, too, were attacked by Israeli aircraft. One of the British Tempests was shot down, killing its pilot. Two of the Israeli Air Force pilots involved in the day's attacks, Chalmers Goodlin and John McElroy, were US and Canadian citizens respectively, fighting in a foreign military and shooting down Allied aircraft.[553]

Not coincidentally, Ben-Gurion had his sights set on the land nearby. He promised to precipitously transform Beersheba, which the UN had allotted to the Palestinians, into "a Hebrew town," and in response to UN demands that Israel withdraw its illegal occupation, he instead promised to seize it through "the largest settlement programme that has ever been carried out in Palestine at one time," and laid out plans "to establish a chain of semi-military settlements in the whole of the conquered [i.e., Palestinian] area".[554]

The prolific *New York Times'* war correspondent, Anne McCormick, tolled the death-knell for a two-state solution in a mid-January 1949 piece. After describing how Israel "overstepped" the Partition and now "claim possession of territory they have conquered," she wrote that there is no Palestine, but rather "there is Israel and an overcrowded remnant of territory that is not and cannot be a state …"

"Israel will break the heart of its friends yet," the *Manchester Guardian* wrote when, on February 10, 1949, the new state declared an unconditional, general amnesty for "forty members of the Stern Gang in custody and many more in hiding." Among them, Count Bernadotte's murderers were freed—even, the paper lamented, as they refused to renounce terrorism. In an internal British memo, Cyril Marriott wrote that the unconditional freeing of its most infamous terrorists "is a cynical admission that the Israeli Government has forgotten the murder of Bernadotte, which in fact I believe they connived at."[555]

An armistice agreement ending hostilities was signed on February 24. It explicitly stated that the cease-fire line agreed to—what became known as the Green Line or, in later political parlance, the "1967 borders"—"is not to be construed in any sense as a political or territorial boundary." It was not a *de facto* legitimization of Israel's illegal conquest beyond the Partition, but temporary lines to end hostilities. Sharett's reaction was typical: now a Knesset member, he quickly disavowed any commitment even to the cease-fire line, saying that Israel's territory will be determined by "possession," not by Partition or any other plan.[556]

Scattered in the heap of Resolution 181's rubble was the credibility of the United States. Palestinians had looked with admiration to the US and its lofty principles, but that respect now lay shattered. When in 1919 the King-Crane Commission sought to understand the desires of the various peoples of the Middle East, the United States was consistently held to be the nation of highest principles.

During the Mandate years, Kermit Roosevelt spoke of the Palestinians' respect for America's ideals, "in the right of people inhabiting a land to determine the future of that land by a free, uncoerced election." One could

> talk to a farmer in a little Arab village in Palestine who has never seen an American, who has never had any contact with American life, and yet he has known over the last years that the people he has most admired in his Arab community, in his larger Arab community, were people who were trained at Americans schools and who told him what the American views on politics, on world order and on the dignity of human beings were.

Their shock at America's betrayal of those principles in Palestine

> is one of the most extreme forms of disillusionment I have seen anywhere in the world. Even without having had any contact with Americans, he still built up this very impressive image of what America stood for, and tears would run down his face as he told you of his extreme disappointment in what he understood American policy to be.[557]

Two and a half years after Israeli statehood, in January 1951, the CIA reported the same American fall from grace in Iraq. Through the end of World War II, "U.S. ideals of democracy, observed both on the American and the world stage, created a confidence in the United States as the one world power which would abide by the principles of right and justice." But its betrayal of those principles made America "the most hypocritical of nations."

Palestine had become an issue larger than itself, the "line in the sand" between centuries of conquest and racial chauvinism, and a more enlightened world that was supposed to have learned the precious lessons of two apocalyptic world wars.

After the first of those wars, the League of Nations planted the roots of the Israeli state while Zionists denied that this was the purpose. Three decades later, after the second of the wars, Resolution 181 acknowledged half the truth: yes, their demand is a ethnically-predicated settler state in Palestine, but some land will be left for the Palestinians themselves, and within the Zionist state, non-Jews will have equal rights. But like the Balfour Declaration, Partition was a strategy, a lie.

"There is no serious difference," British intelligence acknowledged in early 1948, between the positions of the Jewish Agency and the terror gangs regarding Partition:

Partition was a "temporary expedient."[558]

8

Israel *sans frontières*

> The Israeli leaders now state freely, though usually unofficially, their demand for an ever-increasing empire. Their present boundaries are regarded by them as only a beachhead.
> —*CIA report, eleven months after Israel declared statehood, the term "present boundaries" referring not to the borders Israel agreed to with Resolution 181, but to the Armistice Line, which included more than half the land designated for a Palestinian state and which was supposed to be temporary.* [559]

> **Note:** What we know today as the West Bank is called "Jordan" in most source documents after 1948, since it was occupied by that kingdom until 1967. For clarity, however, I refer to it as the West Bank unless quoting from such a source. No clarification is needed for Gaza, then under Egyptian occupation, as the term is ancient.

The year 1948 left in its wake nearly a million Palestinians purged because of their ethnicity and more than four hundred of their villages exterminated, crippling life even for those spared the immediate uprooting. This catastrophe—*nakba*—was for the Zionists "a miraculous simplification of our task," to quote Weizmann. Like Ben-Gurion, he pretended as though the deed had happened of its own accord through some inexplicable intervention of fate. The Israeli press openly applauded the ethnic cleansing of non-Jews, and "natural selection," the Israeli Foreign Ministry predicted, would reduce the refugees to "a human heap, the scum of the earth."[560]

The new state's method was self-perpetuating: its blocking of the refugees' return home, its blanket theft of their property, and its continuing violence against them, all assured the "threat" that it would cite as the justification for further aggression and ethnic cleansing. "No resolution of the United Nations," British officials witnessing the upheaval predicted, will get the Israelis to return the Palestinian land they seized beyond Partition, "or prevent the expansion of the 'beach-head' they have already secured."[561]

MI5, however, suggested that Israel's need for *de jure* recognition would compel it to agree to fixed borders.

> The Americans and the Russians have so far recognised no more than the de facto State of Israel. The de jure State cannot exist until its boundaries are defined...[562]

This made sense—how could any nation formally recognize another without knowing what that nation *is*? Yet today, several decades after most of the world granted Israel *de jure* recognition, Israel is still expanding without national borders, while the Palestinians are called upon to "recognize" this neighbor that occupies and attacks their land, and refuses to state where, or if, it will stop.

A CIA report of March, 1949, presaged the consequences of this sovereignty without borders. Its prophetic title was "A Long-Range Disaster":

> The establishment of the State of Israel by force, with intimidation of Arab governments by the US and the USSR [means that] the Israeli battle-victory is complete, but it has solved nothing. If boundaries to an Israeli state, any boundaries, had been set and guaranteed by the Great Powers, peace might return to the area. On the contrary, we have actually a victorious state which is limited to no frontiers and which is determined that no narrow limit shall be set. The Near East is faced with the almost certain

prospect of a profound and growing disturbance by Israel which may last for decades...[563]

Three months later, the CIA suggested that Israel's poor cooperation with efforts to bring a lasting peace, both at the Lausanne Conference and in talks with Syria and Jordan, was a tactic for continued expansion, and the US State Department as well warned of Israel's wild territorial designs. The British rejected Israel's sincerity for peace, as it continued to violate the Armistice and was "laying claim to everything which they now [illegally] possessed [beyond Partition] and to the Gaza Strip as well."

Reuven Shiloah, the first director of Mossad, told the US that Israel would never relinquish any of the Palestinian land it had seized, and when British authorities in Tel Aviv pressed him on permanent borders, he replied instead that it would always be Israel's right to take more land as necessary. The "ingathering" was not complete, as Mapai argued with a favored messianic word—or in Moshe Dayan's more direct language, "we have not yet determined whether ... our existing borders [Armistice, not Partition] satisfy us..."[564]

For its first eighteen years officially, and longer in practice, Israel enforced martial law based on ethnicity—Jews were exempt. Non-Jews were required to get permits from the military government to leave their village for any reason, paralyzing all aspects of normal daily life—civilian, family, and economic. Farmers or merchants barred from reaching markets because they were not Jewish had no choice but to sell their produce to Jewish merchants for considerably less; and when Palestinian husbands and fathers did get "permission" to leave their village for work, they did so in constant fear of what Israeli soldiers or settlers might do to their families while they were away.[565]

"The Arab community is living in terror," Cyril Marriott reported from Haifa in early 1949.

> [Non-Jewish] workmen are only able to get to work if they produce identity cards at a given office where they have to leave them. A few hours later they are arrested for not having documents of identity. Numbers of young Arabs have recently disappeared ... Arab houses are daily invaded

> by armed Jews and Arab men are increasingly afraid to go to work because of what may happen to their families in their absence...⁵⁶⁶

The "United Nations Assembly," Marriott warned, "should be aware of the barbarous nature of the country now applying for membership."

Yet despite Israel's "barbarous" behavior and its defiance of the international body, on May 11 it was admitted to the United Nations. Israel mollified objections with promises of compliance, but reneged on those assurances twenty-four hours after admission to the world body. It moved government offices to Jerusalem immediately after the UN specifically forbade it (since Jerusalem did not lie in Israel), and continued to racially "purify" the land under its control.⁵⁶⁷

The commonly cited figure of Palestinians ethnically cleansed in 1948, 750,000, is misleadingly low (Eisenhower put it at 900,000), as it includes only those who were pushed over the Armistice Line *and* whose homes and fields lay entirely on the Israeli side of it. That Line is wild and irrational, as it was merely a cease-fire expediency that was supposed to be short-lived, and it lay entirely in Palestinian land—the Israeli side included more than half of the Palestinian side of Partition (one can hardly miss the parallel to today's "separation wall"). Eighty Palestinian villages were orphaned partly in what became the West Bank and partly in a newly-enlarged Israel, separating homes from farming and grazing lands. By 1952, one-quarter of the people in the West Bank who were *not* categorized as refugees were "slowly starving" as a consequence of Israel's intransigence, "and a further substantial proportion are not far above the same level and may soon sink below it," as described in a British report.⁵⁶⁸

The Arab village of Qalqilya, which for generations had lived off its orange groves, is illustrative. The Armistice Line fell between the villagers' homes on the Jordanian-occupied side and their groves on the Israeli-occupied side, and so "the people of Qalqiliya," in the words of Sir John Bagot Glubb, the British soldier, scholar, and author who led the Arab Legion, "are starving in their houses and can see their orange groves only three hundred yards from their houses."

> A great many of these wretched people are killed now picking their own oranges and olives just beyond the line ... If the Jewish patrol sees him he is shot dead on the spot, without any questions.[569]

Nor does the refugee figure record those driven from their homes but still in Israel or on Palestinian land under Israeli control. Israel continued to seize the property of non-Jews, and by April 1949, it had placed 150,000 Jewish settlers in stolen Palestinians' homes—not including the Palestinian homes commandeered by individual settlers under the protection of the state, as continues today in, for example, Hebron and East Jerusalem.[570]

One such "unofficial" post-statehood ethnic cleansing campaign began at six in the morning on April 7, 1949. Groups of about one hundred Israeli soldiers, all armed with Tommy guns, went house-to-house in Arab quarters to commandeer homes of non-Jews as Israeli military police looked on. Non-Jewish families endured "serious Arab baiting" even after being forced from their homes. British witnesses informed the United States, but hesitated to inform the UN Conciliation Commission for fear that "these unfortunate people [be] branded as British stooges" and render their situation even worse. Arab leaders, for the same reason, advised the villagers against any protest. Many Palestinians ethnically cleansed from their homes, but not pushed over the Armistice Line, were used by the state for forced labor and were reduced to sheltering in shacks or caves.[571]

Soon after Israel won membership in the UN, its Air Force began strafing West Bank refugees, killing men, women, and children, as well as their livestock. No Jordanian resistance was possible, as it then had no air force. Seven attacks are recorded in 1950 in which, to quote Glubb, "Israeli fighter aircraft machine-gunned farmers and shepherds (many of them women and children) and herds in the Hebron sector." The spectre of Britain's defence treaty with Jordan made Israeli Air Force (IAF) strafing uncommon after 1950, though the IAF's harassing violations of West Bank airspace remained commonplace.[572]

Palestinian refugee family, 1951.

Fear of ethnic violence by the state continued to dominate the lives of non-Jewish citizens of Israel. Not even the presence of UN observers could protect them from being rounded up by Israeli soldiers and forced into barbed-wire compounds in order to loot their homes ("spoiled of their gold items and of their money by the Jews," to quote one UN witness), before forcing them over the Armistice Line.[573]

One well-documented case is the village of Abu Gosh, whose people had not only tried to make peace with the Zionist settlers during the Mandate, but indeed had provided them with assistance during 1947-1948. Once the Israeli state was established, however, the people of Abu Gosh became victims of mass expulsion and "disappearances." In an "Open letter to the Inhabitants of Israel," dated July 10, 1950, the villagers testified that the IDF had repeatedly

> surrounded our village [and] taken our women and children [and sent them into] the Negev Desert, where they met their deaths ... they rounded up our women, old people, children, the sick, the blind, and pregnant women, using force and blows [and took them] to an unknown destination, and we still do not know what has befallen them.[574] [see also Wadi Araba, pages 291-294, below]

The Israeli justice system was, and remains, an opaque maze of racially angled mirrors designed to offer the illusion of consistency and redress. It is an ever-changing prism of official, administrative, and *de facto* discrimination. The histories of two Christian villages in the far north, Kafr Bir'im and Iqrit, offer a well-documented glimpse at the reality of non-Jewish citizens seeking its protection. During the Mandate, both villages had been known for their friendliness to Jewish settlers and had assisted illegal Jewish immigrants slipping into Palestine through Lebanon. In 1948 the villagers tried to demonstrate their friendliness to the new regime, and greeted its soldiers with fresh bread and salt when they arrived on their sweep across Palestine. When Israel nonetheless forced them from their villages because they were not Jews, they sought redress through the Israeli legal system. The IDF then bombed and levelled both villages. Yet the villagers persevered through the Israeli courts, but were now informed that they could not return home due to a "security" situation. Still they worked within the system, asking the government simply to preserve their title to their land so that when the alleged security issues were resolved, they could return home. Israel, instead, built Jewish-only towns on the ruins of their stolen villages.[575]

For the Zionist narrative to succeed, the hundreds of physically obliterated Palestinian villages had also to be obliterated metaphysically—erased from the map both figuratively and literally. Over their ashes, Israel planted trees or erected new villages, Biblically-suggestive names replacing their Arabic names. For the purpose, in July 1949 Ben-Gurion appointed Israel's first Governmental Names Committee, some of whose members would become important figures in Israel's "narrative"-driven state archaeology.[576]

Jews as well remained victims. Until its ethnic cleansing of 300,000 more Palestinians in 1967, Israel's most precipitous post-1948 ethnic cleansing was of Jews from North Africa and the Middle East. "Jews from Islamic lands did not emigrate willingly to Israel," wrote Naeim Giladi, who had been part of Zionist underground in Iraq. "To force them to leave," he testified, "Jews killed Jews." The most catastrophic purge was Israel's destruction of the ancient Jewish community of Iraq, where until the Zionist purge Jews comprised one third of Baghdad's population.

In mid-October of 1949, the Israeli government issued "gravely disquieting reports of a new wave of persecution against the Jewish minority in Iraq." The World Zionist Organization warned of coming pogroms, and soon the worst was confirmed—or so it appeared. The "pogroms" began by April 8, 1950, with a hand grenade thrown from a passing car into a popular café, Dar El-Beyda, accompanied by leaflets warning Jews to flee Iraq.

Chief rabbi Sassoon Khedduri argued that Jews had lived in peace in Iraq and visited the US Embassy hoping to quell the panic. But such was the alleged emergency that Israel proposed rescuing the entire Iraqi Jewish community by airlift to the new state. The United Jewish Appeal called for "every understanding person in the United States" to donate to the effort, stressing that they were "in a race against time" to rescue Jews who had not yet reached the safety of Israel. The race seemed real: a series of bombings over fourteen months hit Baghdad's American Cultural Center and US Information Service Library, a Jewish-owned automobile company, and Jewish homes. The worst single attack was the bombing of Masouda Shem-Tov Synagogue on January 14, 1951, among whose victims was a twelve year old boy, electrocuted when a grenade felled a high voltage line.[577]

Believing the anti-Jewish violence to be the tragic confirmation of the warnings, Iraqis began forfeiting their ancient homeland by the tens of thousands to become settlers in the Israeli state. Zionism's obligatory Biblical association was not missed: they were the flight of 42,360 Jews from Iraq to Jerusalem two and a half millennia ago, when the Persian King Cyrus freed the Jews who had been exiled by Nebuchadnezzar. The airlift operation was called "Ali Baba," the character who learns the secret phrase "Open Sesame" in the *1001 Nights*, now alluding to the opening of the door to Israel.⁵⁷⁸

The airlift materialized quickly. In May, 1950, the contract for it went to a company called Near East Air Transport (NEAT), and on May 20 the first plane load of Iraqi Jews reached Israel. The small airline's two aircraft, however, were wholly inadequate to keep up with the exodus of people who were now stranded in Iraq after giving up their homes and citizenship—yet Israel insisted that no other airline take part in the allegedly urgent mass human migration. In response to criticism, Israel used a phrase that the Jewish Agency would have railed against a few years earlier: it replied that there was a "regulated plan of absorption" of new immigrants, and this "regulated plan" happened to be "the capacity of the two aircraft provided by Near East Air Transport." By September, the backlog of Jews who were stranded after fleeing "Muslim violence" had created such a humanitarian emergency in Iraq that, in the words of a British witness,

> I can only add that thousands of them literally face starvation, having sold all their belongings and expended the last penny of it, in the expectation of an early departure. [NEAT has] proved utterly inadequate to cope with the situation.⁵⁷⁹

Even after "the onset of winter [further worsened] the sufferings of those Jews," Israel not only continued to forbid any assistance, but indeed threatened that it would impound any aircraft that tried—as it had already done to two aircraft of Britain's Eagle Aviation Limited when they landed in Lydda bringing Jews from Tehran.

Why was Israel claiming an urgent life-or-death crisis to save Iraqi Jews from massacre at the hands of their countrymen, yet threatening other countries not to help save them? Even as the "emergency" now left tens of thousands of them homeless, cold, and starving? As long as Israel blocked any airline but NEAT, money was not part of the equation: no amount of donations raised for this "race against time" could help NEAT ferry the new refugees any faster.

Some premonition of what was going on in Iraq might have been seen in a series of bombings in the West Bank villages of Nablus and East Jerusalem in September (1950), which at first baffled the Jordanians, who suspected communists or fighters loyal to the ex-Mufti, but proved to be a covert Israeli sabotage and espionage operation. And so the "anti-Jewish violence" in Iraq was soon exposed as an Israeli "false flag" operation that imported human facts-on-the-ground while furthering the narrative of a world inhospitable for Jews. NEAT was an Israeli outfit, founded jointly by El Al and the owner of Alaskan Airlines, its name designed to obscure identification.[580]

In the summer of 1950 an Israeli from Acre was recognized in Baghdad by a Palestinian refugee. His arrest led to others and, by June of 1951, to the unravelling of the Iraqi operation. The police were led to a vast cache of arms, maps, and Zionist materials, including 426 hand grenades, 33 Tommy-guns, 186 pistols, 24,764 bullets, 97 machine gun magazines, and 32 daggers, all spread out among three Baghdad synagogues and two houses. Further arrests led to the trials of two accused bombers of what the police called the Shoura and Tnua terror organizations. In confiscated documents, one of the defendants had written that the café grenade that started the panic "had very good effect," and congratulated his colleagues on successfully defeating those Jews who had tried to counter the hysteria. The Zionist terror cell, training for which began at age thirteen, was held responsible for Iraq's "anti-Jewish" bombings.

In response, the World Jewish Congress claimed the scandal was part of an anti-Jewish conspiracy, and blamed the Muslim Brotherhood. But the Iraqi police were in contact with the US Embassy, a CIA official was present, and the British carefully monitored the proceedings, as well as the evidence, protocol, and even the quality of the special court's president. British witness P.A. Rhodes reported that the trial was conducted fairly, that there was no evidence to support Israeli claims that the defendants were tortured or that there was any "irregular procedure" by the court. Nothing, he wrote, suggested that the two principal suspects "were anything but guilty of the charges preferred against them." The explosive devices used in the bombings matched those discovered in the underground caches, and the leaflets warning Jews to flee were written with a typewriter found with the suspects. Among the documents was a letter from Yigal Allon, who would become chief of staff of the IDF and Israeli Foreign Minister, expressing satisfaction that he had been able to transfer arms into Iraq.[581]

The two principal conspirators were sentenced to death. Fifteen of twenty-one accomplices were given sentences as long as life imprisonment, and as short as (in the case of three girls) five months, including time already spent in detention. Six defendants were found not guilty.

In Israel, crowded, dismal refugee camps greeted the approximately one hundred twenty thousand ex-Iraqi Jews ethnically cleansed by Israel, their situation made all the worse when hundreds of their tents were destroyed by a particularly strong mid-December gale. For the sake of the settler state, Zionism had within two years destroyed a vibrant Jewish community dating back two and a half millennia.[582]

When the "false flag" Lavon affair broke a few years later (pages 314-316, below), the Israeli Defense Minister commented that the method had first been tried in Iraq. Teddy Kollek, who was close to then-PM Ben-Gurion, defended the ethnic cleansing of Iraqi Jews by arguing that it was "better for a country to be homogeneous."

The US was not amused. "It was one thing," State Dept official George McGhee remarked, "to take Jews from all over the world who were in distress, but it was another matter entirely to attempt to create circumstances which would stimulate immigration of Jews from areas where they were living in peace." Thus when Israel next set its sight on the Jews of Iran, State Dept. official G. Lewis Jones warned Israel that the US State Department "would not favor a deliberately generated exodus there along the lines of the ingathering from Iraq." Israel refuses to release documents relating to the operation.[583]

Israel also turned to North Africa's Jewish communities to quench its need for ethnically-correct settlers. As described by Hagana member Hanna Braun, sent to Eliat in 1952 to process arriving Arab Jews and teach them Hebrew, the North African immigrants had not abandoned their homes because of persecution, but as a result of Israeli coercion. Since these were not European Jews, they "were sprayed with DDT at the port of entry and then crammed into extremely primitive reception camps," shipped to the army for three years, then settled in the frontier regions to take the brunt of any attack across the Armistice Line.[584]

Although Israel's leaders needed North African and Middle Eastern ("Mizrahi") Jews as human place-holders to secure land, they looked down upon these darker-skinned Jews as a lower caste, an embarrassment. The state minimised the "problem" through a mass kidnapping of thousands of Mizrahi newborns, giving the babies to fair-skinned European ("Ashkenazi") couples and telling the infants' parents that the child had died. This practice—which fits the UN definition of genocide—persisted at least through Israel's first decade.

Israel refuses to open state records about its kidnappings, and in the 1950s the parents, however confused by the events surrounding their newborn's "death," could prove nothing. But bitter resentment against their uprooting and treatment led Mizrahi Jews to form a resistance group named the "Black Panthers." *What did you do, Ben-Gurion?* victims of Israel's anti-Jewish purges railed in song. *Would that we had come riding on a donkey and we hadn't arrived here yet! Woe, what a black hour it was! To hell with the plane that brought us here!*

The final, cynical irony of Israel's uprooting of Middle Eastern and North African Jews from their homelands is that the state now uses it as a racial "settling of scores" for its own ethnic cleansing of Palestinians. The former balanced out the latter—the same injustice having been committed against both "races," the logic goes, the Palestinians have no grievance.[585]

Those uprooted Palestinians had been reassured by the international community of their unqualified right to return home. The moral necessity of this was obvious, and on 11 December, 1948, the UN Security Council passed binding Resolution 194 to reaffirm it. Yet in its early years Israel killed roughly five thousand Palestinians for the attempt. Others were killed in Israel's raids into the West Bank and Gaza Strip.[586]

Alec Kirkbride, British ambassador to Amman, visited the northern West Bank village of Nablus in the summer of 1950 and described the situation there as "gloomy indeed." Its most cultivable land had been taken by Israel, and commodities now had to be imported through

Beirut at great expense. Malaria was increasing, and the refugees were crowded into unfit tents that offered little protection against the winter. Nonetheless, there was calm and order in the West Bank, or as Glubb described it, "the appearance of normality."

> Crime statistics are lower than in the days of the Mandate—apparently in contrast to Israel which seems to be suffering from a crime wave. The low incidence of crime in Arab Palestine is especially remarkable in view of the great fall in the standard of living since Mandate days and the presence of tens of thousands of homeless refugees.[587]

Gaza was more horrific still. As described by a Quaker aid worker, the people of the Gaza Strip

> who owned fields [that are now] in no-man's land ... have, from sheer desperation, plowed ... as close to the Jewish lines as it was possible to go ... In doing so, they braved the very determined efforts of the Jews [who have] shot and killed various men, women, cows, sheep, camels, donkeys, and so forth.[588]

Another Quaker witness described the "wretched cave, tent or hovel" that the displaced "have called home" since their expulsion. The IDF itself was blunt: it had "condemned to complete extinction" those it had made refugees in Gaza, and the Red Cross reported that about ten children were dying every day from hunger and cold. Desperate, some refugees risked a nocturnal crossing to Hebron (West Bank), passing charred animal carcasses that were a constant reminder that they might get blown up by land mines even before risking the IDF. Those who survived were greeted in Hebron by a somewhat less horrific situation and a typhus epidemic. In one incident of May, 1950, recorded without further explanation, "two Egyptian aircraft arrived unannounced at Kolundia [Kalandia, West Bank] and dumped two loads of destitute [Gazan] refugees on the runway." In the north, more stories of desperation: non-Jews ethnically cleansed by Israel into southern Lebanon "had to brave IDF fire when they crossed the lines to forage for food" in what had been their homeland—these the words of an Israeli settler.[589]

A few months after Israel's establishment, the value of property it had stolen from the Palestinians was put at about £P50 million, and Israel's theft of their financial assets was estimated at between £P4 million and £P5 million. When the UN ordered Israel to return the money to its owners, Israel replied that it would agree to do so if any Arab states blocking "Arab" [Palestinian] assets would also return them, "on a basis of equal and reciprocal compensation." Arab negotiators were happy to agree to this—but Israel then claimed that its wording obliged them to return only the *same amount* as what Arab nations had blocked. Only one Arab state had any such account, and the amount was small. The project was dropped.[590]

Economic analysis, indeed, demonstrates that the Israeli state owes its very existence to its wholesale theft of the Palestinians' worldly possessions—land, homes, assets, money, orchards, quarries, 10,000 acres of vineyards, 25,000 acres of citrus groves, 10,000 business establishments, olive groves, and machinery. Despite the massive infusion of foreign capital into Israel and its claims of modern efficiency, it was in the end the Palestinians that saved the Israeli state from stillbirth; and today Israel reaps vast financial benefits through the theft of Palestinian natural resources, and micro-control of the Palestinian economy, taxes, tourism, imports, and exports.[591]

Although the terror gangs of the Mandate era ceased to exist as such, some Lehi veterans formed a new terror group, the Kingdom of Israel (or Tzrifin Underground), supplementing their ranks with sixteen-to-eighteen year olds who were raised with the gang's heroic myths. The Kingdom's repertoire included the bombing of the Czech Consulate (December 5, 1952) and Soviet Legation (February 9, 1953), two attempts on the life of Konrad Adenauer (March 28 and June 24, 1952), and an attack on the violinist Jascha Heifetz for programming Richard Strauss' violin sonata (April 16, 1953). Kingdom of Israel operatives were caught and imprisoned for this new campaign of terror, but only briefly: repeating history, Israel commuted their sentences.

The name *Irgun* did pop up now and then, for example in England on the morning of July 25, 1952, when Harold MacMichael, targeted by a letter bomb five years earlier, received a new threat to his life, "day or night, walking or sleeping," which was signed "I.Z.L." But although a British report that year described the Irgun as "still very much a force," there is little evidence of it beyond a brand franchise, an identity to affix to individual initiatives of extra-state terror.[592]

Aside from some Kingdom of Israel vigilantism along the West Bank Armistice Line, these vestiges of Mandate-era terror militias were short-lived and uninvolved with the new state's expansionism. That expansionism was the charge of the Israeli military, whose recruits were taken on training patrols into Palestinian territory in order to "overcome their conscience," as the marginalized peace group Agudat Ihud put it, and get accustomed to arbitrary killing. When parents who heard of the "training" their children were getting asked Agudat Ihud to bring their complaints to the government anonymously, Ben-Gurion, whose diary proves that he himself ordered such missions, dismissed the accusations as "imaginary and without foundation."[593]

Israel's expulsions of non-Jews continued "at the whim of the Israeli police or District Administration," as Ambassador Kirkbride put it, and by making life so miserable that it is "impossible for any Arab to contemplate spending a lifetime under Israeli rule." But if stories of abuse "reduced the earlier determination of the refugees to go home," it did not stop them. Many tried, despite risking beatings, torture, rape, and murder. In mid-1949, an IDF intelligence officer spoke of the "hundreds" of Palestinians attempting to return home to the villages of Western Galilee (which was supposed to be part of Palestine, not Israel) that were rounded up and "liquidated by military order"—tied to a tree and shot in the head being one documented method. In his study of declassified Zionist archives, Benny Morris determined that

> Israeli troops more or less routinely beat captured infiltrators [people attempting to return home], sometimes torturing them, and occasionally raped and/or murdered them.[594]

This continued with impunity because of "the pervasive attitude among the Israeli public that Arab life was cheap," and that the killing, torturing, beating, and raping of Arab infiltrators was, if not permitted, at least not particularly reprehensible...[595]

Statehood did not end the rape of Palestinian girls and women by Israeli soldiers: in 1950, Ben-Gurion still referred to an IDF battalion that "is prone to" raping and murdering Arab girls.[596]

On August 22, 1949, Israeli soldiers kidnapped a Bedouin girl just after machine-gunning dead a man for sport as he fled, unarmed, up a sand dune in fear, and killing six of the Bedouins' camels. They took the girl, whose age was estimated to be as young as ten but was probably about fifteen, to the IDF camp and began by a public humiliation, stripping her naked and making her stand under a water pipe as the men rubbed her body with soap. Three soldiers then raped her. After the Sabbath meal, the platoon commander got involved: he ordered soldiers to cut her hair and wash what was left in kerosene, and for her again to be displayed naked under the shower pipe. The girl was then gang-raped over a period of three days, at times leaving her unconscious. Pecking order was decided by the commander: Squad A raped her on day one, Squad B on day two, Squad C on day three.

When they finished, they dug her grave right in front of her eyes before shooting her.[597]

In 2003 this atrocity surfaced in the Israeli and British press, reported as though it were a dark secret newly unearthed, a regrettable aberration of the fledgling state, terrible but singular. The state was insulated at the expense of the late war's Jewish survivors: these were IDF soldiers, yes, but they were World War II DPs, and thus they were something apart, of "low professional and moral level," as it was reported. Yet Ben-Gurion's elite Palmach was notorious for mass murder and rape, and "cultured officers" were specifically cited by soldiers as eager participants in such grisly crimes. Thus the settler state's final violence against the girl was the exploitation of her memory for the state's ritual absolution, spinning her murder as an original sin by a wayward relative, the sin now buried in the Negev along with its nameless victim.[598]

Three Palestinian children, two girls and a boy, were abducted from the Gaza Strip by Israeli soldiers on March 16, 1950. The soldiers gang-raped both girls, then murdered all three children. When the villagers responded to the atrocity with an ambush on an IDF car, Israel "defended" itself: it mortared the village. A twenty-six year old Palestinian woman captured by an Israeli patrol near the Armistice line five months later, on August 15, was accused of picking fruit on the Israeli side of the Line (though it was her family's grove). She was taken to a police station and raped by four Israeli constables. When both the Red Cross and UNRWA confirmed the charge, Israel accused the ICRC of disseminating "anti-Israel propaganda" and called for the removal of the Red Cross representative.[599]

Another organization with which Israel was frequently at odds was the Mixed Armistice Commission (MAC), created by the United Nations to supervise the truce that ended the 1948 war. Composed of separate organizations for each of Israel's four *de facto* borders—Lebanon, Syria, Jordan, and Egypt—each of the five countries had a representative, and UN observers monitored the borders and investigated complaints. Records demonstrate that complaints were given a fair hearing and investigators were thorough, though the MAC had no power of enforcement. One of the early issues the MAC investigated became known as the Wadi Araba incident.

In the first days of June, 1950, eighty-seven half-dead naked men and boys as young as seven began turning up on the western frontier of southern Jordan, the Wadi Araba desert region to the south of the Dead Sea. They were the survivors of about one hundred twenty "infiltrators" seized by Israel in various parts of the land under its control and marched into this desert to their likely deaths. Approximately thirty-four of the victims perished, among them at least two girls, one who did not survive the desert and another who the IDF shot dead when she attempted to escape the death march.[600]

Israel had conducted such forced marches during its 1948 ethnic cleansing, in which children and the elderly in particular perished along the way. The Wadi Araba expulsion was exceptional, however, in that many of the victims survived when found by Bedouin and Arab Legion patrols, and their stories were documented and corroborated. Two years into Israeli statehood, these accounts offer an unparalleled examination of Palestinian "infiltrators," who they were, their motivations, how Israel dealt with them, and how Israeli media reported it. Since they were arrested over a wide area and over a period of several months, we can assume that they are a representative sampling of these unfortunate people. Three chroniclers interviewed the survivors: a representative from the International Red Cross, a Belgian observer from the MAC, and a correspondent from *The Observer* (UK). Fifty-one survivors are accounted for in forty-nine interviews. Their stories closely corroborated.[601]

In late May, the prisoners were collected into a camp at Katra (near Rehovot)—"a concentration camp ... run on Nazi lines," as Ambassador Kirkbride described the facility. All were suffering from extreme malnutrition; many had been tortured. Early on the morning of Wednesday, May 31, they were blindfolded and loaded onto two trucks, with no water or other supplies, and driven south with the escort of Israeli soldiers fore and aft. Later in the day, they reached a military camp which they surmised was near Beersheba. An Israeli woman from a southern kibbutz was a chance witness to their arrival.[602]

> Two large trucks arrived, packed with blindfolded Arabs (men, women, children) ... The way the Arabs were crowded together [on the trucks] was inhuman ... Those of us standing nearby had witnessed no bad behaviour on the part of the Arabs, who sat frightened, almost one on top of the other. [Then one or more of the soldiers] jumped up and began to ... hit [the Arabs] across their blindfolded eyes and when he had finished, he stamped on all of them and then, in the end, laughed uproariously and with satisfaction at his heroism...

"I ask," the woman from the kibbutz finished, "does this not remind us exactly of the Nazi acts towards the Jews?" Having already endured the long drive in the heat, the prisoners asked for water. The Israeli soldiers brought water and—the Palestinians' blindfolds now removed so that they could see—"poured it away on the ground in front of the Arabs." None of the roughly sixty people in each of the two trucks were allowed to descend, not even "to relieve nature."

Blindfolded again, they were trucked several more hours. About midnight, blindfolds removed, they found themselves at "completely uninhabited desert." The soldiers ordered them to walk into it. As summarized from the interviews,

> The general direction indicated to them seemed to be south-east. They were told that anyone who ran north would be shot. This procedure was then applied, the men being taken forward in groups of four. As each party ran off into the darkness, bursts of fire were opened on them by the Jews.[603]

The interviewers described the spot as "one of the hottest, wildest and most utterly desolate areas in the world," and "is infested by snakes, wolves and hyenas, so that the missing persons may well have been eaten by wild animals." The post nearest to where they were released was Dhahal, about ten miles away, but none of them found it in under 36 hours since it lay east-north-east. "Others walked 25 to 28 miles and climbed a range of mountains 3000 feet high, before arriving at inhabited country in the vicinity of Shobek."[604]

All were weak from hunger and extreme thirst. Many were suffering from torture, including beatings, whipping, teeth smashed off by rifle butts, hearing loss from beatings on the ears, and fingernails torn out. Some adults who collapsed along the way had to be abandoned by those still conscious in order to save the children among them.

Yet the Wadi Araba incident might have slipped by little noticed had the journalist Philip Toynbee not been passing through Amman and heard of the survivors. The *Observer* published his shocking account in which Toynbee, who had been a supporter of Zionism, now compared the Israeli regime to Nazi Germany.[605]

Who were these "infiltrators?" All but four of the survivors interviewed (these representing 42.5% of those pushed into the desert) had been ethnically cleansed by Israel and were attempting either to reach the West Bank from Gaza, or to reach their homes in an attempt to rejoin their families or retrieve property (hidden cash or grain). Starvation resulting from Israel's ethnic cleansing was the common driving force, fathers or sons hoping to save their starving families. For two of the remaining four, the desert march was itself their ethnic cleansing; they had escaped the 1948 purge. The last two were chance outsiders, a man from Sudan making a pilgrimage to Hebron, and a student at Al-Azhar University in Cairo en route to his home in Tira to get money to complete his studies.

Survivors of the Wadi Araba desert crossing, June 2 or 3, 1950. MS note on photo reads "Group just found being given water by Arab Legion patrol."

After Toynbee's exposé, the Jerusalem Post repeated the government denial. These "infiltrators" posed a grave threat to Israel, yet they had been well treated. Still with three hours before sunset, they had been released to an Arab Legion post directly in front of them. As Israel denied everything publicly, it placated US unease by claiming that an investigation was in progress—and indeed, an internal Israeli memo advised the government simply to "promise an inquiry in order to settle things down."[606]

In the meantime, the systematic expulsion of non-Jews continued: 5,548 people were known to have been pushed over the Line in the half year ending January, 1951, or one every forty-seven minutes. Atrocities were white-washed by the government to the extent of forging victims' statements, and "the brutality," Glubb noted, "is too general to be due only to the sadism of ordinary soldiers". For example, when on the night of October 20, 1950, IDF soldiers seized and tortured seven Palestinians in the (predominantly Christian) town of Jish in upper Galilee, some suffering severe injuries, they did so under the leadership of the local military governor.[607]

On November 2, an Israeli patrol of twelve soldiers penetrated about 400 meters (0.25 mile) into the West Bank and discovered three children from Yalo village collecting wood. One, an eight-year old girl, ran away at the sight of the patrol, escaping with a bullet in her thigh. The soldiers dragged away the other two children, a brother and sister aged twelve and ten, just as their father and uncle rushed to the scene. As described by Glubb, the children were forced into a ditch "and there butchered by one soldier with a sten-gun, while the rest of the patrol looked on. All this was plainly visible to their parents, standing helpless on the border only a few hundred yards away."[608]

The boy was dead, with two bullets in his head and one in his shoulder. The girl—ten-year old Fakhriyeh Muhammad Ali Alayyan—had been shot seven times, but was still breathing. Once the soldiers moved on, her father carried her away, while the uncle carried the boy's body. Fakhriyeh lived several hours, long enough to make a statement to the authorities.

Like Wadi Araba, this atrocity was unusual in that it was witnessed, documented, *and* hit the British press, saddling Israel with another public relations problem. Questions were raised in the House of Commons, and the British Zionist establishment's denials convinced few. Both the MAC and UN observers confirmed the incident as do, we know these decades later, internal Israeli records. As for the children's village, in 1967 Israel ethnically cleansed and levelled Yalo, and today Israel's Canada Park is built on its ruins and those of neighbouring Deir Ayyub and Beit Nuba.[609]

Yalo was targeted again less than three months later, on January 29, 1951. About sixteen Israeli soldiers descended on the village, approaching simultaneously from two directions while attacking with gunfire and grenades. The Tulkarm area was invaded by Israeli soldiers on the night on February 2, and the following day the IDF killed three Palestinians in an attack on Saffa.

The attacks grew bolder. On the night of February 7, the soldiers invaded Sharafat, near Jerusalem, and blew up two houses, killing thirteen and wounding five. Twelve of those killed were women and children, and more than half were under fifteen. Beit Nuba and Emmaus—like Yalo, depopulated, razed, and confiscated by Israel sixteen years later—were next. "In the small hours of the morning of February 9," an Israeli patrol slipped about two kilometres inside Jordanian territory and attacked with Bren and Sten gun fire. They lobbed a grenade into a house, killing a man, his son, and his daughter. The targets were apparently random, and no explanation was offered.[610]

At the MAC meeting later that day, the Israeli representative insisted that the Sharafat massacre be put at the bottom of the list of outstanding matters and walked out when this was not agreed to. The UN Information Officer confirmed that the attack was carried out by the Israeli army with Israeli army equipment, but that "in view of the Israeli delegation's attitude there was no likelihood of M.A.C. being able to do anything in the matter."[611]

The bombing followed "a period of mounting attacks against Arab villages," as the *Manchester Guardian* reported. The paper, which had for years been staunchly pro-Zionist, now suggested that Israel was engaged in a "deliberate terroristic policy" against the Palestinians, whereas *Haaretz* defended the attacks even as it acknowledged that the victims were innocent. Most tellingly, the "liberal" Israeli paper claimed that events perhaps justified "the ultimate acquisition by Israel of Arab Palestine"—that is, that Israel should annex the West Bank (which included East Jerusalem) and Gaza.[612]

A week after Sharafat, Jordanian officials, hoping to establish frontier cooperation, met in Jerusalem with Israel's General Mordechai Maklef, a veteran of notorious Operation Hiram and soon to become Israeli Chief of Staff. When Maklef blamed the troubles on "infiltrators," the Jordanian representatives asked for more information. In response, the General "waved his arm in a noble gesture and said he was prepared to forgive us." Similarly, when at a MAC meeting the Israeli representative was asked why they made their allegations difficult for the MAC to investigate, he answered that since the Arabs knew what they did, why should Israel have to give any details?[613]

The investigative journalist Colin Reid published an analysis of Israel's interaction with the MAC in January (1951). His conclusions mirrored those of British government documents which he could not have seen. "As a matter of policy," he found, "details were not published or reported to the authorities. Only the charge was reported, and often too late to follow up." Israel constantly varied its claims, no two statements coinciding, with even the place names changing, so that a single claim appeared to be many claims. The allegations were filed as much as five months after the alleged incidents, and accompanied by artificial complaints of Palestinian aggression so as to "considerably obscure the issue" to the press. Allegations never bore any date of origin or filing, rarely indicated the date of the act complained of, and were submitted in batches. In concert with these methods, Israel subjected Palestinian charges to "skillfully constructed procedural obstruction."[614]

On April 2, 1951, an Israeli patrol attacked four unarmed Palestinians collecting brushwood near Hebron; two escaped, but the bodies of the other two, aged eighteen and sixty-two, were later recovered by the MAC and IRC investigators. The IDF had cut off their sexual organs, skinned their buttocks, stabbed their sides with bayonets, and fired Sten gun rounds into their skulls.[615]

Ben-Gurion, in New York in May (1951), reiterated Israel's refusal to address the Palestinian land it had stolen beyond the Partition, and stated that it would take all the demilitarized zones as well. It was illegally draining Lake Hula in the north and continued to do so in defiance of the UN and threat of US sanctions, both of which had proven impotent. For a moment, it appeared that Israel had finally gone too far when it pirated aircraft parts from a US vessel, prompting the State Department to withhold arms exports. But this was quickly reversed: the US Congress instead prepared an unconditional grant of $150m to Israel, leading US Secretary of Labor Maurice Tobin, then in Israel, to propose that the grant at least be contingent on Israel abiding by UN Resolutions. This, too, failed.[616]

Idna, the target of several earlier attacks, was invaded again on May 23. On July 11, six to eight Israeli soldiers threw grenades into a house in Khirbet Najjar, located two kilometres (1.24 miles) inside the West Bank, killing an eight-year-old girl and wounding her brother and mother. An Israeli patrol penetrated to the southeastern end of the Dead Sea on September 25 and blew up a house in Ghor Safi village, killing a twelve-year-old girl and her mother as they slept inside, and wounding a boy and two women.[617]

A tragedy unfolded at the end of 1951 which, like the Wadi Araba incident, offers a glimpse inside the Israeli state's need for a perceived external threat, terror in the service of expansionism, and manipulation of news and information. It began with the rape and murder of a young Israeli woman from the town of Malha.

On December 4, eighteen-year-old Lea Festinger disappeared. Twenty-two days later, her body was discovered in a cave. There were no tracks, as rains had flooded the area, no evidence, and no suspects. "Arab infiltrators" were, however, automatically blamed. Similarly, when on the night of December 30 a woman in Jerusalem was murdered, the "notoriously overworked and understaffed" Israeli police blamed "Arab infiltrators" because someone claimed to have seen "men in torn khaki clothes" in the area.

Yet Israel's domestic violent crime was so rampant that when Lea Festinger's body was discovered, even the *Jerusalem Post* warned against using "infiltrators" as scapegoats.

Murder, rape and robbery in Israel have taken on alarming proportions. By no means all the incidents can be blamed on infiltrators or remnants of war psychosis among either immigrants or old timers: to a large extent this is merely a final consequence of the general and contemptuous disregard for law that has grown up around us … we are faced with a political situation in which no crime is too crude or pathological to be exploited.[618]

"Intolerance," as a British report noted, "explodes into violence with appalling ease in Israel," whose domestic murder rate in 1951 was fourteen times England's. Nonetheless, Jordan, aware that West

Bankers were the presumed suspects, immediately asked Israel "for any evidence they might have about the murderer so that steps could be taken." Israel replied that there "was no need for Arabs to bother with evidence," since "we have our own methods of dealing with this sort of thing."[619]

Those "methods" came to pass on the night of Eastern Christmas Eve, January 6: three attacks surrounding Bethlehem, timed to coincide with the start of the great midnight procession to the Church of the Nativity in this predominantly Christian area. One Israeli patrol blew up a house near Beit Jala, about two kilometres west of Bethlehem. Another patrol bombed two houses one kilometre north of Bethlehem, near the Greek Orthodox monastery of Mar Elias. A third IDF patrol crossed three kilometers (1.86 miles) of no man's land in the Latrun Salient and opened fire on the village of Imwas (fifteen years later, Imwas would be levelled on the orders of Yitzhak Rabin).

1952

It happened that some British MPs had come for the Christmas Eve procession, and so there were early outside witnesses to the carnage. The MAC's US Commander E. H. Hutchison was there as well: "No person could live long enough," he wrote, "to become calloused to such a sight" of massacred men, women, and children.[620]

Israeli leaflets, printed on pink paper by cyclostyle, were scattered in Beit Jala and Mar Elias, announcing that the attacks were in retaliation for the rape and murder of the Jewish girl on December 4. The leaflets were identical except for the name of the accused village.[621]

Israel, to be sure, had never named any suspects for Lea Festinger's murderer, and had still never named any suspects when at the next MAC meeting the Jordanian representative put on record the names of the victims of the Christmas Eve massacre. Upon presenting the Committee with the names of the dead, an extraordinary fraud took place right in front of the MAC:

> Some minutes after the occupants of the demolished houses were named in the MAC by the Jordan representative, one of the Israeli representatives left the room and returned with a slip of paper on which were written three names,

allegedly those of the Jewish girl's murderers: they were those of the householders just previously named by Jordan as the victims of the assault. The Senior Israeli delegate then said: "We have the names of the people who carried out [the rape and murder], but I did not want to pass them on before."[622]

And so Israel posthumously framed three of its Christmas eve victims for Lea Festinger's rape and murder. Spreading the lie to the media, Israel announced that the houses blown up on Christmas Eve "appeared to be inhabited by the three infiltrators whose names were given [by Israel to] the Jordanian delegation as responsible." When Ramati, the Israeli representative, was pushed to find those responsible for the massacre, he replied that the MAC only provides for prevention. Nor could Israel make any attempt to discover the young woman's actual murderer, as the attempt itself would contradict its official lie. The MAC chairman suspected that the Christmas eve atrocities were "intended to provoke Arab hostilities which would be capitalised abroad by the Israelis."[623]

A week after the Bethlehem massacre, on 13 January, a father and son working on the lands of Cremisan, the area near Bethlehem known for its wine, were seized by nine IDF soldiers, "taken into the Israel area, and butchered." Five days later, three villagers working a vegetable plot (on the Israeli side, but under agreement) were murdered in similar fashion, "marched a few hundred metres further into Israel [i.e., to make them 'infiltrators'] and gunned down at point-blank range." The same formula was used in the murder of two more villagers the next day. Between February and May, thirty-nine Israeli attacks on the West Bank were recorded, involving the murder of civilians, including farmers asleep in their field, the targeting of UN observers, theft of livestock, and kidnappings.[624]

On May 7, about a kilometre inside Jordanian territory between Qaffin and Nazlot Issa, an Israeli patrol of about thirty-two soldiers opened fire on harvesters at a range of about 200 yards, among them a sixty-year-old woman too feeble to run. On the night of May 20, an Israel patrol laid a delayed-action mine against a house on the outskirts of Qaffin village (northwest Palestine). When it exploded at about 1:30 in the morning, a sixteen-year-old boy and two children aged five and six were killed outright, and a baby of one and a half years died while being extracted from the rubble. The father was asleep in his field, having left the teenage son to take care of the family in his absence. As in distant Bethlehem, leaflets were left behind announcing that the bombing was retribution for the murder of a Jewish girl (presumably Lea Festinger). A senior Belgian UN observer joined those warning that Israel was attacking in order to create a war:

> Jews are deliberately working up the tension and the shooting with a view to provoking the Arab Legion to retaliate and then blaming us and starting up the war again.[625]

Relations between Israel and the United Nations reached a crisis in June of 1952 over Mt. Scopus, an area in northeast Jerusalem that lay on the Palestinian side of the Armistice Line but which Israel occupied. The UN tolerated Israel's occupation of Mt. Scopus with the stipulation that it not be militarized. Israel, however, was digging trenches along the hill, defying UN demands that it stop, and smuggling in weapons. It was caught on June 4, when one of its convoys heading for Mt. Scopus was stopped at the UN border crossing at the Mandelbaum Gate, and a UN guard dipped a test rod into one of the oil drums it was transporting. The rod struck a "heavy object concealed beneath." As the drum was removed from the truck to be checked, the Israeli driver pretended to have engine trouble, pushed the truck to make it roll toward the Israeli check post, jumped in, and escaped with the rest of the evidence.

After much deliberation, the decision was made to open the impounded barrel in front of international observers and representatives from Israel and Jordan, on June 20 at half past noon. For safekeeping until then, it was rolled into the bathroom of the MAC headquarters and locked.

That meeting, however, never took place. As described by US Commander Hutchison, at noon on the appointed day, the door of the MAC office burst open and three Israeli officers, with pistols drawn and escorted by two enlisted men who were holding Thompson sub-machine guns at the ready, marched into the room.[626]

Armed Israeli soldiers prevent international observers and members of the United Nations Mixed Armistice Commission from examining an "oil barrel" Israel was using to smuggle arms to Mt. Scopus in violation of the Armistice.

The Israelis commandeered the UN office, prevented the examination of the barrel, replaced the MAC's key to the bathroom with their own, kept guard over UN personnel and answered the UN's phones. The MAC itself now hijacked by Israel, MAC personnel kept vigil by the door, taking turns throughout the night to prevent any action going unwitnessed. Israel's next move was its smokescreen: it issued an *Aide Memoire* requesting "the immediate replacement of the United Nations Personnel involved in this disreputable incident."

A new date was set—July 10—to open the barrel, now with the presence of the US' General William Riley, Commander of the UN Truce Supervision Organization. With Riley in charge,

Israel had no objections to proceeding. Riley had the dip rod inserted again, confirmed that it concealed contraband, but then to everyone's astonishment, he declared that it would be returned to Israel unopened—"against violent opposition by [MAC chairman Colonel] de Ridder and Sloan and against the views of almost his whole staff." As Hutchison explained, Riley's action made the entire peace-keeping endeavor meaningless, since Israel's violations carried no risk. Foreseeing the barrel incident "win" as another watershed in Israeli intransigence, the British in Jerusalem warned the Foreign Office that "the Israeli use of force has thus paid handsome dividend and I fear the consequences may be far-reaching."[627]

Describing Israel's occupation of Mt. Scopus as "a dangerous anomaly," officials wrote in despair of their inability "to bring the Israelis to heel." Some advocated the suspension of UN convoys to Mt. Scopus until Israel cooperated, but this, too, was not pursued because of the surety that Israel would respond with force. In the words of Commander Hutchison—who by his own account had gone to the Middle East pro-Israel—"had the Jordanians been guilty of these deeds, Israel would have spelled them out in banner headlines from Baghdad to Fresno."[628]

Israel's "passive" ethnic cleansing of non-Jews continued. "Israel intends to make it so uncomfortable for its remaining Arabs," the CIA reported in late 1952, "that eventually they will all try to emigrate." Among those "passive" methods, Bedouin were forced to sign "requests" to move to Jordan under the threat of expulsion to unproductive desert if they refused. In another method, witnessed by Hutchison, the IDF broke and ignited benzene-filled beer bottles over the humps of their camels, burning the animals alive in order to make even the hides unsalvageable. Moshe Dayan stuck to the script of an existential threat: According to future Jerusalem mayor Kollek, Dayan had his soldiers chase Bedouin in jeeps, firing at them and killing several in order to provoke them to attack army patrols—which "was what Dayan was looking for," giving him the "reason" to wage a "mopping up campaign." The commandeering of Palestinian homes by Jewish Israelis continued with impunity, Israel maintaining that it "cannot evict a Jew from a house" once he has gone inside it.[629]

The stranger-than-fiction intrigue of Mt. Scopus continued on the night of December 13, 1952, when Israeli soldiers were caught running an arms cache past the border. They fled, leaving behind six US Army manpacks filled with 1,000 rounds of rifle ammunition, 2,000 rounds of stengun ammunition, six 81mm mortar shells, six 2" mortar shells, three 90-volt dry batteries, twenty-four hand grenades, and a tin of detonators—all destined for Mt. Scopus. Twice during the night, the Israelis attempted to retrieve the arms, but were driven back.

Throughout the next day (December 14), the MAC tried to contact Israeli authorities, but were continually told that no one "was available" to speak to them, the very UN-administered peace-keeping mission that had just foiled their nocturnal arms-running to occupied territory. The ritual obfuscation came the following day, when Israel filed what Hutchison described as "perhaps the most ridiculous allegation received during the history of the [MAC] mission": the culprits were not Israeli, but "Jordanian marauders" who had stolen ammunition from an Israeli army dump and wounded an Israeli soldier.

To the MAC's credit, it nonetheless took the allegation seriously, and had the Israelis submit evidence and walk the investigators through the alleged events. After the Israeli claim proved farcical and the MAC condemned Israel for the breach of the Armistice, Israel responded by launching an international campaign against Chairman de Ridder. Soon, de Ridder needed a bodyguard. The harassment continued, and although de Ridder stood firm, the UN did not. Under what Hutchison referred to as Israel's constant pressure on the UN, he was eventually removed from his position.

The Israeli "smokescreen of words" was described by John Wilson upon leaving the British delegation in Tel Aviv in mid-1953. Israeli officials have built up "a sickening jargon ... the air is thick with propaganda ... Misleading stories and press campaigns are worked up [and] censorship stifles the dissemination of honest news." Several observers noted how the Israeli state, following in the footsteps of the Jewish Agency, conjured such hysteria with its manipulation of the news that it found itself having to take action against the threats it had invented.[630]

The year 1953 brought the fifth year of displacement, poverty, and suspension of normal civilian life. It is about this time that Israeli terror against those it made refugees finally produced the inevitable, and it would seem intended, result: Palestinian reprisal raids were now a threat. As Glubb put it, "Jewish terrorism made the infiltrator into a gunman":

1953

> [T]he infiltrators are the dispossessed ... The creation of a vast horde—nearly a million—of dispossessed, who four years after the battle are still wholly prevented from returning to their lands and villages now lying fallow or given over to Israeli immigrants, [the separation of villages from their fields], all these are Israel's doing; and they have created a landless, and a depressed community of almost ungovernable proportions on the fringes of Israel.[631]

Yet few infiltrators were armed even as late as the Suez Crisis, and fewer still crossed the Armistice with the intent to cause harm. Typical infiltrators, according to British ambassador to Jordan Geoffrey Furlonge, were hungry refugee children risking their lives to steal.

Consistent with expansionist goals, Israel appeared to exacerbate the desperation as the opportunity offered. In Qalqilya (West Bank) there were several impoverished families near the Armistice Line who depended on a single cistern which, according to the MAC, lay well within a twenty-yard uncertainty of the Armistice Line. Once the Line was set more clearly, the cistern ended up three yards into the Israeli side. Israel did not use the cistern, but for the families Israel had displaced, its water meant survival, and so the MAC asked that they be allowed to access it. Israel refused. Any Arab who tried to make the extra few steps to the water, its representative assured the MAC, would be shot dead.

Israeli raids into the West Bank continued. Two IDF paratrooper companies were sent to Idna (Hebron area) and Falama on the night of January 22 with orders blow up houses and kill their inhabitants, but were intercepted by National Guardsmen, though a repeat attack against Falama six days later was more successful. On February 25 an IDF patrol murdered five shepherds, the youngest age thirteen, mutilated their bodies and stole their flock of 177 sheep.[632]

April 22 brought what became known as the "Jerusalem incident," in which both the Jordanians and the Israelis accused the other of initiating a bloody sunset encounter along the Armistice Line. Officially, the UN judged it impossible to determine who fired first; however according to the British General Consul in Jerusalem, the United Nations staff, and both the US and British consuls in Amman, the evidence pointed wholly to Israel. For one, Israeli soldiers knew about the violence in advance. The "lady friend" (as the British Consul described her) of an Israeli soldier stationed at an advanced post happened to be employed at a French convent on the border, and the day before the incident, April 21, he warned her not to go to the convent's garden the next day because "there were going to be manoeuvres." The woman alerted the Mother Superior. Another factor cited is that the Israeli fire was from the first moment coordinated over a wide area. As explained by the senior investigating officer, "judging by his own military experience," he could not understand "how such widespread and simultaneous firing by the Israelis took place unless there had been a pre-set time or signal."

According to Ambassador Furlonge, it was because of General Riley—the same General Riley who saved Israel in the "barrel incident" the previous summer—that the UN was unable to reach a verdict, as he "seems to have resorted to the suppression of evidence" in withholding from the UN such information unfavorable to Israel. Riley then refused to investigate an alleged Israeli attack on Beit Sira on May 17, the refusal, according to Glubb, at Israel's request.[633]

On May 20, small parties of Israelis penetrated into the West Bank and attacked five villages in the Tulkarm area. According to the British in Amman and Nablus, they "laid mines at doors and windows of a house and then lobbed hand-grenades through the windows and directed machine-gun fire at the doors." The next night, Israelis blew up a house in Jaba, near Jerusalem, killing a woman and child; but Israel refused to allow the MAC to investigate, dismissing the attack as an internal matter for Jordan. De Ridder then proposed modifying MAC procedure "to permit UN observers to investigate incidents, although the one party may not agree that incident is a breach of armistice agreement"; Jordan agreed; Israel refused. Finally,

Israel alleged a Palestinian attack that it dated at about the same time as its attacks on Tulkarm and Jaba, thus "balancing" the situation, and then refused the MAC's procedure for investigating its own accusation. Among the continuing attacks, four Palestinian villages were targeted on four successive nights, May 20-23, and Palestinians already reduced to hiding in caves were killed on May 24.[634]

The MAC judged that there was no evidence to link two murders in Beit Jibrin on August 8 to the West Bank, but "reprisals nevertheless followed swiftly." On the night of August 11-12, UN investigators reported that "Israel military forces using demolition mines, bangalore torpedoes, 2-inch mortars, machine-guns and small arms" attacked Wadi Fukin, Surif, and Idna. "Bullet-riddled bodies near the doorways and multiple bullet hits on the doors of the demolished houses indicated that the inhabitants had been forced to remain inside until their homes were blown up over them."

US Colonel T.M. Hinkle reported that the Israeli Air Force's strafing of Gaza resumed in July (1953), and it was this summer that Israel's elite terror militia, Unit 101, began its raids. On August 28, the young Ariel Sharon (then Scheinerman) led Unit 101 in an attack against the Bureij refugee camp in Gaza in an alleged search for "infiltrators," but what the MAC described as "an appalling case of deliberate mass murder." Using automatic weapons, hand grenades, and incendiary bombs, forty-three men, women, children whom Israel had ethnically cleansed five years earlier were killed, and twenty-two seriously injured.

One member of Unit 101 refused to take part in the Bureij massacre due to its barbarity, and when some soldiers questioned Sharon's indiscriminate slaughter of women, he dismissed the victims as Arab "whores." He had a reputation for such dehumanization—Hareetz reporter Uzi Benziman recorded Sharon responding with laughter as he watched a junior officer torment an old Palestinian man and then murder him at close range, and being amused by inventive ploys to murder civilians, such as trapping a peaceful Bedouin boy as he shepherded his flock.

Israel's "balancing" smokescreen to the Gaza refugee camp massacre came three days later, when Tel Aviv radio reported terrible news: "Arabs" had attacked UNRWA warehouses in Gaza. The story served its purpose, but it was a fabrication—that it was "entirely without foundation" came directly from the acting director of UNRWA, Leslie Carver.[635]

The pattern continued. The MAC dismissed Israeli claims that the Israeli village of Ahiezer, near Lydda, was attacked by infiltrators on September 7, 1953, but nonetheless four Israeli patrols crossed into the West Bank in "retaliation," attacking a shepherd, stealing his flock, and abducting a woman who was collecting firewood.

The fate of the twenty-five year old woman kidnapped by the IDF remains unknown. When the MAC demanded that she be freed, Israel replied that she had suddenly died. To demands that her body be returned to her family, Israel replied that she had already been buried.[636]

Israel's ongoing activity in the south, though less visible, would ultimately prove more decisive. A CIA report dated September 20 summarized:

> In the past two weeks, Israeli troops have made almost daily armed incursions into the neutral zone and attacked Arab bedouin settlements. Moreover, the insistence of UN observers that the Israelis leave the zone has apparently been ignored ... [it is] apparently a deliberate move on the part of the Ben-Gurion government to gain control of the El Auja [demilitarised] zone.[637]

October of 1953 began relatively quietly. The MAC condemned Israeli ambushes on October 10 and rejected an Israeli claim of an attack on October 11 for lack of evidence. However, when on October 13 a grenade was thrown into a house in the Israeli town of Yehud, killing a woman and two of her children, the Jordanians themselves acknowledged that West Bank infiltrators might be responsible. Glubb immediately flew to Jerusalem and met with Hutchison. They arranged for the Israelis and their tracking dogs to follow the tracks wherever they may lead. The bloodhounds, however, lost the scent in Rantis, due east of Yehud.[638]

In "retaliation" for the unsolved crime, the following evening, October 14, Sharon's Unit 101 invaded the West Bank village of

Qibya and murdered sixty-nine Palestinians, half of them women and children, and blew up at least forty-five houses. Once again, the victims had been forced to remain in their homes while they were bombed. The roads to Budrus and Shuqba were mined, and both villages were shelled. UN observers who reached the scene about midnight reported that

> about 10 PM Israeli forces, estimated conservatively at 3 companies or 400 men, moved on the village of Qibya ... Forces used demolition bombs, Bangalore torpedoes, hand grenades, automatic weapons and incendiary bombs. Persons attempting to escape were machine-gunned.[639]

For Hutchison, it was "difficult to describe the wanton destruction that had taken place."

> An Arab woman [was] perched high on a pile of rubble. Here and there between the rocks you could see a tiny hand or foot protruding ... the lifeless bodies of her six children. The bullet riddled body of the husband lay face down in the dusty road behind her.[640]

Sharon was obeying orders: Central Command had instructed him "to attack and temporarily to occupy the village, carry out destruction and maximum killing, in order to drive out the inhabitants of the village from their homes." Sharett's diary records the official order for Unit 101 to attack Qibya, as well as Ben-Gurion's approval of the operation. But Qibya became Israel's new public relations scandal, and so in a special broadcast, Ben-Gurion emphatically denied "the false and fantastic tale" that Israeli soldiers committed the massacre. "We have examined the facts in detail," and can categorically state that "not a single unit, not even the smallest, was absent from its barracks." Most extraordinarily, Ben-Gurion, addressing his nation and the world, framed Holocaust survivors for the slaughter.[641]

The MAC acting chairman described Qibya as a "sheer cold-blooded massacre." The US, already alarmed by Israel's continued obstruction of UN personnel and refusal to suspend its illegal diversion of the upper Jordan, described Israel's behavior as "shocking" and "was so disturbed about a whole series of Israeli incidents along the Arab frontiers" that President Eisenhower held up $26 million allocated to Israel for the first six months of 1954, and "urgently" considered Security Council action in consideration of "the inefficiency of past representations to the Israeli government."

This was short-lived: According to Benny Morris, Israel then "promptly and successfully mobilized the pro-Israel lobby in Washington," which caused US officials to grow concerned about its "effect on General Eisenhower's and the Administration's political future." New York Mayor-elect Robert F. Wagner joined Zionist groups in smearing as anti-Semites anyone who called for an investigation into Qibya. Ben-Gurion claimed persecution: "If it is difficult to be a Jew," he said in response to condemnation of the massacre, "then it is even more difficult to be a Jewish state." Ben-Gurion then linked this "difficulty" to "something that happened two thousand years ago in this very country," which the *NY Times* assumed to be a reference to the birth of Christ.[642]

As with previous attacks, the victims were retroactively vilified: Israeli media announced that Qibya was "a nest of marauders." This, too, was a lie: the village had not once figured into the MAC files, or in any incident, since the Armistice was signed four and a half years earlier. When investigations by the American Consulate and US Embassy contradicted Ben-Gurion, the Israeli Foreign Minister blamed the United States for a lack of friendship. The US, he charged, was encouraging "Arab appetites."[643]

The Qibya terror attack "greatly advanced his [Sharon's] professional career," Sharett wrote in his diary. The public relations debacle caused by the massacre lingered, however, and so diversionary "balancing" incidents were needed. There would be two: one eleven days later, and one the following March. On the morning of October 25, an Israeli freight train was hit by a bomb, derailing the locomotive and eleven cars (all empty). Immediately, Israel lodged a "sharp protest against this new Jordanian aggression," and wanted Britain to "reprove Jordan for this latest act of violence [as it was] swift to react to the Kibya incident." The Israeli press stressed how fortunate it was that the "infiltrators" happened not to hit a crowded passenger train.

The train bombing, however, was almost surely a false flag operation. There was no evidence to link it to the West Bank, and in the words of Ambassador Furlonge, "we all here remain firmly of the opinion that the whole thing was a frame-up on the part of the Israelis, who staged it themselves."[644]

Like Deir Yassin in 1948, Qibya appeared to have been calculated to destroy any hope among the survivors that they could ever regain normalcy as long as they were on land wanted by Israel. In Qibya's wake, Israel heightened the psychological terror by continuing military "exercises" with live ammunition right at the Armistice Line, stray bullets hitting Palestinian villages such as Budrus, all to the accompaniment of the IAF's menacing airspace violations. None of this was in response to any Jordanian action. The British ambassador to Israel, Francis Evans, suspected that Israel was now encouraging Jewish settlers to attack Palestinians and then say they had no control over them—this foreshadowing settler attacks in the West Bank and East Jerusalem today.[645]

It is unclear whether surveillance "hiking" teams, like those of the Mandate period, continued on a small scale. In late 1953, three Israeli men and two women were caught by Jordanian police, then killed when they attempted to escape. They carried maps, compasses, and army type water bottles, but no identification papers. Israel claimed they were tourists en route to Petra yet, curiously, did not raise this incident with the MAC, nor explain why Israeli tourists would have thought they could enter Jordan when the reverse would have meant an IDF execution on the spot.[646]

Mount Scopus, which Israel now armed by airdropping cargo by parachute, flared to the fore again on November 1, 1953, when a time bomb destroyed part of the eight-inch diameter pipe that was Arab Jerusalem's only water pipeline. UN observers followed the tracks of the attack to Mount Scopus, where Israel blocked them from any investigation. The British on the scene suspected that the sabotage was intended to provoke Palestinians to attack Mt. Scopus.[647]

More raids filled the night of December 21-22. A party of about four Israelis "blasted open door of house selected apparently at random and murdered women inside with automatic fire [and then] murdered two unarmed Arabs running to the scene" to help. Two more homes were sprayed with bullets, but the occupants had escaped. Near Tarqumiya, a Bedouin village was attacked with Sten guns, submachine guns, and a grenade.

The "balancing" allegation came on December 28: Israel announced that an Arab had murdered an Israeli "engaged in marking the demarcation line." A meeting was immediately arranged for 17:00 hrs at the scene of the alleged murder. The UN representative and the Jordanian delegate were present and waited two hours for the Israeli representative, who failed to come. The meeting was set again for the next day, but the UN and Jordanian representatives again waited in vain for the Israeli representative. At a MAC meeting on December 30, the Israeli representative, asked why he twice failed to show up at the meeting arranged to examine his own allegation, replied that he was both times "unavoidably late."[648]

The era's most infamous attack against Israeli civilians occurred on the night of March 16-17, 1954. An Israeli bus on an unscheduled run from Eilat to Tel Aviv was barbarously attacked while traveling through Scorpion's Pass (Ma'ale Akrabim) in the Negev. Eleven people were murdered; three survived. Israel realized that the atrocity could, as Hutchison put it, "wipe the Qibya massacre from the Israeli slate"—but only if it could be shown that the murderers came from the West Bank or Jordan, rather than from Gaza or the southern Negev, as was far more likely. Israel however immediately insisted that this was the case, and its military delegate even handed Hutchison the names and locations of the culprits, with the odd instructions that it not be given to the MAC, as that would "delay the proceedings." Hutchison and Glubb nonetheless accommodated him and within a half hour launched a massive search. Just before midnight, failing even to find anyone who recognized the names, they widened the scope.

As they searched, Israel manufactured a media coup that would "make the MAC look ridiculous unless the vote went to Israel," as Hutchison put it: the headline of the morning's Jerusalem Post and a second front-page article were fabrications, with fabricated citations, planted to create the "fact" that the murderers were from the West

Bank or Jordan, and that the MAC knew this. Now armed with the Israeli public's manufactured belief, Israel put "intolerable pressure" on the MAC chairman that a vote blaming Jordan be concluded immediately, without investigation—PM Sharett threatening the chairman that "he would not like to see the press the following day" if the commission did not do as instructed. Jordan, meanwhile, made available trackers, officers, and an airplane for the search, sent forces to the adjacent Jordanian area, and offered a large monetary reward for information.[649]

The blackmail to frame the West Bank or Jordan failed. No determination was made—all possibilities (including the West Bank and Jordan) remained open. Israel quit in protest and launched a campaign of intimidation against Hutchison who, like de Ridder before him, soon needed a bodyguard. Israel blocked UN personnel and tracking dogs from circling the area of the crime, and when a solitary piece of evidence, a skull cap that fit the description given by one of the survivors, was discovered to the west of the crime scene (indicating assailants from Gaza or the Negev), an Israeli watcher took it and planted it to the east, in order to implicate Jordan or the West Bank. The CIA reported that there was no evidence to support the Israeli contention, and four independent sources cited a Black Hand Gang, formed by Bedouin who had been the victims of Israeli violence, as the likely perpetrators. As with the murder of Lea Festinger, Israel's need to manufacture "facts" to serve its expansionist goals meant that the actual murderers must never be found. The Scorpion's Pass massacre remains unsolved.[650]

At about midnight on March 28-29, an Israeli force of about 200 men penetrated 3.5 km (2.2 miles) east of the Armistice Line and attacked the West Bank village of Nahalin, killing nine and wounding fourteen. Reminiscent of the Mandate gangs' habit of targeting first responders, the soldiers hid a grenade and a prepared charge of TNT that blew up an Arab Legion vehicle rushing to the scene. UN investigators were there within three hours, but the Israeli representative failed to attend the MAC meeting called about the incident, despite several attempts to secure his participation. In a confidential memo from the British Consulate-General in July,

1954, T. Wikeley voiced "doubts regarding the sincerity of Israeli protestations for peace ... until the boundaries of Israel have reached the Jordan."

> [These doubts] have been strongly reinforced by the disgusting manner in which the United Nations Truce Supervision Organisation is being treated by the Israel Military authorities and in the Israel press ... Far from pointing to a desire for peace, this can most easily be interpreted as an indication of a wish to stop unwelcome investigations which U.N. observers are constantly making, or trying to make, along the Israel frontier ... the repeated Israeli requests for a peace meeting with Jordan are no more than a tactical manoeuvre aimed at the Security Council...[651]

"It is the deliberate intention of the Israelis," concluded British Lt.-Col R. J. Gammon in reporting one of the continuing IDF mortar attacks on the West Bank, "to provoke the Arab Legion into crossing the frontier in retaliation," and "in this they may well succeed." US intelligence as well continued its bleak assessment of Israeli intentions.[652]

When on July 2, 1954, bombs exploded inside the post office in Alexandria, the Egyptian government's ability to control terrorism was thrown into doubt. Whether the attacks were by the Muslim Brotherhood, as some claimed, or the Communists, as others alleged, Egypt was obviously not stable, and the British, who were considering withdrawing their military from the region, now had second thoughts. Matters worsened twelve days later as bombs exploded inside US cultural centers in both Alexandria and Cairo. The events bolstered Defense Minister Lavon's case when at a news conference on July 19 he warned that Israel must act aggressively to defend itself from its neighbours—and, significantly, that Israel's borders (Armistice Line) "should not be regarded as unchangeable."[653]

On July 23, the Egyptian bombers targeted cinemas in Cairo and Alexandria, and a railroad yard in Alexandria. But then the nascent wave of terror abruptly ended: As one of the bombers neared the next target, the British-owned Rio Cinema in Alexandria, his device exploded prematurely. Soon, thirteen men and one women were in custody, charged with espionage and terrorism against Egyptian, American, and British civilian targets, including a cinema, library, and an American educational center. Egypt was now certainly foremost in Lavon's thoughts, because the suspects were neither Communists nor Islamic radicals, but Jews and Israelis. The bombings—by Israel's Unit 131, created in 1948 to conduct sabotage and "black propaganda"— were what the CIA called a "sabotage operation against US and UK installations," a bungled false-flag operation that soon became known by Lavon's name*.[654]

Egypt's arrests ignited charges of anti-Semitism. The Political Director of the World Jewish Congress warned the British government that he feared large-scale anti-Jewish campaigns in Egypt, and others warned of a wave of pogroms. Rabbi Nahum, chief rabbi of the Jewish communities in Egypt, responded with the following statement:

> I consider it my duty to declare that there is no racial terror against our communities in Egypt. On the contrary, and especially under the present regime [Nasser], the Egyptian authorities have repeatedly shown their sympathy for Egyptian Jews.[655]

Much the same was reported by T. W. Garvey from the British Embassy in Cairo. "Anti-Semitism as known in Europe had no real parallel" in Egypt, and "successive Egyptian governments and this one in particular, made a special point of religious toleration." Nonetheless the Israeli government pressured Britain to intervene to free the suspects and to "mobilize the support of world opinion" against the Egyptians. A guilty verdict, Israel warned, could "provoke extremely violent reactions in Israel." The typical view of the Western public was likely that expressed by the *Manchester Guardian*: the accusations against the defendants were too outrageous to be plausible. "What conceivable benefit

---

* Lavon's signature was allegedly forged on the orders authorizing the false flag operation, which was code-named Operation Susannah. TNA FO 371/151273, declassified in September, 2013, states that the Head of Military Intelligence who submitted the plan to Lavon, Benyamin Givli, was then Israel's Military Attaché in London. The document also records an alleged 1960 Israeli attempt to assassinate Egyptian president Nasser.

could Israel have gained," it asked, from bombing American and British facilities?⁶⁵⁶

The answer, however, soon became clear. In the blunt words of the CIA, Israel staged "Arab" bombings "to embitter relations between Egypt and the West." Domestically, Israel used its strict news censorship to keep its denials credible, and did not admit the Affair to its own citizens until 2005, when it honored the operatives at a Jerusalem ceremony and bestowed certificates of appreciation upon three who were still alive. Israel's archives relating to the operation remain secret.⁶⁵⁷

Israel was "determined to get revenge," as Teddy Kollek put it, against Egypt for its execution of two of the "Lavon" bombers. The pretexts came the following February 23 and 25, 1955, when maps and documents were stolen from an Israeli military facility, and a bicyclist was murdered near Tel Aviv, which Israel blamed on infiltrators from Gaza. With this scorecard in hand, Israel staged a brutal attack against Gazan civilians on February 28, the bloodiest against the coastal strip since the 1948 war.⁶⁵⁸

Israel's pretexts, however, altogether failed to explain the massacre, and so Ben-Gurion concocted an official lie to quell the international condemnation. An Egyptian patrol, the new story went, had ambushed an IDF patrol inside Israeli territory, and so in self-defense the Israeli unit had chased the Arabs back into Gaza. The soldiers were ordered to repeat the story to UN observers if questioned. Privately, Sharett doubted that anyone would believe it, and he was correct: "the pretence deceived no one and was at once abandoned," as the British Embassy in Tel Aviv put it. For the first time, both the US and the USSR voted to censure Israel.⁶⁵⁹

Israel's cross border raids continued during the heat of the Lavon conspiracy. Among them, on September 11, 1954, settlers from the Mevo Beitar cooperative fired on Palestinian children swimming in a reservoir roughly a half km inside the West Bank, severely injuring a twelve and a thirteen-year-old. No action was taken against the culprits.⁶⁶⁰

The morning after the trial for the "Lavon Affair" bombers began in Cairo, December 12, 1954, a Syrian passenger plane left Damascus on a routine, scheduled flight to Cairo. It flew west over Lebanon, and once it was well over the Mediterranean, it turned south. A US businessman onboard estimated that they were about 70 miles offshore when, without warning, Israeli fighter planes intercepted the aircraft and forced it to land in Lydda—an air piracy "without precedent in the history of international practice," the State Department informed Sharett. Israel claimed that the plane was intercepted over its "sovereign" territory in Acre (actually Palestinian, but seized in 1948), roughly 60 kilometer (37 miles) south of where, according to the American witness, it crossed the coast on its westward course from Damascus. Common speculation at the time was that Israel wanted the passengers as hostages to secure the release of five Israeli soldiers whom Syria had just captured in the Golan Heights changing batteries in Israeli bugs on Syrian telephone lines.[661]

In December, a young Israeli man and woman infiltrated Jordan to the southeast of the Dead Sea. Like the "Petra tourists" two years earlier, Israel behaved as though they should not meet the same end as a Palestinian infiltrating Israeli-controlled territory. When in February 1955 they failed to return, UN observers asked local Bedouins' assistance. The UN/Bedouin team found their bodies, but no clue as to what had happened. In response, an Israeli military patrol penetrated 15-20 kilometers (9-12 miles) inside the West Bank, kidnapped six random Bedouin, brought them to the Israeli side and murdered five of them, four with knifes, one with firearms. One was sixteen years old. They sent the sixth back to announce that the five were executed in revenge for the two Israeli "tourists." Israel gave wide publicity to the (unsolved) murder of the two, yet inexplicably did not file a complaint with the MAC "on which UN observers can initiate their normal investigations." Ben-Gurion prevented the soldiers from being tried for the Bedouins' murders, and Lt.-Col R. J. Gammon speculated that this tactic—"abduction of isolated peasants near the border and their subsequent murder on Israeli territory"—was replacing the tactic of fewer, larger attacks on West Bank soil.[662]

British officials hoped never to have to make good on the defense treaty they maintained with Jordan, avoiding the issue by parsing words: was Israel "attacking" Jordan, or merely "raiding" it? The military nonetheless took the defense pact seriously, in part because a destabilized Jordan would invite Soviet intrigue. In early 1954, as the "Lavon"' operatives planned their bombings, the British developed secret plans to destroy the entire Israeli Air Force, as well as key Israeli military and communication installations, in order to stop Israeli aggression. In preparation, Britain moved one armored squadron, consisting of about 20 tanks and 100 men, from the Suez area to supplement its small garrison at Aqaba.[663]

A summary of plans dated April 27, 1955 read :

> Neutralise the Israeli Air Force using all the planned reinforcements and operating from the following bases Nicosia Abu Sueir Fayid Amman and Mafraq. Conduct operations against military targets in Israel in particular centres of communications and oil installations.[664]

Britain had been giving military aid to Israel even as it protested Israeli crimes and soul-searched its obligation to come to the West Bank's defense. Only in October 1953 did it acknowledge to itself that "Israel's military strength was at least partly due to our assistance" and speak of discontinuing that aid.[665]

Military force was also being considered to stop Israeli aggression against Gaza, and its maneuvers inside the UN's El Auja demilitarized zone, a turtle shell shaped area whose bottom was the Egyptian border. The area was in fact integral to Gaza and was supposed to be Palestinian, but what we know as the "Gaza strip" was all that remained after 1948.[666]

In April 1955, the US State Department advised the British Foreign Office that the UK "should consider urgently what action we should be prepared to take if Israel made a deliberate attempt to alter her existing frontier with Egyptian occupied territory [the Gaza Strip]," the "we" suggesting joint US-UK action against Israel. Four months later, the Foreign Office indeed proposed enlisting the help of the United States in an attack on Israel to halt its aggression against Gaza.[667]

> 2. Our outline plan based on the assumptions in paragraph one above is contained in the following paragraphs.
>
> 3. Air.
>
> (a) Neutralise the Israeli Air Force using all the planned reinforcements and operating from the following bases Nicosia Abu Sueir Fayid Amman and Mafraq. Conduct operations against military targets in Israel in particular centres of communication and oil installations.
>
> **TOP SECRET**

Extract from a document dated April 27, 1955, from G.H.Q. Middle East Land Forces, to Ministry of Defence, London, regarding British plans to attack Israel.

By 1955, Israel was treating the DMZ as its sovereign territory. It built a military camp (which it called it a "kibbutz") and planted minefields (which it called "non-military"). Egypt had no such militarization of the DMZ nor claimed it as its territory. It had however placed cement markers in the south, indicating its view of the (imprecise) Egyptian-DMZ border. After some back-and-forth, on November 2, Israeli soldiers took over the DMZ's UN compound and wiped out the Egyptian post, massacring about fifty Egyptians. Hoping to repeat its earlier success in commandeering Mt. Scopus, Israel forced out the UN peacekeepers, who continued their work as best they could from Gaza.[668]

Finally, to create what the CIA called "a rise in war fever," on December 27 all Israeli newspapers carried an alarming report— "inspired by the Israeli army," in the CIA's judgement—that predicted a considerable increase in Arab military strength and warned of Israel's increasing vulnerability. Israel further inflamed the "fever" by moving personnel and vehicles to the Negev for what it called "maneuvers" to be held in January or February 1956. All news was spun as bad news: When General Glubb, long a thorn in Israel's side, was dismissed from his post in March, the Israeli press now warned that the "threat to Israel, with Glubb's departure, has increased ominously."[669]

1956

But in the end, in a historical irony, the bungled "Lavon Affair" influenced the course of events roughly as intended, if circuitously. Israel's massacre in Gaza on February 28, in retribution for Egypt's execution of two of the "Lavon" terrorists, was the spark that ignited the Gazan powder keg that Israel had created—what the CIA at the time called "more than 200,000 Palestinian Arab refugees, deeply embittered and frustrated after more than six years in camps," and whom the United Nations had failed to protect "against Israeli attacks." Gazan refugees rioted against the Egyptian regime for its inability to defend them, Nasser stopped secret peace talks he was holding with Israel, the British and Americans stopped their "Project Alpha" initiative to bring a lasting peace, Fedayeen groups formed and attacked southern Israel, and these in turn provided Israel's pretext for its next occupation of Gaza in which hundreds more civilians were killed. Pressure on Nasser to purchase weapons heightened, and unable buy them from the US, he concluded an arms deal with Czechoslovakia. "It is no flight of fancy," Britain's Ambassador in Israel reported in 1956, "to suggest that Israel, by her attack on Gaza in February [28, 1955], was herself responsible for Egypt's decision in August to accept Communist arms."

The US feared Soviet influence in the region and was furious at Nasser (though Israel had also bought arms through Czechoslovakia in 1948). His hopes for a US loan to build a high dam at Aswan now looked all but dead, contributing to his decision to nationalize the Suez Canal. When on July 26, 1956, Nasser announced this move, he sealed his fate. His relationship with the West was poisoned, and "regime change" was the solution: PM Eden looked to military action to oust him.[670]

Thus Britain, instead of attacking Israel to defend Jordan or Egypt, joined with Israel and France against Egypt in Operation Musketeer, creating the war known as the Suez Crisis. Yet Britain's seemingly antithetical options—destroying Israel's military, versus joining forces with it against Egypt—were kept alive simultaneously. These remarkable instructions were written by the Chiefs of Staff Committee:

> If these operations [British neutralizing of Israeli Air Force and communications] are ordered while Musketeer [British-Israeli-French attack against Egypt] is still held in readiness they [attacks against Israel] will take priority and consequent delay to Musketeer will be accepted.[671]

Britain's assault against Israel would delay, but not necessarily stop, its collaboration with Israel against Egypt afterwards. After Musketeer, which was to be launched on September 15, was postponed "due to political factors," top British military figures continued to discuss logistics and circulate plans for a British attack on Israel. If the attack against Israel was commenced, squadrons in Malta, Germany, and Cyprus that were in place for Musketeer would be used, but without compromising their readiness for Musketeer should it be enacted afterwards.[672]

Nor the opposite: the launching of the "Musketeer" attack against Egypt would not mean that Britain would not attack Israel afterwards. The seemingly irreconcilable contradiction is caught in this instruction from the Ministry of Defence on October 18, a scant eleven days before Israel invaded Egypt in step one of Musketeer:

> We are advising Ministers that, once Musketeer is launched, we should avoid all hostilities with Israel until after Egypt had capitulated or we could dispose our maximum air effort against Israel.[673]

Among the many twists that the British had to weigh were that if during Musketeer Jordan were to support Egypt, Britain might, ironically, be bound to attack Jordan; and since Cyprus remained an important base for both Musketeer and an attack against Israel, a British attack on Israel would risk an Israeli attack and French losses on that island.[674]

In the build-up to Suez, Israeli attacks against the West Bank continued. About twenty Palestinians were killed in a raid on Hebron on September 11, and about ninety lay dead after an assault against Qalqilya on the night of October. 10 But a renewed Jordanian request for British protection following the Qalqilya attack was moot: on October 29, Israel invaded Egypt. Muskateer had begun.[675]

This first move in the new conspiracy to destabilize Egypt was accompanied by one of the better documented Israeli massacres against non-Jews within Israel (rather than cross-Armistice into Palestine). Israel had maintained a 6:00 PM curfew on the village of Kafr Qasim (since non-Jews were under martial law), but at 4:45 that afternoon the villagers were informed that the curfew was now 5:00, effective immediately. Many of the villagers were out in the fields and could not possibly be informed of the change and be back in fifteen minutes. Over the next hour, twenty-two children aged eight to seventeen, six women (one of whom was pregnant), and nineteen men were shot dead by Israeli soldiers as they returned home from the day's labor.

After the Suez Crisis, Israeli forces remained in Gaza and began the large-scale execution of civilians and soldiers. According to the UN's figures, within the first three weeks of its occupation of Gaza the Israeli military killed 447-550 civilians "in cold blood and for no apparent reason," in the words of the head of the Egyptian-Israeli Mixed Armistice Commission (EIMAC). Between 49 and 100 more refugees were killed when Israel seized Rafah in the first two days of November, and a few hundred people, about half of whom were refugees from 1948, were executed by Israeli troops upon capturing Khan Yunis on November 3. When Israel cited Palestinian "fedayeen activity" to justify its occupation and assault on Gaza, the US Eisenhower Administration "derided" Israel's explanation; in response, the *Jerusalem Post*, which the CIA considered to reflect the voice of the government, accused the United States of being "singularly unfriendly," a "crystallization of [US] policy against Israel."

Israel used the attack against Egypt to seize the Sinai, which it intended to annex. For Eisenhower, the celebrated general of World War II, Israel had finally gone too far. He threatened to stop US underwriting of Israel if it refused to vacate the Sinai, and unlike all such US threats before and after, this one time this one president did not back down. Privately, Administration figures like Secretary of State Dulles were warning that Israel was effectively running US foreign policy; and the pressure on Eisenhower to yield to Israel was so great that on February 20, 1957, he appeared on national television to explain what in any other situation would not need explanation: why a nation should not be permitted to seize and annex land by force of arms, or to impose conditions on its own withdrawal. Ben-Gurion stood fast, telling the world that Eisenhower's demands "place me under great moral pressure … as a man and a Jew, the pressure of the justice for which my people were fighting." Israel, Ben-Gurion suggested, was the victim of discrimination "because we are few, weak and perhaps isolated." Ultimately, with face-saving diplomacy, Israel withdrew.[676]

With the conclusion of Suez, its first post-statehood war, Israel had fully established its techniques of expansion and racial cleansing that continue to serve it today: its maintenance of an existential threat, both as the natural consequence of its aggression and of provocation for the purpose; its expropriation and squandering of the moral weight of historic anti-Semitism and the Holocaust; its dehumanization of the Palestinians; its pretence as the prophet-state of Jews; and its seduction of its Jewish population with the perks of blood privilege. The myths that had once roused terrorists to action were now the narrative of the state, and this narrative-myth remains Israel's most powerful weapon. Were this book to continue into the ensuing decades, the circumstances and personalities would change, but the psyche and inertia of a settler movement determined to "regain" a "racially pure" land to which it claims messianic entitlement, would be ever-constant.

9

Postscript: Segue to Today

After the Suez Crisis, the situation in Israel-Palestine returned to normal—"normal" being the chokehold under which Palestine has been suffocating since early 1948. To the international community, this unrelenting crippling of Palestinian life is static, and therefore it is peace. The ever-present, untenable injustice remains, a permanent state of normalized violence festering until Israel's next move. With the Six Day War of 1967, Israel ethnically cleansed three hundred thousand more Palestinians and occupied what remained of their land. That war brought new American capitulation as Israel launched a sustained, deadly attack on the USS *Liberty* by both air and sea, which the Johnson Administration called an "accident" as it tried to silence the survivors. More UN Resolutions, now pale ghosts of their 1948-1949 ancestors, were passed and ignored. The stranglehold on Palestine and Palestinians tightened, and the violent "peace" returned once more. Again in 1980, when Israel "annexed" East Jerusalem, several explicit Security Council Resolutions demanded it cease the expulsion of non-Jews and destruction of non-Jewish archaeological sites. Even though these Resolutions explicitly warned Israel that its rush to create "facts on the ground" would change nothing, they too quickly joined their predecessors in the graveyard of unrequited demands.[677]

Since every new Israeli defiance has been answered with weakened demands, Israel has since its birth been rewarded for its non-compliance. With every newly emasculated ruling, the previous, unenforced ones are forgotten, effectively "giving" Israel the difference. The "clock is restarted" regarding non-compliance, until the next, ever weaker and equally unenforced rulings incrementally "lower the bar" of what is, futilely, demanded of Israel. The settler state's crowning achievement was the Trojan horse known as the Oslo Accords, which effectively gave official sanction to everything it had imposed by force.

Nor are Palestinians alone made to pay for the settler state: Generations of Egyptians in particular have been condemned to the tyranny of pro-Israel regimes imposed upon them by United States money and force, a crushing obstacle to any popular, democratic "Arab spring."[678]

Israel's strangling of Gaza—profound, unremitting violence, even when it is not dropping bombs or shooting its farmers and fishermen—and its violent subjugation of East Jerusalem and the West Bank, are all sold as the unwanted burden placed upon a peace-seeking democracy saddled amidst uncivilized neighbours. We are conditioned to accept all this as we are conditioned to accept everything in Israel-Palestine: Israeli invasions are self-defense, and Palestinians resisting its invasions are terrorists. In the aftermath of 1967's newly-widened occupation, Avraham Shalom, former head of Shin Bet (Israel Security Agency), complained of a lack of purpose "because [Palestinian] terrorism hadn't developed." Intensified Israeli provocation was the answer: then, "luckily for us," Shalom continued, "terrorism increased."

When Hamas or fringe groups in Gaza retaliate against Israeli attacks, Israel alerts the world to the "terror attack" and "defends" itself by carnage against the very population Israel holds captive in the coastal enclave. In the wake of its "Cast Lead" operation (December 2008 – January 2009), Israel left behind what was supposed to be its worst nightmare—a vast stockpile of unexploded ordnance (UXO) *inside Gaza*—yet for fourteen months, Israel steadfastly blocked UN bomb experts from neutralizing this huge stockpile of explosive devices that Israel itself put there. It actively *prevented their destruction*, insuring that the vast cache of explosives would be taken by Hamas and, more dangerously for Israel, fringe groups—as, of course, happened. Soon, Israeli headlines decried "terrorism" when white phosphorus was fired into southern Israel.

With well over ten thousand Palestinians killed by Israel since the Oslo Accords, the US media religiously confine the discourse to two options: Most pundits, and the US Congress, offer unqualified support for Israeli attacks, while dissenting commentators suggest that Israel's actions might have been "disproportionate"—justified, yes, but perhaps a bit too much "defense." The spectrum of permissible debate lies entirely in the realm of narrative; what is actually happening remains unspoken. "Self-defense" is never questioned: Israel invokes it to block the rebuilding of the homes it bombs and the sewage plants it destroys, to keep out the doctors who care for its victims, to stifle access to food and potable water (95% of which in Gaza is now undrinkable), and above all to squash any form of Palestinian self-sufficiency or achievement.[679]

Addressing the root causes of the so-called "conflict" is and always has been in Israel's hands. Palestinians have no chips to bargain away except their inalienable right to justice. No Palestinian has ever occupied or laid siege to Israel. No Palestinian has ever controlled who may, and who may not, enter Israel, blocked Israeli students from pursuing their education or blocked Israeli musicians from performing or athletes from competing. Palestinians have never commandeered Israeli aquifers, decided for Israelis whom their elected leaders may be, whether they may see a doctor or travel to their own country or visit their family. Palestinians have never stopped Israeli children from playing the violin or Israeli schools from teaching Israeli history. No Palestinian has ever forbidden Israelis from putting a desk or books in a schoolroom or eating lentils or using shampoo without conditioner—all this an infinitesimal taste of Israel's totalitarian grip.

Palestinians have no Israeli prisoners to release, and the one time they did, he was an invading soldier. Yet whereas his capture (and ultimate release) became an international *cause célèbre*, we are unaware of and/or untroubled by the several thousand Palestinian civilians that are in Israeli dungeons at any one time, including hundreds of children, many tortured, and many held indefinitely without charge. Nor are we troubled by the IDF's nightly raids through the occupied West Bank to pull sleeping youths from their homes for allegedly resisting Israel's occupation of their villages. Through the kaleidoscope of the narrative that informs our morality, the capture of a single invading Israeli soldier is an act of terrorism, whereas the decades of Israeli prisons brimming full of Palestinian civilians kidnapped on Palestinian soil merely confirms the violent existential threat that is Israel's ever-present burden.[680]

When Palestinians are asked to compromise, what is actually meant is for them to give up yet more—even this they have done, but with political Zionism's original, unshakable goal not yet fully achieved, the "peace process" is and has always been a time-buying fraud. A solution will require untangling the injustice back not to 1967, but to 1947, and reconciliation with the truth back to the events of 1914-1917. The moment the ethno-nationalist movement of Zionism set sights on Palestine as a settler state based on claims of genetic entitlement, there was no other possible outcome but the tragedy seen in today's headlines. Terrorism—political violence against civilians—is the only means through which an indigenous population can be subjugated, dehumanized, and displaced.

This, stripped of all baggage, is the reality of today's Israel-Palestine "conflict."

Bibliography

Abu El-Haj, Nadia, *Facts on the Ground: Archaeological Practice and Territorial Self-Fashioning in Israeli Society*, [University of Chicago Press, 2002]

Abu-Lughod, Ibrahim (ed.), *Transformation of Palestine* [Northwestern University Press, 1987]

Anglo-Palestinian Club, *Palestine 1917-1944. Pamphlet No. 2. A Review by Sir Wyndham Deedes, The Hon. R. D. Denman, M.P., Mrs. E. Dugdale, Victor Gollancz, S.S. Hammersley, M.P. Sir Andrew McFadyean* [The Narod Press, London]

Arab Higher Committee, *Palestine The Arab Case, Being a statement made by the Delegation of the Arab Higher Committee before the first committee of the General Assembly of the United Nation's Organization on 9th May, 1947* [Cairo, Costa Tsoumas & Co., 1947]

Arab Higher Committee Delegation for Palestine, *The Black Paper on the Jewish Agency and Zionist Terrorism*, memorandum to *The United Nations Delegations*. Submitted by *The Arab Higher Committee Delegation for Palestine* 4512 Empire State Building, New York, NY. 12 March 1948. Copy examined: BL.

Bailes, Jon (ed.), Aksan, Cihan (ed), *Weapon of the Strong: Conversations on US State Terrorism* [Pluto, 2013]

Baumel, Judith Tydor, translation Dena Ordan, *The "Bergson Boys" And the Origins of Contemporary Zionist Militancy* [Syracuse University, 2005]

Bell, Bowyer, *Terror out of Zion: Irgun Zvai Leumi, LEHI, and the Palestine underground, 1929-1949* [St. Martin's 1977]

Ben-Yehuda, Nachman, *Political Assassinations by Jews: A Rhetorical Device for Justice* [SUNY Press, 1993]

Benziman, Uzi, *Sharon: An Israeli Caesar* [London: Robson Books, 1987]

Bishop, Patrick, *The Reckoning: Death and Intrigue in the Promised Land* [Kindle edition, HarperCollins, 2014]

Black, Edward, *The Transfer Agreement: The Dramatic Story of the Pact Between the Third Reich and Jewish Palestine* [Dialog Press, 2009]

Black, Ian, and Morris, Benny, *Israel's Secret Wars: A History of Israel's Intelligence Services* [Grove Press, 1992]

Burt, Leonard, *Commander Burt of Scotland Yard, by Himself.* [Heinemann, 1959]

Braun, Hanna, *Weeds Don't Perish*, Garnet Publishing, 2011. Also the author's conversation with Ms. Braun in London in 2007.

Brenner, Lenni, *Zionism in the Age of Dictators* [Croom Helm, 1983 / Kindle, Amazon Digital, 2015] — *51 Documents: Zionist Collaboration with the Nazis* [Barricade Books, 2010]

[British government], *Palestine Pamphlet Terrorist Methods With Mines and Booby Traps*. Headquarters, Chief Engineer, Palestine and Transjordan. December 1946.

Central Intelligence Agency, *The Consequences of the Partition of Palestine*, ORE 55, 28 November 1947 Copy No. 35.

Cesarani, David, *Major Farran's Hat: The Untold Story of the Struggle to Establish the Jewish State* [Da Capo Press, 2009]

Chomsky, Noam, *Fateful Triangle: The United States, Israel, and the Palestinians* [South End Press 1999]

Clarke, Thurston, *By Blood and Fire: The Attack on the King David Hotel* [Hutchinson, 1981]

Cohen, Michael, *Churchill and the Jews, 1900-1948* [Frank Cass, 2003]

Cohen, Stuart A., "A Still Stranger Aspect of Suez: British Operational Plans to Attack Suez," in *The International History Review*, Vol. 10, No. 2, May, 1988 — *English Zionists and British Jews: The Communal Politics of Anglo-Jewry, 1895-1920*, Princeton University Press, 1982

Davis, Uri, *Apartheid Israel* [Zed Books, 2003]

Dieckhoff, Alain, *The Invention of a Nation*. [Columbia University Press, 2003]

Dreyfus, Laurence, *Wagner and the Erotic Impulse*, [Harvard University Press, 2010]

Ehrlich, Mark Avrum, Encyclopedia of the Jewish Diaspora: Origins, Experiences, and Culture, Vol 1 [ABC-CLIO, 2008]

Elkins, Caroline (ed.), and Pedersen, Susan (ed), S*ettler Colonialism in the Twentieth Century: Projects, Practices, Legacies* [Routledge, 2005]

Ernst, Morris, *So Far So Good* [New York, Harper & Brothers, 1948]

Eveland, Wilbur Crane, *Ropes of Sand, America's Failure in the Middle East* [W W Norton & Co, 1980]

Feldman, Ilana, Governing Gaza [Duke University, 2008]

Filiu, Jean-Pierre, *Gaza: A History* [Comparative Politics and International Studies, Oxford University Press, Kindle Edition, 2014; translated by John King]

Fischbach, Michael R., *Records of Dispossession: Palestinian Refugee Property and the Arab-Israeli Conflict* [Columbia University Press, 2003]

Frantz, Douglas, & Collins, Catherine, *Death on the Black Sea* [HarperCollins, 2003]

Friedmann, Robert R. (ed), *Crime and Criminal Justice in Israel: Assessing the Knowledge Base Toward the Twenty-First Century* [State University of New York Press, 1998]

Gallagher, Nancy, *Quakers in the Israeli - Palestinian Conflict: The Dilemmas of NGO Humanitarian Activism* [American University in Cairo Press, 2007]

Gat, Moshe, *The Jewish Exodus from Iraq, 1948-1951* [Routledge 1997]

Giladi, Naeim, *Ben-Gurion's Scandals: How the Haganah and the Mossad Eliminated Jews*. [Dandelion Enterprises, 2006]

Golani, Motti, Palestine Between Politics & Terror [Brandeis University, 2013]

Gorny, Joseph, *The British Labour Movement and Zionism, 1917-1948* [Rutledge, 1983]

Greenfield, Murray, and Hochstein, Joseph, *The Jews' Secret Fleet: The Untold Story of North American Volunteers who Smashed the British Blockade*. [Gefen Publishing, 2010]

Grodzinsky, Yosef, *In the Shadow of the Holocaust: The Struggle Between Jews and Zionists in the Aftermath of World War II*. [Common Courage Press, July 1, 2004]

Grossman, Avraham, *Pious and Rebellious: Jewish Women in Medieval Europe*. [University Press of New England, 2004]

Herzl, Theodor, *Diaries of Theodor Herzl* [Grosset & Dunlap 1962]

— *Zionist Writings. Essays and Addresses. Volume 1: January 1896 - June, 1898.* Translated by Harry Zohn [NY, Herzl Press, 1973]

Hirst, David, *The Gun and the Olive Branch: The Roots of Violence in the Middle East* [Nation Books, 2003]

Hope Simpson, Sir John, Palestine. *Report on Immigration, Land Settlement and Development. Presented by the Secretary of State for the Colonies to Parliament by Command of His Majesty*. October, 1930.

Hutchison, Elmo Harrison, *Violent truce: A military observer looks at the Arab-Israeli conflict, 1951-1955* [Calder, 1956]

Institute for Palestine Studies, Arab Women's Information Committee, *Who Are the Terrorists? Aspects of Zionist and Israeli Terrorism* [Beirut: 1972]

Irgun Zvai Leumi, *Official Report of the Proceedings at a Conference between Representatives of the United Nations Special Committee on Palestine and of the Irgun Zvai Leumi, held in Palestine on 24 June, 1947. Published by the Diaspora Headquarters of the IRGUN ZVAI LEUMI By Authority of the High Command in Eretz Israel.* Copy examined, TNA, FO 371/61866. [Typewritten, not printed.]

Jeffries, J.M.N., *Palestine: The Reality* [1939; facsimile, Delhi, 2015]

Jewish Agency for Palestine, *Memorandum on Acts of Arab Aggression to Alter by Force the Settlement on the Future Government of Palestine Approved by the General Assembly of the United Nations, submitted to the United Nations Palestine Commission by the Jewish Agency for Palestine*. [Lake Success, New York, February 2, 1948. Copy examined: BL]

Jewish Legion, *Report of the Conference between Representatives of the United Nations Special Committee on Palestine and the Commander and Two Other Representatives of the Irgun Zvai Leumi*. [London: Published by the Jewish Legion, November, 1947] [Copied examined: TNA, KV 5/39]

Kapeliouk, Amnon, "New Light on the lsraeli-Arab Conflict and the Refugee Problem and Its Origins," in *Journal of Palestine Studies*, Vol. 16, No. 3, Spring, 1987.

Karmi, Ghada, *In Search of Fatima* [Verso, 2009]

— *Married to Another Man: Israel's Dilemma in Palestine* [Pluto, 2007]

Kesaris, Paul (ed), Dobrosky, Nanette (compiler), *A guide to the Microfilm Edition of U.S. State Department Central Files Palestine, United Nations Activities, 1945-1949* [University Publications of America, 1987]

Khalidi, Thabet, *The Rising Tide of Terror or Three Years of an "Armistice" in the Holy Land.* [Ministry of Foreign Affairs, Amman, 1952]

Khalidi, Walid, *All That Remains: The Palestinian Villages Occupied and Depopulated by Israel in 1948* [Institute for Palestine Studies, 2006]

— "Revisiting the UNGA Partition Resolution," *JPS*, XXVII, no.1 (Autumn 1997), 5-21.

Kirkbride, Alec, *From the Wings: Amman Memoirs 1947-1951* [Routledge 1976]

Kister, Joseph, *The Irgun the Story of the Irgun Zvai Leumi in Eretz-Israel* [Ministry of Defence Publishing House, 2000]

Koestler, Arthur, *Promise and Fulfilment Palestine 1917-1949* [Macmillan, 1949]

Kolsky, Thomas, *Jews Against Zionism: The American Council for Judaism, 1942-1948* [Temple University Press, 1992]

Lavie, Smadar, *Wrapped in the Flag of Israel: Mizrahi Single Mothers and Bureaucratic Torture* [Berghahn Books, 2014]

Lazin, Fred A., "Refugee Resettlement and "Freedom of Choice' - The Case of Soviet Jewry," Center for Immigration Studies [June 2005]

Lilienthal, Alfred M., *What Price Israel?* [Infinity Publishing, 2004]

Maov, Zeev, *Defending the Holy Land: A Critical Analysis of Israel's Security and Foreign Policy* [University of Michigan Press, 2006]

Masalha, Nur, *Expulsion of the Palestinians, the Concept of "Transfer" in Zionist Political Thought, 1882-1948* [Institute for Palestinian Studies, 1992 /2001]

Maxwell, ex-Sergeant Max, "An Explosive Situation," [personal account of the bombing of the Mallnitz train on August 12, 1947]. Accessed online January 20, 2012; and subsequent email exchanges with Mr. Maxwell.

Medoff, Rafael, *Militant Zionism in America: The Rise and Impact of the Jabotinsky Movement in the United States, 1926-1948.* [University of Alabama Press, 2006]

Menuhin, Moshe, *The decadence of Judaism in our time* [Beirut Institute for Palestine Studies, 1969]

Morris, Benny, *The Birth of the Palestinian Refugee Problem, 1947-1949* [Cambridge University Press, 1989]

— *The Birth of the Palestinian Refugee Problem Revisited* [Cambridge University Press, 2004]

— *Israel's Border Wars, 1949-1956: Arab Infiltration, Israeli Retaliation, and the Countdown to the Suez War* [Oxford: Clarendon Press, 1993]

— *Righteous Victims: A History of the Zionist-Arab Conflict, 1881-1998* [Vintage ed, 2011]

— *1948: A History of the First Arab-Israeli War* [Yale, 2009]

Morris, Ira R.T., & Smith, Joe Alex, *"Dear Mr. President ..." The Story of Fifty Years in the White House* [Julian Messner, 1949]

Murray S. Greenfield & Joseph Hochstein, *Jews Secret Fleet* [Gefen, 1996]

Nasr, Kameel B., *Arab and Israeli Terrorism: The Causes and Effects of Political Violence* [McFarland & Company, 2007]

Neff, Donald, *Fallen Pillars: U.S. Policy Towards Palestine and Israel Since 1945* [Institute for Palestine Studies, 2002]

Nicosia, Francis R., *The Third Reich and the Palestine Question* [Transaction Publishers, 2000]

Pappé, Ilan, *The Idea of Israel: A History Of Power And Knowledge* [Verso, 2014]

— Out of the Frame [Pluto, 2010, Kindle]

— *The Ethnic Cleansing of Palestine* [Oneworld Publications, 2007]

— *The Making of the Arab-Israeli Conflict 1947-1951* [I.B. Tauris, 1992]

— *A History of Modern Palestine* [Cambridge University, 2008]

Pedahzur, Ami, and Perliger Arie, *Jewish Terrorism in Israel* [Columbia University Press, 2011]

Pedahzur, Ami (ed.), and Weinberg, Leonard (ed), *Religious Fundamentalism and Political Extremism* [Frank Cass, 2004]

Polkehn, Klaus, "The Secret Contacts: Zionism and Nazi Germany, 1933-1941," in *Journal of Palestine Studies*, Vol. 5, No. 3/4 (1976), 54-82

Pragnell, F. A., *Palestine Chronicle, 1880-1950: Extracts from the Arabic Press Tracing the Main Political and Social Developments* [Pragnell Books, 2005]

Quigley, John, *Palestine and Israel: A Challenge to Justice* [Durham and London: Duke University Press, 1990]

Qumsiyeh, Mazin B., *Popular Resistance in Palestine: A History of Hope and Empowerment* [Pluto Press, 2006]

Rabinovich, Itamar, and Reinharz, Jehuda (eds), *Israel in the Middle East: Documents and Readings on Society, Politics, and Foreign Relations, Pre-1948 to the Present* [Brandeis University, 2007]

Reinharz, Shulamit, and Schor, Laura S., *The Best School in Jerusalem: Annie Landau's School for Girls, 1900-1960* [HBI Series on Jewish Women, Brandeis University, 2013]

Rhett, Maryanne A., *The Global History of the Balfour Declaration: Declared Nation* [Routledge 2015]

Rogan, Eugene, *The Arabs a History* [Basic Books, 2011]

Rokach, Livia, *Israel's Sacred Terrorism: A Study Based on Moshe Sharett's Personal Diary and Other Documents* [Assn of Arab-American University Graduates, 1985]

Roosevelt, Kermit, *The Arab Position on Palestine*, Presented at the National War College, Washington, DC, 24 November, 1948

— *Partition of Palestine A Lesson in Pressure Politics*, The Institute of Arab American Affairs, NY, February, 1948

Rose, John, *The Myths of Zionism* [London: Pluto Press, 2004]

Ryan, Joseph L, "Refugees Within Israel The Case of the Villagers of Kafr Bir'im and Iqrit," in *Journal of Palestine Studies*, Vol. 2, No. 4, Summer, 1973, 55-81

Said, Edward, *Orientalism* [Vintage Books, 1979]

Sand, Schlomo, *The Invention of the Jewish People* [Verso, 2009]

Scott, James M., *The Attack on the Liberty: The Untold Story of Israel's Deadly 1967 Assault on a U.S. Spy Ship* [Simon & Schuster, 2009]

Schwartz, Ted, *Walking with the Damned* [New York: Paragon, 1992]

Segev, Tom, *One Palestine, Complete: Jews and Arabs Under the British Mandate*

[Picador, 2001]

Sharett, Moshe, The 1953 Qibya Raid Revisited: Excerpts from Moshe Sharett's Diaries Introduced by Walid Khalidi and Annotated by Neil Caplan. In *Journal of Palestine Studies*, XXXI, no. 4 (Summer 2002), pages 77-98.

Shlaim, Avi, "The Protocol of Sèvres, 1956: Anatomy of a War Plot," in *International Affairs*, 73:3, 1997, 509-530

Sitkowski, Andrzej, *UN Peacekeeping: Myth and Reality* [Praeger, 2006]

Smith, Charles, *Palestine and the Arab-Israeli Conflict: A History with Documents* [Bedford/St. Martin's, 2010]

Stein, Kenneth W., "The Jewish National Fund: Land Purchase Methods and Priorities, 1924-1939," in *Middle Eastern Studies*, Volume 20 Number 2, 190-205, April 1984.

Sternhell, Zeev (translation D. Maisel), *The Founding Myths of Israel* [Princeton University Press 1999]

Strawson, John, *Partitioning Palestine Legal Fundamentalism in the Palestinian-Israeli Conflict*. [Pluto, 2010]

Tamari, Salim, (ed.), Jerusalem 1948: The Arab Neighbourhoods and Their Fate in the War. [Inst for Palestine Studies, 2002]

Teveth, Shabtai, *Ben-Gurion and the Palestinian Arabs: From Peace to War* [Oxford University Press, 1985]

Tomes, Jason, *Balfour and Foreign Policy: The International Thought of a Conservative Statesman* [Cambridge University Press, 1997]

Veracini, Lorenzo, *Israel and Settler Society* [Pluto, 2006]

Wagner, Steven, "British Intelligence and the Jewish Resistance Movement in the Palestine Mandate, 1945-46," in *Intelligence and National Security*, Volume 23, Issue 5, 2008, 629-657

Walton, Calder, *Empire of Secrets: British Intelligence, the Cold War, and the Twilight of Empire* [Overlook, 2013]

Wendehorst, Stephan E. C., *British Jewry, Zionism, and the Jewish State, 1936-1956* [Oxford University Press 2011]

Wilson, Major-General Dare, *With 6th Airborne Division in Palestine 1945-1948* [Gale and Polden Ltd, 1949 /Kindle, 2008]

Wistrich, Robert S., *From Ambivalence to Betrayal: The Left, the Jews, and Israel* [Studies in Antisemitism, University of Nebraska Press, 2012]

Zertel, Idith, *Israel's Holocaust and the Politics of Nationhood* [Cambridge University Press, 2005]

Sources used at The National Archives (Kew)

ADM 116/3690
AIR 2/98
AIR 5/1155
AIR 8/1895
AIR 81/7
AN 2/204
CAB 104/7
CAB 104/8
CAB 128/18-0027
CAB 128/29-0015
CAB 128/29-0027
CAB 128/29-0030
CAB 128/6-0012
CAB 128/6-0013
CAB 128/9-0006
CAB 128/9-0030
CAB 128/9-0033
CAB 129/10-0038
CAB 129/14-0014
CAB 129/16/0049
CAB 129/16/3
CAB 129/17-0045
CAB 129/18-0007
CAB 129/19-0011
CAB 129/2-0015
CAB 129/21-0012

CAB 129/32-0010
CAB 129/74-0046
CAB 129/75-0035
CAB 129/75-0036
CAB 129/76-0037
CAB 129/77-0027
CAB 129/9-0019
CAB 129/9-0023
CAB 129/9-0025
CAB 158/1
CAB 195/02/0058
CAB 195/13-0057
CAB 195/14-0006
CAB 195/5-0006
CAB 195/8-0037
CAB 21/2567
CAB 21/58
CAB 23/4
CAB 23/4-0001
CAB 23/4-0019
CAB 23/78-0014
CAB 23/89-0006
CAB 23/94-0006
CAB 23/97
CAB 24/1
CAB 24/2

CAB 24/8
CAB 24/9
CAB 24/18
CAB 24/22-0017
CAB 24/24-0003
CAB 24/24-0004
CAB 24/26-0015
CAB 24/263-0020
CAB 24/263-0055
CAB 24/27-0058
CAB 24/27-0093
CAB 24/270-0008
CAB 24/272-0015
CAB 24/278-0028
CAB 24/278
CAB 24/28-0063
CAB 24/282-0005
CAB 24/36-0032
CAB 24/4-0014
CAB 27/1
CAB 65/34/21-0001
CAB 65/48-0009
CAB 66/13/48-0001
CAB 66/58-0028
CAB 67/4/17-0001
CAB 79/48

CAB 80/98/33
CAB 95/14
CN 5/2
CO 1069/732
CO 1069/734
CO 1071/305
CO 1071/306
CO 1071/307
CO 1071/308
CO 1071/309
CO 1071/310
CO 323/1603/3
CO 323/1605/2
CO 323/1605/4
CO 323/1606/1
CO 323/1606/3
CO 323/1607/1
CO 323/1652/43
CO 537/1709
CO 537/1711
CO 537/1712
CO 537/1715
CO 537/1720
CO 537/1723
CO 537/1729
CO 537/1814
CO 537/1820
CO 537/1821
CO 537/1838
CO 537/2270
CO 537/2285
CO 537/2288
CO 537/2292
CO 537/2295
CO 537/2297
CO 537/2303
CO 537/2366
CO 537/3854
CO 537/3855
CO 537/3856
CO 537/3857
CO 537/3858
CO 537/3860
CO 537/3861

CO 537/3872
CO 67/373/9
CO 730/153/5
CO 730/175/10
CO 733/190/5
CO 733/250/1
CO 733/272/12
CO 733/275/4
CO 733/283/12
CO 733/302/6
CO 733/316/11
CO 733/333/8
CO 733/370/11
CO 733/380/1
CO 733/401/19
CO 733/415/4
CO 733/420/19
CO 733/439/20
CO 733/439/20
CO 733/441/4
CO 733/443/18
CO 733/443/19
CO 733/443/21
CO 733/444/17
CO 733/446/11
CO 733/446/4
CO 733/449/34
CO 733/456/9
CO 733/456/10
CO 733/456/11
CO 733/456/12
CO 733/456/2
CO 733/456/3
CO 733/456/4
CO 733/456/6
CO 733/456/7
CO 733/456/8
CO 733/456/9
CO 733/457/11
CO 733/457/12
CO 733/457/13
CO 733/457/14
CO 733/457/2
CO 733/457/3

CO 733/457/4
CO 733/457/5
CO 733/457/6
CO 733/457/9
CO 733/458/13
CO 733/463/21
CO 733/477/3
CO 733/477/4
CO 733/477/5
CO 733/478/1
CO 733/478/2
CO 733/478/3
CO 733/490/3
CO 733/58
CO 73325813
CO 79347
CO 967/103
CO 967/96
CRIM 1/1951
DEFE 4/76
ED 49/10397
EF 5/12
FCO 141/14270
FCO 141/14271
FCO 141/14280
FCO 141/14283
FCO 141/14284
FCO 141/14286
FCO 141/14290
FCO 141/14292
FO 1018/70
FO 1020/361
FO 1020/1774
FO 1020/2279
FO 1071/39
FO 1093/330
FO 1093/444
FO 1093/508
FO 1103/1087
FO 122/3
FO 141/1001
FO 141/666
FO 141/805
FO 262/1741

FO 266/120
FO 226/306
FO 369/4021
FO 371/102121
FO 371/104735
FO 371/104779
FO 371/104781
FO 371/104782
FO 371/104785
FO 371/104788
FO 371/104789
FO 371/104791
FO 371/108548
FO 371/110941
FO 371/111069
FO 371/111098
FO 371/111101
FO 371/111104
FO 371/114788
FO 371/114789
FO 371/115816
FO 371/115898
FO 371/115905
FO 371/121692
FO 371/121744
FO 371/121776
FO 371/121794
FO 371/121804
FO 371/151273
FO 371/23245
FO 371/32662
FO 371/40125
FO 371/40126
FO 371/40127
FO 371/40129
FO 371/40130
FO 371/40131
FO 371/45376
FO 371/45377
FO 371/45378
FO 371/45381
FO 371/45382
FO 371/45383
FO 371/45385

FO 371/45386
FO 371/45387
FO 371/45406
FO 371/52530
FO 371/52563
FO 371/60138
FO 371/60786
FO 371/61761
FO 371/61768
FO 371/61770
FO 371/61771
FO 371/61773
FO 371/61776
FO 371/61783
FO 371/61865
FO 371/61866
FO 371/61914
FO 371/61915
FO 371/64126
FO 371/67796
FO 371/67813B
FO 371/68502
FO 371/68504
FO 371/68512
FO 371/68648
FO 371/68649
FO 371/68650
FO 371/68651
FO 371/68663B
FO 371/68674
FO 371/68697
FO 371/75192
FO 371/75340
FO 371/75344
FO 371/75350
FO 371/75365
FO 371/75376
FO 371/75377
FO 371/75387
FO 371/75396
FO 371/75397
FO 371/75399
FO 371/75400
FO 371/75401

FO 371/75402
FO 371/75455
FO 371/82176
FO 371/82619
FO 371/82703
FO 371/82706
FO 371/89806
FO 371/91376
FO 371/91383
FO 371/91385
FO 371/91386
FO 371/91387
FO 371/91402
FO 371/91692
FO 371/91715
FO 371/91725
FO 371/97020
FO 371/98484
FO 371/98490
FO 371/98492
FO 371/98493
FO 371/98767
FO 608/99
FO 624/191
FO 684/10
FO 78/5479
FO 800/221
FO 800/484
FO 800/485
FO 800/486
FO 800/487
FO 816/179
FO 83/1723
FO 800/484
FO 881/4907
FO 905/111
FO 917/2315
FO 919/5
FO 921/156B
FO 953/728
FO 954/19A
GFM 33/97
HO 45/25586
HS 4/115

HW1/2498
KV 2/1390
KV 2/1435
KV 2/2252
KV 2/2264
KV 2/2956
KV 2/3170
KV 2/3171
KV 2/3176
KV 2/3266
KV 2/3428
KV 2/3680
KV 2/3779
KV 3/41
KV 3/41
KV 3/437
KV 3/438
KV 3/439
KV 3/440
KV 3/441
KV 3/56
KV 3/67
KV 4/467
KV 5/11
KV 5/14
KV 5/29
KV 5/30
KV 5/31
KV 5/32
KV 5/33
KV 5/34
KV 5/35

KV 5/36
KV 5/37
KV 5/38
KV 5/39
KV 5/4
KV 5/40
KV 5/41
KV2 2251
KV2 2252
OS 3/419
PREM 11/2691
PREM 11/945
PREM 8/1251
PREM 8/1275
PREM 8/860
TS 13/3127
TS 27/175
TS 27/198
WO 169/48
WO 169/148
WO 169/183
WO 169/22957
WO 169/24225
WO 169/23031
WO 169/23233
WO 169/4334
WO 193/68
WO 201/230
WO 208/1705
WO 208/1706
WO 261/562
WO 261/564

WO 261/566
WO 261/571
WO 261/647
WO 261/648
WO 261/656
WO 261/657
WO 261/658
WO 261/659
WO 261/660
WO 274/79
WO 275/27
WO 275/29
WO 275/30
WO 275/31
WO 275/32
WO 275/33A
WO 275/33B
WO 275/34
WO 275/35
WO 275/36
WO 275/38
WO 275/58
WO 275/64
WO 275/73
WO 275/83
WO 275/86
WO 275/121
WO 32/11347
WO 32/11352
WO 32/21899

End Notes

BL = British Library
CIA = Central Intelligence Agency (US)
JTA = Jewish Telegraphic Agency
LOC = Library of Congress (Washington, D.C.)
NYT = New York Times
TNA = The National Archives (Kew)
ZOA = Zionist Organization of America

Introduction

1. TNA, FO 1093/330.
2. TNA, KV 5/34, 112a. See also FO 371/68504, 17-18.
3. TNA, CO 733/477/5, 148.
4. See Bibliography for works by Lilienthal, Menuhin, and Pappé. For extending terms of classified Zionist documents, see e.g., Barak Ravid, "State archives to stay classified for 20 more years, PM instructs," in *Haaretz*, July 28, 2010.
5. By the mid nineteenth century, more than half of the Jews in Palestine were foreign-born. Population figures from Itamar Rabinovich and Jehuda Reinharz (eds), *Israel in the Middle East: Documents and Readings on Society, Politics, and Foreign Relations, Pre-1948 to the Present* (The Tauber Institute for the Study of European Jewry Series), as cited on Jewish Virtual Library, accessed 4 Nov 2015; the c1900 figure from Justin McCarthy's study as cited in Wikipedia, "Demographic history of Palestine," accessed July 23, 2016.
6. "The bride is beautiful, but she is married to another man," was a cable sent by two Rabbis in Palestine in 1897, reporting on the feasibility of establishing a Zionist state. See Ghada Karmi's *Married to Another Man* [Pluto Press, 2007]; Benny Morris, *Revisited*, 5-6, argues that while "the evidence for pre-1948 Zionist support for 'Transfer' really is unambiguous,"

the ethnic cleansing of 1948 was not "tantamount to a master plan." This argument defies the unequivocal deliberateness and years of planning behind what happened, and fails to explain why, if it was not the "plan," Israel to this day steadfastly blocks the refugees' return. Morris, indeed, "bemoans the fact that the job was left unfinished" (2004 interview, "Survival of the fittest," Ari Shavit, in *Haaretz*, January 8, 2004, haaretz.com/survival-of-the-fittest-1.61345 retrieved June 16, 2014. For Palestinian agricultural and industrial productivity expanding markedly in the nineteenth century, before Zionist presence, see e.g., Smith, *Palestine*, 22-23.

7. Regarding the common use of "terrorism" for violence against the military, for example, the bombings of the 1995 Oklahoma City bombing and the 1983 Beirut US Marine compound bombing, which were government and military targets respectively, are usually referred to as terrorism.

8. Virtually all Zionist leaders subscribe to all these justifications against democracy, but specific mention in this book includes Weizmann claiming "Arabs" are inferior people and so do not deserve a vote he and Begin arguing that all Jews are, by blood, "nationals" of Palestine; all, including Ben-Gurion, arguing that Jews were a majority in a vast Biblical realm, and that this gives alleged descendants the right to "return"; and Ben-Gurion arguing explicitly (and all others at least implicitly) that the Zionist state is not bound by the norms governing any other nation. International Humanitarian Law prohibits "acts of terrorism" against persons not or no longer taking part in hostilities. https://www.icrc.org/eng/resources/documents/faq/terrorism-faq-050504.htm (accessed Mar 2, 2015). The US Joint Chiefs of Staff definition: Terrorism is the unlawful use of violence or threat of violence, often motivated by religious, political, or other ideological beliefs, to instill fear and coerce governments or societies in pursuit of goals that are usually political. (Joint Publication 3-26, Counterterrorism, 24 October 2014). For further discussion on definitions of "terrorism" (no variation of which would affect this book's working definition), see Cihan and Bailes, Introduction to *Weapon of the Strong*; Sulzberger was also an important US judge at the turn of the twentieth century; Richard P. Stevens, "Zionism as a Phase of Western Imperialism," in Abu-Lughod, *Transformation*, 40-41; TNA, FO 608/99, 281-295, esp 287-288; Jewish Legion, *Report of the Conference...*; FO 1093/330, after 48, 12; UNSCOP A/364/Add.2 PV.19 (7 July 1947). Many Zionist leaders distrusted democracy even within the Jewish community. It was for Ben-Gurion an enemy in the "building of Eretz Israel by the Jewish people"; he and others argued that Zionists knew what was best for Jews and thus did not require their majority support (see e.g., the Begin "conference" with the UNSCOP committee in the present book, in TNA, KV 5/39, and Sternhell, *Founding Myths*, 190-191).

9. TNA, FO 371/91715, 29; for more Zionist settler analogy to European colonization of America, e.g., NYT, Jan 27 1947; The Israeli state's claim on language enables its Ministry of Defense to publish a book glorifying even the most ghastly terrorism of the Mandate period (Kister, *Irgun*).

10. TNA, CO 733/316/11, 4-6. See also Wasif Jawhariyyeh, *Storyteller of Jerusalem: The Life and Times of Wasif Jawhariyyeh, 1904-1948* [Olive Branch, 2013], 228-229.

11. Regarding the far more lenient treatment of Jews, the opposite claim was (and is) sometimes made, apparently based on a *Jewish Chronicle* report from 11

February 1944 alleging a few cases in which Arabs received lesser sentences than Jews had for the same charges. These specific cases involved possession of pistols and bullets. See TNA, FO 371/40126, "Discrepancies between sentences awarded in Palestine to Jews and Arabs for similar offences." A telegram 299 commented on the "circumstances of the cases in question."

12. One may find a two or three percent disparity in published percentages for the Partition. The reason is that Resolution 181 established an international zone comprising Jerusalem and Bethlehem, and so some figures tally Israel and Palestine combined as slightly short of 100%, while others, such as that quoted herein, exclude it, dividing the remainder; *NYT*, 19 Jan 1949, 10 Jan 1949. For Britain's claim that it bore no responsibility to keep peace Palestine when it decided to end the Mandate, see e.g., FO 800/487, 55.

13. Regarding Israel and foreign aid to the Palestinians, see also Jonathan Cook, "Study: At least 78% of humanitarian aid intended for Palestinians ends up in Israeli coffers," *Mondoweiss*, 8 March 2016; Amira Haas, "Not an internal Palestinian matter," *Haaretz*, 4 Oct 2006.

14. Although British reports usually used the generic "Arab," one clear example of the deliberate use of "Palestinian" is seen in a report about the bombing of the King David Hotel in July of 1946, which uses the term "Palestinian employees" (rather than "Arab employees") to account for nearly half of the fatalities; TNA, WO 275/58, 6 Airborne Division, Intelligence Summary No. 3 (to 26 July 46).

Chapter One — The Third Temple

15. Anstruther Mackay, "Zionist Aspirations in Palestine," *The Atlantic Monthly*, July 1920.

16. *Falastin*, 3 Nov 1922, quoted from *Palestine Chronicle*.

17. For an analysis of Zionism's settler colonialism, see Robinson, *Citizen Strangers*. For similarities to traditional settler ventures, see, e.g., Veracini, *Israel and Settler Society*; Ben-Gurion quote, NYT, 8 Jan 1937; this was to the Peel Commission, and his use of the word "mandate" in regard to the Bible was a play on the British *Mandate*; Also, e.g., Jewish right to take Palestine "is based on the ancient mandate of the Bible" in TNA, WO 275/121, Appendix A, The Voice of Israel.

18. For Weizmann, CO 537/1711, 29; for Lehi, Pedahzur & Perliger, *Jewish Terrorism*, 11; Weizmann warned Churchill in 1946 that failure to accede to Zionists' demands for ethnicity-based minority rule in Palestine would mean the "destruction of the Third Temple," thus "destroying the last hope of hundreds of thousands of Jews throughout the world." Ben-Gurion, singing "the song of Moses and the Children of Ancient Israel," spoke of IDF conquests that "will become a part of the third kingdom of Israel" and of "IDF divisions [who] extended a hand to King Solomon" (Sand, *Invention*, 108). Judaism and the Bible are invoked even for the names Israel assigns its wars; Genesis, the Biblical six days of Creation, is invoked in the name "Six Day War" (1967 war; Rabin chose the name. See Michael Oren, *Six Days of War*, 309 [Ballantine, 2003]); more recently, "Cast Lead," Israel's 2008-2009 attacks against Gaza, refers to a Hanukkah festival; and "Pillar of Cloud," its 2012 assault against Gaza, is a reference to the Biblical Exodus; Moshe

Dayan equated the Suez War with the Exodus, and the 1948 and 1967 wars with the conquest of Canaan (Sand, *Invention*, 112); Zertal, *Israel's Holocaust*, 93; Congressional Record, 1922 House of Representatives, June 30, 1922B, *National Home in Palestine for the Jewish People, cont. Pages 9809–.9820.*

19. Herzl, *Diaries*, 283. Regarding the fight between adopting Hebrew or Yiddish, etc., as the settlers' "native" tongue, see Dieckhoff, *Invention of a Nation*, ch 3.

20. For Jacob Melnik, see *The Jewish Transcript*, Seattle, 11 Feb 1938, and after the appeal, Evening Telegraph & Post, Dundee, Jan 30 1939, Nottingham Evening Post, Jan 30 1939; a comprehensive account is in The Kentucky Jewish Chronicle, Feb 25, 1938; Grossman, *Pious and Rebellious*, 68; Irgun/Torah, KV 5/40, Principles of Hebrew Freedom Mov't.

21. Ben-Gurion, "The Redemption," *Der Yiddisher Kempfer*, 39, 16 Nov 1917 (Quoted from Zertal, 93); For Meinertzhagen, TNA, FO 608/99, 510.

22. 'Jewish" citizenship most recently reaffirmed in 2013; see *Haaretz*, Supreme Court rejects citizens' request to change nationality from 'Jewish' to "Israeli," 3 Oct 2013; The Israeli government does not recognize an Israeli citizenship. (See Jonathan Ofir, "Israelis Don't Exist," in *Mondoweiss*, 25 March 2016). Regarding the Jewish Brigade and Jewish "nationality," see TNA, WO 193/68, Minute Sheet 35, MS, verso Israel has, in a few test cases precipitated by individuals to contest the state on this issue, denied citizenship to a "Jew" who has converted to another religion and legally challenged his Israeli identity on that account; For Hagana, NYT, 8 Mar 1948; Ben-Gurion to Amos, 1937, I have used the new, critical translation by JPS; underlined 'obliged' is original; For an analysis of the various genetic theories being flaunted since the mid nineteenth century regarding blood descent and the Jewish "race," see Sand, *Invention*, esp ch 5.

23. Special Committee on Palestine Verbatim Record of the Nineteenth Meeting, Held at the Y.M.C.A. Building Jerusalem, Palestine, Monday, 7 July 1947; Ben-Gurion also applied ethnicity arguments to the Palestinians: at his UN testimony, he argued that since the Palestinians are "Arabs," and there were already many lands with "Arabs," that therefore "they" (the "Arabs") already had sovereign land and didn't need Palestine; Regarding medieval mapmakers, depending on the geographer and, ultimately, on the viewer, *mappaemundi* could represent a spherical earth, where Palestine formed the central vantage point; or a flat earth, in which case Palestine's middle-earth location was literal. For PEF, Abu El-Haj, *Facts on the Ground*; Begin, Irgun Zvai Leumi, *Official Report*. The Palestine Exploration Fund's Biblical mind set is evident even into the Mandate period; see e.g., TNA, CO 1071/305, *Report on his Britannic Majesty's Government on the Administration Under Mandate of Palestine and Transjordan for the year 1924*, 5.

24. Segev, *Complete*, 394; in TNA, FO 919/5 (loose), is a telegram dated July 15, 1938, sent to London by Lipman Schalit (who apparently was attending the Conference), which says that Roosevelt could grant five years' quota to German Jewish emigrants to be used right away, without going through Congress; Ben-Gurion quote, Rose, *Myths*, 145; Brenner, *51 Documents*, 149 & 159 n23; "If I knew that it would be possible to save all the [Jewish] children in Germany by bringing them over to England, and only half of them to Eretz Israel, then I would opt for the second alternative"; Braun

(*Weeds*, 66) states that Ben-Gurion expressed this "more than once"; Also see Segev, *Complete*, 394; Segev, a staunch supporter of the Israeli state, nonetheless notes 1930s Zionists' "tendency to see the Jews of Europe as 'human material' necessary to establish the state, rather than seeing the state as a means to save the Jews."

25. Grodzinsky, *Shadow*; Irgun, Herzog, TNA CO 537/1705; KV 5/34, 8c; CO 733/415/4, 20-24; CIA, *Consequences*, 14; Weizmann, TNA, FO 608/99, 281-295; Ben-Gurion, Quigley, *Challenge*, ch 3; Ernst, *So Far So Good*, 173-177; also TNA, FO 800/487, 110. Regarding Zionism's need to confine Jewish settlement to Palestine alone, in 1940 Sharret allegedly deflected criticism by saying that he welcomes all plans for Jewish colonization in countries other than Palestine because any such endeavor is doomed to fail (TNA, WO 169/148, "Situation Report," 2).

26. Braun, *Weeds*, 82-83; and the author's conversations with Ms. Braun in London, 2007.

27. Masalha, *Expulsion*, 7; Erskine B. Childers, "The Wordless Wish: From Citizens to Refugees," in Abu-Lughod, *Transformation*, 166; Richard Crossman, Palestine Mission: A Personal Record (1947), 159, quoted in Quigley, *Challenge*, ch 3; Rothschild, TNA FO 608/99, 218; at a meeting with British officials on March 22, 1919; For early Palestinian resistance, Qumsiyeh, *Resistance*, 41.

28. Asher Zvi Ginzberg (pen-name Ahad Ha'Am), see Menuhin, *Decadence*, 63-64; and others.

29. Nathan, see NYT, 18 Jan 1914 (also note "arrogant Zionist activity" and "overwrought Jewish nationalist chauvinism"); for Eduard Bernstein, see Wistrich, *Ambivalence to Betrayal*, 147.

30. T. E. Lawrence, letter to Sir Mark Sykes, 9 Sep 1917; TNA, CO 733/272/12; Traveller was Laurence Oliphant in 1882, in the Plain of Esdraelon; see Quigley, *Challenge*, ch 1.

31. For JNF, see e.g., Stein, "The Jewish National Fund," 190-205; Hope Simpson, ch 5.

32. Hope Simpson, ch 1.

33. Confirmation of Simpson, e.g., CO 733/283/12, penciled 50-51; field mice, Hope Simpson, ch 1; Sharett, TNA, PREM 11/945, 24.

34. Lewis French, *Supplementary Report on Agricultural Development and Land Settlement in Palestine*; TNA, CO 733/272/12 (Parkinson quote from verso of penciled '11').

35. At the time (1895), Herzl wrote in context of a proposed Zionist colony in Argentina. *Diaries*, vol. 1 88, 90. For Ben-Gurion, see Erskine B. Childers, "The Wordless Wish: From Citizens to Refugees," in Abu-Lughod, *Transformation*, 168. Labour, *ibid*, 174, and Gershon Shafir, in Elkins / Pedersen, *Settler Colonialism*, 41-46. Other techniques, such as pouring gasoline on Arabs' produce, further starved out the native population (see, e.g., Pappé, *Ethnic Cleansing*).

36. *Falastin*, 25 Mar 1924, in *Palestine Chronicle*.

37. Regarding Sir Ellis Kadoorie, the author examined Kadoorie's original will in Kew, FO 917/2315; TS 27/175, letter by J.E. Shuckburgh from Downing Street, 24 May, 1923; TS 27/198; "Mrs. Bertha Guggenheimer Leaves $125,000 Bequests," JTA, March 14, 1927. The fund's administrator was Stephen Wise, then acting president of New York's Jewish Institute of Religion; for Zionist reaction, see Segev, *Complete*, 390-391.

38. Ben-Gurion, *Palestine Royal Commission Notes of Evidence*.

39. J.A. Constitution, see Article 3, sections d & e; John Ruedy, "Dynamics of Land Alienation," in Abu-Lughod, *Transformation*, 130.

40. Israel, Law of Return, 2nd amendment, 1970, section 4.a.

41. Reagan, see, e.g., Lazin, *Refugee Resettlement*...; Today, Israeli global "ownership" of Jews can be seen, for example, in its blocking of Jews of any nationality from entering the Arab old city of Hebron in the Palestinian West Bank (e.g., in November, 2014 the author, entering the old city to teach violin, was detained by two IDF soldiers for refusing to deny that he is Jewish, and was freed only by stating that he is Christian).

42. Herzl, *Zionist Writings*. 167; also *The World*, October 15, 1897, quoted from Dreyfus, *Wagner*, 165-166.

43. *London Standard*, 6 Sep, 1897, 5.

44. TNA, CAB 24/28/0063, 2; CAB 24/4/0014, 7. For support of Zionism among Nazis, see e.g., Nicosia, *Third Reich*, 19-21.

Chapter Two — Zionism and the British Mandate to 1938

45. TNA, FO 608/99, 277-288.

46. TNA, FO 371/68649, 43.

47. Yitzhak Epstein, *The Hidden Question*, Aug 1907 (lecture delivered at the Seventh Zionist Congress in Basel, 1905).

48. Chamberlain, see Abu-Lughod, *Transformation*, 35, 37; Herzl, *Diaries* (Lowenthal), 412, 407; Herzl, *Jewish State*; For same principle espoused by Weizmann, see CO 733/443/18, MS '25 To JS MacPherson' in upper left; See also Weizmann comment in CO 733/443/18, E 2399/87/31, verso, regarding psychological value of Palestine as Jewish settler state; Herzl pushing for Jewish settlement in the Sinai, FO 78/5479; Post-World War I Cyprus still proposed as part of a "Greater Palestine," see FO 608/99, letter from David Treitsch.

49. Cohen, *English Zionists and British Jews*, 83-84; also *Cheltenham Chronicle and Gloucestershire Graphic*, 12 Sep 1903. East Africa was the immediate target site in 1903.

50. 1905 Aliens Act. For quotes, Tomes, *Balfour and Foreign Policy*, 201; Cohen, *Churchill and the Jews*, 19. Abu-Lughod, *Transformation*, 45-46; Asquith said Lloyd George supported Zionism to keep the French away from Palestine.

51. TNA CAB 24/4/0014, 4; CAB 21/58; CAB 24/28/0063, 3; CAB 24/4/0014, 2; CAB 21/58; See also Bentwich quote from 1909 commingling Jews and nationality; the original proposed clause would have guaranteed "the rights and political status enjoyed in any other country by such Jews who are fully contented with their existing nationality and citizenship." Regarding the

Zionists' attempt to have the Balfour Declaration read "re-establishment" rather than "establishment," in 1935 the British government's unabashedly pro-Zionist report on Palestine and Trans-Jordan referred to the "re-settlement" of the "Jewish people" in Palestine (TNA, CO 1071/310, 19); For Weizmann's wish that the Balfour Declaration refer to the "Jewish race," see Rhett, *Balfour*, 31-32.

52. Montefiore, TNA CAB 21/58, 80-81; Montagu, letter to Robert Cecil, 1st Viscount Cecil of Chelwood, Sep 1917, CAB 24/27/0093, "Memo on British Government's Anti-Semitism." Regarding Zionism and the US entry into World War I, Patrick Bishop (*Reckoning*, K Locations 175-176) writes that "...pro-Zionist declarations were thought useful to coax a reluctant United States into the fray," without further explanation; James A. Malcolm, twelve-page typewritten document entitled "Origins of the Balfour Declaration Dr. Weizmann's Contribution," London, 1944, The British Museum, reprinted by the Institute for Historical Review, 1983; TNA, KV 2/3171, letter from Malcolm to Weizmann, 18 June, 1948.

53. Weizmann, CAB 24/4/0014, 5.

54. Cabinet meeting of 3 Sept 1917, see TNA, CAB 23/4, large 25, 80.

55. TNA, CAB 23/4, large 25, 80; Proskauer, FO 800/486, 137; Strawson, *Partitioning Palestine*, 33; for Rothschild-Weizmann letter of 3 Oct 1917, FO 371/61783, penciled "59" upper right; in this letter, Rothschild and Weizmann also noted that their "extensive propaganda for a Jewish Palestine" was carried out with British approval.

56. TNA, FO 608/99, 106, 475-484; As reported by British Major-General Thwaites in February of 1919, Weizmann "wants to be able to give an assurance to the Jews throughout the world [that] a Jewish country will be established in, say, one or two years [i.e., by 1921]."

57. TNA, FO 608/99, 106, 114, 153; The new term "Jewish Commonwealth" apparently originated with the American Jewish Congress.

58. *ibid*, 104.

59. *ibid*, 513; for Meinertzhagen's anti-Semitism, see e.g., Segev, *Complete*, 95.

60. For Meinertzhagen, TNA, FO 608/99, 514; Britain did not release the Meinertzhagen document because it presumed that Britain would be the Mandatory power in Palestine, which was not yet legally official; Sir Erle Richards, among many others, explicitly states that no Jewish state was promised and indeed would be contrary to pledges given to Arabs (4 Feb 1919); FO 608/99, 15; Weizmann quote, FO 608/99, 281-295.

61. TNA, FO 608/99, 286-288, 281-283, obvious typos corrected.

62. TNA, FO 608/99, 385, 388, and others. Ilan Pappé records what appear to be later instances of this: "In 1920 and 1921, these protests [against Zionism], especially in urban centres such as Jerusalem and Jaffa, turned violent as a result of either Zionist provocation, as in the case of Jerusalem in April 1920..." (*Idea Of Israel*, 35); TNA, FO 608/99, 387.

63. TNA, CAB 21/58, 18; CO 730/153/5, type-written page beginning Sir S. Wilson, and MS page preceding it; CO 730/153/5, early MS pages.

64. NYT, 5 March, 1919; Kahn's letter delivered on 4 March.
65. TNA, FO 608/99, 218, at a meeting with British officials on 22 March 1919.
66. Said, *Orientalism*, Vintage Books,1979; Jaffa Moslem Christian Committee, Mar 1919, TNA, FO 608/99, 222, 235.
67. Anti-Zionist prohibition, TNA, FO 608/99, 192, 196 and others; Weizmann, FO 608/99, 103; Rothschild, FO 608/99, 214, 217 (at a meeting with British officials, 21 Mar 1919); Jaffa governor, Segev, *Complete*, 87; Christian-Muslim exclusion, Abu-Lughod, *Transformation*, 58; regarding the prohibition of anti-Zionist articles, even Emir Feisal, for his own political calculations, wanted them stifled (see FO 608/99, 196); According to Jeffries (*Palestine*, 312), attempts to stifle the native Arabic led Jaffa Municipality to pass a by-law making Arabic compulsory on all signboards (in addition to Hebrew and English), but the Zionist Commission intervened and forced the cancellation of the Jaffa by-law.
68. Landau, see Reinharz /Schor, *Best School*, 92-93; Segev, *Complete*, 299, 210; Ben-Yehuda, *Assassinations*, 66-67, 137-140.
69. NYT, Dec 3 1922. Typo in original, "The word is askew..." Introduction by Mideast correspondent William Ellis. Also see Smith, *Arab-Israeli Conflict*, 81-82; King-Crane Report, section E, 3. 1919; The British War Office claimed in 1947 that "Nobody really knows" what happened to the King-Crane Report after it was handed to the Secretariat of the US Delegation in Paris by August 28, 1919, while suggesting that it might have saved the British from the quagmire they then founds themselves in, had it been heeded (UK War Office in 1947, WO 261/566, Fortnightly Intelligence Newsletter No. 37, 1 - 14 Mar 47).
70. King-Crane Report, E, 3. Most people in the region wanted independence. US stewardship was second choice, British stewardship third.
71. TNA, FO 608/99, 486-488. Report by H. D. Watson, Major-General, Chief Administrator, 16 August, 1919.
72. Report by Sd Major J. N. Camp, 12 Aug 1919, Jerusalem. Ironically, neither realized that it was ultimately for defense against the Zionist settlers, not against the Palestinians, that the British would send more troops.
73. TNA, FO 608/99, 511-513.
74. King-Crane Report; Segev, *Complete*, 119.
75. Churchill, quoted from: Official Records of the Second Session of the General Assembly, Supplement No. 11 Untied Nations Special Committee on Palestine, Report to the General Assembly, Volume 1; Cabinet report, 1923, CO 733/58, 321.
76. French, Lewis, "Supplementary Report on Agricultural Development and Land Settlement in Palestine," Director of Development, Jerusalem, April 20, 1932; Weizmann, CAB 24/263/0020, 6.
77. TNA, CO 733/250/1, penciled '2', '9'; regarding Zionists' refusal to work with Palestinians, see also reference in *Report on his Britannic Majesty's Government on the Administration Under Mandate of Palestine and Transjordan for the year 1926*, 60, which cites strikes stemming from "the refusal of Jewish labourers to work with Arabs" (TNA, CO 1071/306).

78. MS letter, Paul Siegel, July 18 1937, Albacete, Spain. Elmer Holmes Bobst Library, NY. Downloaded Nov 1, 2011. I am grateful to Prof. Francis Manasek for bringing this letter to my attention. For references to the violence and chaos within the Jewish settlements, see e.g., TNA, WO 169/183.
79. Nicosia, *Third Reich*, 53. Business interests also led some German Jews even to refute claims that the Nazis were ill-treating Jews; see Nadan Feldman, "The Jews Who Opposed Boycotting Nazi Germany," *Haaretz*, 20 Apr 2015.
80. Nicosia, *Third Reich*, ch 3, and 50, 63; Black, *Transfer Agreement*; Brenner, *51 Documents*; Polkehn, "Secret Contacts," 72. When on 8 September 1939 Haavara announced its closing, it had transferred US $35 million, which is about $600m in 2016 dollars, using the value of 1936 dollars (see Jewish Telegraphic Agency, 10 Sept 1939); Brenner, *Age of Dictators*, Kindle 2559-2561; My thanks to Joseph Massad, Professor of Modern Arab Politics and Intellectual History, for his email correspondence regarding the Brenner reference, May 2016.
81. Brenner, *51 Documents*, 115-118; Nicosia, *Third Reich*, 62; It is not clear to what extent Polkes was operating independently or representing the Hagana. Brenner, quoting the custodian of the Hagana records, said the files on Polkes are closed "because it would be too embarrassing" (*51 Documents*, 111, 117). There is inconsistency in records as to whether Polkes went with Eichmann to Egypt, or met him there again after travelling separately.
82. Report of the Palestine Royal Commission, Chapter XXII.
83. NYT, 8 Jan 1937 (note error in Ben-Gurion quote, where (as quoted) he refers to the Basel program of 1897 as being forty years before the Balfour, Declaration (1917), when he obviously meant before the present (1937); Interestingly, a year earlier, Weizmann told the Cabinet that he did not remember using the phrase "there would be the Jewish National Home" and wanted it omitted from the record. TNA, CAB 24/263/0020, 6.
84. Segev, *Complete*, 403-404; Morris (*Righteous*) translation: "This is more than a state, government and sovereignty—this is national consolidation in a free homeland."
85. For the 1933 news photo, TNA, CO 733/333/8; Morris, *Righteous*, ch 4 (During the first six months of 1936, approximately two hundred Palestinians, eighty Jews, and twenty-eight British personnel died); NYT 27 Oct 1946.
86. TNA, CO 537/2303, penciled "12"; red "49"; ADM 116/3690, "Report of Proceedings 'Malaya' No. 04895/9"; "Report of Proceedings 'Malaya' No. 04967/9"; CO 733/316/11, letter, penciled "Dear Eddie" (red "6"), p3; statement by F.A. Buckley, No. 04895/9. The demolition operation began at 16:45 on Thursday, 25 August, 1938. "Minesweepers" were not abolished until January 1940 (see TNA, WO 169/148, Notes on G.O.C.'s Conference Held at Force Headquarters on 19 Jan 40, 4).
87. Palestinian terrorism, TNA, MS, N. Ollerenshaw, CO 733/477/3, 196-205; Zionist terror, CAB 67/4/17/0001, 1; War Cabinet, Palestine, W.P. (G.) (40) 17, Jan 1940, 3; for example of Irgun records, see pages 63-64, above.
88. Morris, *Righteous*, K location 3174; Both Morris, and (contemporary) *Falastin* (in *Palestine Chronicle*), date the Ramataeem attack on 17 April (and the *Falastin* identifies it as a Friday, which would be the 17th), though the Irgun's

dating in Kister (*Irgun*) is the 16th; TNA, CAB 67/4/17; Kister, *Irgun*, 246.

89. A British War Cabinet Report dated January, 1940, cites an incident of October 5, 1939, in which 43 armed and uniformed Irgun were caught, and a large cache of weapons and explosives discovered in a nearby settlement, as Britain's first confirmation of the Irgun as a specific organization; This may have made it bureaucratically official, but British records well before this date cite the Irgun by name and as responsible for terror attacks; TNA, CAB 67/4/17; Kister, *Irgun*, 246.

90. TNA, CO 733/370/11, especially Dispatch No. 383 Reference No. K/50/38; Kister, *Irgun*, 249; NYT, 12 Apr 1938.

91. Kister, *Irgun*, 251; Pedahzur & Weinberg, *Religious Fundamentalism*, 100-101; By 1939, more than 60 terror attacks against Palestinian civilians are known. Hoffman, *Anonymous*, records the April 21 attempted bus attack and claims that the bombers intended to blow up a bus whose passengers included certain "Arabs" who, the bombers claimed, were responsible for an attack against Jews. Even if the claim of guilty Palestinians on that bus were correct, and even if one forgets the majority of the victims would have been innocent passengers, Hoffman's position is untenable, as the bombers then targeted a different bus after failing to hit the first. (k1736 etc); Bell, 42.

92. TNA, ADM 116/3690, No. 191/9862; see also beginning (unnumbered) pages.

93. Falastin, 7 July 1938, in *Palestine Chronicle*.

94. TNA, ADM 116/3690, No. 191/9862; see also beginning (unnumbered) pages.

95. NYT, 9 July 1938; Kister, *Irgun*, 251 (which cites an attack at the Jaffa Gate at 10 July, but this is presumably a misdating for July 8).

96. TNA, ADM 116/3690, SECRET. H.M.S. "REPULSE" at Haifa, 3oth July, 1938. For Tel Aviv attack, Hoffman, *Anonymous*, k1896, cites a bombing in Tel Aviv on 23 July 1938 in which twenty-three Jews were injured.

97. TNA, KV 5/34, 10AB; Bell, *Terror*, 42-43; Kister, *Irgun*, 252.

98. TNA, for Irgun attacks against the British by 1938-39, see CO 733/456/6, leaf 2, MS annotation; for Britain deciding on Palestinian representation, see e.g. CAB 104/7, Cabinet, "Minutes of a Meeting of Ministers...," 13 Oct 1938, Annex III.

Chapter Three — While the War Raged, 1939-1944

99. Quoted in NYT, 12 Nov 1944.

100. Jabotinsky was active in the US in 1926 (see Medoff, *Militant Zionism*, 5-6).

101. Lehi "Pro-Axis," TNA, KV 5/34, 430x, 'C.O. file 75969 (7a)'; FO 371/40125, Inward Telegram 372; For Nazi collaboration, see also Rogan, *The Arabs*, 248, and Brenner, *51 Documents*; Exploiting Britain's vulnerability during the war, see Yellin-Mor, MS letter, in Brenner, *51 Documents*, 307; This differed from Ben-Gurion's plan only in that Ben-Gurion advocated striking right after D-Day, rather than during the war.

102. TNA, KV 5/34, 7a, KV 5/31, 143a; WO 275/121, 'The Stern Group'.

103. Targeting anyone in uniform is implicit in most relevant TNA documents; see also Ben-Yehuda, *Assassinations*, 190; Regarding most targets of assassination

were Jewish, the numbers demonstrate this, and also see Friedmann, *Crime*, 162.

104. TNA, KV 5/34, 72A; FO 371/23244. There was continuing violence against civilians, both Palestinians and Jewish settlers, during early 1939, not all clearly political. For a detailed record, see e.g., MacMichael's reports in FO 371/23244; FO 371/23245, 14-15.

105. White Paper related violence, FO 371/23245, 15, 20; FO 371/23244, 83, 85, 88, 89, 109; on 18 May in Tel Aviv, Revisionists and Hapoel (sports association) stoned one another; NYT, "Twenty–Five Hurt in Palestine Riot," 18 May 1939.

106. TNA, FO 371/23244, 109, 110; FO 371/23245, 17, 18; Rex Cinema, KV 5/34, 54a; FO 371/23245, 18, says "a third bomb failed to explode" (instead of half failed). In Bethlehem's Ghirass Cultural Centre, among a series of old photographs, are two showing an explosion at the "Riex movie," with the date 1946. The author could not corroborate an attack on the Rex Cinema in 1946.

107. TNA, FO 371/23244, 115, 131, 135; Communications sabotage, see also Bell, *Terror*, 48.

108. TNA, FO 371/23244, 131, 135 (which records a "Jewess arrested placing time bomb near central prison Jerusalem" on 9 June 1939, but this is also probably the same as the attempted attack on the Arab market); also regarding that attempted bombing 9 June 1939, another later British report mentions an incident a year earlier: "in 1938 a Jewish girl still in her teens had been arrested with a bomb which was to have been exploded in a public place in Jerusalem" (TNA, report by R. Newton, FO 371/45382), but this is probably a mis-dating for this 1939 incident; Jewish origin of bombs, "Time-Bomb in Basket," the *Times*, 10 June 1939.

109. TNA, FO 371/23244, 141, 142, 146, 152 (which cites the 10 June attack in Tiberias, with some ambiguity as to whether the seven dead is (as it seems) just from that land mine attack, or includes the day's other attacks).

110. TNA, FO 371/23244, 141, 142, 146, 148, 154; Regarding the execution of five villagers of Belad es Sheikh (Balad esh Sheikh), a Telegram from the High Commissioner of June 14 1939, in FO 371/23244, states only that "the village headman reported that the perpetrators were Jews," as this was before the Zionist gang confirmed that they had done it; "More Terrorism in Palestine," the *Times*, 16 June 1939.

111. TNA, FO 371/23244, 156, 167; The 19 June market attack is surely the one cited in Kister (*Irgun*) as 20 June, and that Hoffman (*Anonymous*) refers to (k2209) but does not date. The British same-day report is certainly the correct dating.

112. TNA, FO 371/23245, 21, 22, 23; FO 371/23244, 109, 110, 115, 131; FO 371/23244 141, 142, 146, 148, 154, 156, 167, 173, 177, 181, 184; WO 169/148; For an example of Palestinians working to capture Palestinian gangs, FO 371/23244, 138; "Jewish Terrorism in Palestine," the *Times*, 26 June 1939; British documents record instances of Palestinian villagers working together to capture remaining Palestinian gang leaders, with no parallel effort of the Jewish settlements; For a record of the "background" ongoing (lessening) Palestinian and (increasing) Jewish violence during 1939, see TNA, FO 371/23244 and FO 371/23245.

113. TNA, FO 371/23245, 24, 25; FO 371/23244, 179, 186, 190, 198, 213; "Jewish Terrorism Another Bomb Outrage in Jerusalem," the *Times*, 7 Jan 1939; Bell,

Terror, 48; Pedahzur & Weinberg, *Religious Fundamentalism*, 99-102; A British corporal was murdered because he "was a trickster in the pay of the Jewish Agency ... the second traitor to be done away with,"TNA, KV 5/34.

114. Irgun record of attacks, TNA, KV 5/34, 10AB, and Kister, Irgun, 254-256. A slight variation of the British record is preserved in TNA, FO 1093/330, "Notes on Illegal Jewish Organizations," 8.

115. Bell, *Terror*, 42, 48; Kister, Irgun, 256-257 (in which the Irgun claims six victims on July 20), 259; TNA, FO 371/23244, 246, 253; WO 169/148, 'Secret High Grade Cipher Message, red '3a' at upper-right; FO 371/23245, 2 (which dates the failed cricket bombing at August 6), 6, 36, 38, 110; KV 5/34, 10AB (8); CO 733/415/4, 20-24; Ben-Yehuda, *Assassinations*, 155-156; Bell, *Terror*, 48; Pedahzur & Weinberg, *Religious Fundamentalism*, 99-102; the audience at the failed cricket match bombings (5 Aug) were "men women and children of the European community"; for Irgun interview, KV 5/34, CO 733/415/4, 11-13, 15 Aug 1939; the Irgun member interviewed gave his name as Yardany.

116. Kister, *Irgun*, 256-257 (in which the Irgun claims six victims on July 20), 259; TNA, FO 371/23244, 221, 246, 253; FO 371/23245, 2 (which dates the failed cricket bombing at August 6), 6, 36, 38, 110; Interview, 15 Aug 1939; the man gave his name as Yardany; KV 5/34, CO 733/415/4, 11-13; KV 5/34, 10AB (8); CO 733/415/4, 20-24; Ben-Yehuda, *Assassinations*, 155-156; for Irgun Biblical justification, TNA, KV 5/34, 10AB. Explosions alerted the British to one Irgun contingent undergoing military-style drills on 18 November, comprised of thirty-four men aged sixteen to twenty-five, and two women aged seventeen and eighteen. Irgun drill was at Mishmar Hay Yarden Colony - WO 169-148, High Grade Cipher Message, blue '38a' at top.

117. For a show of Jewish Agency cooperation with enlistment, see TNA, WO 169/148, 'Supplementary Summary 1," which is then qualified "Summary of Intelligence," 18th Sept 1940, 2.

118. TNA, WO 169/183, Weekly Progress Report (up to 24 Feb 40); Lydda Area, Intelligence Summary, week ending 24 Feb 1940; week ending 16th March 1940.

119. TNA, WO 169/183, Weekly Progress Report (up to 9th March 1940); the Jewish constable was not expected to survive and was too injured to make a statement, but the British attributed the assassination to retribution for the arrest of the Histadrut officials (Intelligence Summary week ending 16th March 1940); Weekly Progress Report up to 23 March, & 30 March, 1940: TNA, WO 169/183, Weekly Progress Report (up to 9 March 1940); Lydda Area, Intelligence Summary, week ending 24 Feb 1940; Intelligence Summary, week ending 3 May.

120. TNA, WO 169/183, Weekly Progress Report (up to 9th March 1940); Lydda Area, Intelligence Summary, week ending 24 Feb 1940; Intelligence Summary, week ending 3 May; Letter from the High Commissioner, October 16, 1939; KV 5/34, 10AB.

121. Irgun enlistment, TNA, KV 5/34, 15a; Palmach, CO 537/1715, 'Memorandum'; Hagana secrecy and the assassination of suspected informants, WO 275/121, "What's What," item 5; TNA *(ibid)* mentions the need of interning all

Germans in Jaffa and the Enclosed Colonies, "especially the women."

122. TNA, WO 169/148, "Political Situation"; "Situation Report," '128a' in pencil upper-right; *Pum*, see TNA, WO 169/183, Weekly Progress Report (up to 11th May, 1940); the soldier assassinated on 11 May was AMPC, 401 Auxiliary Military Pioneer Corps; note that Ben-Yehuda (*Assassinations*, 161) cites three Hagana assassinations in May, 1940, with one on the 11th perhaps being a duplication. For Axis attacks, see WO 169/148, "Secret 104 196' and subsequent pages.

123. *Patria*, CO 733/446/4, Letter to MacMichael, signed Alan Rose, A.J. McNeil, L.J. Edwards, 3; Hoffman (*Anonymous*) omits this attack and cites the less deadly King David Hotel bombing in 1946 as the most deadly terror attack to that time.

124. TNA, WO 169/148, "War Diary," 14 December, 1940; Arthur Koestler, *Promise and Fulfilment*, New York, The Macmillan Company, 1949, 60; Regarding spinning incident in relation to the Masada, see Meir Chazan, "The Patria Affair: Moderates vs. Activists in Mapai in the 1940s," in *The Journal of Israeli History*, Vol.22, No.2 (Autumn 2003), 61–95 [Frank Cass, London]; regarding Masada in the "Israel of the Bible," the Masada is not mentioned in the Bible, but the alleged event was recorded by Josephus during the period of 'Biblical' Israel. All modern sources noted (e.g., Wikipedia, last accessed 6 June 2016), state that the Hagana's responsibility for the bombing was not established until conceded by alleged bomber Mardor in 1957. Although the British were uncertain of the bombers' identity in their initial investigation, the Hagana's responsibility was soon established (e.g., TNA, CO 733/457/12, Intelligence Summary No. 8/45, 3-4).

125. TNA CO 733/446/4, letter from Mac Michael, C.S.499; TNA, CO 733/457/12, Criminal Investigation Department, Jerusalem, 24 April, 1945, Secret Document, 3-4; CO 733/457/12, Jewish Affairs, Terrorism, Intelligence Summary No. 8/45, esp 3-4; CO 733/446/4, red '10.2.41', begins "I am sorry to have delayed...." There was opposition from the British command to allowing the *Patria* survivors to remain, based on the fear that "it will be spread all over the Arab world that Jews have again successfully challenged decision of British Government," CAB 66/13/48/0001.

126. The quote "read like a summer camp brochure" is from Frantz & Collins, *Black Sea*, 78; TNA FO 371/32662, penciled '127'; Giladi (*Scandals*) says 769 passengers, Frantz & Collins (likely the more accurate source) says 781; Both British records and Frantz & Collins, 216, state that Britain refused them entry because they were nationals of a country at war with Britain, proceeding direct from enemy territory. Giladi insinuates that the Jewish Agency had 25,000 entry permits available but refused to use them for the *Struma* passengers. The author found no evidence of this in the British archives (see FO 371/32662, 97, verso, although Robert Weltsch also spoke of the Jewish Agency's refusal to consider any non-Palestine means to save the refugees; See TNA, FO 371/32662, 66 for British explanation of refusal to admit *Struma*'s passengers; For British attempt to admit children aged 11-16; see *ibid*, 96; See also CO 733/446/11, CO 733/449/34; The cause of the sinking was hotly disputed, but recent research, and the recovery of the wreck, convincingly point to a Russian torpedo as the cause (Frantz & Collins, *Black Sea*).

127. For a show of Jewish Agency cooperation with enlistment, see TNA, WO 169/148, 'Supplementary Summary 1,' which is then qualified "Summary of Intelligence," 18th Sept 1940, 2, which states that "the so-called registration at the beginning of the war was purely a political gesture…" Regarding Czech military service, TNA, WO 169/183, Intelligence Summary, week ending 3 May; WO 169/4334, Appendix 'A' to Weekly Intelligence Summary week ending April 8 1942; for Hagana against Allied recruitment, see e.g. WO 169/4334, week ending 10 June 42; Jabotinsky and Trumpeldor, among others, were lobbying for a segregated "Jewish" army by 1914 (WO 32/11352).

128. See Giladi, *Scandals*; TNA, FO 1093/330, Lehi's Communique No. 21/41, dated 1 August, 1941, 3; CO 733/420/19 (released as a result of the author's F.O.I. request), also cites new evidence for the Mufti's close involvement with the Italian fascists in 1940; on November 16 of 1940, S.E.V. Luke noted that "possible action against [the Mufti] was discussed with the Secretary of State a few days ago, [and] it was decided that the only really effective means of securing a control over him would be a military occupation of Iraq"; the same day, H.F. Downie stated that "We may be able to clip the Mufti's wings when we can get a new Government in Iraq. F.O. [Foreign Office] are working for this." For Zionist move to get Iraqi Jews to move to Palestine, see FO 371/98767, Special Court Judgement in Zionist Activity Case, in *The Iraq Times*, 20 Dec 1951.

129. FO 1093/330, "Notes on Illegal Jewish Organizations" (11).

130. TNA, FO 1093/330, Note of Meeting Held of New Court, St. Swithin's Lane, E.C., on Tuesday, September the 9th, 1941 at 2:30 p.m.

131. Bell, *Terror* (73) states that Lehi's "electronically [sic? electrically?] detonated bomb blasted across the road—and missed." In the same year, Lehi attempted, but failed, to assassinate Alan Saunders, a British official, for his role in sending illegal immigrants to Mauritius; Lehi assassinated one of its first members, Abraham Wilenchik, after his release from British detention; Some say he had given information in exchange for his release, but others maintain that he tried to quite the gang, and his murder was a warning to other members that "only death would release from the organization" (See Ben-Yehuda, *Assassinations*); TNA, WO 169/4334, High Grade Cypher ref 35a; Weekly Intelligence Review No. 9; CO 733/439/20, verso of leaf with MS '2'; TNA, CO 733/457/9 38, verso; TNA, CO 733/439/20, No. 580 Secret; WO 169/4334, Weekly Intelligence Review No. 14; Hoffman, *Anonymous*, K2526.

132. TNA, CO 733/444/17, FO 371/68697, Ref. 3/315/48; for Proskauer, FO 800/486, 137.

133. TNA, WO 169/4334, Weekly Intelligence Report no. 21; G.S.I. Palestine Base & L of C 1-30 April 1942.

134. TNA CO/733/439/20, Cypher Telegram No. 523. Note that at least three different versions of the attempted assassination of McConnell exist; Ben-Yehuda, *Assassinations* (172), citing Eliav and Ha'aretz, says that the bomb was rigged to the car's back wheel, that the servant backed the car out of the garage for McConnell, and the device exploded as intended, save for the wrong victim; Bell, *Terror* (73) claims that "the Arab" had "seized the opportunity to curry favor" with his boss by opening the car door for him, and "as he swept open the door with a grand gesture … a small package

tumbled in front of him [and] McConnel [sic] was left "standing over his shattered corpse"; The author has dismissed Bell's account as an ethnically condescending embellishment; and has opted for the British account over Ben-Yehuda's (in principle credible) account because it relies on Lehi's operative Eliav, but the British, not Lehi, were the ones on the scene after the explosion; WO 169/4334, High Geade Cipher ref 13a; Weekly Intelligence Reviews No. 22, 24; G.S.I. Palestine Base & L of C 1-30 April 1942; 1-31 May 1942; also the *Times*, 24 April 1942.

135. TNA, KV 5/34, 15a.

136. TNA, WO 169/4334, Weekly Intelligence Review, week ending 17 June 42; Weekly Intelligence Reviews No. 27.

137. TNA, WO 169/4334, G.S.I. HQ Palestine ... 1-30 Sept 1942, Summary no. 11; G.S.I. Palestine Summary No. 10; Weekly Intelligence Review No. 39; for disillusionment with Mufti, WO 169/4334, Weekly Intelligence Review No. 9, ending 21 Jan 42; CO 733/420/19, declassified in July 2014 as a result of the author's F.O.I. request, cites new evidence for the Mufti's close involvement with the Italian fascists as well (1940). There were signs that the Mufti, whose meeting with the Nazis is still used to smear the Palestinians, was at this time (1942) losing support. As one once-ardent follower explained, the struggle was for independence, not replacing one oppressor with another.

138. TNA, WO 169/4334, G.S.I. HQ Palestine, Summary No. 12 (1-31 Oct 1942); Weekly Intelligence Summary No. 40; the author assumes that the 4 Oct meeting cited in this document is not the same as the similar (but undated) meeting cited in the September Summary no. 11 in the same folder (WO 169/4334), whose coverage ended 30 September; Weizmann, conversation with Isaiah Berlin, on or about May 18, 1943 (CO 733/443/18, E 2399/87/31, verso, and otherwise untitled 'Copy').

139. TNA, WO 169/4334, Weekly Intelligence Review No. 42 week ending 25 Nov 42; Summary No. 14.

140. TNA, WO 169/4334, Weekly Intelligence Review No. 6, week ending 1 Jan 1942; CO 733/443/21, letter from Elias N. Koussa; Palestinian enlistment figure quoted in Khalidi, and in Kimberly Katz and Salim Tamari, *A Young Palestinian's Diary, 1941-1945: The Life of Sami 'Amr*, 31 [University of Texas Press, 2010].

141. TNA FO 371/40129, Cypher Telegram No. 117; CO 733/458/13, Outward Telegram No. 117; FO 1093/330, Extract From Security Summary Middle East No. 131; *ibid*, Most Secret, Ref No.C.S.573/1, red '31', esp 2. Regarding sabotage training sought from the Allies, for example two ex-S.O.E. agents (Special Operations Executive, a WWII espionage and sabotage unit against the Axis powers) on leave on Denmark were "approached by some Jews who wanted them to give instruction in sabotage methods." (They were "of a pretty tough variety, although one of them like Bach and the other Nietsche.") See TNA, KV 4/467, 294 Liddel Diaries, entry August 13, 1946.

142. TNA FO 1093/330, Following upon the High Commissioner's; *ibid*, letter from Robert Scott to "My dear Boyd," unnumbered, "MOST SECRET 21st January 1942" at top.

143. TNA, KV 5/33, 37a, 38a, 35a (10 pages) London, "from our Palestine representative on the Jewish situation, as viewed by him." The report is dated 28 May 1943 but is said to be from observation in January. Also see

FO 1093/330, Latest Aspects of the Palestine Zionist-Arab Problem, 6; for charge against Hunloke, see Nigel West, *The A to Z of Sexspionage*, Scarecrow Press (2009), 132-133 (Hunloke was cleared).

144. TNA, FO 1093/330, The Jewish Situation, The Hagana; CO 733/458/13, "Dr. Altman" (red '21', etc).

145. Moshe Arens quote from foreword in Baumel, *Bergson Boys*, xii; TNA, KV 2/2251, 25305/PS; CO 733/458/13, Extract from a memorandum submitted for pre-censorship by Mr. Gershon Agronsky; FO 371/40129, letter dated 4.9.43. The friend was J. H. Dayag, 3 Antolsky St. (*sic* Antokolsky), Neveh Bezalel, Jerusalem.

146. *ibid.*; TNA, FO 371/40129, letter dated 4.9.43; extra comma in original: "… San Francisco, Houston, (Texas) and…"

147. *ibid.*

148. TNA, FO 371/40129, penciled '16', Robert Scott, Acting Chief Secretary; (written "organizers," not the British "organisers"); Capitalization "HER" original. Cited in WO 208/1705, penciled '68', cited as appearing in NYT, 30 April 1943; the author did not see this ad on the NYT's online resource for this date, but the transcript is specific and the ad surely appeared about this date in a major US paper; For Jewish Authority connection, KV 2/1435, '1642'; FO 371/40129, penciled '11', January 3, 1944; CO 733/457/5, Note on Visit to the United States, 3; Biltmore Program.

149. PICME (British Political Intelligence in the Middle East) WO 208/1705, P.I.C. Paper No. 35; TNA WO 208/1705, An Estimate of the Possibility that the Jews in Palestine May Use Force in 1944 to Achieve Their Political Aims (pencil '46'); Similarly, in Apartheid South Africa, opponents of the racial system were smeared as anti-Christian (see, e.g., Davis, *Apartheid*, 4-5).

150. As Idith Zertal has written, Zionists' associating themselves with Jews struggling in the Warsaw ghetto trivialized the reality of life under Nazi occupation; Zertel, *Israel's Holocaust*, 26-29, 35; "We fought here and they fought there," in the words of a Palmach commander in Palestine. Edelman, *The Ghetto Fights*, published by The Bund, Warsaw, 1945.

151. Zertal, *Israel's Holocaust and the Politics of Nationhood*, 29-30; for Eliezer Livneh quote, at a symposium in 1966, Polkehn, *Secret Contacts*, 54; Lilienthal, *What Price*, 29; Brenner, *51 Documents*, 211-212.

152. Brenner, *51 Documents*, 212. Brenner states that Yehuda Bauer, in his *From Diplomacy to Resistance*, explains Gruenbaum's behavior this way: Gruenbaum had no hope of saving European Jews and thought the money would be wasted, but had to "go through the motions" of trying.

153. TNA, CAB 66/37/25, 14; FO 371/45377, 84; FO 371/45377, pencil '84'; also see KV 2/1435, '1642', esp verso; FO 1093/330, red '44', Inner Zionist General Council and Non-Cooperation; Dr. Senator is described as a non-Zionist.

154. TNA, FO 1093/330, red '48'; *ibid*, Latest Aspects of the Palestine Zionist-Arab Problem (In the original, one typo: "find themselves *in* anachronism"); *US Office of Strategic Services Foreign Nationalities Branch Files 1942-1945* (Congressional Information Service, 1988) lists two reports by this name, INT-18JE-242 (July 19) and INT-18JE-251 (July 25); the Kew document cited here would appear to be an earlier draft than either; String-bound

between red '48' & '46' when examined; War Cabinet, CAB 66/37/46, 2; In the words of MP Lt.-Col. Victor Cazalet, the Zionist establishment in Palestine was seen as "a kind of Nazi-Gestapo run organization" - Aug 2 1943, CAB 95/14, 74.

155. TNA, FO 1093/330, *ibid.*

156. TNA, FO 1093/330, *ibid.*

157. TNA CO 733/456/2, Fortnightly Report ending 31 Jan 1944, 'IV'; KV 5/36, *Herut*, no. 59, July, 1946; TNA, FO 371/45377, 84, Running Diary of Political Developments in Palestine; the 1943 campaign to prevent Jewish-Gentile friendships was launched in September. Also see Sand, 291.

158. TNA, KV 5/39, Report of Conference, 2; also note FO 371/40126, Inward Telegram 695, in which in May 1944 MacMichael reports the feeling in Palestine that the war was merely an "irksome complication" to nationalist aims.

159. TNA, FO 371/40125, Inward Telegram No. 217; CO 733/443/18, red '60'; *ibid*, red '30.8.43', verso, others; *ibid*, red '50'; Weizmann allegedly claimed to have gotten Roosevelt's promise to guarantee the funds. Shertok (Sharett) was also involved *ibid*, letter to Hayter/Campbell/Wright; Churchill confirms that he was the origin of the plan *ibid*, red '5', red '6'; Also see Monroe, *Philby of Arabia*, 221-225; CO 733/443/19, Weizmann to S. Welles, 13 Dec 1943; *ibid*, Aide Memoire, Riyiadh, 20 Aug 1943.

160. TNA, CO 733/456/6, Extract from Middle East telegram 0/72248; FO 371/40125, penciled '32'; CO 733/456/2; CO 733/458/13, Intelligence Summary No. 3/44; CO 733/457/9, Summary of Terrorist Outrages, 1944; CO 733/456/6, Inward Telegram, MS 143. Also CO 733/456/2, Fortnightly Report Jerusalem District ending 15 Feb 1944; For Latrun, TNA FO 1093/330, red '51'; FO 371/40125, penciled '33', & Inward Telegram 238.

161. TNA, CO 733/456/6, Inward Telegram No. 238; FO 1093/330, 'Palestine, Jewish Terrorism'; CO 733/456/6, Inward Telegram No. 205; CO 733/456/2, Fortnightly Report Jerusalem District ending 29 Feb 1944; Fortnightly Report Jerusalem District ending 15 Feb 1944; Kister, *Irgun*, 257 February, 1944; Bell, *Terror*, 113; CO 733/457/9, Summary of Terrorist Outrages, 1944; KV 5/34, 'Jewish Newsletter No. 10'; FO 371/40125, penciled '34', & Inward Telegrams 217, 238; Also FO 1093/330, 'places must be known to many' at top.

162. The *Times*, Feb 19 1944; TNA, WO 208/1705, P.I.C. Paper No. 35, 4; NYT April 1944; TNA FO 371/40130, letter from Rachel Yarden (MS '64' at top); for White Paper as anti-Bible, e.g., CO 733/456/2, Jerusalem Fortnightly Report for the Period 16 - 31 October, 1944; and *ibid*, 1 - 15 September, 1944, Chief Rabbi Herzog; "writing on wall," WO 193/68, MO/5 Loose Minute Sheet 305 (January, 1944).

163. Kister, *Irgun*, 112; TNA, CO 733/456/6, Inward Telegram No. 207; CO 733/456/2, Fortnightly Report Haifa District ended 15 Fed 1944; CO 733/456/6, Extract from Middle East Telegram 0/72248; FO 371/40125, Inward Telegrams 217, 257; CO 733/456/6, MS '18'; CO 733/456/6, MS '2' with date 13.2.44, and following page; *ibid*, Inward Telegram No. 205; CO 733/456/6, penciled '133'; *ibid*, typewritten '(7) Paragraph 1' under MS notes; CO 733/456/6, MS red '9', '8', '24'. Note that CO 733/457/9, Summary of Terrorist Outrages, and FO 371/40125, Inward Telegram No. 217, date the

murder of Green and Ewer at Feb 14-15, while other sources cite a day earlier, probably due to a day difference between the attack and their succumbing to the wounds; CO 733/457/9, Summary of Terrorist Outrages, 1944; CO 733/458/13, Extract from HC Pal tel 258; CO 733/456/2, Fortnightly Report Haifa District ended 29th Feb 1944; CO 733/456/2, Extract from Middle East Telegram 0/77252; *ibid*, Inward Telegram No. 257; CO 733/456/6, MS '120'; CO 733/456/2, Fortnightly Report Jerusalem District ended 29 Feb 1944; CO 733/456/2, Fortnightly Report Lydda District ended 29 Feb 1944; CO 733/456/6, MS '56', Extract from telegram No. 384; FO 371/40125, Inward Telegram 269; Also see Bell, *Terror*, 114; CO 733/456/2, Fortnightly Report for Haifa District ended 29 Feb 1944; FO 371/40125, penciled '52'; Kister, *Irgun*, 258.

164. NYT, Feb 26, 1944; TNA, CO 733/457/5, as reported in 1944 by a contact called "Y 32," R. C. Catling, "Notes on Visit to the United States," p6. Also Brenner, *51 Documents*, 198; CO 733/457/5, Telegram No. 784 ('C.S. 679/7' at top); the inclusion of non-Zionist Jews in the governing bodies of the Jewish Agency after 1929 similarly served to bring it new sources of revenue; see Abu-Lughod, *Transformation*, 132; and TNA, CO 733/457/5, R. C. Catling, 'Notes...'.

165. Regarding the "hiking groups" that were part of military gathering intelligence about Palestinian villages and population prior to 1948, my thanks to Dr. Rona Sela for sharing her knowledge via email correspondence and a meeting in Tel Aviv, November, 2012. This information was published in Rona Sela, *Made Public—Palestinian Photographs in Military Archives in Israel* (Israel: Helena Publishing House, 2009); TNA, CO 733/456/2, Fortnightly Report Jerusalem District ended 15 Feb 1944; FO 371/40125, Inward Telegram 340; Pappé, in JPS, 11-13; See also the Hagana operations chief's acknowledgment of a "map in which the strategic character of every Arab village, and the quality of its inhabitants, were indicated" (Erskine B. Childers' "The Wordless Wish: From Citizens to Refugees," in Abu-Lughod, *Transformation*, 178); Pappe, *Ethnic Cleansing*, 18-22; Quigley, *Challenge*, ch 3 (who does not connect the simulated attacks with the hikers); FO 1093/330, "Palestine, the Jewish Defense Forces" (penciled '22'), 5-6. Centers cited are "Aylet es Shahar" and "Ain Aaaron near Ain Geb."

166. Restaurant, TNA CO 733/456/2, Fortnightly Report Jerusalem District ended 15 March 1944, 2; CO 733/456/6, typewritten '(7) Paragraph 1' under MS notes; CO 733/456/2, Fortnight Report Lydda District ended 14 March 1944; *ibid*, Fortnightly Report Haifa ended 31 Mar 1944; CO 733/456/6, Inward Telegrams 3384, 362, 340; Note that in CO 733/456/6, blue leaf with type-written "2nd March" at top, the murder of a Jewish CID is cited on March 15, which to avoid the risk of duplication I have assumed to be the same as cited elsewhere on Mar 13; However, CO 733/456/7, Inward Telegram No. 1586, cites two British police killed on Mar 15, hence I have assumed that at least one is not a duplication; FO 371/40125, Inward Telegram 362; CO 733/457/9, Summary of Terrorist Outrages, 1944; media clippings in CO 733/456/6, e.g. "Bomb Outrages in Palestine," News Chronicle, the *Times*, Mar 25 1944; Bell, *Terror*, 115-117; Kister, *Irgun*, 258.

167. TNA, CO 733/457/5, Extract From Top-Secret Telegram No 409 from Palestine dated 2 April 1944; CO 733/456/6, Inward Telegram No. 372, esp

verso; *ibid*, Inward Telegram No. 363; also FO 371/40125, Inward Telegram No. 363, 372; MacMichael proposed that the Agency has "a real chance of saving their face before the world" by "handing over the guilty," which it had the power, but not the will, to do.

[168.] TNA, CO 733/457/5, "Extract From Top-Secret Telegram No 409 from Palestine Dated 2.4.44"; CO 733/456/2, Fortnightly Report Nablus District ended 30 Nov 1944; CO 733/456/3, Fortnightly Report Jerusalem District ended 31 Jan 1945; CO 733/457/12, Intelligence Summary No. 8/45, esp 3; On April 2, addressing a fund-raiser to bring Jews to Palestine (only to Palestine); CO 733/456/6, JTA Bulletin Vol XXV. No. 80; *ibid*, penciled '17' upper right; *ibid*, red 40; see also KV 5/34, O.F. 608/1; Jewish Agency agreed to "help" fight terrorism if the British would agree to give it 25 to 50 anonymous firearms permits, and then it would conduct an investigation autonomously; the Agency would share limited information of its choosing with the police, who would have to agree not to search settlements for illegal arms; CO 733/456/6, '221522' at top next to "Most Secret Cipher Telegram"; *ibid*, '436585' at top next to "Most Secret Cipher Telegram"; For transcript of discussion among Mapai leaders regarding cooperation with British, see CO 537/1814, "Speech Delivered by Eliezer Kaplan... 22.10.46"; Anglo-Palestinian Club, *Pamphlet No. 2*, 1944.

[169.] TNA, CO 733/458/13, Palestine Censorship, red '57', 3-4. CO 733/456/2, Fortnightly Report, Jerusalem, end 31 July 1944; Fortnightly Report, Gaza, end 15 May 1944; FO 371/40126, Inward Telegram 695; this telegram from MacMichael states that some segments of the Yishuv were nervous about the Labour Party motion, as it gave the public the impression that there was no available space left in Palestine. Public protestations from Zionist spokespeople that they did not want to expel the Arabs is consistently contradicted behind closed doors.

[170.] TNA, FO 371/40125, Inward Telegram 409, 431, 448, Cypher Telegram 214749, 223481; CO 733/456/2, (Haifa District) Fortnightly Report for the period May 1 - April 15, 1944; CO 733/456/7, Inward Telegram No. 1586; CO 733/456/6, JTA Bulletin Vol XXV. No. 80, 3; *ibid*, Palcor Bulletin, 3 April 1944, 3; CO 733/456/2, Fortnightly Report Lydda District ended 15 April 1944.

[171.] TNA, CO 733/456/6, Inward Telegram No. 448; CO 733/456/7, Inward Telegram No. 1586, esp verso; CO 733/456/2, Fortnightly Report Haifa District ending 31 May 1944; *ibid*, Fortnightly Report Lydda District ending 15 May 1944; CO 733/456/6, Inward Telegram No. 591; Kister, *Irgun*, 258.

[172.] TNA, CO 733/456/6, Inward Telegram No. 639; which puts a question mark by the "17th May" date; but the subsequent events (2:30 AM on the 18th) support that date. Police at the nearby Ramallah police station, who had heard the explosion, arrived followed the sound and found the Arabs that had been targeted. The assailants had left behind a small amount of gelignite. This attack is briefly cited in Bell, *Terror*, 120; CO 733/456/6, red MS 'Extract from HC Pal tel 695 Sec. of 29.5.44' and '78'; FO 371/40125, Inward Telegram 591; CO 733/456/2, Fortnightly Report Jerusalem District ended 15 July 1944; CO 733/456/7, Inward Telegram No. 875; *ibid*, "Terrorist Activities," red '109' upper left; For Arab identity, see CO 733/456/7, Inward Telegram No. 930, verso; In Kister, *Irgun*, 258, the Irgun identifies one destroyed building as the

Jaffa District Intelligence Command, which I have assumed to be the same the Kew records' District Police Headquarters; Bell, *Terror*, 120; CO 733/456/7, Inward Telegram 1586; FO 371/40126, Inward Telegram 695, 875, 930.

173. TNA, CO 733/456/2, Fortnightly Report, Lydda, end 15 July 1944; Fortnightly Report, Jerusalem, end 15 July 1944.

174. TNA, CO 733/456/2, Fortnightly Report, Jerusalem, end 31 July 1944; FO 371/40126, Inward Telegram 814; CO 733/456/6, penciled '102'.

175. TNA, WO 193/68, '81E'; For Jewish Brigade, CAB 66/51/44; Sternhell, *Founding Myths*, 31; Segev, *Complete*, 393, quoting from Ben-Gurion, *Memoirs*, vol III, 24, 38, 41, 64, 85; FO 1093/330, red p '7', esp 2. Since the beginning of the war, as the Nazis were overrunning Poland and the darkest days of European Jewry were dawning, Ben-Gurion opposed a general conscription of Jews to fight Hitler, as this would detract from what he called "Zionist considerations." Future PM Sharett, addressing Jewish recruits as the war raged two years later, spoke of Jewry's "tragic alliance with Britain in this war" (that the fight against the Axis had put them on the same side as the British), and stressed that they would later use British military training to make the people of Palestine "reckon with us."

176. TNA, WO 193/68, penciled 118, SD2/6005; CAB 66/27/12; WO 193/68, penciled '305', blue MS notes at bottom and verso; FO 1093/330, Latest Aspects of the Palestine Zionist-Arab Problem, esp 7; *ibid*, 'No. 1541 Most Secret' from MacMichael, verso; "The extreme Zionists contemplate the use of armed force for the attainment of their objectives. They have already large quantities of illegal arms. What they need is training [and the Hagana,] whose threat, already formidable, would be strengthened by the existence of an official Jewish army." CAB 66/27/12; WO 193/68, Army Secretariat, Reference W.P. (44) 344. A.C.S./B/969; CO 733/456/2, Fortnightly Report Nablus District ended 30 Nov 1944.

177. Dated 4 March, 1942. TNA, FO 371/32662, penciled '93', '101'.

178. TNA, FO 371/40127, Inward Telegram 1081. Ben-Gurion speech in Haifa, August 21, 1944. TNA, CO 733/457/4; As example of Ben-Gurion against Partition, WO 208/1705, red '16A', among many others; NYT, "A Zionist Army?," Jan 26 1942; TNA, CO 733/456/2, Fortnightly Report Nablus District ended 30 Nov 1944; Fortnightly Report Jaffa District ended 30 Nov 1944; NYT, Jan 22 1942; The idea of a "Jewish army" to establish an ethnicity-based national identity dates back at least to 1914; in January 1917, Joseph Trumpeldor petitioned the British government for the establishment of a Jewish Regiment in language that took the concept of a Jewish 'nation' for granted. See TNA, WO 32/11352, red '3A' at top'; FO 371/32662, penciled '76'; Ben-Yehuda, *Assassinations*, 120; Grodzinsky, 50, etc.

179. TNA, CO 733/457/3, "Report on the attempt to assassinate the High Commissioner of Palestine"; TNA, CO 733/457/3, Inward Telegram No. 994; TNA, CO 733/456/2, Lydda District Fortnightly Report ended 15 Aug 1944. MacMichael had already survived several assassination attempts. Among the assailants' unspent weaponry discovered nearby was a US grenade. One of the British reports states that it was the driver who was shot in the lung, but I have gone according to MacMichael's statement in FO 371/40126, Inward Telegram 984. The A.D.C. was a Major Nicholls.

180. Sir Harold MacMichael decided in 1943 that as result of "severe disorders" upon search at Ramat Hakovesh that no further searches of Jewish settlements would be made. See e.g., TNA, CO 733/456/8, penciled 14 upper-right; CO 733/456/9, light penciled '99' at top, letter from Sgd John A. Rocke, 4 November, 1945; CO 537/3854, Intelligence Summary No. 2/46, 2; FO 371/45377, Running Diary of Political Developments in Palestine (MS '82' at top); CAB 158/1, "Annex Organisation of Illegal Immigration"; FO 371/40127, Inward Telegram 1081.

181. TNA, CO 733/456/7, red no. 111, 113, 114; FO 371/40127, Inward Telegram 1051; FO 371/40127, Inward Telegrams 1235, 1238; Bell, *Terror* (120) cites Irgun attacks on March 23 on CID barracks in Jaffa, Abu-Kabir, and Neve Shaanan. I have assumed these are the same I have cited.

182. TNA, KV 5/34, Inward Telegram 1051; FO 371/40127, penciled '20' top-right; Inward Telegram 1288; CO 733/456/2, Lydda Fortnightly Report ended 31 Aug 1944; Kister, *Irgun*, 258.; KV 5/34, Inward Telegram No. 1051; CO 733/456/2 Lydda Fortnightly Report end 31 Aug 1944; CO 733/456/2, Nablus Fortnightly Report, end 30 Nov 1944, *ibid*, Haifa Fortnightly Report, end 30 Sept 1944; CO 733/457/9, red '38'; NYT, Sept 29 1944; Kister, *Irgun*, 259. TNA, also records this theft. For Al Capone quote, see Segev, *Complete*, 475; bands of Jewish youth, TNA, CO 733/456/2, Lydda District Fortnight Report ending 15 August 1944; rumors of Partition, Lydda District Fortnight Report ending 31 August 1944.

183. TNA; KV 5/34; CO 733/456/2; WO 208/1705, penciled '9'; WO 208/1705, 17A; Ramat Hakovesh is cited as the "recent experience"; this a reference to the extreme reaction of the settlers to the British attempt to search that settlement in November of 1943. Also see WO 208/1705, P.I.C. Paper No. 35.

184. TNA, WO 208/1705, No. 1259; Weizmann, FO 371/40129, 98A.

185. TNA, WO 208/1705, Cipher Telegram 1259; CO 733/457/9, 'Important Notice' with MS '4' in upper right; also FO 371/40127, Inward Telegrams 1300, 1299, 23, 1282,

186. TNA, WO 208/1705, Cipher Telegram 1259, from the Officer Administering Government (O.A.G.).

187. TNA, WO 208/1705, Cipher Telegram 1259; CO 733/456/2, Jerusalem Fortnightly Report, 16-31 Oct., 1944

188. CO 733/457/9, Inward Telegram 1245 (also in FO 371/40127); TNA, CO 733/456/2, Lydda District Report Fortnight ended 30 Sept 1944

189. TNA, WO 208/1705, "An Estimate of the Possibility that the Jews in Palestine May Use Force in 1944 to Achieve their Political Aims," 4 (C. D. Quilliam, 15 Feb 44).

190. September, 1944. TNA, CO 733/456/2, Gaza District Fortnightly Report No. 138; For Zionist and Israeli tactic of creating a threat against which to defend itself, see Postscript; CO 733/456/2, Jerusalem Fortnightly Report, ended 31 Oct 1944.

191. The scale of these terror attacks made it "sufficiently evident," a secret telegram to the Secretary of State for the Colonies read, that they were "not attributable to an isolated small gang of terrorists, but are planned and executed by a

192. formidable organization, which is able to command a considerable force of well armed men." TNA, CO 733/457/9, 'No. 1245'; TNA, CO 733/456/2, Lydda Fortnightly Report Ended 30 Sept 1944; TNA, CAB 67/4/17/0001, 3.

192. Hikers, TNA, CO 733/456/2, Nablus Fortnightly Report ending 31 Oct 1944; CO 733/456/4 Nazareth Fortnightly Report, ended 31 Oct 1945, 2.

193. For records in Kew regarding Moyne, see e.g. CO 733/456/2, CO 733/457/13, and especially FO 141/1001, which contains the statements of the witnesses.

194. House of Lords Debate, 9 June 1942, vol 123 cc179-210.

195. Ben-Yehuda, *Assassinations*, 207; CIA, N-193, "American Zionists Intercede with Egyptian Authorities on Behalf of Moyne Assassins," 9 Feb 1945, declassified Feb 2002.

196. Jewish Agency, TNA, CO 537/1711, 112; TNA, CO 537/1712, "Jewish Agency and Hagana Anti-Terror Campaign"; *ibid*, MS '121'; *ibid*, 118; Also Ben-Yehuda, *Assassinations*, 210, who refers to it as "settling scores." For claimed cooperation, see TNA, CO 537/1814 'Report on a meeting of I.Z.C. Held on 29.10.46'. TNA, KV 3/41, Zionist Subversive Activities, 22; also KV 2/1435 333B; CO 537/1711, 'Cooperation by the Jewish Agency'; For Fishman and Gruenbaum, TNA, CO 733/457/9, "Jewish Reaction to the assassination of Lord Moyne," 4-5; NYT, "Churchill Warns Jews to Oust Gangs," 18 Nov 1944; Postage stamps, Ben-Yehuda, *Assassinations*, 210. For Herzog, Kister, *Irgun*, 121.

Chapter Four — The War Ends, 1945

197. Ernst, *So Far So Good*, 176-177. See also TNA, FO 800/487, 110.

198. CIA, N-193, "American Zionists Intercede with Egyptian Authorities on Behalf of Moyne Assassins," 9 Feb 1945, declassified Feb 2002.

199. TNA, CO 537/1715, 262/10/5/GS, esp 6; FO 1093/330, "Sir W. Battershill" at top, verso, suggests that Roosevelt did not think Palestine was the best solution for the problem of Jewish DPs, and Colonel Hoskins states that Roosevelt favored a Jewish-Christian-Muslim trusteeship, but felt the Zionists would not agree; CO 733/443/19, "Palestine Question" (red '77A'); CO 733/456/3, to Chief Secretary, 21 Apr 1945; WO 208/1705 16A, "Note No. 1" (red '16A'); CAB 66/37/46; CO 733/457/14, letter from Liddell to Eastwood (red '1'); CAB 66/37/46, p2; WO 208/1705 , "Note No. 1" (red '16A'); CO 733/457/12, Intelligence Summary No. 8/45, esp 3, re 'The Time Factor in Zionism." Ben-Gurion, speaking in February, 1943: "The weeks and months following the collapse of the Hitler régime will be a time of uncertainty in Europe and even more so in Palestine, and we must exploit this period in order to confront Britain and America with a *fait accompli*." (CAB 66/37/46, 2).

200. TNA, FO 371/40127, 75156/151E/44, letter dated 8 September 1944; Inward Telegram 977; CO 733/457/5, Catling, 'Note on Visit to the United States. Sept. 29 - Oct. 10 1944', esp 2; *ibid*, John Harington, "Top Secret" to Cecil, 8 Dec 1944 (red "36"); *ibid*, Agenda, red '35'; *ibid*, Telegram No. 784 (red '34'); CO 537/1720, C.S.728/11 (red '4'), contains samples of propaganda in which "imaginary atrocities were painted in glaring colours," collected

during an attempt to search settlements to June 29, 1946, e.g.: *Children and old people, men and women—pregnant—cripples and invalids were beaten up cruelly with rifle butts, bayoneted, maltreated and hit on all parts of their bodies until they fell unconscious. All were dragged over the ground and the stones or loaded like cattle on trucks... Suckling babies were torn from their mothers arms in cold blood ...children were being carried away ... their cries being heard from a distance...";* See also *ibid,* "Copy Statement," for similar from the Yishuv's leaders, indistinguishable from what the Irgun or Lehi were printing. CO 733/457/14, MS, begins "Jacob Meridor" (red '1945'); *ibid,* letter from Liddell to Eastwood (red '1'); letter, 3 May 1945 (red '2').

201. TNA, CO 733/456/3, Fortnightly Report, Haifa, ending 15 May 1945; *ibid,* Fortnightly Report, Lydda, ending 15 May 1945; for May 13, Hoffman, *Anonymous,* k4491; TNA, KV 5/34, Cipher Telegram 21.5.45 (MS '49A'); *ibid,* 45AC; CO 733/456/8, Palestine Outrages 1945 (red '49'); re hiking parties, CO 733/456/3, Fortnightly Report, Samaria (Nablus), end 15 May 1945; CO 733/456/8, Palestine Outrages 1945 (red '49'); KV 5/34, Cipher Telegram 21.5.45 (blue '49A'); CO 733/456/3, Fortnightly Report, Galilee, end 31 May 1945; *ibid,* Fortnightly Report, Lydda, end 31 May 1945; CO 733/456/8, Palestine Outrages 1945 (red '49'); Kister, *Irgun,* 260-261.

202. Shertok, TNA, FO 371/45377, Inward Telegram H.C.757; CO 537/1715, chart, '30. Aug 45' upper left; KV 5/29, Interview No. 8 with Kollek, ref DSO/P/13576; *ibid,* Extract from ... Palestine Summary No. 47.

203. TNA, CO 733/456/8, Palestine Outrages 1945 (red '49'); The battery "aligned in the direction of the King David" surely corresponds to the statement by Teddy Kollek that an Irgun mortar had been discovered near a YMCA (see TNA, KV 5/29, interview, 15.9.45); Clarke (*Blood and Fire*) cites this as a King David Hotel bombing stopped by the Agency.

204. TNA, KV 5/34, Extract Relating to O.F. 608/1 (blue MS '57B'); CO 733/456/8, begins "This Telegram should," dated 25.8.45; *ibid,* letter, G.H. Hall to Earl Winterton, MP, 15 Nov 1945. Some records cite Constable Hill, but Wilde is correct.

205. TNA, CO 733/456/8, letter, signed Francis James Bloor, Frederick John Popkins, R.L. Creese, dated 12.10.45.

206. Kister, *Irgun,* 261; TNA, KV 5/29, "Command Announcement" MS '81a'; All four piers had been mined, but two charges exploded. CO 733/456/8, red '29'; *ibid,* red MS '23.7.45' upper right, begins "(24). This telegram"; *ibid,* Palestine Outrages 1945 (red '49').

207. Former Congressman and Senator from Iowa, Guy Gillette. JTA, Aug 2, 1945; TNA, KV 3/56, "Jewish illegal immigration to Palestine" ('96c'), 20; KV 5/29, Inward Telegram 1149; Regarding the explosives theft on Aug 13, contradictory report from interview with Kollek, saying gang found no detonators - see KV 5/29 ('54B' upper right) verso; *ibid,* Jew Shot in Zichron Yaacov (MS '50B'); *ibid,* Inward Telegram 1149; CO 733/456/8, Palestine Outrages 1945 (red '49'); See JTA, Aug 23 1945.

208. TNA, CO 733/456/4, Gaza Fortnightly Report No. 160. Item 199 refers to "a separate report [that] has been submitted to you on the subject" of hiker, but which the author has not been able to locate. The Nablus report's

"Masherik" is now commonly spelled Mashriq, presumably refers to area east of Nablus; *ibid*, Fortnightly Report, Nablus, ending 30 Sep 1945.

209. TNA, Palestine Discount Bank, Sept 2 '45, KV 5/29, 'Command Announcement' MS '81a'; *ibid*, "Extract," Defense Security Office, DSO/B/2/5 (2 sides); *ibid*, Interview with Kollek ('54B' upper right); CO 537/1814, letter, H.L. Brown to T Smith, P.F. 46863/B3a/HLB.

210. TNA, KV 5/29, "Command Announcement" MS '81a' ("Zichon Moshe" Street in document).

211. TNA, KV 5/29, "Extract," Defense Security Office, DSO/B/2/5 (2 sides); CO 733/456/8, Palestine Outrages 1945 (red '49') (The British records lists the Sept 28 incident as an "outrage" (terror attack) and specifies one of the three assailants as having been identified as a Jew.)

212. TNA, KV 5/36, & WO 261/562, *Palestine: Statement of Information Relating to Acts of Violence;* Also Hoffman, *Anonymous*, k4839.

213. TNA, FO 371/45383, Inward Telegram No. 1531; Magnus, WO 261/571, Fortnightly Intelligence Newsletter No. 54.

214. JTA, July 3 1946, suggests that Athlit doubled as a prison, which the British deny, though it may have been use at times to detain people (see WO 275/38 Operation at Givat Haim, 26th Nov 1945); TNA, CO 733/456/4, Fortnightly Report 1-15 Oct 1945 (there is no explanation for the presence of the Christian woman in the clearing camp); FO 371/45381, Outward Telegram 1572; Inward Telegram 1433; FO 371/45383, Inward Telegram 1531; CO 537/1715, "Illegal Zionist Armed Forces in Palestine and the Complicity of the Jewish Agency," esp Appendix to Part I, & penciled page 6; CO 733/456/8, Palestine Outrages 1945, esp '6th Oct'; *ibid*, letter from G.H. Hall, red '69'.

215. Kister, *Irgun*, 261; TNA, FO 371/45381, Inward Telegeam 1441, 1440; CO 733/456/4, Jaffa District, Report 16-31 Oct 1945; *ibid*, Gaza Fortnightly Report No. 160; CO 733/456/8, "Palestine Outrages 1945," red '49', verso; TNA, KV 5/29, 59A; FO 371/45383, Inward Telegram 1531.

216. TNA, FO 371/45382, penciled '233', "Note of a Verbal Report made to the Secretary of State by Mr. R. Newton ... 17th October, 1945."

217. TNA, *ibid*, ('Note of a Verbal Report...'); CO 733/456/4, Fortnightly Report ending 15 Oct 1945, verso; CO 733/456/4, District Report, Jaffa, 16-31 Oct 1945, Ref S/7/38 ("sabateurs" in the document).

218. TNA, CO 733/456/8, Palestine Outrages 1945, verso, and Inward Telegram 1566; Kol Israel, see Statement of Information Relating to Acts of Violence (WO 261/562 and others); CO 733/456/4, Fortnightly Report ending 31 Oct 1945; A train carrying stone was also fired on near Tantura; see CO 733/456/8; CO 733/456/8, Cipher Telegram, 351075 red '54'; *ibid*, Cipher Telegram, 350892; *ibid*, Inward Telegrams 1549, 1566; repeated in FO 371/45383; According to Kister (*Irgun*, 128) the attacks of 31 Oct 1945 were not coordinated among Irgun-Lehi-Palmach, but were independent, unknown to each other, timed for the Balfour Declaration anniversary. Egged bus documents, CO 733/456/10, Summary of Documents Seized at Birya Settlement on 27.2.46.

219. Bevin meeting, see TNA, FO 800/484, 46; CO 733/457-11, Inward Telegram

1549; CO 537/1715, "Illegal Zionist Armed Forces in Palestine and the Complicity of the Jewish Agency," esp Part II; *ibid*, red '48', No. 5 (1 Nov 1945); *ibid*, '(b) Kol Israel Broadcasts...'; *ibid*, 'No. 5' 1 Nov 1945 'To London from Jerusalem'.

220. KV 5/39, Jewish Legion, *Report of the Conference*; FO 371/45387, Inward Telegram 1710, 2; FO 226/306, Army Signal In, No. GI/63977.

221. TNA, CO 733/457/11, after red '10'; Outward Telegram 3 Nov 1945; Wagner, 21 June, 1946, FO 371/52530, Cable and Wireless Limited, stamped 21 June 1946, penciled '76'; Sharett speech June 19 1946, TNA, FO 371/45378, penciled "55"; FO 371/45378, marked 'No. 743', British Embassy, Washington, D.C., July 1, 1945; CO 733/457/11, Outward Telegram, 3 Nov re No. 1549; *ibid*, letter by Bevin about meeting with Weizmann and Sharett, 2 Nov 1945.

222. TNA, CO 537/1715, "Illegal Zionist Armed Forces in Palestine and the Complicity of the Jewish Agency," esp 3-4; CO 733/456/4, Report for Period 1-15 Nov 1945, esp 2; CO 733/456/9, Inward Telegram 1625; *ibid*, Inward Telegram 'Not numbered' (red '86'); FO 226/306, Telegram, No. 509, 15 Nov; *ibid*, Army Message In, GO/63204; FO 371/45386, Inward Telegram (unnumbered, penciled '141'); WO 275/38, Events in Tel Aviv on 15.11.45; NYT, Nov 15 1945; Kister, *Irgun*, 261.

223. TNA, CO 733/456/9, Inward Telegrams 1677, 1680; *ibid*, Inward Telegram 'Not numbered' (red '88'); some repeated in FO 371/45386; CO 733/456/4; Fortnightly Report ending 30 Nov 1945, and others; CO 537/1715, "Illegal Zionist Armed Forces in Palestine and the Complicity of the Jewish Agency," esp Part II; FO 371/45387, Inward Telegram, 1680; CO 733/456/9, various cables, penciled 68-74, Outward Telegram 1906; FO 371/45386, Meyer Levin, NY Post, Nov 20 1945.

224. TNA, FO 1093/508, "Top Secret" / begins "Ben Gurion returned," esp p6 (in the original, "succeed" is "suceed"); FO 371/45382, penciled '233', "Note of a Verbal Report made to the Secretary of State by Mr. R. Newton ... 17th October, 1945"; KV 2/1435, '1642'. David Low satirised Zionism's need for anti-Semitism in a cartoon published in the *Evening Standard* on 22 Nov 1946. A man standing on a street corner is being observed by two Zionist terrorists hiding in the shadows. "What, he's not anti-Semitic?" one exclaims, obviously troubled. "We'll soon alter that." In another *Evening Standard* cartoon (3 Jan 1947), labelled "The Dark Mirror," Low shows a Zionist terrorist looking at himself in a mirror. His reflection is a monster labelled "Anti-Semitism."

225. TNA, CO 733/456/4, Chief Secretary 26 Nov 1945; *ibid*, Fortnightly Report ending 15 Nov 1945; TNA, KV 2/1435, 67191 CIRCUS 51a; KV 3/347; FO 371/45387, various cables to Bevin.

226. Kister, *Irgun*, 262; TNA, CO 733/456/9, Inward Telegrams 1840, 1845; *ibid*, Outward Telegram, 2063; CO 537/1715, "Part II - The Outrages," penciled 5-8; The Irgun cites an attack on Army Camp in north Tel Aviv on Dec 27 as its first naval action. Attacks that day on what it called Intelligence Headquarters in Jerusalem and in Jaffa were said to be a collaborative effort with Lehi (Kister, 131, 262), also confirmed by pamphlet bombs dropped on 2 Jan 1946; CO 733/456/10, Palestine Situation / Terrorist Outrages (red '6'); Inward Telegrams 27, 26; regarding charges of pervasive anti-Semitism and fascism among British

personnel cited, e.g., by Hoffman (*Anonymous*), see CO 733/456/10, Cypher letter from Washington to Jerusalem, red '2', Inward Telegram 21, and cypher message about US radio commentator Walter Winchell.

227. CO 537/1715, "Illegal Zionist Armed Forces in Palestine and the Complicity of the Jewish Agency," esp Part II; CO 733/456/4, Fortnightly Report through 31 Dec 1945; CO 733/457/11, Inward Telegram 1840; CO 733/456/9, Inward Telegram 1840; NYT 4 Jan 1946; NYT, 31 Dec 1945; CO 537/3854, Intelligence Summary No. 2/46, esp "ONLY SO Proclamation"; Note total casualties unclear, but one (incomplete?) tally recorded ten people were killed and twelve wounded in one day; CO 733/456/9, esp Inward Telegram 1845; CO 733/456/10, Palestine Situation / Terrorist Outrages (red '6'); Kister, *Irgun*, 262; The Palestinian telephone operator killed in the 27 Dec 1946 attack was Coustandi Eissa Ghaneim.

228. TNA, CO 733/457/11, Cabinet 1 (46); CO 537/1711, Co-operation by the Jewish Agency in suppression of terrorism, esp 4-5; press clippings; KV 3/56, Outward Telegram 1414. Regarding JA refusal to use the post- White Paper quota of 1500 a month, see Churchill's letter, FO 800/484, MS, 8, item 3; WO 275/38, Incident in Tel Aviv Monday 31 Dec 45; WO 169/23031, Monthly Summary No. 4, Jan 46; No. 7, Apr 46, p4; Appendix B 21.4.46.

229. TNA, KV 2/1435, 67191 CIRCUS 51a; Moshe Sneh was a proactive advocate for seeking support from the Soviet Union.

230. re Sneh's overtures to Soviet sponsorship, TNA, KV 2-1390; TNA, CO 537/1715, 75156/151/J.B. (red '77'), page "D" at top. This particular document is undated. Most dated documents from the cache are from late 1945, but in any event this document and the penciled annotation can not be later than the summer of 1946. Also see TNA, KV 4/467, for Jewish Agency terror link.

231. Plan of action is from "B.L." (translated from the Hebrew) dated Dec 19 1945. TNA, CO 537/1715, 75156/151/J.B. (red '77'), esp 2,3,5; *ibid*, Inward Telegram 1279: News reports misquoted the letters and made the Hagana appear more cooperative; That Zionism would require force, not political argument, was commonly expressed, e.g. Mr. Golomb of the Histadruth Executive in July of 1942 (See CAB 66/37-46, 2). Having the Jewish National Fund purchase land was at odds with the Irgun's belief that the entire region belonged to Jews by right and did not have to be purchased back.

Chapter Five — Race for Fanaticism, 1946

232. epigram: Letter, written in Hebraico-Yiddish, to a friend in New York, Grodzinsky, *Shadow*, 134.

233. TNA, CO 537/1715, letter, C.W. Baxter to T. Smith (red '82'); CO 733/457/12, Criminal Investigation Dept, Jewish Affairs. Terrorism, esp 3-4. The threat of using terrorism to stop Jews from leaving Palestine was expressed by saying the Hagana's sinking of the Patria would be eclipsed to intimidate Jews in Palestine against leaving (see Kew, CO 733/457/12, Criminal Investigation Department, Jerusalem, 24 April, 1945, Secret Document, 3-4); Ben-Gurion quote, Segev, *Complete*, 471, quoting from CZA S25/6090; Zertal eloquently points out that for these people just freed from unspeakable horror, then put into a new totalitarian environment, there was no such thing as free will or

free choice.

234. The sole post-Holocaust survey of DPs' wishes, before substantial Zionist intervention in the camps, was conducted in Dachau among 2,190 Jewish survivors. Fifteen percent expressed a desire to emigrate to Palestine. The rest wanted to return home or emigrate to the US (Grodzinsky, 41). This same opinion is voiced by several independent first-hand sources, among them Ernst (*So Far So Good*, 171).

235. TNA, FO 1093/508, "Top Secret / Ben Gurion returned to Palestine...," esp 6-7; Grodznski 60, 129-130; TNA, KV 3/41, "Zionist Subversive Activities," (blue '7a'), esp p8; KV 3/437, draft of address, "We have been considering...," (blue '100[N?]') esp third page. An example of an Irgun pamphlet printed in several languages and disseminated in the camps, such as one distributed at the DP camp in Linz Bindermicht, US Zone of Austria: It implored Jewish youth to fight to take "our homeland in its historical frontiers ... the state of Erez-Izrael must be given back to the Jewish nation, as the Almight promised the Jewish people." With the phrase "ki kecha ulezerache nattati et haaretz hazot'. KV 5/38, "Subject: Jewish Pamphlet," penciled '323'. In KV 3/41 there is a note that many Jewish DPs were in UNRRA camps, not Zionist-run camps; however, the influence of the Zionist remains the same, and other documents suggest strong Zionist influence even in the UNRRA camps. Regarding Churchill-Truman correspondence, FO 800/484 MS 9.

236. Grodzinsky, *Shadow*, 76-77 (September 1945); Bergen-Belson was also called Hohne Camp by MI5's 1946 report. TNA, KV 3/56, Report on a Tour of M.I.5 Liaison Officer in France, Germany, Austria and Italy between 5 September, 1946 and 8 October 1946, esp 4,6; violence against DPs, Grodzinsky, *Shadow*.

237. NYT, Feb 18 1946, which quotes 90% wanting to go to Palestine; for 100%, see Morris, *1948*, 46.

238. TNA, FO 371/75340, Policy of HM Government in Relation to Palestine 1945-1948 (52A), esp 3; Re US coercion, see also Lord Moyne's comments to the War Cabinet, 10 Dec 1943, in CAB 95/14, 31.

239. TNA, KV 3/56, Report on a Tour of M.I.5 Liaison Officer in France, Germany, Austria and Italy between 5 September, 1946 and 8 October 1946, esp 4,6; CAB 158/1, Annex, Organisation of Illegal Immigration.

240. NYT Feb 25 1946; Grodzinsky, *Shadow*.

241. TNA, CO 537/1705, letter, Chief Rabbi Herzog; Grodzinsky, *Shadow*.

242. *ibid*; Note quoted extract reads "with 1,000-500 children" but the latter number is surely a typo for "1,500").

243. *ibid*.

244. *ibid*.

245. *ibid*; Herzog's view of assimilation is also clear in his scathing condemnation of Reform Judaism: "[Reform Judaism] is a malignant growth eating away at the very vitals of what is holiest and dearest to Israel and jeopardising the continuity of our great God-inspired history. Reform inevitably leads to assimilation, and it has been aptly described as a back-door way to total

apostasy from Judaism." (Quoted from *The Jewish Post* (Indiana), 7 June 1946, quoting *London Jewish Chronicle*)

246. *ibid*.

247. One of the children "rescued" from his adoptive home was Yossi Peled, former IDF general and politician. Grodzinsky (*Shadow*, 50) cites an interview with him, his sister, and the daughter of their Belgian adoptive family, in which both of the Peled children's parents are said have perished in the Holocaust. The present author noted that the Wikipedia entry on Yossi Peled (accessed 9 May, 2013, again 17 May, 2014) states that Peled's mother survived the death camps and that it was she, with the Jewish Brigade's help, that "reclaimed" him, and then they made *aliyah*. The Wikipedia entry appears to be based on Peled's profile in the Israel Ministry of Foreign Affairs (accessed as above). The author contacted Prof Grodzinsky, who replied that he can produce the source with Yossi Peled's sister's testimony, and that Peled's story is well-known in Israel and does not include his mother. Prof Grodzinsky stated: "Further, the Wikipedia version raises a question: if his mother reclaimed him, how did he end up without her at kibbutz Negba? He was in the kibbutz by himself." Prof Grodzinsky found a web page that "fixes" this part of the story, placing his mother with him in the kibbutz. He also found that the Likud party's website (in Hebrew, no longer accessible), had stated that "Peled was raised as a Christian child up to age 8, at which point his mother arrived with soldiers of the Jewish Brigade to return him to the bosom of Judaism." The present author also noted that Wikipedia and the IMFA date his birth at 1941, raising the additional question as to why the mother wait four years after the end of the war before retrieving her children. *My thanks to Professor Grodzinsky for his kind assistance.*

248. Grodzinsky, *Shadow*, 94, 51, 90-91. The cited example of contact forbidden with surviving family is the orphanage in Selvino, northern Italy. TNA, CO 537/1705/0003. John Gutch, who would survive the King David Hotel bombing, reacted angrily to the kidnappings, writing that it "illustrates only too clearly the fact that Zionist Jews are not in the least interested in the happiness and comfort of Jews ... Such bigotry and callousness are difficult for us to appreciate"; There appear to have been two contemporaries named John Gutch with British military careers, causing some confusion; the present Gutch was best known in his day for his career in the Solomon Islands.

249. Ernst, *So Far So Good*, 173; TNA, FO 800/487, 110, 211.

250. Lilienthal, *What Price*, 26-27; Regarding Roosevelt's quip about Wise, the President worried that Wise might pass by Joseph Proskauer, president of the American Jewish Committee and influential critic of Zionism, outside his office; Menuhin, *Decadence*, 96; Ernst, *So Far So Good*, 176.

251. NYT 27 Oct 1946.

252. TNA, KV 5/29, '69C'; *ibid*, DSO/P/2131/D.3. ('Lochmei Herut Israel'); FO 1093/508, red '64'; CO 537/1709, C.S. 731; The British, aware that Jews were being murdered if they were suspected of working with the British against terror, tightened the small pool of individuals privy to their identities. The caution was vindicated when documents seized in a raid of the Jewish Agency included records of the Agency's spies. TNA, CO 537/ 1715, "Top Secret: Memorandum" begins "following are further," see item 4.

253. In correspondence with the British, Sharett presented new arguments, not cited in 1944, as to why the Brigade should not be disbanded. See, e.g., TNA, CO 537/1821, letter, Shertook to Bevin; CO 537/1821, MS page with penciled '5' upper left, begins *immigration and the recent seizure*; *ibid*, Loose Minute to SD2/7580'A', & *ibid*, penciled '27 End'.

254. TNA, CO 537/1820, Palcor Bulletin, 3 Jan 1946, 3, 5; CO 733/456/10, Inward Telegram 45, 55; 51; Outward Telegram 95; WO 275/73, chart 31 Oct /1 Nov; KV 5/34, blue '70d', blue '73c'; According to Circus (MI6), "a large number of Palmach men" reportedly joined in the attack; CO 537/1709, C.S. 731; CO 537/ 1715, "Top Secret: Memorandum" begins "following are further," see item 4.

255. TNA, CO 537/1715, "Illegal Zionist Armed Forces in Palestine and the Complicity of the Jewish Agency," esp Part II; CO 733/456/10, 330/169/GS; Inward Telegram 95; Outward Telegram 118; Kister, *Irgun*, 262; NYT Jan 20 1946.

256. *ibid*.

257. TNA, CO 733/456/10, 75156/151A; CO 537/1715, "Illegal Zionist Armed Forces in Palestine and the Complicity of the the Jewish Agency," esp 16; Kister, *Irgun*, 132, 262; for yarn theft, TNSAA, WO 169/23031, Monthly Summary No. 4, Jan 46; The radar station at Mount Carmel was also known as the RAF Experimental Station in Haifa.

258. Kister, *Irgun*, 262; TNA, WO 169/23031, Monthly Summary No. 5, Feb 1946; CO 733/456/10, Inward Telegrams 220, 214; KV 5/35, O.F.608/1 "IZL and LHI," 6; CO 537/1715, chart, "20 Feb 46" upper left; KV 5/30 Statement Relating to Acts of Violence, esp 7; also summarized in CO 733/456/10, "Extract from Palestine Tel. 349..." (red '36').

259. TNA, CO 733/456/10, Cypher Telegram marked D.T.O. 161330B (red '21'); Inward Telegram 260; "Extract from Palestine Tel. 349..." (red '36'); Ben-Yehuda, *Assassinations*, 217-218; TNA, KV 5/29, OF 85/22(1)B.1.B.; *ibid*, '78a'; *ibid*, Extract '68b'; KV 2/3428 (leaf 13A for connection with Manchester paper).

260. TNA, KV 5/29, 373/2/1/GS; CO 537/1715, Statement Relating to Acts of Violence; CO 733/456/10, Inward Telegram 614, Inward Telegram 289; British record cite attacks at three separate locations: Shafr Amr, Kfar Vitkin, and Sarona; See also NYT Feb 22 1946; CO 537/1715, "Illegal Zionist Armed Forces in Palestine and the Complicity of the Jewish Agency," esp 16-22; CO 733/456/10, Inward Telegrams 289, 301, 311, 319, & "Extract from Palestine Tel. 349..." (red '36'); CO 537/1715, Top Secret: Memorandum, begins "Following are further," esp 2; WO 169/23031, Monthly Summary No. 5, Feb 1946.

261. Cunningham, in a telegram dated 19 February; TNA, CO 537/1711, Inward Telegram 281; Already in the early 1950s, British records speak of Israel's government using the country's media to create mass hysteria of an alleged threat, then finding itself forced to take action against that "threat," lest it lose credibility. This is repeated quite explicitly, e.g., in 1956 (see FO 371/121692, report from British Embassy, Tel Aviv, February 20, 1956, 2).

262. NYT 23 Feb 1946, Masada, the youth organization of the ZOA, announced

the campaign at their eleventh annual national convention.

263. Kister, *Irgun*, 132, 262-263; TNA, CO 537/1715, Statement Relating to Acts of Violence, 7, cites seven aircraft destroyed and eight damaged; another report says seven aircraft destroyed and fifteen damaged; I have used the figures in TNA, CO 537/3854, MS.11750 /AOC.215 Feb 26, as it seemed to be the final British tally. WO 275/34, Appendix A in "General Report on Terrorist Activities in 6 Airborne Divisional Area in 1946"; the NYT cites fourteen aircraft destroyed, eight damaged beyond repair (NYT 27 Feb 1946); TNA, CO 733/456/10, Cipher Telegram 363920; *ibid*, Inward Telegram 320; CO 733/456/10, Official Communiqué (penciled '52'); Summary of Documents Seized at Birya Settlement on 27 February 46, and subsequent pages through '79'; Inward Telegram 352.

264. TNA, CO 733/456/10, Extract from Palestine Tel. 349 (red '36'); CO 537/1715, "Top Secret / Illegal Zionist Armed Forces in Palestine and the Complicity of the Jewish Agency," esp 8; CO 537/1821, 92275/1/SD1a; ibid, penciled "27 End"; Kister, *Irgun*, 263; NYT 7 Mar 1946; CO 733/456/10, Inward Telegrams 376, 502; According to WO 275/73, chart, "31 Oct 1 Nov" (1945), the railway station at Sukreir was bombed on 27 Mar, without casualty or damage; for a list of minor incidents for March 1946, see WO 169/23031.

265. TNA, WO 275/73, chart 1; CO 733/456/10, Inward Telegrams 542, 546; KV 5/35, 104AB; *ibid*, 101z; WO 169/23031, Monthly Summary No. 7, Apr 46, p4; Kister, *Irgun*, 263.

266. TNA, CO 733/456/10, Inward Telegram 613, 614; WO 275/73, chart, '31 Oct / 1 Nov' (1945); WO 275/34, Appendix A in "General Report on Terrorist Activities in 6 Airborne Divisional Area in 1946" cites an attack on the "3 CON DEPOT armoury," which I have assumed to be the same attack as on the Army Convalescent Depot. This report estimated 20 "armed Jews" rather than 10-15 for the second Nathanya attack.

267. TNA, CO 73/456/10, Inward Telegram, 664; According to WO 275/34, "General Report on Terrorist Activities in 6 Airborne Divisional Area in 1946," Appendix A, the Tel Aviv station bombing was a diversionary tactic for the police station attack; Kister, *Irgun*, 263.

268. TNA, KV 5/29, Inward Telegram 687; *ibid*, "Mourning Notice"; CO 537/3854, 75156/151; *ibid*, Cypher Telegram, IZ 2315; *ibid*, Outward Telegram, 739; WO 169/23031, Monthly Summary No. 7, Apr 46; CO 733/456/10, Attack on Airborne Car Park TEL AVIV 25 Apr 46; Appendix with Statements; Outward Telegram 739; Inward Telegram 687; for minor incidents see WO 169/23031, Diary of Events - April 1946.

269. HMS *Chevron*, TNA, CO 733/456/10, Inward Telegram 737, 749.

270. TNA, KV 5/35, Extract from report forwarded by D.S.O. Palestine re Jewish affairs, DSO/P/17478/P2. Capitalization original; WO 261/562.

271. *ibid*.; CO 537/1711, "3. Situation in Palestine."

272. TNA, WO 275/58, Intelligence Summary No. 3, ... up to 26 July 46.

273. TNA, CO 733/456/10, Inward Telegram 737; CO 733/456/11, red '73'; CO 537/1711, C.O.S. 534/6; *ibid*, letter, L.G. Hollis to PRIME MINISTER; *ibid*, Cypher Telegram, 972/CIC 4 May; CO 537/1711, "3. Situation in Palestine,"

"Annex II," "Enclosure to Annex II"; *ibid*, for Ben-Gurion directing the Hagana, upper left "Top Secret 95"; *ibid*, letter, Weizmann to Churchill, April 14 1946.

274. TNA, CO 733/456/11, red '73'; CO 537/1711, C.O.S. 534/6; *Palestine Statement of Information Relating to Acts of Violence*, Colonial Office, July, 1946. Its most damning evidence was intercepted Agency telegrams and broadcasts by Kol Israel. The case was further supported by printed materials: the Irgun's Herut, Lehi's Hamaas, and the Eshnav of the Jewish Resistance Movement (a Hagana-Irgun-Lehi alliance). TNA, KV 5/36, Statement of Information Relating to Acts of Violence; WO 261/562, Historical Record July - Sep 1946.

275. TNA, KV 5/30, "Extract," DSO/B/2/5, '97z', verso & following; WO 169/23031, Monthly Summary 8, May 1946; WO 275/34, Appendix "A" 613/A/GSI; WO 275/73, chart, "31 Oct / 1 Nov"; CO 733/456/10, Inward Telegram 847; Kister, *Irgun*, 263.

276. TNA, CO 733/477/3, Main Terrorist Incidents; CO 733/456/10, Inward Telegram 935; KV 5/35, DSO/B/2/5, Rescue by the LHI, 6; WO 169/23031, Monthly Summary 9, June 1946; Re clinic incident, some documents say Irgun (KV 5/30, O.F. 606/1 '96B'), but Lehi is surely correct (KV 5/30, B.3.a., 92a); KV 5/35, blue '91ZA', etc; *ibid*, blue '96'; WO 169/22957, Report on the Train Sabotage on 10 June 46; WO 275/73, chart '1 Nov 45'; CO 733/456/11, C.S. 759 (red '86').

277. TNA, CO 733/456/11, Report, C.S. 759, red '86'; WO 275/73, chart, '11 Jun 46'; KV 5/30, press clippings; CO 537/1712, '135' upper right; KV 5/38, 162a; WO 169/22957, red 'J58' at top, and North Palestine Dist Weekly Int Review No 11.

278. TNA, CO 733/477/3, Main terrorist incidents 1 June 1946 -6 Mar 1947; CO 733/456/11, pencil 131 red 86; *ibid*, red '89', 22 August, 2946 [sic]; *ibid*, '128' upper right; *ibid*, "Acts of Sabotage," penciled '99' (one Bedouin was stabbed and seriously wounded); FO 371/52530, Inward Telegram 985, 987; WO 169/22957, North Palestine Dist Weekly Int Review No 11.

279. TNA, FO 371/52530, Inward Telegram not numbered but penciled '70'; FO 371/52530, Cipher Telegram (373476 at top); WO 169/22957, North Palestine Dist Weekly Int Review No 11; CO 537/1711, red '112'; *ibid*, letter, Weizmann to Churchill, Aril 14 1946, esp 2.

280. TNA, CO 537/3854, SF.209/Palestine/Supp/B3a/JCR (red '20'); KV 5/35, JTA, '98W' (The JTA reported attack as Irgun, but British believed it was Lehi, seems to be confirmed in CO 537/3854 red '20', and MS annotation KV 5/35 JTA blue '97'; WO 169/22957, Incidents night 17/18 Jun; CO 537/1715, Statement Relating to Acts of Violence, p8; FO 371/52530, Inward Telegram 989; for other attacks of June 17-18, see WO 169/22957, Outline report of incidents night 17/18 June 46; KV 5/35, 'Kol Israel Broadcast Gives Reasons For Attacks'.

281. TNA, CO 733/456/11, 106; Kidnapped officers, see also WO 169/22957, J81, & North Palestine Dist Weekly Int Review No 11; KV 5/35, 97B (JTA Bulletin); *ibid*, 'O.F.608/1', IZL and LHI, esp 6; CO 733/477/3, Main Terrorist Incidents; CAB 129/10/0/0038; FO 371/52530, Inward Telegram 992; CO 537/1711, Inward Telegrams 1100, 993; KV 5/35, 98W (Attack

on Haifa Railway Workshops); CO 537/1711, 1071 (red '49'); *ibid*, Inward Telegram 993; WO 275/58, 6 Airborne Division, Intelligence Summary No. 1 (27 Jun - 11 Jul 46); kidnapped officers' release, WO 275/58, 6 Airborne Division, Intelligence Summary No. 1 (27 Jun - 11 Jul 46); my description of the wooden box as coffin-like is based on several British reports describing a box used at the scene of the kidnappings in which stretchers were seen hidden and which was believed used for the abductions. The men were believed to have been held at 9 Salameth Road, Givat Moshe Qtr, Tel Aviv.

[282.] TNA, CO 537/1715, 262/10/5/GS, Criminal Investigation Dep't, esp 7,11,12; Kolsky, *Jews Against Zionism*, 143-144.

[283.] TNA, WO 275/58, 6 Airborne Division, Intelligence Summary No. 4 (up to 9 Aug 46).

[284.] TNA, KV 5/30, 107 (DSO/P/20054/S.1.); WO 169/23031, Monthly Summary 9, June 1946; Re insurance & diamonds, see also WO 275/79, 317 Airborne Field Security, Report No. 44, week ending 9 Sep 47. Diamond firms with British insurance were targeted, and after receiving the insurance money the owner would repurchase the merchandise from the gangs; KV 2/1435, letter, Kellar to Smith, 229a; WO 275/58, 6 Airborne Division, Intelligence Summary No. 1 (27 Jun - 11 Jul 46).

[285.] TNA, FO 371/67813B, Z 6069, Jewish terrorism in Italy.

[286.] TNA, KV 5/37, "Extract from MITROPA"; The leaflets mentioned were taken at Bad Gastein. The document cites a "Bagola" branch of the Irgun, of which the author found no further trace but the name apparently (?) from Ilo Bagola, an African-American Christian said to have joined the Zionist cause in the early twentieth century.

[287.] TNA, KV 5/36, 107x (Irgun posters); *ibid*, Palestine Statement of Information Relating to Acts of Violence; WO 261/562, Historical Record July - Sep 1946.

[288.] TNA, WO 261/562, Historical Record July - Sep 1946. Op Agatha; WO 275/27; WO 275/29, Operation Agatha, Instruction No. 68; CO 537/1711, *HQ Palestine and Transjordan Operation Agatha 29 June - 1 July 1946*, 3-5; *ibid*, Inward Telegram 1056; Telegram from Prime Minister To the President of the United States; Draft Oral Statement ... (60th Conclusions: Minute 3, 20 June, 1946); *ibid*, Inward Telegram 1007; The British records refer to leakage from an Operation Broadside, which appears to have been another name for Agatha. Broadside was a "theory, then widespread in the Yishuv and repeated in Israeli historiography," of a large-scale plan (Motti Golani, *Palestine between Politics and Terror, 1945-1947*. Brandeis University Press, 2013, 92-93). For the pamphlet *Palestine Statement of Information Relating to Acts of Violence*, see TNA, CO 537/1715, WO 261/562.

[289.] TNA, CO 537/1711, *HQ Palestine and Transjordan Operation Agatha 29 June - 1 July 1946*, p12, 5; WO 275/29, Operation Agatha, Instruction No. 68, 2; CO 537/1715, Telegram No. 1130 / no. 1077 Case Against Jewish Agency; *ibid*, From High Commissioner No. 1038. Some documents alluded to a previously unknown terror group called Kotzer, which the British thought was named for the initial letters of the Hebrews words meaning "Military Reserve Group"; Wise and Truman, see FO 371/52563, letter from Secretary of State James F. Byrnes to Wise, October 24, 1946, and accompanying correspondence from Wise.

290. TNA, CO 537/1711, *HQ Palestine and Transjordan Operation Agatha 29 June - 1 July 1946*, esp 10-11 (note "the childrens [sic] see-saw"); CO 537/1712, 'Jewish Agency Policy'.

291. TNA, CO 733/456/11, Inward Telegram 1175; WO 275/58, 6 Airborne Division, Intelligence Summary No. 2 (12 Jul - 19 Jul), & No. 1 (27 Jun - 11 Jul 46). For specific reference to pressure against Czechs joining the Czech Army, see e.g., WO 169/148, Summary of Intelligence, 8 June 1940, section 75.

292. Rogan, *The Arabs*, 250 (and many others); TNA, KV 5/36, 110b; 113 (DSO/P/18281/14/P2); 112 (O.F.608/1/B.3a/JCR) re claim that between 10-11 the morning of the bombing, the Irgun informed all Jewish institutions of a more aggressive stance; Cunningham quote, FCO 141/14292, letter to Creech Jones, 30 October 1946; WO 261/562, The Attack on the King David Hotel; WO 275/33A, "Translation of One of the Documents Found in Meir Garden on 30 July 46"; Somewhat clarified in CO 537/1715, Inward Telegram 1257; KV2 2251, 25a; KV 5/30, Summary of a letter from D.S.O. Palestine ref. DSO/P/S1; KV 5/36, 112z; 114 (Irgun Zvai Leumi); Irgun *Communique*, KV 5/36. Among the leads given the British after the King David attack, one ex-corporal named Jewson identified four individuals who he claimed were involved with terrorism, including the pilot of a training plane and a former doctor of philosophy in Vienna who now extorted money for the Hagana. The following appeared in a special edition of *Falastin* (in *Palestine Chronicle*) on 22 July 1946: *All the employees of the second grade utterly condemn that appalling campaign which was directed at the general secretariat in Jerusalem and which as a result many of its members met their death with many of their companions of the employees of the first grade while they were carrying out their duties with all loyalty. The association has no doubt that all members of the public will express the most heartfelt sympathy at this dark hour to the families of the victims who were killed by the most repulsive act of barbarity that can be described. Under these circumstances the association offers with a wounded heart its deep condolences to the families of the victims and to His Excellency the head of the government works this momentous calamity.*

293. TNA, KV2 2252, '100a'; CO 537/1715, '58'; Begin & the Knesset was on 18 Oct 1950.

294. TNA, WO 275/58, 6 Airborne Division Intelligence Summary No. 4 (through 9 Aug 46); KV 5/36, Extract GI/33879; KV 2/1435, 264c; Mr. Ted Steel, interview with the author in Knighton, Wales, August 3, 2014; a friend of his, Hilda, was a sergeant in charge of the ATS girls (Auxiliary Territorial Service); CO 537/3854, red '2A.J. Kellar' in upper left; CO 537/3854, 'Top Secret & Personal ... 21.1.46'; A rumor was spread that the British knew of the King David attack in advance; see CO 733/478/2, red '31', where a misquoted British officer may have been the gossip's origin. For an improbably detailed reconstruction of alleged warning calls, see Clarke, *By Blood and Fire*, which presents a moment-to-moment record of the alleged caller's precise movements and thoughts. For record of the Irgun's fake bomb scares around the time of the King David bombing, see, e.g., TNA, WO 275/121.

295. E.g., Hoffman (*Anonymous Soldiers*) cites the King David attack as the most deadly to that time. It is also said that the neighboring Post Office and French Consulate received warning calls; this is true, but they were received after the

main explosion. TNA, WO 261/562, The Attack on the King David Hotel.

296. TNA, KV 2/1435, Robertson to Smith, 264C; For Iltyd Clayton, CO 733/478/2, letter from Cairo, 26 July 1946; CO 733/478/2, 112A (eight dots at end in original).

297. TNA, WO 261/562, Historical Record July - Sep 1946 Op Shark; WO 275/31; WO 275/32; Cesarani, *Hat*, 41; CIA Documents; KV 5/30, Press section; Counterfeiting equipment and counterfeit bonds, Jewish Virtual Library, accessed June 15 2014; KV 5/37, Kellar to Smith, 126B; TNA, KV 5/36, Herut No. 59. The Anglo-American loan was approved in July despite American Zionists' attempts to stop it (Medoff, *Militant Zionism*, 143-144). Wise was the only prominent Zionist not openly opposing the loan. See also FO 800/485, 159.

298. TNA, WO 275/73, chart, "11 Jun 46"; KV 5/36, 115z; KV 3/56, Outward Telegram, 1414.

299. TNA, HO 45/25586.

300. TNA, KV 3/56, Outward Telegram (no marking); KV 5/36, Extract, JTA, OF.608/1; WO 275/121, Periodical Intelligence Review, Period Ended 29 Aug 1946; CO 733/456/11, Cipher Telegram, 42257G(0)4, & Inward Telegram 1355; CO 537/2292, Inward Telegram 1400, & letter, Glutch to Smith, C.S. 728. Some sources (e.g., Wikipedia) date the Empire Rival attack at August 22; British records state that the charges were placed at 22:45 on the 21st. Hagana responsibility, WO 275/58, Intelligence Summary No. 6, 6; For HMG policy bringing illegal immigrants to Cyprus, see WO 261/562, "G Branch," Historical Record July - Sept 1946 Illegal Immigration. For reasons that the author could not determine, the exact timing of the announcement commuting the death sentences was crucial, and the British took measures to insure that word did not leak out early; KV 5/38, "Jewish Interest in Atomic Fission."

301. TNA, KV 3/437, 46A, media reports; Medoff, *Militant Zionism*, Ch. 8; NYT Nov 11 1946; TNA, FO 800/486, 106, 128; PM quote: Dr. Nahum Goldmann made the proposals on behalf of the Agency. TNA, FO 800/485, 194 (No. 1218). This document refers also to telegrams 606 & 607, which the author has not been able to locate. Re Golda Meir and Jewish Agency's instance on global control of Jewish presence at the London Conference, see interview transcript in WO 261/562.

302. TNA, KV 5/30, media reports; FO 371/52560, Outward Telegram 1683; NYT 11 Sep 1946; Haifa-Kantara Line bombings 8-9 Sept were reported as between Rehovoth and Bir Yaacov (destroyed in three places), between Kfar Jinnis and Ras El Ain, and near Qalqilya. CO 733/456/11, Inward Telegram 1453 (Tarshiha is "Acretarshiha," Qalqilya is "Kalkiliya"); *ibid*, Letter to Alec Kirkbride (E 8911/4/31); WO 275/73, chart, '1 Nov 45' upper left; chart, 9 Sept 46; WO 261/562, Terrorist Activities from 8 Sep - 30 Sep.

303. TNA, KV 5/30, media reports; Letter to Trafford Smith, 120B; CO 733/477/3. KV 5/37, Cipher Telegram 58248/G(0); CO 733/456/11, Inward Telegram 1466. British documents record a very different account of Sergeant Martin's assassination than that in Bowyer Bell (167) and cited by Ben-Yehuda (*Assassinations*, 225). That account has the assassins posing as tennis players who kill Martin as he walks past the court. According British documents, three Jews in a Buick car drove up to Martin, two exited

the car while the driver remained at the wheel, and fired seven shots, five bullets hitting Martin in the back. Instead of dying on the spot as per the Zionist account, British records have him surviving for two hours, dying in the hospital. Bowyer Bell's dating the assassination at 10 August is surely in error. Yitzhak Shamir = Itzhak Yazernitzky-Shamir.

[304.] TNA, CO 733/456/11, Inward Telegram 1496; KV 5/37, Inward Telegrams 1487, 1455; Cipher Telegram 380587; Inward Telegram 1466; blue 136B; blue 133D; WO 261/562, Terrorist Activities from 8 Sep - 30 Sep; CO 733/477/3, HO 45/25586, *Jewish Struggle*; Perhaps these four Arab deaths from the bank robberies were confused with those from the train incident of the same day?; NYT Sep 14 1946; Bevin & Byrnes, TNA, FO 800/486, 123; WO 275/121, Periodical Intelligence Review Period Ended 8th October 1946.

[305.] TNA CO 733/456/11, Inward Telegram 1552, 1528, 1599; KV 5/37, Cypher Telegram blue 136; *ibid*, Inward Telegram 1528; WO 275/73, chart, '8/9 Sept' upper left; '18/19 Feb' upper left; WO 275/121, Periodical Intelligence Review Period Ended 8th October 1946. WO 261/658, Intelligence Summary No. 12, up to 4 Oct 46; CO 733/456/11 puts the Haifa-Kantara line bombing on Sep 24 (night of the 23-24) Irgun records cite the 23rd Kister, *Irgun*, 265); WO 261/647, HQ South Palestine District, Intelligence Summary No. 16, period ending 29 Sep 46; KV 5/37, Secret Telegram Received in Cipher 136; Inward Telegram 1528; CO 733/477/3, Main Terrorist Incidents during the Period 1 June - 6 March 1947; KV 5/30, Inward Telegram 1603; dogs, see WO 261/647, HQ South Palestine District, Intelligence Summary No. 16, period ending 29 Sep 46; FO 371/52560, Inward Telegram 1599 cites 50 lbs explosives in the 29 Sept 1946 Haifa oil dock incident, though another British report estimated 40 lbs; Inward Telegram 1603.

[306.] NYT 26 Sep 1946; Bevin, TNA, FO 800/486, MS '123' at upper right.

[307.] TNA, FO 800/486, 16.

[308.] TNA, WO 275/121, also WO 261/564, 'Text of an address given by a Jew before an audience at a dominion club'.

[309.] *Ibid*. ('Text of an address…'); As regards Zionist interference with the emigration of Jewish DPs to Australia, Klaus Neumann, in *Across the Seas - Australia's Response to Refugees: A History* (Black, 2015), states that many Jewish leaders were against Jewish immigration "either because they feared the emergence of anti-Semitism or because they were committed Zionists."

[310.] TNA, WO 261/562, "G Branch," Historical Record July - Sept 1946, Intelligence Newsletter 34 June - 7 July [1946]; and others; WO 275/121, Periodic Intelligence Review, Period Ended 12 Sept. 1946.

[311.] TNA, KV 5/30, 128z 'Terrorist Methods'; WO 275/58, and WO 261/656, Intelligence Summary No. 12 (to 4 Oct 46); WO 261/647, Intelligence Summary No. 17, ending 28 Oct 46.

[312.] TNA, WO 275/121, Periodical Intelligence Review Period Ended 8th October 1946; *ibid*, Monthly Air Letter No. 1. October - 1946; L.H.I. Bulletin No. 1, Nov 1946; TNA, CO 733/456/11, Inward Telegram 1634 (also in FO 371/52560); CO 537/1814, P.F.93,666/B.3.a/DJS; KV 5/37, "Notes on a Conversation between the D.S.O. and Z on 7 October 1946"; CO

733/456/11, Inward Telegram 1634; WO 275/58, Intelligence Summary No. 13 (to 11 Oct 46).

313. TNA, KV 5/30, Inward Telegram 1647; CO 733/456/11; WO 261/564, Summary of Major Incidents During the Quarter Ending 31 Dec 46; WO 261/656, Road Mining Incidents in Division Area since 16 Jun 46; FO 371/52560, Inward Telegram 1647; Kister, *Irgun*, 265; L.H.I. Bulletin, No. 1, Nov 1946.

314. TNA, CO 733/457/12, Inward Telegram 1441; CO 733/477/3, Main Terrorist Incidents during the Period 1 June - 6 March 1947; WO 261/564, Summary of Major Incidents During the Quarter Ending 31 Dec 46; Ben-Yehuda, *Assassinations*, 227-230; CO 733/456/11, Inward Telegram 1958; WO 275/73, chart, "8/9 Sept" upper left (places time at night of 21st-22nd); FO 371/52563, C.S. 421, No. 1563; WO 275/58, Intelligence Summary No. 15 (to 25 Oct 46), No. 14 (to 18 Oct 46); some duplication in WO 261/656; WO 261/647; Intelligence Summary No. 17, period ending 28 Oct 46; L.H.I.-Bulletin, no. 1, Nov 1946, 10; TNA, WO 27/121, Monthly Air Letter No. 1. October - 1946; FO 371/52563, Inward Telegram 1767; WO 261/564, Fortnightly Intelligence Newsletter No. 27.

315. TNA, FCO 141/14286, Telegram No. 2078, 1803, 1676; FO 371/52563, Inward Telegram 2078; Gillette's ads on the 23rd, see FO 371/52563, letter from the British Embassy in Washington, 25 October 1946.

316. Silver, NYT Oct 27 1946. Some works cite what is claimed to be Silver's actual quote about refugees at the 49th ZOA Convention, wrongly attributing it to this NYT article; The author could find no source for the alleged quote, "...are we again, in moments of desperation, going to confuse Zionism with refugeeism, which is likely to defeat Zionism? Zionism is not a refugee movement." Also TNA, WO 275/58, Intelligence Summary 22 (to 13 Dec 46); for Silver claiming the Agency to be representative body of all Jews, see e.g., NYT, 27 Jan 1947.

317. Regarding the Lehi attack on the 29th near Wilhelma, the *NY Times* reported what was likely the same attack, "some miles north of Tel Aviv"; NYT Oct 31 1946; L.H.I.-Bulletin, no. 1, Nov 1946, p10-11; TNA, WO 27/121, Monthly Air Letter No. 1. October - 1946; CO 537/1712, OF.607/1/Link/B.3a/HPC; KV 5/31, 138; FO 371/52563, Inward Telegram 1777; L.H.I.-Bulletin, no. 1, Nov 1946, p11; Kister, *Irgun*, 265; TNA, CO 733/456/11; CO 733/456/11, Inward Telegram 1777; See *Palestine Pamphlet*, 17, for seventeen injured; WO 275/79, 317 Airborne Field Security Section, Report No. 1, for the week ending 5 Nov 1946.

318. TNA, CO 733/456/11, Inward Telegram 1780; WO 275/121, Monthly Air Letter No. 1. October - 1946; Ben-Yehuda, *Assassinations*, (242) says the attack commenced at 2:00, not 3:00. The NYT account (31 Oct 1946) cites three Jews in the taxi when apprehended, not four that Ben-Yehuda cites as captured. The document in WO 27/121 cited herein states that three men were arrested but that "the girl seems to have escaped"; FO 371/52563, Inward Telegram 1780. A slightly different account of the 30 Oct attack is found in WO 261/564, Historical Record Oct-Dec 1946, Attack on Jerusalem Station on 30 Oct 46. It has Constable Smith leaving the first suitcase outside without destroying it, the second suitcase exploding and killing him, then the first exploding outside, and after that the third suitcase (inside).

319. TNA, FO 371/60786, From Rome to Foreign Office, No: 1618; KV 5/38, 158A; NYT, Nov 1 (report that a passer-by was too injured to be questioned), & Nov 5 1946; Kister, *Irgun*, 191; A newsreel (unidentified) from the time states that two people were killed in the Rome bombing. TNA, FO 371/60786, ZM 3734 No. 1649 ("Ineretz" [sic, "in Eretz"]).

320. TNA, FO 371/60786, ZM 3734 (3684, & No. 1652).

321. TNA, CO 537/2295, "Your telegram No. 2017 paragraph 2." Sanctuary in Vatican City was said to be the goal of the suspect killed while escaping.

322. TNA, CO 537/2295, '28.12.46' upper right; The suspect who was killed was Israel Epstein; some documents note that Italian police believed there was insufficient evidence to bring him to trial, but he was being held, apparently, for extradition back to Palestine; CO 537/1729, Appendix I, "The National Military Organisation in Palestine"; FO 371/67796, British Embassy Rome, 37/199/47; FO 371/102121,British Legation Tel Aviv WT1651/1; *Daily Express*, 18 , April 1952; JTA, 21 April 1952; NYT, 18 April 1952.

323. L.H.I.-Bulletin, no. 1, Nov 1946, 9; TNA, KV 5/38, Cipher Telegram G(0)1 73795; *ibid*, Inward Telegram, 1783; WO 275/58, Intelligence Summary No. 16 (to 1 Nov 46); HO 45/25586, *The Jewish Struggle*, No. 1, Dec 1945.

324. TNA, FO 371/61865, Cairo to Foreign Office No. 331; letter to Mr. Mayhew, "Barc., Dec. 5th, 1946"; KV 3/437, 46A, 45A, 44A; Sneh, FO 371/52563, letter from the British Embassy in Washington, dated 26 October 1946, and note to Trafford Smith, dated 31 October, 1946.

325. TNA, WO 261/658, Extract from Notice Issued by the Stern Group; KV 5/38, Cipher Telegram G(0)1 73795; FO 371/52563, Inward Telegram 1783; CO 733/456/11, Inward Telegrams 1793, 1783; the *Times*, Nov 19 1946; FO 371/52563., Inward Telegram 1803.

326. TNA, FO 371/52563, Inward Telegrams 1795, 1815, 1826; CIA documents; TNA, WO 275/79, 317 Airborne Field Security Section, Report No. 1, for the week ending 5 Nov 1946; CO 733/456/11, Inward Telegram 1795, 1805, 1815; WO 275/73, chart, "9 Sept 46"; KV 5/38, Inward Telegrams 1805, 1826, 1815; *ibid*, 162a, 1556; CO 733/477/3, Main Terrorist Incidents during the Period 1 June - 6 March 1947; WO 275/73, chart, "9 Sept 46"; WO 275/58, Rail Sabotage in Divisional Area Since 7 Nov 46. Note that the L.H.I.-Bulletin, no. 1, November, 1946, p11 claims that Lehi cut cables on the 6th, but I have assumed it is the same as the British report of the 5th. *Falastin*, in *Palestine Chronicle*, 4 Nov 1946.

327. TNA, KV 5/31, '136b'; *Palestine Pamphlet Terrorist Methods With Mines and Booby Traps*, 5; Note that the two Palestinians killed on 3 Nov was reported as two people killed "on Arab land."

328. TNA, WO 275/79, Capt. J. Linklator, 317 Airborne Field Security Section, Report No. 1, for the week ending 5 Nov 1946.

329. TNA, CO 733/456/11, Inward Telegrams 1841, 1854; WO 275/121, Air Headquarters Levant, Monthly Air Letter - November 1946; L.H.I.-Bulletin, no. 1, Nov, 1946, p11. Also NYT Nov 12 1946; FO 371/52563, Inward Telegram 1854; KV 5/38, 160c, etc; WO 275/73, chart, "9 Sept 46" upper left; The *New York Times* reported "Three Zionists drove up in a black police-type truck..." (NYT 12 Nov 1946).

330. TNA, CO 733/456/11, Inward Telegram, 1854 (One further attack on Nov 11 was thwarted); Kister, *Irgun*, 266; WO 275 73, chart, '11 June 46' upper left; *ibid*, chart, '8/9 Sep' upper left; *ibid*, '11 Nov 46' upper left; L.H.I.-Bulletin, no. 1, telegraph wires on the 11th, 11; the Rosh Ha'Ayin attack is report by Kister and does not appear to be a duplication of the "El Ain" attack recorded the previous day.

331. FBI, Irgun files, News Chronicle, Nov 11 1946; L.H.I.-Bulletin, no. 1, Nov, 1946, 7; TNA, CO 733/457/13, S.F.57/2/11(2)/B.1.B/JCR, red '10'.

332. Lehi, L.H.I.-Bulletin, no. 1, Nov 1946, 7; for Nakam, see e.g. Jonathan Freedland, Revenge, The Observer, July 2008.

333. TNA, FO 371/61761, Wichita Beacon, 14 Nov 1946; For the forming of Political Action Committee for Palestine, see NYT, 13 Feb 1946.

334. TNA, CO 733/456/11, Inward Telegram 1871, 1876, 1926, 1904, 1898; FO 371/52563, Inward Telegrams 1871, 1876, 1886, 1898; 'Times, 19.11.46'; Illustrated London News, Jan 11 1947; WO 275/73, chart, '11 Nov 46' at upper left; Lehi claims it cut telegraph wires on the 11th (L.H.I.-Bulletin, no. 1, Nov 1946, p11); FBI, *Irgun*; Lehi's report of what appears to be the same 13 Nov attack cites the death of the two policemen, but not the four Arab civilians (L.H.I.-Bulletin, no. 1, Nov 1946, 11, item 25); WO 274/79 Airborne Field Security, Report No. 3, week ending 19 Nov 46; KV 3/437, 63c; Six Palestine Officers Killed in Ambushing of Railway Patrol, Washington Evening Star, 13 Nov 1946; CO 733/477/3, "Main terrorist incidents during the period 1 June, 1946 - 6 March, 1947," esp penciled '220'; WO 275/121, Monthly Air Letter - November 1946; NYT, 18 Nov 1946; Kister, *Irgun*, 267; *Falastin*, in *Palestine Chronicle*, 19 Nov 1946.

335. Kister, *Irgun*, 267; TNA, CO 733/456/11, Inward Telegram 1931A; WO 275/73, chart, '11 Nov 46' at upper left cites a mine discovered at Ras Al Ein on November 19, blown up *in situ*; I have omitted it to avoid risk of duplication; NYT, Nov 20 1946; TNA, FCO 141/14286, Telegram No. 1858.

336. TNA, CO 733/456/11, Inward Telegrams 1938, 1958, 1986, 2015; *ibid*, DTO 210920B; CO 733/477/3, penciled '220'; WO 275/121, Monthly Air Letter - November 1946; KV 5/31, 137a, 136b; KV 5/38, 166c; CO 537/1712, OF.607/1/Link/B.3a/HPC; What I have cited as Petah Tiqva appears as "Sht Ha Tiqua" in the MS WO 275/73, chart, '11 Nov 46' at upper left; NYT, Dec 1 1946.

337. TNA, CO 733/456/11, red '163'; These letters held by the National Archives are presumably those that Segev (*Complete*, 482) says Kollek saw while in London.

338. TNA, FO 371/61768, letter, Mrs. W Talhouse, 21 Feb 47.

339. TNA, KV 5/31, '136b'; NYT, Dec 5, 1946; TNA, CO 537/1712, Anti-Partition Feeling in Palestine; FCO 141/14286, Cunningham, Telegram No. 1769 (1727).

340. *Palestine Pamphlet Terrorist Methods With Mines and Booby Traps*. Headquarters, Chief Engineer, Palestine and Transjordan. December 1946.

341. L.H.I.-Bulletin, no. 2, Dec, 1946, 14; TNA, CO 733/456/11, Inward Telegram 2032; FO 371/61761, penciled '197'; CO 733/477/3, penciled '220'. The British pamphlet was *Palestine Pamphlet Terrorist Methods With*

Mines and Booby Traps; WO 275/121, Section II, Terrorist Activities.

342. TNA, WO 261/647, Report - 252 Field Security Section 7 Dec 46, and others; CO 733/456/11, Inward Telegram 2050; FO 371/61761, penciled '196', '197'; WO 261/648 (the single sheet in this folder had been extracted from WO 261/647 and relates to the 5 Dec '46 attack); CO 733/477/3, penciled "220" (this document states that the truck, rather than the taxi, ran over the island regarding the Dec 5 incident); WO 275/121, Section II, Terrorist Activities, which is more detailed but somewhat ambiguous in referring to the occupants of "the other two vehicles" (i.e., one taxi and one truck) being booby-trapped after the explosion from the crashed taxi, then stating that both taxis were destroyed *in situ*, leaving the truck unexplained. Another slight variation to the incident is in WO 261/564, Report on Incidents in Jerusalem 5-6 Dec 46; *ibid*, The Stern Group attack on HQ South Palestine District, Sarafand 5 Dec 46; Regarding Syrina, the first relief to reach the DPs stranded on Syrina was the Greek destroyer Themistocles; FO 371/52563, Inward Telegram 2133.

343. TNA, FO 371/52563, Inward Telegram 2023; WO 261/564, Fortnightly Intelligence Newsletter No. 30; NYT, 13 Dec 1946; TNA, CO 733/456/11, Inward Telegrams 1496, 2213; WO 275/121, Section IV - Political Affairs. The children were kidnapped for an alleged theft of arms. Note that on 10th December Cunningham (FO 371/52563, Inward Telegram 2078) comments that there had been no terror attack for four days due to the Zionist Conference in Basle that began on the 9th, but omits that at least one was intended, the failed terror attack of the 8th; FO 371/52563, Inward Telegram 2133.

344. WO 275/79, 317 Airborne Field Security Section, Report No. 7, week ending 17 Dec 46.

345. TNA, WO 275/79, 317 Airborne Field Security Section, Report No. 7, week ending 17 Dec 46; WO 275/58, Intelligence Summary No 53 (to 20 Dec 46); No. 22 (to 13 Dec 46); Report No. 8, week ending 24 Dec 46; WO 261/659 (only two sheets in folder).

346. Jews are not Zulus, see TNA, WO 275/58, Intelligence Summary 25, 8-9; WO 275/58, Intelligence Summary No. 24; CO 733/477/3, penciled '221'. Date of incident obliterated by punch hole; subsequent incident is 26.12.46; NYT, Jan 5 1947; TNA, WO_261-657 (the single sheet in the folder had been extracted from WO 261/656 and relaest to the floggings of 29 Dec '46); CO 733/456/11 (repeated in FO 371/61761), Inward Telegram 2213 (When the Irgun attacked the Ottoman Bank in Jaffa on the 13th, the British caught one of the participants, a sixteen year old boy. He was given 18 lashes ("strokes of the cane," as a manuscript note clarifies), an extreme punishment of a child that boomeranged with the Irgun's retaliatory caning of British military men.); NYT, Jan 1 1947; "We would have been greatly disappointed," a spokesman for the US' Political Action Committee for Palestine said, "if the kidnapping and floggings had not been carried out." For any new flogging of a gang member, the Irgun promised, a British officer would be assassinated.

Chapter Six — "A Besieged Garrison," 1947

347. The Consequences of the Partition of Palestine, CIA, ORE 55, 28 November,

1947, 8-9. DOC_0000256628

[348.] TNA, KV 3/41, "Notes on the security situation in Palestine..." ("Top Secret Cream" in bold red); CO 537/1712, "Berl Locker on Rabbi Aba Hillel Silver"; FO 371/61865, "Zionist Advertisements in US Press"; ACJ, see NYT, 14 Feb 1947.

[349.] TNA, WO 275/58, Intelligence Summary No. 30 (up to 16 Feb 47).

[350.] TNA, WO 275/34, 'Report on the Incidents Night 2/3 Jan 47'.

[351.] TNA, CO 733/477/3, Main terrorist incidents ... 1 June, 1946 - 6 March 1947; NYT 3 Jan 1947; TNA, WO 275/34, Report on Incident evening 2 Jan 47; WO 275/34, "Report on the Incidents Night 2/3 Jan 47"; FO 371/61761, Inward Telegram No. 22; WO 275/79, 317 Airborne Field Security, Report No. 10, week ending 7 Jan 47, Appendix 'B'; WO 261/656, Report on Flamethrowers used by Terrorists on 2 Jan 1947 During the Attack on Citrus House MR12941634.

[352.] TNA, CO 733/477/3, Inward Telegram 22; CO 733/477/3, Main terrorist incidents ... 1 June, 1946 - 6 March 1947, p3; WO 275/121, Monthly Air Letter - January 1947. Some incidents of Jan 2 have not been cited here to avoid the risk of duplication, as it is not always clear whether similar incidents are variant reports of a single incident.

[353.] TNA, WO 275/34, Report on Incident evening 2 Jan 47; TNA, WO 275/34, "Report on the Incidents Night 2/3 Jan 47"; WO 275/58, Intelligence Summary No. 25; NYT 3 Jan 1947.

[354.] TNA, WO 275/34, "Third Incident" ('-2-'); CO 733/477/3, Inward Telegram 22; WO 275/58, Intelligence Summary No. 25 (repeated in WO 261/656).

[355.] TNA, WO 275/58, Intelligence Summary No. 26 (to 10 Jan 1947); NYT 6 Jan 1948; Kister, *Irgun*, 268; TNA, CO 733/477/3, Inward Telegram 31, 35; FO 371/61761, penciled '228', '233'. On 6 Jan 1947, A heavy utility police vehicle was stolen in Tel Aviv on the 11th, the driver dragged from the vehicle and held captive.

[356.] TNA, CO 733/478/1, *Daily Telegraph* 27 Jan 1947 quotes a figure of £200,000; the pound was worth just over US $4; FO 371/67796, Amended Distribution (18/2/47); Telegram, Rome to Foreign Office 22 Jan 1957; CO 537/2295, Amended Distribution (18/1/47).

[357.] TNA, CO 733/477/3, Bomb explosion District Police Headquarters 12 January, 1947 ('318'); Cipher Telegram 391390; L.H.I.-Bulletin, no. 3, January, 1947, 15; CO 537/2285, Inward Telegram 94074 G(O)I; FO 371/61761, penciled '239'; WO 275/121, Monthly Air Letter - January 1947; pamphlet, *For the Record*.

[358.] TNA, WO 275/79, various; re sex workers, 317 Airborne Field Security Section, Report No. 11, week ending 14 Jan 47, & No. 26, ending 29 April; Wiretapping, see Airborne... Report No. 23, week ending 8 Apr 47.

[359.] TNA, WO 261/566, The Kidnapping of Mr. H.A.I. Collins and Judge Windham; CO 733/477/3, Inward Telegram 177 (which says 'H.A.I. Collins'); Irgun confirms reason for kidnappings, see WO 275/79, 317 Airborne Field Security, Report No. 16, week ending 18 Feb 47; CO 733/478/1, Daily Sketch 29 Jan 1947; WO 275/121, Monthly Air Letter, January, 1947.

360. TNA, CO 733/478/1, *News Chronicle* 29 Jan 1947 ('35'); CO 537/2285, *Evening Standard* 30 Jan 1947; *The Star* 30 Jan 1947. For Gruner not having applied to Privy Council, WO 261/566, Fortnightly Intelligence Newsletter No. 34.

361. TNA, CO 733/477/3, Inward Telegram 177.

362. TNA, CO 733/478/1, News Chronicle 28-1-47; meeting of January 20, 1947. CO 537/2285, "Cable and Wireless," from Cunningham to S. of S. Colonies (2 pages). CO 537/2285, 142/67/GS 23 Jan 1947, attachment, 2-3;

363. TNA, WO 261/573, "Government of Palestine indictment of Jewish Agency as a result of outrages." Typo in the original: "political interate."

364. TNA, CAB 128/9/0/0022, 145; CO 537/2285, 142/67/GS, 7 Jan; No.C.S.759; 142/67/GS, 23 Jan; Inward Telegrams 239, 299; Plenum meetings of the Va'ad Leumi in which cooperation in the fight against terror was refused is cited for 20 January and 5 February, but it is not clear whether the Feb 5 is the same cited elsewhere as 3 Feb; Archbishop of New York, Dr C. F. Garbett, in *Diocesan Leaflet* for February, 1947. Safed, TNA, WO 275/34, "Third Incident" ('-2-').

365. TNA, CO 733/478/1, the *Times*, 27 Jan 1947 (red '5' at top); CO 733/478/1, *Daily Telegraph*, January 28, 1947.

366. TNA, CO 733/478/1, (red '5' at top).

367. NYT, 8 Feb 1947; TNA, FO 371/61761, penciled '201', verso; NYT 15 Feb 1947; Heyd is 'Heydt' in the document; KV 2/1435, typed '459', '460'; Lebanon, see also KV 2/1435, '460' at top, and KV 2/1435, typed '460' (page begins "I think you will...").

368. TNA, WO 275/79, 317 Airborne Field Security, Report No. 15, week ending 11 Feb 47; WO 261/660, Report on illegal immigrant ship "Merica." Broken bottle and tins would also be used by passengers of the *Runnymede Park*, suggesting that this was taught on the ships; WO 275/58, Intelligence Summary No. 34 (up to 14 Mar 47), No. 35 (up to 21 Mar 47). A contrasting immigration enterprise was the Abril, a German-built converted motor yacht owned by a US shipping company. The ship was well supplied, well-endowed with all American equipment, clean, and its cargo of immigrants acquired in Bouc (southern France) were cooperative. They possessed faux landing documents issued in Paris by Bergson's Hebrew Committee for National Liberation.

369. Hashomir Hatzair Gazette, 12 Feb 1947; TNA, WO 275/121, Air Headquarters Levant, Monthly Air Letter, February, 1947; CO 733/477/3, Inward Telegrams 372, 379 (also in FO 371/61768); CO 733/477/3, Inward Telegram 322; WO 275/73, chart, 18/19 Feb upper left; WO 261/660, Intelligence Summary No. 30, No. 31, No. 32; WO 275/79, 317 Airborne Field Security, Report No. 17, week ending 25 Feb 47; WO 261/566, Fortnightly Intelligence Newsletter No. 36 (15 - 28 Feb 47); NYT, Feb 21 1947; CO 733/477/3, Inward Telegrams 381, 444, 446, 448; continuing sabotage of oil pipelines, see WO 275/79, 317 Airborne Field Security Section, Report No. 13, week ending 28 Jan 47, & Report No. 18, week ending 4 Mar 47, & No. 20, 18 Mar. Re: pipelines sabotaged at Endor village, Wadi Malka, Haifa, the pipeline attack dated by the author as on the night of

the 19th is dated by Hoffman (*Anonymous*) on the night of the 20th, but this is doubtful, as the event is recorded in the NYT on the 21st; Most sources cite third floor or Barclay's Bank, while WO 261/566, Summary of Major Incidents, cites the second floor; for Gruner's sister, WO 275/58, Intelligence Summary No. 30 (up to 16 Feb 47).

370. TNA, WO 275/79, 317 Airborne Field Security, Report No. 18, week ending 4 Mar 47.

371. For Irgun "hell," TNA, FO 371/61866, Irgun, "To the People and the Youth!"; "besieged garrison," CAB 129/17/0/0009, 60; TNA, CO 733/477/3, Main terrorist incidents during the period 1 June, 1946 - 6 March 1947 (penciled '222').; Inward Telegrams 451, 454, 462; WO 261/566, HQ British Troops in Palestine & Transjordan G Branch ... Incidents in Jerusalem 1-2 Mar 47; Pikovsky's printing press was at 6, Keren Kayemeth Street (see also incident in TNA, CO 537/3856, Summary of Events, 1 February, 1948).

372. TNA, CO 733/477/3, Inward Telegrams 451, 454, 462; Outward Telegram 437; sheet marked '(4) 222'; CO 537/3854, Inward Telegram 453; CO 733/477/3, "Main Terrorist Incidents during the Period 1 June, 1946 - 6 March 1947," 3; WO 275/79, 317 Airborne Field Security, Report No. 18, week ending 4 Mar 47; WO 275/58, Intelligence Summary No.33; WO 261/566, Summary of Major Incidents; Hoffman, *Anonymous*, K8404: Kister, *Irgun*, 269. Casualty figure for the attacks of March 1 vary, likely because of people dying of their wounds after the initial reports; I have used the times of the various attacks to avoid duplication of the same attack described differently by different sources. For Jewish witness to the March 1 Haifa attack, see WO 275/79, Report No. 18, week ending 4 Mar 47, Para 8(g); and Report No. 54, week ending 19 Nov 47, 4-5.

373. TNA, WO 275/79, 317 Airborne Field Security, Report No. 18, week ending 4 Mar 47; WO 275/58, Intelligence Summary No.33; CO 733/477/3, Inward Telegrams 473, 484, 491; *ibid*, penciled '222' upper right; also in FO 371/61770; NYT, Mar 5 1947; WO 27 4/79, 317 Airborne Field Security, Report No. 19, week ending 11 Mar 47; WO 261/660, Intelligence Summary No. 33, WO 275/79, 317 Airborne Field Security, Report No. 18, week ending 4 Mar 47, & Report No. 19, week ending 11 Mar 47; WO 261/566, Summary of Attacks by Armed Jews...

374. TNA, boycott, FO 371/61770, penciled '212'; London terror cell, KV 3/441, S.F.218/UK/Link.

375. TNA, KV 3/441, "Part 1 (A)" (blue 9A); The British were at a loss to explain how the Colonial Club bomb was planted, and indeed had at first not realized that the explosion was from a bomb.

376. Cesarani 83-86, TNA, KV 3/41, Zionist Subversive Activities (7a), p11-12; Walton, *Empire of Secrets*, 79; KV 3/439, Jewish Terrorist Activities in Britain (219z), KV 3/438 157a.

377. TNA, CO 733/477/3, Inward Telegrams 506, 512, 753; CO 733/477/3, Inward Telegram 517; Kister, Irgun, 270.

378. NYT, Mar 9 1947; CO 537/2270, "Secondment of Army Officers to Palestine Police"; For dating of previous, see CO 537/2270, letter to Eric Speed, red '7'.

379. TNA, CO 733/477/3, Inward Telegram 533, 542.

380. TNA, CO 733/477/3, Inward Telegram 533, 542; NYT, 15 Mar 1947; TNA, CO 733/477/3, Inward Telegram 545; WO 261/566, Fortnightly Intelligence Newsletter No. 37 (1 - 14 Mar 47); WO 275/73, chart, 18/19 Feb upper left; TNA record says three charges explode on the oil pipeline near Haifa, and the Haifa-Kantara line blown up near Rehovoth. The Irgun also records demolishing the oil pipeline in the Haifa area on Mar 14 (Kister, *Irgun*, 270); WO 275/79, 317 Airborne Field Security, Report No. 20, week ending 18 Mar 47; WO 275/58, Intelligence Summary No. 34; TNA, WO 261/660, Intelligence Summary No. 34, which suggests that the oil pipeline attack of March 14 was the work of the Hagana, unaware that the Irgun would take credit.

381. Kister, *Irgun*, 270; TNA, WO 275/79, 317 Airborne Field Security, Report No. 20, week ending 18 Mar 47; CO 733/477/3, Inward Telegram 577; WO 261/660, Intelligence Summary No. 35; CO 537/2285, Bucharest to Foreign Office No. 264; The Irgun denied responsibility for the Press room bombing (FCO 141/14286, Telegram No. 648, item 7, and WO 275/79, 317 Airborne Field Security, Report No. 20, week ending 18 Mar 47; WO 275/58, Intelligence Summary No. 35 (up to 21 Mar 47); WO 261/660, Intelligence Summary No. 34, No. 36.

382. TNA, CO 733/477/3, Inward Telegrams 600, 679, 577, 689; WO 275/58; WO 275/79, 317 Airborne Field Security, Report No. 22, week ending 1 Apr 47.

383. TNA, CO 733/477/3, Inward Telegram 696, 734; Kister, *Irgun*, 271.

384. Kister, 270; TNA, CO 733/477/3, Inward Telegrams 696; Kister, *Irgun*, 271; TNA, CO 733/477/3, Inward Telegrams 699, 700; CIA; L.H.I.-Bulletin, no. 5, June, 1947, 16 (not numbered); WO 275/79, 317 Airborne Field Security, Report No. 22, week ending 1 Apr 47; Morris, *1948*, 39.

385. TNA, CO 733/477/3, penciled 228, 227, 226, 225 (N. Ollerenshaw.) Underline original. A widow's MS letter is preserved in CO 733/477/4, penciled '150'.

386. TNA, CO 733/477/3, MS notes, 15156/151A, penciled 196-205.

387. TNA, WO 208/1705, 5397 cipher 16 Jan ('18a'); ADM 116/3690, 'Report of Proceedings "Malaya" No. 04895/9' for reports of Arab assistance, and non-assistance.

388. TNA CO 733/477/3, letter 75156/151A/47; CO 537/3854, Despatch No. 24.

389. TNA, CO 733/477/3, Inward Telegram 721; Kolsky, p160-162. American Jewish Conference Bulletin April 4, 1947. Lilienthal, *What Price*, 28; A year later, one month and three days after Israel's declaration of statehood, a much different Displaced Persons Act passed which limited Jewish immigration.

390. TNA, WO 275/79, 317 Airborne Field Security, Report No. 22, week ending 1 Apr 47, which states the Galilee attack of 1 Apr was carried out by 3 Lehi members dressed as Arabs; CO 733/477/3, Inward Telegrams 725, 734; FO 371/61866, Outward Telegram 549; Inward Telegram 579; WO 275/79, 317 Airborne Field Security, Report No. 23, week ending 8 Apr 47.

391. TNA, KV 5/4, "The Betar Organisation." The Betar premises were at 20 Heathland Road, Stoke Newington, N. 16; CO 733/478/1, Outward

Telegram 184; Tom Segev, "A British Memoir On Dov Gruner," *Haaretz*, May 2, 2008. At writing, Gruner's execution is commonly placed at April 19, but this is surely wrong. He was executed on the 16th. Outward Telegram in CO 537/2295, red '10', dated the 16th at 12:35 PM states that he "and three other Jews were executed in Palestine this morning, at 8 a.m. local time," and other British records corroborate this; one indicates that Jewish shops closed in protest on 17 April, after the execution (FO 371/61773, Cypher, penciled '70'); and an Airborne Field Security report state that he was transferred to Acre on 15 April and hung "four hours after the week began," in context meaning Wednesday the 16th (WO 275/79, 317 Airborne Field Security, Report No. 25, week ending 22 Apr 47).

392. TNA, KV 3/438 152a; Burt, *Commander Burt*; Cesarani, *Hat*, 86-87; Yinon Royhman, "What connects Molotov, Lehi underground?" ynetnews.com 11.05.06. KV 3/441; EF 5/12, begins "On 15th April 1947, a time bomb"; "Outrage, June 1947, Postal Packets";* KV 3/41, p 11 begins "More spectacular." For security after the Dover House bombing, see CAB 21/2567, "Establishment Department Notice"; "Instructions to Doorkeepers"; 1460/1/47 Security; For idea that bomb was not meant to go off, and that Eliav was wanted for the King David Hotel bombing, see KV 3/441, 2a; and KV 3/438 131b. (* This document refers to a bombing by Zionist terrorists in London on April 16 ("outrage at Dover House on 16/4/47," but this is surely an error for the 15th.)

393. L.H.I.-Bulletin, no. 5, June, 1947, 15 (underline original). TNA, FO 371/61865, Letters from British Consulate-General Chicago, April 17, 1947; British Embassy, Athens, 3 March, 1947; British Embassy Buenos Aires, 24 February, 1947; WO 275/79, 317 Airborne Field Security Section, Report No. 25, week ending 22 Apr 47; British Embassy Santiago; Note in French from the Irgun to British Counsel; FO 371/61866, British Embassy, Bogata, 29th April, 1947; "From Addis Ababa to Asmara," 'E4054'.

394. TNA, CO 733/477/3, Inward Telegram 825, 829, others in same collection; also in FO 371/61773. Red Cross depot, see britishforcesinpalestine.org/events47.html, accessed 14 Mar 2016; events 16 April, *Falastin* quoted from *Palestine Chronicle*, 17 April. Regarding the No. 61 Field Dressing Station attack, the Irgun claimed it also bombed the camp headquarters.

395. TNA, CO 733/477/3, Inward Telegrams 841, 852

396. TNA, CO 537/2285, Inward telegram 845. Original: "...detonated the [sic] mines..."; FO 371/61773, Inward Telegram 851; CO 733/477/3, Inward Telegram 834.

397. TNA, CO 733/477/3, Inward Telegrams 829, 841, 834, 877. In original: "...detonated the [sic] mines..."

398. TNA, CO 733/477/3, Inward Telegrams 841, 852, 857; also in FO 371/61773; WO 275/79, 317 Airborne Field Security Section, Report No. 26, week ending 29 Apr 47.

399. CIA documents; TNA, CO 733/477/3, Inward Telegram 863, 856, 841; Lehi Bulletin 5, June 1947, p16 (not numbered).

400. TNA, CO 733/477/3, Inward Telegrams 874, 864, 1045, 1050, 901 (901 also in FO 371/61776); Lehi Bulletin 5, June 1947, p16 (not numbered).

401. TNA, CO 733/477/3, Outward Telegrams 911, 903; MS notes penciled '126'; CO 537/3854, Despatch No. 24; FO 371/61771, Inward Telegram 919, 921.

402. TNA, CO 537/3854, typewritten letter to "Sir T. Lloyd" from "TS" (probably Trafford Smith of the Colonial Office). The US loan to Britain's war-ravaged economy was the context of British fear of offending the Zionists.

403. TNA, CO 733/477/3, 146,145; 118, 969, 962, 937 (which states three cases of "armed Jews" setting fire to shops); copies of same documents found in FO 371/61776; WO 275/73, chart, '18/19 Feb' at upper left; WO 275/121, Air Headquarters, Levant, Monthly Air Letter - June, 1947; WO 275/121, Current Palestine Affairs, Section III; NYT, May 19 1947; May 15 1947.

404. TNA, CO 733/477/3, Inward Telegrams 969, 988; WO 275/73, chart, '11 Nov 46' upper left; The destination of the civilians' train was listed as '614 AOD'; identity of 614 AOD as being near Haifa taken from http://cosmos.ucc.ie/cs1064/jabowen/IPSC/php/place.php, accessed 8 December 2013; WO 275/79, 317 Airborne Field Security, Report No. 29, week ending 20 May 47. I have omitted the murder of a plain-cloth Palestinian constable in Haifa on 19 May, probably while attempting to make an arrest, because the British were unsure of the identity of the assailant (FO 371/61776, Inward Telegram 1007).

405. New York Post, 14 May 1947.

406. Medoff, *Militant Zionism*, 196-198.

407. E.g., for Baruch Korff's American Political Action Committee for Palestine. TNA, CO 967/103, '357d'; Ads, e.g., June 30 and October 7, 1947. FO 371/61866, OF.85/19/B.3.a/HLB; TNA, CO 967/103, letter,'357e'; letter, 'C.S. 679/7'. The Palestine Relief Committee operated out of an office at 123 West 44th Street in New York City. "It does seem to us fantastic," the British complained from Jerusalem, "that the Americans, while associating themselves with appeals for peace in Palestine, should allow" the terror organization to openly fund-raise.

408. TNA, CO 733/478/3, 'Anti-Terror League, Palestine'; CO 537/1712, O.F.85/11/B.3.a./PS. The author could find no mention of this Anti-Terror League in the published literature. An internet search (10 May 2015) reveals only a listing in St Antony's College (Oxford), Middle East Centre, Jerusalem and the East Mission Collection, Box 70, 70/2.

409. TNA, WO 275/79, 317 Airborne Field Security, Report No. 29, week ending 20 May 47; CO 733/477/3, Inward Telegrams 988, 1018, 1007 (also in FO 371/61776); KV 3/438, 157a.

410. Kister, *Irgun*, 272; WO 275/79, 317 Airborne Field Security, Report No. 31, week ending 3 June 47; TNA, CO 733/477/3, Inward Telegrams 1050, 1053, 1088, 1094 (also in FO 371/61776); WO 275/73, chart, '11 Nov 46' upper left. The Irgun records (in Kister) what appear to be these same attacks all on June 3.

411. TNA, KV 3/56, "Organisation of Illegal Immigration"; For Jewish Democratic Front, FO 1071/39, Foreign Office 22 May 1947, MS '36' at top; see also Ehrlich, *Encyclopedia of the Jewish Diaspora*, 962.

412. TNA, KV 3/56, SF.215.B3A.DJS, 5, 22; WO 275/79, 317 Airborne Field

Security, Report No. 30, week ending 27 May 47; Report 31, week ending 3 June 47; "Definition of a Zionist" is from WO 275/121, January 1947 report, Section IV, Political Affairs.

413. TNA KV 3/439, Jewish Terrorist Activities in Britain (blue '219z'); KV 3/438, 157a; KV 3/441, '9a'.

414. *ibid*; also Yinon Royhman, "What connects Molotov, Lehi underground?" ynetnews.com 11.05.06. Knut is also spelled Knout, Knuth.

415. TNA, EF 5/12, "Outrage June, 1947, Postal Packets"; A piece of the original carbon paper used to obscure the bomb mechanism is preserved in this folder in TNA. Two months after the letter bomb, MacMichael received a threatening message type-written on an American anti-British cartoon mailed from Los Angeles. Cartoon was from a Drew Pearson article. Regarding the letter bomb thrown in the pail of water, accounts differ as to whether the secretary or the MP threw it into the water.

416. NYT, June 7 1947; TNA, EF 5/12, "Outrage June, 1947, Postal Packets"; Letter, Ref 865,258/35; Cesarani, *Hat*, 117-118; Walton, *Empire of Secrets*, 80; Kenya bomb may have been brought by the bomber, not mailed there. TNA, CO 537/2297, letter from H.L. Brown, red '6' upper right; another from Brown, red '1'.

417. Ira Morris, 229-230. Lehi is said to be the origin of the anti-Truman letter bombs, but the author was unable to find any confirmation of this.

418. Kadima Building, see NYT June 18 1947; CO 537/2366, "Appendix "B" Translation of Handwritten documements [sic] ..."; "allowd" and "inportnce" [sic] in the transcript; also "questions as also." After their mission the "Theater" spies proved useful in a "stitching group," perhaps to do with processing their data. The publisher and the author would be very interested to learn if any of the women who were the "Theater spies" are known to be alive and can be contacted. For association with JA's liaison officers, FCO 141/14284 [F]rom the High Commissioner for Palestine, No. 169, 9th July, 1947, 2, item 5.

419. Regarding secrecy of Irgun-UNSCOP, meeting is merely "alleged" in TNA CO 537/2303, red '49' upper right, 2; FO 371/61866, Letter, Ministry of Defense, 1 October 1947; KV 3/439, Metropolitan Police, 257c; KV 5/39, Jewish Legion, *Report of the Conference...*; Note also allusion to meeting as a rumor, in FCO 141/14286, Telegram, No. 1283, item 3. Regarding Begin's Biblical geography, "Dan" is usually identified as Tell el Kadi, now northern Israel and southern Lebanon.

420. TNA, WO 275/121, Air Headquarters Levant, Monthly Newsletter, June, 1947, 6; WO 275/79, 317 Airborne Field Security, Report No. 32, week ending 10 Jun 47.

421. TNA, WO 275/121, Air Headquarters Levant, Monthly Newsletter, June, 1947, 6,7,8; FCO 141/14284, Monthly Report for June, 1947, from the High Commissioner for Palestine; WO 275/79, 317 Airborne Field Security, Report No. 33, week ending 17 Jun 47; The Irgun (Kister, p272) dates the Hagana discovery of its tunnel at June 19; See also TNA, FO 371/61776, Inward Telegram 1170 (Hagana agent misspelled 'Zev Werber').

422. Regarding the attack in Jordan Book Shop, what is surely the same incident is dated 19 June in TNA, WO 275/121, Air Headquarters Levant, Monthly

Newsletter, June, 1947, 8; I have trusted the dating in FO 371/61776, Inward Telegram 1200; WO 275/79, 317 Airborne Field Security, Report No. 34, week ending 24 Jun 47.

423. TNA, WO 275/121, Air Headquarters Levant, Monthly Newsletter, June, 1947, 8; CO 733/477/3, Inward Telegrams 1116, 1119, 1140, 1181, 1200, 1232 (some also in FO 371/61776); FCO 141/14284, Telegram, No. 1226 (from the High Commissioner), p2, and No. 1283, p1; KV 3/439, Jewish Terrorist Activities in Britain (blue '219z'), esp 5.

424. "Hanover Trial Linked to Zionist Terrorism," NYT, Sep 4 1947; TNA, WO 275/79, 317 Airborne Field Security, Report No. 35, week ending 1 Jul 47; CO 733/477/3, Inward Telegram 1242 & 1250 (also in FO 371/61776); WO 275/73, chart starting "29 June 47" in upper left; also WO 275/121, Air Headquarters Levant, Monthly Newsletters; WO 275/121, Air Headquarters Levant, Monthly Newsletter, June, 1947, p9.

425. TNA, KV 3/41, "Zionist Subversive Activities," blue '7a', esp 9-10; MI5 reported that terror activity in Austria was greater than in Germany, but less was known about it.

426. TNA, FCO 141/14284 Telegram, 'No. 1283 Top Secret Immediate'; Zertal, 46; TNA, WO 208/1705, P.I.C. Paper No. 35, 3-4; CAB 129/12/0/0020, p4; KV 2/1435, typed '460' ("Zionists of the stamp of BEN GURION," a British correspondence wrote, are "humanitarians only for the purpose of propaganda."); for Farran, Cesarani, *Hat.*, who makes a compelling case for Farran's guilt; the present author interviewed an acquaintance of Major Farran from the late 1940s in Palestine, Ted Steel, who did not believe the murder charge.

427. Zertail, 48; TNA, KV 2/1435, 548a; Normally, Britain sent would-be immigrants to facilities in Cyprus or Mauritius, but the Exodus passengers were returned to southern France, from where they had embarked; refused to land there, then to the British Zone of Germany.

428. Zertal, 50, 178. For Israeli theft of Holocaust survivor funds, see Norman Finkelstein, *The Holocaust Industry* [Verso, 2000]. Survivor quote from Daniel Gordis, "What Israel Owes Holocaust Survivors," *Bloomberg*, 16 Apr 2015. Recent reports claim that some newborns of Holocaust survivors were stolen and sold by the state, this allegedly occurred both in Israel and in the DP camps in Cyprus. See "Dozens of Ashkenazi Babies Mysteriously Disappeared During Israel's Early Years," *Haaretz*, 12 Aug 2016.

429. This account was published in the Daily Telegraph & Morning Post on October 3, 1947, without authorization. Transcript consulted is in TNA, WO 275/64, Fortnightly Intelligence Newsletter No. 52, 8-11 (also in WO 261/571). Meyerson, see FCO 141/14286, Telegram (Cunningham), No. 1572, 23.8.47, 2, item 8.

430. TNA, CO 537/2303. One Kew document cites the date as July 10, but another on the 12th, as does Kister's listing of Irgun records 272, and this squares with the day of the week (Thursday) in 1947. The kidnapping presumably happened in the early hours of the 13th. TNA, CO 537/2303, 330/364/GS ('55' upper right), 14 pages. The pamphlet, *For the Record*, misdates the abduction as 17 July.

431. TNA, CO 733/477/3, Inward Telegrams 1351, 1378, 1361 (also in FO

371/61776); also see FCO 141/14284, Monthly report for July, 1947. One of the two constables shot on July 19 in Haifa did not die immediately, but succumbed to his wounds later.

432. TNA, WO 275/121, Monthly report for July, 1947, and Section III.

433. KV 3/41, "Zionist Subversive Activities," blue '7a'; CAB 21/2567, E75/19; KV 3/439, Jewish Terrorist Activities in Britain (blue '219z'); KV 3/438 178a. Grenade and detonator figures vary slightly.

434. KV 3/439, Jewish Terrorist Activities in Britain (blue '219z'), 4, 8; KV 2/3171; KV 3/438, blue '180', etc; KV 2/3779, at top: 'PF.93044', type begins 'B.4.d report on movements'; KV 2/3779, at top: 'PF.93044', type begins 'B.4.d report on movements'; *ibid*, "Northoit Airport / Metropolitan Police," dated 25 Jan 1948; KV 3/438 178a.

435. TNA, FO 371/61776, Inward Telegram 1384; WO 275/79, 317 Airborne Field Security, Report No. 37, week ending 22 Jul 47; FO 371/61776, Inward Telegram 1384; CO 733/477/3, Inward Telegram 1398 (also in FO 371/61783); FCO 141/14284, Monthly report for July, 1947, and Section III.

436. Casualty figures quoted in CIA Documents On Truman & Zionist Terrorism and http://www.jewishvirtuallibrary.org/jsource/History/brits.html (accessed 15 Sept 2012, again March 13 2016 at http://www.jewishvirtuallibrary.org/jsource/History/timeline.html#brits2). Donald Neff cites sixty-five deaths (Hamas: A Pale Image of the Jewish Irgun And Lehi Gangs, WRMEA, May/June, 2006); Giladi, *Scandals*, 76-77; FCO 141/14284, C.S. 699, No. 212, 9th September, 1947, 4; The *Empire Lifeguard* was used once after the attack to transport 500 (elsewhere: 485) Jewish orphans from Cyprus. These and other orphans the British did not count as part of the quota. Citing no casualties: NY Times; Greenfield & Hochstein, *Jews Secret Fleet*, 114; Moshe Nachshon, "This is the Way it Was," palyam.org/English/IS/Nachshon_Moshe, retrieved 15 Mar 2016. Regarding the number of immigrants on the *Empire Lifeguard*, the allegedly first-hand account of Moshe Nachshon says 750 immigrants (which was Britain's monthly quota), while other contemporary sources, such as the JTA Daily News Bulletin of 24 July says 300, as does the non-contemporary book by Greenfield & Hochstein. Retribution for the Exodus debacle was the alleged motivation for bombing the vessel, though preparations for the bombing long predated the Exodus' Haifa landing. The bombing forced the British to stop using its own ships to transport Jewish immigrants to Palestine.

437. TNA, CO 733/477/3, Inward Telegrams 1398, 1412, 1423 (also in FO 371/61783). Police car was also targeted on July 24 1947; WO 275/79, 317 Airborne Field Security, Report No. 38, week ending 29 Jul 47.

438. Kister, *Irgun*, 194; TNA, CO 733/477/3, Inward Telegram 1431 (also in FO 371/61783); WO 275/86, "Sabotage of Cables"; WO 275/121, Monthly report for July, 1947, and Section III.

439. Kister, *Irgun*, 276; TNA, CO 733/477/3, Inward Telegrams 1438, 1448, 1451, 1477 (also in FO 371/61783).

440. TNA, CO 537/2303, 330/364/GS at upper left, total 14 pages; CO 537/3854, Outward Telegram 1708; Some sources, e.g., NYT, 1 Aug 1947, say one of the two bodies was booby-trapped, while others, e.g., author's interview

441. CIA docs; TNA, WO 275/121, Current Palestine Affairs, 2; HO 45/25586, begins ' "Jewish Struggle" had now reached 7 issues'; *ibid*, "Metropolitan Police,""1 Jauary [194]7'; *ibid*, 'Extract from Parliamentary Debates, 29.3.45, Coles 1522-3'; *ibid*, "Lesse's Bureau of Anti-Jewish Information"; *Christian Patriots*: Copies examined in BL; NYT, 1 Aug 1947. In Palestine, the "reports of increasing anti-Semitism in Britain" allowed the scandals of Jewish terrorism to be "relegated to the background," British intelligence noted; *Falastin*, 31 July 1947, quoted from *Palestine Chronicle*; Retaliation was not, the Irgun announced, the reason for the hangings of the two sergeants; the executions were a 'normal' action of the of the Irgun "court."

442. NYT, Aug 14 1947; Kister, *Irgun*, 194, & 275 (where Sacher is "British Officers Club"); TNA, KV 3/41, "Zionist Subversive Activities," blue '7a', esp 9-10; FO 371/64126, 'C10934'; KV 3/438. Kister, *Irgun*, 274; TNA, CO 733/477/3, Inward Telegram 1501 (also in FO 371/61783); WO 275/79, 317 Airborne Field Security, Report No. 39, week ending 5 Aug 47.

443. TNA, CO 733/477/3, Inward Telegrams 1502, 1511, 1517 (also in FO 371/61783).

444. *ibid*, Inward Telegram 1517. An accomplice in the Ajami incident escaped.

445. TNA, CO 733/477/4, Inward Telegram 1525 (also in FO 371/61783); WO 275/121, Current Palestine Affairs, 6 (which dates the Aug 9 attack as Aug 7); NYT, 10 Aug 1947.

446. *ibid*, Inward Telegram 1537 (also in FO 371/61783); The Hawari café is called "the Gan Hawaii night club" in WO 275/121, Current Palestine Affairs, 2; FCO 141/14284, C.S. 699, No. 212, 9th September, 1947, 2-3; From High Commissioner for Palestine, No. 1651; C.S. 699/2 No. 1572.

447. TNA, CO 733/477/4, Inward Telegram 1547, 1554, 1559 (also in FO 371/61783); WO 275/79, 317 Airborne Field Security, Report No. 40, week ending 12 Aug 47.

448. TNA, FO 1020/2279, "Statement on Oath by P/267936 Cpt. R. Wilson."

449. TNA records cite 130 men + 40 women aboard the Medloc train, while the NYT quoted 175 people on the train, so I have assumed five were crew: NYT, 14 Aug 1947; TNA, FO 371/64126, 'C10934/10522/3'; TNA, FO 1020/2279, letter from explosives expert Franz Kubicek, 13 Aug 1947; *ibid*, "Statement on Oath by P/267936 Cpt. R. Wilson," esp 2; TNA, FO 1020/1774, penciled '21A'; FO 1020/2279; NYT, Sep 4 1947; NYT, 16 Aug 1947; KV 3/41, "Zionist Subversive Activities," blue '7a', esp 9-10; ex-Sergeant Major Bob Maxwell, "An Explosive Situation," in *The Rose & The Laurel, Journal of the Intelligence Corps*, 1995. Since the bomb could not be hidden on the trestle itself, the saboteurs had opted for firm ground between two sets of trestles rather than risk discovery. The partial explosion hit the outside track, thus pushing the train inward.

450. TNA, FO 371/64126, 'C10934' appears to date a Velden attack August 15 [unclear]; the '5' should be a '3' (it is not a second attack); NYT Aug 14 1947; NYT 17 Aug 1947; NYT 20 Aug 1947.

451. TNA, FO 1020/1774, 'Note by Brigadier Waghorn. Bombing of Medloc "C" '; Letter, Schmidt, blue '51A' upper right; Minutes of Meeting, '30B' upper right. Efforts were made to replace the coal-hungry pilot trains with lighter draisines where possible, or electric locomotives where there were steep gradients.

452. NYT, Aug 14 1947; Kister, *Irgun*, 194, & 275 (where Sacher is 'British Officers Club'); TNA, KV 3/41, "Zionist Subversive Activities," blue '7a', esp 9-10; FO 371/64126, C10934; CIA docs; TNA, CO 537/1814, 'Speech Delivered by Eliezer Kaplan ... 22.10.46'.

453. *ibid*, Inward Telegrams 1547, 1554, 1559, 1570.

454. The idea of boycotting Jewish citrus crop was encouraged by Henry Gurney, Chief Secretary to the Palestine Mandate. TNA, CO 537/2303, red '29', '30', black '7' for UK cash advances on citrus.

455. TNA, CO 733/477/4, Inward Telegrams 1537, 1566 (also in FO 371/61783).

456. "Irgun Denounces Killing of Arabs," *The Daily Worker*, Aug 18 1947; TNA, WO 275/121, Current Palestine Affairs, 2, which states that the Hagana's Aug 15 attack in Petah Tikvah was in retaliation for the Aug 10 café attack allegedly by Arabs, and that the Hagana apologized for the murdering the wrong people; *ibid*, p6; CO 733/477/4, Telegram 1570; FCO 141/14284, C.S. 699, No. 212 9th September, 1947; C.S. 699/2 No. 1572; In Zurich, the General Zionist Council met and, "under the pretext of avoiding civil war" among the Yishuv (as a British report put it), did "their best to block effective counter-terrorist action."

457. TNA, CO 733/477/4, Inward Telegrams 1570, 1579 (also in FO 371/61783); Thomas Reynolds, "Hagana Warns Irgun to Desist," Chicago Sun, 9 Nov 1947; NYT, June 12 1947.

458. Regarding beginnings of anti-Jewish Palestinian violence, possible exception is the August 10 café attack (perpetrators unknown, but based on precendent it may have been a Zionist attack to jump-start ethnic violence); TNA, CO 733/477/4, Inward Telegrams 1576, 1579, 1592, 1598, 1605, 1632, 1689, 1717; WO 275/121, Current Palestine Affairs, p2; FCO 141/14284, C.S. 699/2 No. 1572, p1-2; for a list of incidents of violence between Palestinians and Jewish settlers during this period, see WO 275/121, Jewish-Arab Incidents. Regarding Lehi threats against Jewish civil servants, on the night of 4 Sept the gang warned twenty Jewish members of the staff of the Income Tax Department in Tel Aviv to quit their jobs.

459. TNA, FO 371/61915, letter, "Inverchapel"; *ibid*, letter, penciled '22'; NY Sun, June 24 1947; the *Times*, Sep 9 1947; TNA, KV 3/41, Zionist Subversive Activities, 11; NYT Sep 9 1947; Cesarani, *Hat*, 117, 151.

460. TNA, KV3/439, MS note dated 23 Aug '47. The word "the" in "the Colonial office" is surmised, as it is punched through; 3 Sep 1947 postal bomb, TNA, KV 3/439, 220B.

461. TNA CO 733/477/4, Inward Telegram 1717; WO 275/83, "Minutes of a Meeting Held in the Refinery Superintendent's Office ... 15th September 1947." The Irgun reference in Kister, *Irgun*, 275, for this day simply states "Three fuel containers blown up during curfew in Haifa"; CO 733/477/4, Inward Telegram 1808; WO 275/64; Fortnightly Intelligence Newsletter No.

51, 4-6. (of the two police murdered in the chase after the bank robbers, one was reported killed, the other as "not expected to recover." The author could find no further record of the alleged 'Lameri' branch of the Hagana; FCO 141/14284, No. 1850.

462. NYT, Sep 30 1947; TNA, WO 275/64, Fortnightly Intelligence Newsletter No. 52, 4 (repeated in WO 261/571);

463. TNA, CO 733/477/4, Inward Telegrams 1842, 1836; *ibid*, Colonial Office Telegram No. 1827; Kister, *Irgun*, 275; TNA, WO 275/64, Fortnightly Intelligence Newsletter No. 52, p5; WO 275/73, "Railway Sabotage," 1947; for the military advocating using "armed Jews," "thugs," and "murderers" instead of "terrorist," because it "invests the individuals concerned with a certain amount of glamor," see WO 275/86, "Stern and Irgun" (red '40').

464. TNA, CO 537/3854, 330/424/GS. The number of rounds is based on the expended cartridges recovered by the British in the morning; Irgun-Lehi meeting, KV 5/39, 200z; Military report, WO 275/64, Fortnightly Intelligence Newsletter No. 52, 4; American Consulate, see WP 275/64, Fortnightly Newsletter No. 53, p2; Irgun banners, *ibid*, 5; WO 261/571, Fortnightly Intelligence Newsletter No. 54, 6.

465. TNA, WO 275/79, 317 Airborne Field Security, Report No. 54, week ending 19 Nov 47; Report No. 42, week ending 26 Aug 47; Content of sex workers' spying forms based on a questionnaire confiscated from an Irgun member that was believed to be similar to that given the women.

466. TNA, WO 261/573, 1 March 1948, "Government of Palestine indictment of Jewish Agency as a result of outrages," 2.

467. TNA, CO 733/477/4, Inward Telegrams 2071, 2139; Early reports about the oil workers say that one survived the attack, but from later correspondence it is clear that he died within a few days; The brother of one of the murdered oil workers wrote to Parliament asking what so many others had: why was Britain so powerless against Jewish terrorism? The reason, an MP replied, was again "the constant refusal of the Jewish community and their organizations to afford them any measure of co-operation." TNA, CO 733/477/4, Inward Telegram No. 2150; *ibid*, red MS '2426' at top; Regarding the four oil workers, another report identified the cinema as the May Cinema (WO 275/79, 317 Airborne Field Security, Report No. 54, week ending 19 Nov 47); Nov 20, WO 261/571, Fortnightly Intelligence Newsletter No. 55 (8-21 Nov 1947), 1, 6; CO 733/477/4, 75156/151A/47; *ibid*, 75156151A/47; CO 733/477/4, Inward Telegram No. 2155; Leaflets from Tel Aviv, KV 3/439; Hebrew Legion, KV5/11, '100' at top; *Aliyah*, WO 275/79, 317 Airborne Field Security Section Report No. 54 for the week ending 19 Nov 47; Lehi "school," TNA, WO 261/571, 'Search for Stern Gang School'. Note that the sentence "some three hundred carefully selected young Jews, earmarked and trained for service with HAGANA" continues to the page end "and that most......." but the next page (3) is missing from the National Archives.

Chapter Seven — Partition, the "temporary expedient," 1947-1948

468. Kermit Roosevelt, *The Arab Position* (address to National War College), 1948.

469. Under Secretary of State Sumner Welles, quoted in Quigley, *Challenge*, ch 4; also Roosevelt, *Pressure Politics*. Ben-Gurion quote, Morris, *Birth* (1989) 24; CIA, *Consequences*, 8-9; Roosevelt, *Arab Position*, 9; Cadogan was then the United Kingdom's representative to the United Nations. TNA, CAB 129/21/0/0009, 4. Foreign Office, 18 September, 1947; for earlier discussion of Arab and Jewish cantons in a single state, see CO 733/283/12. Also see CAB 95/14 for a collection of related Partition papers.

470. TNA, CAB 129/21/0009, Cabinet / Palestine / Memorandum by the Secretary of State for Foriegn Affairs / C.P. (47) 259, esp 5 ('52 stamped at upper right) (18 September, 1947).

471. TNA, FCO 141/14286, telegram 2285; FCO 141/14284, Monthly Report for November, 1947 (No. 295); WO 261/571, Fortnightly Intelligence Newsletter No. 56, 5,6,7; WO 275/79, 317 Airborne Field Security, The UNO Decision; WO 261/571, Partition of Palestine.

472. Quigley, *Challenge*, ch 3; Ben-Gurion to Amos, new, critical translation used. See JPS Responds to CAMERA's Call for Accuracy: Ben-Gurion and the Arab Transfer," in Journal of Palestine Studies Vol. XLI, No. 2 (Winter 2012), 245–250. Also also Shabtai Teveth, 188; Brenner, *51 Documents*, 117.

473. TNA, FO 1093/330, "Outlines of Zionist Policy," especially ch 2, "Jewish State." See also FCO 141/14284, Monthly Report for June, 1947, 1, item 2 suggesting the same tact regarding statehood, Partition, and land allocation when the UN deliberated Palestine's fate.

474. TNA, CO 733/456/3, Fortnightly Report, Jerusalem, end 15 Dec 1944; FO 371/45376, Inward Telegram 1768, 3.

475. Begin & Partition, e.g., TNA, KV 5/37, blue '136b'; Tel Aviv Mayor, CO 537/1712, "Top Secret / Jewish Agency Policy," 3; Hashomer Hazair, *ibid*, also Penkower, Monty Noam, *Decision on Palestine Deferred: America, Britain and Wartime Diplomacy, 1939-1945*. [Routledge, 2002]; FO 371/45376, Memorandum by the S of S, 6th page, penciled '65' and containing points 18, 19, 20.

476. *Jewish Standard*, TNA, KV 5/39, A. Abrahams, "Irgun and Partition."

477. Jewish Struggle, TNA, HO 45/25586; ZOA, see NYT Oct 27 1946; TNA, KV 5/31, Bulletin of the Fighters for the Freedom of Israel; *ibid*, Palestine The I.Z.L. and the Jewish Agency, (vi), (vii), (viii);

478. TNA, FO 371/75344, "Brief for UN Political Dept on Item 18...," 2; FCO 141/14284, No. 1992.

479. TNA, CAB 129/16/0049, p3 UN, A_364_Add.2 PV.19, 7 July 1947; Arab Higher Committee, *Palestine The Arab Case*, 26; Roosevelt, *Arab Position*, 4-5; Husseini, WO 261/571, Fortnightly Intelligence Newsletter No. 56; Alon's statement is widely quoted, e.g., Abu-Lughod, *Transformation*, 178-179.

480. CIA, *Consequences*.

481. TNA, WO 275/79, 317 Airborne Field Security, Report No. 56, week ending 3 Dec 47; WO 261/571, Partition of Palestine, after Fortnightly Intelligence Newsletter No. 56.

482. For Israeli provocation to elicit a response against which it must defend itself

by aggression, see also Ilan Pappé, *Ethnic Cleansing*, especially chapter 4. which draws on Zionist archives unavailable to this author; also Zeez Maoz, *Defending the Holy Land*, and the Postscript to this book; Kapeliouk, *New Light on the Israeli Arab Conflict*, 17; British report, see TNA, Fortnightly Intelligence Newsletter No. 57, 2; Cunningham, FCO 141/14284, telegram No. 2413; WO 261/571, Partition of Palestine; Agency refusal to move to Tel Aviv, FCO 141/14284, No. 2345. Palestinian anti-Jewish violence is commonly said to reemerge on November 30, since it was the day after Resolution 181's passage and the UN precedent of a Zionist state (there was also Jewish anti-Arab violence that day). It was however in mid-August, with UNSCOP's announcement of its recommendations, that a Zionist state was widely understood as inevitable, and that the beginnings of this violence date, as cited in chapter 6, page 226.

483. TNA, WO 261/571, Resume of the major acts of Arab and Jewish violence during the period 5-19 Dec 1947; WO 275/64, Fortnightly Intelligence Newsletter No. 57, 2-3; also in WO 261/571.

484. Haifa bus attack, TNA, FCO 141/14284, telegram No. 2413, 2; WO 275/31, Illegal Appropriation of Land Appx 'B' to 3 Para Bde; CO 733/477/4, Inward Telegram 2509; NYT Dec 13, 20, 21, 24, 13 1947; Pappé, *Cleansing*, 57; For British report on Khisas attack, WO 275/64, Fortnightly Intelligence Newsletter No. 58, 6; For Khisas, also see Khalidi, *All That Remains*, 465-6; for Abdullah and prediction of no Palestinian state, WO 261/571, Fortnightly Intelligence Newsletter No. 57, 6 Dec - 18 Dec 47, esp 2; Quigley, *Challenge*, ch 5; pamphlet, *For the Record* dates the café attack as Christmas eve, whereas TNA documents say the 25th. For the issue of Zionist provocation in December 1947 with the specific purpose of igniting a civil war from which the new Israeli state would have to 'defend' itself through ethnic cleansing, land confiscation, and ethnically-selective martial law, see, e.g., Pappe, *Ethnic Cleansing*, especially ch 3; and Amnon Kapelionk. "New Light on the Arab-Israeli Conflict and Refugee Problems and Its Origin," in *Journal of Palestine Studies* 16, no. 3 (Spring 1987): 16–24.

485. TNA, CO 733/477/4 penciled '34', Inward Telegram, To the Secretary of State for the Colonies; "cooperating" is corrupt but intent clear; pages out of order in Kew but identity of quoted page seems clear.

486. Wilson, *6th Airborne*, kindle 2640-2641.

487. Szyk cartoon in *The Legionaire* (correct spelling), 13 Feb 1948. Copy examined: TNA, KV 5/11; British humour re anti-Semitism smear, see WO 261/571, Fortnightly Intelligence Newsletter No. 56, 'Tailpiece'.

488. TNA, Pappé, *Cleaning*, 59; Also TNA, KV 5/39, '203a' re Hashomer and Haifa; NYT Dec 31 1947; NYT Dec 30 1947; UN A_AC.21_SR.16 21 Jan 1948; TNA, CO 537/3855 Inward Telegram 2525; *ibid*, Summary of Events, 29 Dec 1947 (red '1').

489. Res 181 placed Jaffa as an Arab enclave separated from the rest of Arab Palestine. In 1946, the British had discussed connecting Jaffa to Arab Palestine, but this was not done because it would then cut the Zionist state in two, "and so created for the Jews the difficulty which it solved for the Arabs." See TNA CAB 128/6/0/0009 219; UN, A_AC.21_SR.16 21 Jan 1948; Pamphlet, *For the Record*; TNA, KV 5/39, blue '203a'.

490. Provocation, see TNA, WO 275/64, Fortnightly Intelligence Newsletter No. 58, 1; WO 275/83, 317 Airborne Field … Report on CRL Massacre; Pappé, *Cleaning*, 59; Also TNA, KV 5/39, '203a' re Hashomer and Haifa; NYT 31 Dec 1947; NYT 30 Dec 1947; UN A_AC.21_SR.16 21 Jan 1948; TNA CO 537/3855 Inward Telegram 2525; *ibid*, Summary of Events, 29 Dec 1947 (red '1'); WO 275/83, Report on Rioting at GRL Refinery on 30 December 1947. Benny Morris (Revisited), while acknowledging that "what Arabs did to Jews was barely relevant" in regard to "how and why the Palestinian refugee problem came about" (7), begins the post-181 descent into chaos with an Arab attack against two buses the day after the vote (30 Nov), then effectively jumps to 1948 (65) having mentioned nothing of Zionist provocation that was calculated to cause the civil war.

491. NYT, 5 Jan 1948; Pappé, *Cleansing*, 59-60; NYT 7 Jan 1948; NYT 5 Jan 1948; UN, A_AC.21_SR.16 of 21 Jan 1948; Krystal dates the attack January 4, but most sources say the night of January 5-6. See also Karmi, *Fatima*, 86-89, who mentions the torrential rains that night; Jerusalem Quarterly… Qatamon, 1948 The Fall of a Neighborhood. Quoted from Krystall, "The De Arabization of West Jerusalem." Attacks of Dec 31 & Jan 1, see WO 275/64, Fortnightly Intelligence Newsletter No. 57, p7-8. About the timing of the Hagana attacks on Balad esh Sheikh and Wadi Rushmiyya, Pappe dates these as roughly simultaneous on Dec 31, whereas British records places Balad esh Sheikh at 01:00 on Jan 1. I thus felt it safe to assume that they occurred on the night of the 31st-1st, just around midnight; WO 275/64, Fortnightly Intelligence Newsletter No. 58; The Balad esh Sheikh massacre, as reported by the British, "was carried out simultaneously from two sides by a party of 32 [Hagana]. A gang of 12 took up positions and opened fire from the hills to the West of the village, while a second group numbering some 20 persons entered the village from the South, firing SMGs and throwing grenades."; Pamphlet, *For the Record*. Straight-forward, detailed record of early 1948's daily anti-Jewish and anti-Arab carnage can be found in TNA records, for example CO 537/3855 and WO 261/573. The history of the 1948 war itself is beyond the scope of this book, except to cite civilian terror's evolution into the arsenal of the Israeli state.

492. TNA, WO 275/64, Fortnightly Intelligence Newsletter No. 59, 6.

493. TNA, KV 5/39, blue '203a'; NYT, Jan 5 1948; Pappé, Cleansing, 60; Kim Philby was John Philby's son; NYT 7 Jan 1948; Kister, 202; NYT 5 Jan 1948; UN, A_AC.21_SR.16 of 21 Jan 1948; Krystal dates the attack January 4, but most sources say the night of January 5-6. See also Karmi, *Fatima*, 86-89, who mentions the "howling, icy wind" and "torrential rain" that night; Jerusalem Quarterly… Qatamon, 1948 The Fall of a Neighborhood. Quoted from Krystall, 'The De Arabization of West Jerusalem'. Attacks of Dec 31 & Jan 1, see Fortnightly Intelligence Newsletter No. 57, 7-8; CO 537/3855, Summary of Events - 4 Jan 1948; The attack on the 'Old Serrai' completely destroyed the Social Welfare Offices. WO 261/573, Fortnightly Intelligence Newsletter No. 59, 5, which claims that the Semiramis Hotel attack was not authorised by the Agency.

494. NYT 7 Jan 1948; Re Semiramis, Ghada Karmi, who lived in Qatamon at the time of the bombing, also dismisses the Hagana's claim. She writes that "Arab journalists were in the habit of staying at the Semiramis and it was a

well-known meeting place for activists of all political persuasions" (Karmi, *Fatima*, 89); NYT, 27 Feb 1957.

495. TNA, CO 537/3855, Summary of Events, 7 January, 1948.

496. UN, A/AC.21/SR.16, 21 Jan 1948; for the reaction in the Zionist press of the Semiramis bombing, see TNA, WO 275/64, Fortnightly Intelligence Newsletter No. 59, p9.

497. Re new Mallnitz threat, the "vengeance" was alleged to be for the imprisonment of one Gonsior Henoch; See TNA, FO 1020/1774, Cipher Telegram INT/B/1106, 6 Jan 1948; FO 371/68648, letter from Hector McNeil to S of State; James Reston, NYT 27 Jan 1948; Also see TNA, FO 371/68648, Wash. to F.O. No. 422. In London on January 21, a bomb was allegedly discovered at the Arab Office in Chelsea (KV 3/440, 277A); Sales of Auster aircraft, FO 800/487, 91, etc.

498. TNA, FO 371/68648, Inward Telegram to Commonwealth Relation Office (No. 121).

499. Jewish Agency, *Memorandum on Acts of Arab Aggression*; TNA, FCO 141/14286, Cunningham telegram 1119.

500. Krystall, "De Arabization of West Jerusalem"; Tamari, Salim, (ed.), *Jerusalem 1948*, ch 4, esp 94-95; Morris, *Birth*, 52.

501. FO 371/68648, Cypher 816 (penciled '43'); *ibid*, Telegram, UK Delegation to UN, No. 462, p2; FO 371/82703, Monthly Situation Report for the Jordan, Dec 1949, 2; CIA, *Possible Developments*; CIA, *Aims of the Revisionists*; TNA, FO 371/68649, Telegram No. 5459; For early mention of Abdullah deal, see WO 261/571, Fortnightly Intelligence Newsletter No. 57, 6 Dec - 18 Dec 47.

502. Re "various forms of pressure," TNA, FO 371/61914, FO to Jedda (penciled '7'); NYT 8 Mar 1948; NYT 9 Mar 1948; 1948⊠ 2014 dollar conversion based on dollartimes.com; Hagana set up recruiting centers, see Wendehorst, *British Jewry*, 263.

503. Posterity has laid blame on British irregulars and Arabs for the Ben Yehuda attack; a document preserved in TNA, alleging to be by investigators hired by the Jewish Agency and Va'ad Leumi, categorically dismissed any Arab involvement, putting all blame on the British, probably wrongly and for strategic reasons; TNA, CO 537/3858, "Report of the Committee" (red '66'), esp p6; For pamphlet, *ibid*, 'The British League Palestine Branch'.

504. TNA, CO 733/477/5, Inward Telegram 834; All the victims appear to have been Arab civilians. Both the *Times*, 2 Mar 1948, and UN Palestine Commission Daily News Summary 23, 1 Mar 1948, describe the victims as British military, apparently in error, as the British telegram in TNA citing the dead specifically states that British military personnel "were not (repeat not) injured."; Salam Building, NYT 4 Mar 1948.

505. NYT 23 Mar 1948; Kister, *Irgun*, 277; KV 5/31, Extract OF 606/1, '159z', spelled "Farren [sic] Group," but as the 'Farran Group' by the Irgun, e.g., KV 3/440, 278ab, Irgun letter, p3; Regarding Roy Farran, the present author interviewed an acquaintance of Major Farran from the late 1940s in Palestine, Ted Steel, who did not believe the murder charge; while Cesarani's account, *Major Farran's Hat*, is fairly incriminating.

506. Arab Higher Committee Delegation for Palestine, *The Black Paper*, dated 12 March, 3. Distribution of pamphlet reported by NYT May 14 1948. For "Science Corps of the Hagana," see Pappé, *Ethnic Cleansing*, 100-101. TNA, FCO 141/14286, Telegram, No. 1293, 8.5.48, 2, item 5. For article reporting typhoid outbreak in Acre, NYT, 6 May 1948. Morris, *Revisited*, states that the Acre epidemic may have been the result of poor sanitary conditions resulting from the displacement of people, but health officials determined that the infection was water borne, not due to crowded or unhygienic conditions. Further dispelling Morris' contention, roughly the same number of Palestinians and British soldiers were infected, and there was no outbreak in the more dire conditions in other Arab cities. Naeim Giladi, the participant in the biological attacks quoted herewith, was with the terror organizations and records the use of bacteriological warfare in Acre, Gaza, and in the depopulating of Palestinian villages; See AMEU, *The Link*, Volume 31, Issue 2, April-May, 1998, and Giladi, *Scandals*. Some reports use the word 'typhus' when 'typhoid' is surely what is meant; my thanks to Prof. Francis Manasek for this correction.

507. CIA, *Consequences,* 14; TNA, WO 261/571, Fortnightly Intelligence Newsletter No. 54, 8 Nov 1947.

508. Transcript of videoed interview of Yerachmiel Kahanovitch, filmed in Kibbutz Degania, 23 July 2012. He was part of Operation Broom and Operation Dani. English translation by Ami Asher. Published in *Zochot*. Accessed October 18, 2012.

509. *ibid*.

510. *ibid*.

511. *ibid*.

512. Rapes in 1948, see Morris, *Revisited*, and his interview with Ari Shavit, "Survival of the Fittest." Pappé, *Ethnic Cleansing*, 209.

513. Ernst and Bevin, TNA, FO 800/487, 110. When Ernst "talked to people over there about what Britain had done in the spite of the attack by his fellow Jews upon us, they had scarcely believed it."

514. UN Palestine Commission Daily News Summary 23; NYT, 13 Apr 1948; Kapeliouk, *New Light on the Israeli Arab Conflict*, 17.

515. British intelligence report is in the Weekly Intelligence Appreciation of April 17; TNA KV 5/39, blue 214a; FCO 141/14286, Telegram (from Cunningham), No. 1023; Davis, *Apartheid*, 21-22, 25. Using the coordinates of 31°47'8.5"N , 35°10'40.7"E for Deir Yassin, the Yad va-Shem structure lies 1.25 km from what was the village's center.

516. TNA, FO 371/68649, Dept notice from British Emb, Ref 3/144/48, esp 2; *ibid*, Draft Brief for SS for Discussion with PM and Minister of Defense on April 15, and *Aide-Memoire*; *ibid*, Conversation with US Amb (E 4887/1078/G).

517. TNA, FO 371/68649, R.H. Hadow to P. Mason (UN), 2 May, 1948; FBI, Americans for Haganah Incorporated.

518. TNA FO 371/68504, Inward Telegram 1076.

519. TNA FO 371/68649, E5020, penciled '54' & '55'.

520. TNA, FO/371 68649, Record of Conversation PM and SS with US Ambassador 28 Apr 1948 (penciled '110').

521. TNA, CO 537/3861, Inward Telegram 1232.

522. TNA, CO 537/3861, Outward Telegram 1698; Inward Telegram 1232; CO 733/477/5, Inward Telegram 1194; NYT 2 May 1948; Kister, 202.

523. TNA, FCO 141/14286, Cunningham telegrams 1119 (8 May 48), 1211 (30 May 48).

524. TNA, FCO 141/14286, No. 1119, "My telegram No. 1023," Weekly intelligence appreciation, 2.

525. *Ibid.*

526. TNA, KV 3/440, 277A, and follow-up 278A; No record was found of the truth of the Feb 23 (alleged) bomb by the Colonial Office. There was a fake bomb planted by the Colonial Office on 20 August 1947, what the Office described as a "nose-thumbing" gesture in support of Palestinian (Zionist) terror. (See NYT 20 Aug 1947)

527. NYT: 8 Mar 1948; 18 Mar 1948; 22 May 1948; 21 May 1948.

528. The author tried unsuccessfully to gain access to TNA document MEPO 2/8766, "Murder of Francis Rex Farran by parcel bomb posted by terrorist organisation at Codsall, Staffs 3 May 1948," under a FOI request. It is listed for declassification in 2029, the year someone documented in the files turn 100 and is considered deceased; Cesarani, 193. TNA EF 5/12, 'The Star, Poison Bomb Secrets Out'; KV 3/440, 302a; KV 3/440 299g.

529. Neff, *Pillars*, 65.

530. CIA, Clandestine Air Transport Operations (DOC_0000655104).

531. Erskine B. Childers' "The Wordless Wish: From Citizens to Refugees," in Abu-Lughod, *Transformation*, 187, 182; Quigley, *Challenge*, ch 10; TNA, FO 371/68649, British Emb doc 3/175/48, penciled 136, esp 3; Morris, *Birth* (1989), 200 note 4; TNA, FO 371/68649, penciled 33, 136-137; Ben-Gurion himself gave orders to ethnically cleanse villages, though even three decades later, in 1979, the Israeli government barred Yitzhak Rabin, a commander in 1948, from stating this (NYT 23 Oct 1979).

532. TNA, EF 5/12, Daily Telegraph, 12 May 1948; NYT 12 May 1948; Segev (*Complete*, 480) writes that Barker himself, not his wife or the maid, noted the rigged envelope; the author has trusted TNA docs; TNA, EF 5/12, "Statement of Dr. Watts," p2; *ibid*, 'To the Superintendent' from Surray Constabulary, 13 May 1948. The Lord Speaker is written as 'Lord Chairman of the House of Lords'.

533. TNA, EF 5/12, news clippings; Some published reports (e.g., *Daily Mail*) stated that it is the sodium cyanide that cause the devices to explode in contact with water, but this is incorrect; sodium cyanide does not explode in water (my thanks to Prof. Francis Manasek for this correction); *ibid*, note that "Statement of Dr. Watts," 2, says "it badly bent a ¾ inch steel plate," whereas "Letter Bombs," 16 June 1947, cites a ¼ inch plate.; *ibid*, letter to Dr. Watts (upper right 292,569), MS doc beginning "Telephone message," cite the Atlas Powder Company (Wilmington, Delaware), Dupont, and Hercules Powder Company; *ibid*, letter, Venizia Giulia Police Force (red '1'); *ibid*, CRDD

Reference X12/123, "Outrage, June 1947, Postal Packets," esp 5.

534. TNA CO 537/3860, red '68', '56', '50'; NYT 15 May 1948; *Declaration of the Establishment of the State of Israel*; Kapeliouk, *New Light on the Israeli Arab Conflict*, 3; Herzog, re Hagana-Irgun merger, TNA, FCO 141/14286, Cunningham telegram 1119; KV 5/31, Stern Gang Broadcasts ('168A'); Ernst FO 800/487, 198.

535. TNA, FO 371/68650, Telegram 6612 (penciled '125'); CIA, Possible Developments from the Palestine Truce, 31 Aug 1948 (DOC_0000258353).

536. TNA, boycott, FO 371/68650, penciled '108' and others. Rabbi Baruch Korff, free after his attempted raid on London several months earlier, also bought full-page New York ads in June to announce the dissolution of his Political Action Committee for Palestine. Korff blamed the US Department of Justice, which had ordered the Committee to register as a foreign agent, which he refused to do. See TNA, FO 371/68650, after penciled '105', NY Post, 1 June 1948.

537. Cabinet memorandum, CAB 129/29/0018, 5

538. TNA, CRIM 1/1951 (for arrest, "Copy Charge," 8); Cesarani, *Hat*, 199-200; Walton, *Empire of Secrets*, 94; Canberra Times, 16 Dec 1948.

539. TNA, KV 2/3171, The Activities of Mr. Cyril ROSS (dated May, 1949, attachment to CD/99 of 31.3.50); and others, e.g., 22a; 20a contains transcripts of intercepted phone calls that included reference to "Daniel," the same name Sneh contacted in an intercepted telegram in 1946; and reference to the fear of blackmail, and (separately) de Beers (presumably the diamond firm).

540. Roosevelt, *Arab Position*.

541. TNA, KV 5/31, press clippings, esp Daily Telegraph.

542. TNA, Cyril Marriott, Consul-General in Haifa, FO 371/75192, Haifa to F.O. no. 262, penciled 3.

543. Bernadotte plan, CAB 129/29; Schwartz, 304-307; Newspaper report, KV 5/32, 217a; Jerusalem, *ibid*, 222a; Schwartz, *Walking With the Damned*, 304.

544. Kirkbride, *From the Wings*, 108-110; UN, S/1098, 2 Dec 1948 (letter, Acting Mediator); FO 371/82703, Monthly Situation Report for June, 1950, esp p2; Letter Dated 29 November 1948 from the Acting Mediator Addressed to the Secretary-general Transmitting a Report on Truce Violation by Jewish Forces on 23 September 1948.

545. Morris, *Revisited*, 4, 469-470; FO 371/111104; letter T. Wikeley, R1091/160, esp p2.

546. Pappé Ethnic Cleansing 196; UN Conciliation Commission for Palestine, The Dawaymeh Massacre, 14 June 1949, testimony of Hassan Mahmaud Ihdeib, the Mukhtar of the village; Morris, *Border*, 469.

547. UN Conciliation Commission for Palestine, The Dawaymeh Massacre, 14 June 1949; Morris, *Revisited*, 469-470;

548. Officer in Op Hiram was Yosef Nahmani; Morris, *Revisited*, 500; Zertal, 171

549. Ricky-Dale Calhoun, "Arming David: The Haganah's illegal arms procurement network in the United States 1945-1949," in Journal of Palestine Studies Vol. XXXVI, No. 4 (Summer 2007), 22–32; TNA, KV

2/2264, Extract, "202b," (surname misspelled "Koller"); *ibid*, "S.F.76/Palestine/4/B3a/MCSP (blue "190a[?]"; these state that British Secret Intelligence Service reported that Teddy Kollek, according to sources of "unknown reliability," purchased a million dollars of radar equipment which was shipped to Israel by way of Mexico, but the US authorities stopped the same path for fifty tanks he had bought. Unable to get them to Israel, he sold them to China and, having come to the notice of the FBI, returned to Israel; KV 2/1390, W.1239, "192a"; KV 5/40, "Statement by Mr. Menachem Begin...19th Septembre[sic], 1948, esp p2.

550. TNA, KV 2/2251, "76c," "76b," "77w," "77y"; FO 371/68512, MS "38 upper right. FO 371/68697, letter, ref 3/315/48, 3 December, 1948; KV2 2251, 78a; NYT, Nov 27 1948; NYT, Dec 3 1948; NYT, Dec 4 1948. Note that NYT article with photo of Begin in motorcade is misdated as Nov 28 in KV 2/2251.

551. TNA, KV 2/2252, JTA extract 7.12.49; KV 2/2251, JTA extract 23.12.48 (pencil "796); KV 5/40, Voice of Jerusalem (blue "266a").

552. TNA, FO 371/75340, '74-75' in upper right. British report, preliminary memo from Harold Beeley to Bernard Burrows suggests their (and probably especially Beeley's) authorship.

553. TNA, CAB 129/32-0010, 69; PREM 8/1251, "Historical memorandum ... Since 1945," esp 8; FO 371/75402, Draft Statement re 5 RAF planes, & more; FO 371/75400, Cypher MS.10019, etc; TNA, FO 371/75402 Cypher Telegram No. 99. See also FO 800/487, 293-295.

554. FO 371/75377, Jeru to FO (pencil '3'); PREM 8/1251, "Historical memorandum ... Since 1945," esp 6; While the British Cabinet expressed continued bewilderment at the Security Council's refusal to take action against Israel's invasion, the US was supporting Israel's admission to the United Nations even as it was "simultaneously refusing to comply" with the Security Council.

555. Manchester Guardian, 12 Feb 1949; TNA, FO 371/75192, Haifa to F.O. no. 262, penciled 3.

556. NYT, 19 Jan 1949; Jan 10 1949; TNA, FO 371/75344, Cipher No. 611; Sharett, e.g. at the Knesset 15 June 1949.

557. Roosevelt, *Arab Position*, 3.

558. King-Crane, Aug 28 1919; CIA, National Intelligence Survey, Iraq, Jan 1951, declassified Oct 2005; KV2 2251, "The I.Z.L. and the Jewish Agency," verso.

Chapter Eight — Israel *sans frontières*, 1949-1956

559. CIA, "A Long-Range Disaster," Information Report, Mar 1949 (declassified date illegible on pdf examined, DOC_0000107452).

560. For Weizmann, Fischbach 8; Israeli Foreign Ministry, Quoted from Kapeliouk, *New Light on the Israeli Arab Conflict*. "The [Palestinian] refugees will find their place in the diaspora. Those who can resist will live thanks to natural

selection, the others will simply crumble. Some of them will persist, but the majority will become a human heap, the scum of the earth and will sink into the lowest levels of the Arab world." Israel State Archives, Ministry of Foreign Affairs, Files-refugees, no. 2444/19. For Israel's claim, after its 1967 conquests, that Jordan is Palestine, see TNA, FCO 93/3271.

561. TNA KV 2/1435, typed '460' (page begins "I think you will...").

562. TNA J. C. Robertson, May 19, 1948, KV 2/1435, PF.46863 (592, 593, 594) (One error in Robertson's statement: Russia had already accorded Israel *de jure* recognition); Also see Cabinet report CAB 129/32/0010, 63.

563. CIA, Information Report, Along Range Disaster, Mar 1949, 2 (declassified date illegible on pdf examined, DOC_0000107452).

564. CIA, Review of the World Situation as it Relates to the Security of the United States, 13 June, 1949, 13-14 (DOC_0000215472), declassified July 1998; TNA FO 371/75350, Minute of Meeting With Mr Lewis Jones of US Embassy; FO 371/75350, E8707, stamped '148'; KV 5/40, Reports on Possible Developments (blue '284'); FO 371/75344, Tel Aviv to F.O. Sir K Helm No. 655; FO 371/91376, British Legation Tel Aviv EE1084/6; Rabinovich-Reinharz 97-98.

565. Quigley, *Challenge*, ch 14; Even when martial law was lifted in name in 1966, non-Jewish areas remained "closed" and thereby under near-military control.

566. TNA FO 371/75192, Haifa to F.O., E4575, penciled 11, 2 (8 April 1949).

567. TNA FO 371/98484, Palestine Question Before the UN ME 105/52 es 1, 8 (unnumbered); Pappé, Making of the Arab-Israeli Conflict. Rationalizations for admitting Israel to the UN despite its intransigence ranged from France's, whose representative argued, without apparent irony, that perhaps Israel might cooperate if admitted; to the United States', that the Assembly itself was not directly concerned with compliance (even though it is a condition of membership).

568. TNA, FO 371/104778; FO 371/91387; FO 371/91386; Morris, *Border Wars*, 4, 36, 37; For Eisenhower figure on refugees, see The *Times*, "U.S. Willing to Guarantee Arab-Israel Borders," 27 Aug 1955, quoting Dulles, speaking "with the authority of the President."

569. TNA FO 371/91385, E1091/23.

570. John Ruedy, "Dynamics of Land Alienation," in Abu-Lughod, *Transformation*; Quigley, *Challenge*, ch 12-13.

571. TNA FO 371/75192, Haifa to F.O., No. 507, penciled E6; *ibid*, Jewish squatters, penciled '7'; Quigley, *Challenge*, ch 12-13; Pappé, *Idea*, 288.

572. TNA, FO 371/104791, Notes and Jordan - Israel Border Relations June 1952 to October 1953 (which includes summaries of earlier years), 13; secret report by Sir John Bagot Glubb, 15 Oct, 1949, FO 371/75344; Morris, *Border*, 191.

573. Morris, *Border*, 149, 146-147. IDF records confirm such thefts; see e.g., Morris, 151.

574. Israeli Ministry of Foreign Affairs, Abu Ghosh - The Saga of an Arab Village, 1 June 2000; Morris, *Border*, 149, 146-147, 151-152.

575. Ryan, *Refugees*, 55-81. See also Quigley, *Challenge*, ch 12-13.

576. El-Haj, *Facts on the Ground*, 91-94.

577. NYT 18 Oct 1949, 26 Jan 1951; Giladi, *Scandals*, ch 4; Regarding Iraq, Giladi is largely corroborated in Eveland, *Ropes of Sand*, 48-49; Also Quigley, *Challenge*, ch 2; For Hagana member in Eliat, Braun, *Weeds*, 82-83, and the author's conversions with Ms. Braun in London, 2007; TNA, CO 733/420/19. A temporary suppression of Zionist material in Iraq following the 1929 disturbances in Palestine was cited as anti-Semitism. The 19 Oct 1934 issue of *The Jewish Chronicle* claimed that "the Iraqi Jewish population is living in a state of perpetual fear," CO 733/275/4, 39.

578. NYT 22 May 1950; NYT 20 Jan 1951.

579. TNA CO 67/373/8, stamped '4'; NYT May 22 1950; The flights were routed via Cyprus because Iraq would not allow direct flights to Israel; CO 67/373/8, British Legation, 1572/31/50; *ibid*, 'Enclosure No. 1 in Henry Mack's Despatch No. 230'.

580. TNA FO 371/82703, Monthly Situation Report, Jordan, for Sept 1950, British Legation Amman, esp 2; Morris, *Border*, 198; According to one of the operatives, the Zionist movement even paid some Iraqi newspaper "large payoffs" to publish anti-Jewish propaganda demanding that Jews be expelled (Giladi, *Scandals*, 200); TNA, CO 67/373/8, letter by Moshe Shohet, stamped 35-37; See *ibid*, letter, Henry Mack, stamped 58-61, for movement from Iraq through Iran to Israel. For N.E. Air Transport, see also Moshe Gat, *Exodus from Iraq*, 88 (TNA documents also cite the Alaskan Airlines link).

581. Hirst, *Gun and Olive Branch*, 282-283; TNA, FO 371/91692, penciled E133; FO 371/98767, Q1571/2; ibid, The Baghdad Trials (4pp); *ibid*, EQ1571/20; ibid, The *Iraq Times*, penciled 101; letter from P.A. Rhodes, 26 Jan 52 (penciled '110'); Eveland, *Ropes of Sand*, 49.

582. TNA, FO 371/98767, Q1571/2; ibid, The Baghdad Trials. Synagogues with arms caches were Masooda Shantobe, Hakham Hestel, Ezra Daood, plus the house of Eliahu Gurgi Abid, and another house in Faraj Alla Wahbi's quarter. NYT June 30 1951; Dec 17 1951; Dec 18 1951. Figure of 120,000 Iraqi Jews who fled to Israel is derived from "a leading Iraqi Jew who was a Director-General of the Iraqi Ministry of Finance" (FO 371/98767, letter from P.A. Rhodes, 8 Feb 1952); 5000 were said to be left.

583. Mordechai Ben-Porat quote from the blurb to his book *To Baghdad and Back: The Miraculous 2,000 Year Homecoming of the Iraqi Jews* (Gefen Books, 1998): "Between the years 1949 and 1952, over 130,000 Jews immigrated to Israel from Iraq, thanks largely to the efforts of emissaries from Israel and activists of the "Halutz" Movement in Iraq. This astounding Zionist accomplishment, known as Operation Ezra and Nehemiah, gave a final and glorious curtain call to the ancient Babylonian exile"; TNA, FO 371/98767, EQ 1571/18 (penciled '117'); Eveland, *Ropes of Sand*, 48-49, and Naeim Giladi, *Scandals*, ch 7-8; McGhee, see "Memorandum of Conversation, by the Assistant Secretary of State for Near Eastern, South Asian, and African Affairs (McGhee)," 11 June, 1951, Foreign Relations of the United States 1951, vol. 5, 707, at 710 (1982); Jones, see "Memorandum of Conversation by the Director of the Office of Near Eastern Affairs (Jones)," August 2, 1951, Foreign Relations of the United States 1951, vol. 6, 813, at 815 (1982); both quoted in Quigley, *Challenge*, ch 12.

584. For Hagana member in Eliat, Braun, *Weeds*, 82-83, and the author's conversations with Ms. Braun in London, 2007; for reports on "Oriental" Jews in Israel in 1982, after the election of Begin, see TNA, FCO 93/3191; Protest song excerpted from Hirst, *Gun and Olive Branch*, 290.

585. For a summary of what is known about the state's kidnapping of non-Ashkenazi babies, see Jonathan Cook, "The shocking story of Israel's disappeared babies," in *Al Jazeera*, 5 Aug 2016, who draws from Shoshana Madmoni-Gerber's book, *Israeli Media and the Framing of Internal Conflict: The Yemenite Babies Affair* [Palgrave Macmillan; 2009]. One rationalisation offered for the kidnappings of the newborns was to give them to Holocaust survivors unable to have children due to the emotional trauma they had suffered; but even if this argument had any merit, it is contradicted by the fact that Holocaust survivors themselves were victims of a similar scheme. Some had their babies stolen by state institutions and sold, and were similarly told that their child had died (see Endnote 428). Israel's use of its injustice against North African and Middle Eastern Jews to justify its injustice against the Palestinians has been known for some time, but was made an official device in 2012 (see, e.g., Judy Maltz, "In Bid to Counter Palestinian Efforts, Israeli Diplomats Told to Raise Issue of Jewish Refugees," in *Haaretz*, 11 Sep 2012).

586. Pappé, *Idea of Israel*, 38, or Kindle 635; For "infiltration" to retrieve belongings, e.g., TNA FO 371/111101, The Star in the East, 10; FO 371/98492, Israel Respects an Armistice, 3.

587. For Kirkbride, TNA FO 371/82706, T1017/1, esp 4 (July 1950); see also FO 371/75455, and FO 371/75344, Secret report by Glubb, 15 Oct 1949.

588. Morris, *Border*, 31.

589. Morris, *Border*, 43; TNA FO 371/82703, Monthly Situation Report for May 1950, British Legation Amman, esp 2; Red Cross figure cited in *Falastin* 28 Feb 1949 (in *Palestine Chronicle*), in Filiu, *Gaza*, 70, and Gallagher, *Quakers*, 64; Typhus, see Palestine Chronicle, 28 Feb 1949 (in *Palestine Chronicle*).

590. TNA, FO 800/487, 241. Regarding value of £P, a 100 pound note was equivalent to 40 months wages of a skilled worker in Palestine (wikipedia.org/wiki/Palestine_pound, accessed 5-27-13); UN General Progress Report and Supplementary Report of the United Nations Conciliation Commission for Palestine Covering the Period from 11 December 1949 to 23 October 1950, Chapter III, point 35 etc (A/1367/rev.1); Quigley, *Challenge*, ch 12.

591. John Ruedy, "Dynamics of Land Alienation," in Abu-Lughod, *Transformation*, esp 134-136.

592. TNA, KV 5/41, J.C. Gove, blue 318a; Kent County Constabulary, blue 316a; Pedahzur & Weinberg, *Religious Fundamentalism*, 31-33, 175,176; Yossi Melman, Inside Intel Time Bomb, in *Haaretz*, August 13, 2009.

593. Pedahzur 31, 176; Benziman, *Israeli Caesar*, 54-55. Some sources (e.g., Benziman, *Israeli Caesar*, 55) state that Unit 101 was composed entirely of kibbutzim and settlers, with no ex-Mandate militants, but Morris (Border Wars) cites an ex-Palmach member in Unit 101's raid of Bureij on Aug 28'53; Morris, 239-241; for Agudat Ihud see also Morris, *One State, Two States*, Yale, 2009, 48-50; When some parents who heard of the "training" their sons were getting asked Agudat Ihud to bring their complaints to the government, Ben-

Gurion dismissed the accusations as "imaginary and without foundation." His diary proves that he himself ordered such missions. Curiously, in the early 1950s Israeli officials told the American consul general in Jerusalem that the "Israeli terrorists" (i.e., rogue groups, not the IDF) are responsible for some of the trouble and might be trying to precipitate war between Israel and Jordan, though this defense is not cited later in the MAC meetings. The claim is recorded by the CIA: CIA-RDP79T00975A001100590001-4.pdf. The same documents claims that Glubb suspected the Stern Gang in attacks in 1953, but this is probably a reference to the Kingdom of Israel.

594. TNA FO 371/82706, T1017/1, From a report by Alec Kirkbride, British ambassador to Amman, visiting "West Jordan" (Palestine). See also FO 371/75455; Morris, *Border*, 167. It should be clarified that not only were the 'infiltrators' people attempting merely to return to their own homes, but they were not even infiltrators according to the Armistice terms, which specified that it must involve "warlike acts or acts of hostility" (TNA, FO 371/104779, ERL091/82, 2).

595. Morris, *Border*, 166-167.

596. Ben-Gurion's diary, in Morris, *Border*, 167-168; For rapes in 1948, see Morris, *Revisited*, and his interview with Ari Shavit, "Survival of the Fittest"; Morris, *Border*, 470; Pappé, *Ethnic Cleansing*, 209.

597. According to a soldier eye-witness, the Bedouin man had a rifle which he deliberately threw to the ground at the sight of the soldiers, and ran in fear. The soldier who gunned him down simply recorded that he was "armed" (See Haartez, article cited below).

598. Transcript of videoed interview of Yerachmiel Kahanovitch, filmed in Kibbutz Degania, July 23, 2012. He was part of Operation Broom and Operation Dani. English translation by Ami Asher. Published in Zochot, Accessed October 18, 2012. For "cultured officers," Morris, *Border*, 470; for rapes in 1948, see Morris, *Revisited*, and his interview with Ari Shavit, "Survival of the Fittest." Pappé, *Ethnic Cleansing*, 209.

599. For media reports, Chris McGreal, "Israel learns of a hidden shame in its early years," in The Guardian, 4 Nov 2003, and Aviv Lavie, Moshe Gorali, "I saw fit to remove her from the world," Haaretz, Oct. 29 2003; The 26 year old woman was Khadija bint Suleiman. See FO 371/104791, Notes on Jordan - Israel Border Relations June 1952 to October 1953; FO 371/91385, E1091/7,

600. Toynbee, in his *Observer* piece, cites the daughter of a mason who was arrested with his daughter, the latter "shot dead while trying to escape." She thus appears not to be the same girl cited in other testimony, who "died on the way" (i.e., perished in the desert). FO 1018/70, "To: O.C. Police, Amman"

601. TNA FO 371/91387, letter, M.T. Walker, 15 June 1951, S103/5/33/51; Forced marches, see NYT Oct 23 1979; Three folders in TNA contain the Wadi Araba files, duplicated: FO 624/191, FO 905/111, and FO 1018/70.

602. TNA FO 371/82703, Monthly Situation Report, Jordan, June, 1950; Morris, *Border*, 147-148. (The eye witness from the kibbutz witnessed most likely this incident, else a similar mass expulsion with a month)

603. Morris, *Border*, 147-148; TNA FO 1018/70, Incident in the Wai Araba, 1-2

604. TNA, FO 1018/70, Incident in the Wai Araba, 1-3.

605. *The Observer*, 11 June, 1950, "A Tragic Change of Role"; Morris, *Border*, 161, 163. Philip Toynbee was the sone of the historian Arnold Toynbee, but unlike his father had been a supporter of Israel.

606. "Infiltrators Not Maltreated Army Declares," June 15 1950. TNA FO 1018/70, Incident in the Wai Araba, Appendix II; Morris, *Border*, 161, 163.

607. TNA, FO 371/91385, E1091/1; see also FO 371/82703, Monthly Situation Report Oct 1950; for fabricating victims' statements, see Morris, *Border*, 150. The soldiers accused the men in Jish of "buying smuggled shoes."

608. TNA, FO_371-104791, penciled 75, or Notes on Jordan-Israel Border Relations, June 1952 to October 1953, 13; One British record records "3 children, a boy of 12 and two girls of 8," but Morris says the girls were eight and ten; One source says three bullets in the girl's back and one in her neck; Also uncertainty as to whether both parents, or just the father, witnessed the murders. FO 371/98492, penciled 71; FO 371/82703, Monthly Situation Report Nov 1950, esp p2.

609. TNA, FO 371/98490, penciled 56; Quigley, *Challenge*, ch 16.

610. TNA, FO 371/91385, Sharafat and Falama Atrocities; Fourteen telegraph were rigged with delayed action explosives, but four did not explode; *ibid*, E1091/8, E1091/18; FO 371/104791; Morris, *Border*, 194; TNA, FO 371/98492, penciled 71.

611. Azmi Nashashibi, Chairman of the Jordan delegation to the MAC, claimed that Ramati had been well-known as a member of Lehi and after statehood became a member of the radical Expansionists. The author could not confirm this. See TNA, FO 371/91385, E1091/17, E1091/19; FO 371/91385, E1091/10; The Jerusalem Post published a letter from several associates of Hebrew University strongly criticizing their government's behavior. See FO 371/91385, To The Editor of the Post, etc.

612. TNA FO 371/91385, Appendix "A," Sharafat admitted to be a "reprisal"; *ibid*, E1091/13

613. TNA FO 371/91386, letter from Glubb to Kirkbride, 17 Feb 1951; FO 371/91385, E1091/23 (letter from Glubb, 8 Feb 51).

614. TNA, FO 371/91385, E1091/1; Regarding "balancing" complaints, see FO 371/104791, Note on Jordan - Israel Border Relations June 1952 to October 1953. For example, in early 1953, Israel flew numerous air sorties over the whole of Jordan's lines of communication. Each time Israel did so, it filed a complaint alleging that Jordan—whose fleet consisted of a small number of passenger aircraft and unarmed Austers—had violated Israeli airspace.

615. TNA, FO 371/98490, penciled 56; *ibid*, photographs of the atrocities stored. Morris, *Border*, 171, while confirming the murder of both, cites the mutilation and "15 sten gun rounds" for the older man without specifying the methods against the 18 year old.

616. TNA, FO 371/91715, R10345/2 (4pp); FO 371/91383, E1083/358; CIA, SE-13, 24 Sept 1951, p20; R10345/9, letter, P.S. Stephens; R10345/10, letter, J.E. Chadwick.

617. TNA, FO 371/75344; FO 371/98492, penciled 71-72; FO 371/75344 cites two girls and the mother in the Ghor Safi attack; one of the wounded may have died later, but the author has used the lesser figure.

618. TNA, FO 371/98490, "Reprisal on the Innocent," 2 (penciled 24); J Post, *ibid*, penciled 35, 101 (Jan 4, 1952).

619. TNA, FO 371/98490, penciled 104; Israeli murder rate based on Israeli State Yearbook for 1952: TNA, FO 371/104791, Jordan - Israel Border Relations June 1952 to Oct 1953, p7 (penciled 69); FO 371/75344, Secret report by Glubb, 15 Oct 1949; FO 371/91387, E1091/54, p2; FO 371/98490, report by A.R. Walmsley, 9 Jan 1952, 1091/1/52.

620. TNA, FO 371/98490, "Reprisal on the Innocent," penciled 23-28; Morris, *Border*, 204, and the previous TNA document, whose details differ slightly but without real contradiction; Hutchison, 14 ("no person could live long enough to become calloused to such a sight").

621. The leaflets left at the scenes of the Christmas Eve massacres were in rough Arabic, printed on pink paper by cyclostyle. The same leaflet, for the same crime, was printed separately for two villages, Beit Jala and Mar Elias. Translation follows: *On December 4, 1951, people from the residents of Beit Jala* [or *Mar Elias* on the leaflets left in that village] *killed a Jewish girl near Bayt Waghan after they had committed a crime which cannot be forgiven. What we've done now is the punishment of that horrible crime and we will not stay silent as we always have* [literally] *arrows for them. May the listeners listen.* [Translation Rawan Yaghi.]

622. TNA, FO 371/98490, penciled p '26'; see also *ibid*, E 1091/3.

623. Benny Morris (*Border*, 61 etc), has a confused account of the Christmas Eve attacks. He states that Lea Festinger's murderer(s) was the so-called (Arab) Mansi gang, because "on 8 January 1952, Israel passed their names to the Jordanian authorities," unaware of the document that exposes this fraud (TNA, FO 371/98490, penciled '26'). Yet elsewhere he states that the Mansi gang were not among the bombing's victims, though the names passed back to the MAC were specifically of Christmas Eve victims—that was the whole point. Western diplomats never accepted Israel's post-facto claim, the US consul-general for example noting that Lea Festinger's Israeli boyfriend had never been cleared of suspicion (Morris, *Border*, 204); FO 371/98490, E1091/2.

624. TNA, FO 371/104791, Note on Jordan-Israel Border Relations June 1952 to October 1953, esp 14; Morris, *Border*, 171; TNA, FO 371/98492, penciled 84-86.

625. TNA, FO 371/98492, Appx "B," p2, penciled 72, and others; Appx "C" contains an Israeli Army response, as quoted in Haaretz, much of it demonstrably false; FO 816/179, MS letter, 10301/31A, 10pp; For a different view re tactic of provocation, FO 371/111104, 1033/231/54.

626. TNA, FO 371/98493, E1091/83; Hutchison, 25

627. TNA, FO 371/98492, Cypher, No. 127, penciled 97-98.

628. TNA, FO 371/98492, E1091/58, esp 2; *ibid*, "Secret - Jerusalem – Barrel"; To justify commandeering the UN office, Israel claimed that it lay on the

Israeli side of the Line, which was irrelevant (the international status and inviolability of the UN office was implicit in the agreements) and ironic, since the UN and Jordan had accommodated Israel by allowing it access to its facilities there. See Kirkbride, *From the Wings*, 101, on the Jordanians agreeing to Bernadotte suggestion that they allow the Mt of Olives to be UN administered, and how after his assassination "in some mysterious manner" the Israeli police guard allowed there to prevent looting changed to be a company of Israeli infantry when the Armistice was signed.

629. CIA, Current Intelligence Bulletin, 23 Oct 1952, declassified Oct 2003 (RDP79T00975A000900110001-9); TNA, FO 816/179, 10301/124, esp p2; Camels, see Hutchison, captions between 136-137; Morris, *Border*, 229; Hanna Braun served under Dayan and wrote that he would "boast freely of his fear-striking tactics" (*Weeds*, 80).

630. TNA, FO 371/104735, 10117/2/53, penciled 34-37; FO 371/104791, penciled 80; FO 371/104785, R1091/273; R1091/277; FO 371/98493, E1091/84; FO 371/104791, Note on Jordan-Israel Border Relations June 1952 to October 1953, esp 11-12; UN, Security Council, S_PV.630 27 Oct 1953. Regarding the repeatedly documented IDF policy of Palestinians being forced to remain in their homes as they were blown up, the opposite is stated in Thomas Mitchell, in *Israel's Security Men* (McFarland & Co., 2015). Mitchel writes that the Israeli soldiers called for people to vacate their houses and only afterwards "discovered" that "some 69 had remained." The same claim is made in Samuel Katz, *Israeli Elite Units since 1948*, 10. Regarding the Israeli government's control of the domestic media, and thus of its population's beliefs and attitudes, see Ilan Pappé's *Israel Out of the Frame* [Pluto, 2010].

631. UN, Security Council, S/PV.630, 27 Oct 1953; Morris, *Border*, 51; TNA FO 371/104791, "Note on Jordan-Israel Border Relations June 1952 to October 1953," p2; Syrian border, e.g., TNA, FO 371/104788, penciled 14-20, 27. Few 'infiltrators' armed, see Morris, *Border*; children crossing the line, see British Ambassador Geoffrey Furlonge, TNA, FO 371/104779, letter, March 9, 1953.

632. Hutchison 120-121; TNA, FO 371/104785, R1091/278; For ongoing Syrian border clashes, FO 371/104788, penciled 14-20, 27; Morris (who states that very few "infiltrators" crossed with the intent to do harm), *Border*, 172, 213; TNA, FO 371/104782, R1091/168; hiding in caves, R1091/169.

633. TNA, FO 371/104781, 1062/126, letter to the Foreign Office from the British Consulate in Jerusalem, dated 11 May, 1953; British Embassy, Amman, Despatch No. 62; British Embassy, Tel Aviv, 20th May, 1953; also see Cypher/OTP No. 274; Beit Sira, FO 371/104781, Cypher/OTP No. 69, May 22, 1953.

634. TNA, FO 371/104781, Cypher/OTP No. 273, No. 65, No. 64, No. 66; FO 371/104782, Mr. Walmsley, ER1091/168, 24 May 24 1953, and ER1091/169, 25 May, 1953.

635. Morris, *Border*, 191-192, 240; Benziman, *Israeli Caesar*, 50, 56-57; TNA, FO 371/104788, "ISUM 134," penciled 8; Telegram, penciled 63. Unit 101 was composed principally of Israelis from the kibbutzim and settlement movement, not ex-members of the pre-state gangs.

636. Report by Glubb, 15Oct 1949, TNA FO 371/75344; FO 371/104788, 'ISUM 135', penciled 14, and others.

637. CIA, Current Intelligence Bulletin, 20 Sept 1953, declassified July 2004 (RDP79T00975A001300080001-8).

638. TNA, FO 371/104791, "Note on Jordan-Israel Border Relations June 1952 to October 1953," p12; Khalidi-Caplan, Sharett Diary, 81; Hirst, *Olive Branch*, 307.

639. TNA, FO 371/104788, penciled 29; *ibid*, penciled 106.

640. Benziman, *Israeli Caesar*, 53; Hirst, *Olive Branch*, (who says Qibya dead is 66) 307-308; Alternate translation of Ben-Gurion speech, FO 371/104789, penciled 153; Hutchison (who estimated 250-300 well-trained soldiers), 163, 44.

641. Morris, *Border*, 245; Hirst, *Olive Branch*, 307-308; Benziman, *Israeli Caesar*, 54–55; TNA, FO 371/104789/1091/408. Zertel (*Israel's Holocaust*, 176-178) also notes the framing of Holocaust survivors.

642. TNA, FO 371/104788, R1091/353; *ibid*, R1091/364; Morris, *Border*, 250; NYT, Oct 26 1953, Oct 19 1953; Eveland, *Ropes of Sand*, 75-77, who cites Britain's Archbishop of York as one victim of the "anti-Semitism" smear for raising the issue of Qibya.

643. TNA, Report by Sir John Bagot Glubb, 15th Oct, 1949, FO 371/75344; Sharon later claimed that he had thought the houses were empty; For infiltration, Morris, *Border*, 245; CIA, Current Intelligence Bulletin, 21 Oct 1953, declassified Dec 2003 (RDP79T00975A001300340001-9).

644. Benziman, *Israeli Caesar*, 56-57, Morris, *Border*, 240; TNA, FO 371/104789, penciled '120', '202', '203'; FO 371/104779, R1091/82; FO 371/104789, penciled '120', '168', '202'; FO 371/104791, Notes on Jordan - Israel Border Relations.

645. TNA, FO 371/104788, R1091/365, penciled '150'; *ibid*, R. Makins, penciled '143'; FO 371/104791, penciled '81', & others; *ibid*, letter, A.R. Moore, penciled '88'; NYT, 19 Oct 1953.

646. TNA, FO 371/104788, 'ISUM no. 133', penciled '10'-'11'.

647. TNA, FO 371/104791, R1091/452c, R1091/447.

648. TNA, FO 371/104791, R1091/471; FO 371/111098, HQ Arab Legion Intelligence Summary No. 150, p2; *ibid*, No. 151, p2.

649. CIA, Current Intelligence Bulletin, 23 Mar 1954, declassified Sep 2003 (RDP79T00975A001500090001-5); That Jordanians were not responsible was subsequently supported in CIA, Current Intelligence Bulletin, 4 Apr 1954, declassified Sep 2003 (RDP79T00975A001500210001-1); Morris, *Border*, 294-300; UN, Security Council S//3252 (19 June 1954); Hutchison, *Violent Truce*, 47-54.

650. Hutchison, *Violent Truce*, 47-54; TNA, FO 371/111101, R1091/77, 1032/87/54, and others; among Israel's misrepresentations noted by Hutchison, Dayan claimed that the Scorpion's Pass attack was political (=West Bank) because the victims were not robbed, but this, according to Hutchison, was a fabrication, that the victims had clearly been robbed.

651. TNA, FO 371/111098, Incidents Report 163, p5; Incidents Report 164 (which cites an ambush on the vehicle rather than land mine); UN Sec

Council s/3251; TNA, FO 371/111104, R1091/160, letter by T. Wikeley, British Consulate-General Jerusalem, July 20, 1954.

652. TNA, FO 371/111104, R/1091/172, and R1091/178. Fabrication, in a report filed about an incident he witnessed near Sheikh Mathkoor in Hebron District on August 13 of 1954; Israeli soldiers crossed the Armistice Line in the Hebron District on August 13 of 1954, murdered one Palestinian with a 2" mortar, and presumably kidnapped another who had taken refuge in a cave; *ibid*, Extracts from Colonel Gammon's Frontier Report; CIA, *National Intelligence Estimate Number 36-54 Probable Developments in the Arab States* (declassified Sep 1997); This September CIA National Intelligence Estimate remarked on Arab countries' overtures to improving relations with Israel and finding solutions, but "the Israelis have not, however, shown a like tendency to reasonableness and compromise."

653. TNA, FO 371/108548, E1571/1(c); Morris, *Border*, 317; Black-Morris, *Secret Wars*, 107-110; CIA, Current Intelligence Bulletin, 22 July 1954, declassified Oct 2003 (RDP79T00975A001600500001-8).

654. CIA, Central Intelligence Bulletin, 15 Dec 1964, declassified May 2005 (RDP79T00975A008000360001-3); Some sources cite twelve men and one women arrested by Egypt when the Lavon Affair broke, but the figure of fourteen people is cited in, e.g., TNA, FO 371/108548, E/1571/9.

655. TNA, FO 371/108548, E1571/1; "Confidential Mr. Barnett Janner"; 'YZEP V EGYPT'; Wikipedia's entire entry on Rabbi Nahun relies on a single, online source by Victor D. Sanua, who suggests that much of the Rabbi's words against Zionism were imposed on him by the Egyptian government. British source makes no reference to this, and the Egyptian Jewry had a long history of opposition to Zionism, cited by Zionist leaders themselves.

656. TNA, FO 371/108548, E/1571/9; E1571/2; E1571/3; E1571/19/a.

657. CIA, Central Intelligence Bulletin, 15 Dec 1964, declassified May 2005 (RDP79T00975A008000360001-3); CIA, Current Intelligence Bulletin, 1 Sept 1954, declassified Jan 2004 (RDP79T00975A001700560001-1); "Israel honors 9 Egyptian spies," Reuters, Mar 30 2005; Barak Ravid, "State archives to stay classified for 20 more years, PM instructs," in *Haaretz*, July 28 2010 (the Lavon Affair is specifically cited).

658. TNA FO 371/151273, declassified in September, 2013; Rabinovich and Reinharz, *Israel in the Middle East*, 114-115; Morris, *Border*, 324.

659. Morris, *Border*, 327; TNA, FO 371/121692, John Nicholls, letter from British Embassy, Tel Aviv, No. 24 (1013/56), p2.

660. Morris, *Border*, 312 n132.

661. Nasr, 51, cites the first known hijacking as having taken place in Peru in 1931. NYT, Dec 29 1954, Dec 15 1954, Dec 14 1954, Dec 13 1954. Also Chomsky, *Triangle*, 77.

662. TNA, FO 371/115898, Press Release No 60; Morris, *Border*, 384, who acknowledges that the murdered bedouin had nothing to do with the deaths of the hikers, but does presume, without indicating why, that bedouin were responsible.

663. For parsing of the legal obligation to come to Jordan's defense, see e,g. TNA,

FO 371/111101; CIA, Current Intelligence Bulletin, 28 January 1954.

664. CIA, Current Intelligence Bulletin, 28 Jan 1954, declassified Jan 2004 (CIA-RDP79T00975A001400350001-7); TNA, PREM 11/945, IZ 4753.

665. TNA, FO 371/104789, Secret From Amman to Foreign Office, October 24, 1953.

666. See CIA, Current Intelligence Bulletin, 20 Sep 1953, declassified July 2004 (CIA-RDP79T00975A001300080001-8); Sitkowski, *UN Peacekeeping*, 46-48.

667. TNA, PREM 11/945, letter, 'Action in the Event of Israeli Aggression'; AIR 8/1895, TS 47304 415/3; AIR 8/1895, 'Israeli Aggression - United States Assistance PJ (55)54(Final)'.

668. TNA, FO 371/115905 / FO 371/104788; FO 371/121692, John Nicholls, letter from British Embassy, Tel Aviv, No. 24 (1013/56), 4,6; Morris, *Border*, 357-359.

669. For "rise in war fever," see CIA, Current Intelligence Bulletin, 30 Dec 1955, declassified Mar 2004 (CIA-RDP79T00975A002300390001-3); Such reports, according to the CIA, were "inspired by the Israeli army"; CIA, Current Intelligence Bulletin, 8 Mar 1956, declassified Jan 2003 (CIA-RDP79T00975A002400430001-7); Sitkowski, *UN Peacekeeping*, 46-48.

670. For Project Alpha, Morris, *Border*, 330; CIA, Current Intelligence Bulletin, 6 Mar 1955, declassified Sep 2002 (RDP79T00975A001900270001-1); Cohen, 264; TNA, FO 371/121692, John Nicholls, letter from British Embassy, Tel Aviv, No. 24 (1013/56), p3-4, who also wrote that "There is no reason to doubt Colonel Nasser's assertion that the raid [of February 28] convinced him that Israel's intentions were aggressive ... and that this led him in the end to the now notorious arms deal with Czechoslovakia."

671. TNA, DEFE 6/39, Annex to J.P.(56)Note 9, '33' at top right.

672. TNA, DEFE 6/39, Note by General Sir Charles Keightley, who was C-i-C of Musketeer; *ibid*, Aid to Jordan in the Event of Israeli Aggression Note by the Directors of Plans, '30' at top right; ibid, '32' at top right; FO 371/121535, From: Ministry of Defence, London, to G.H.Q. Middle East Land Forces (Main). Commander-in-Chief, Mediterranean, 18th October, 1956.

673. *ibid*.; similar in FO 371/121535.

674. TNA, AIR 8/1895, "Exclusive for C.A.S.—from CINC" ('27' at top); DEFE 6/39, Aid to Jordan in the Event of Israeli Aggression Note by the Directors of Plans, '30' at top right.

675. Morris, *Border*, 397-398, suggests that perhaps talk of the attack on Israel was kept alive to the end because Britain could not reveal its contradictory arrangements with Israel and France; but as quoted herein, top secret British documents that had no need for any such pretence continued to deal seriously with the raid on Israel. For US correspondence regarding Suez, see TNA, FO 371/121794; British records, see e.g. WO 32/21899; Jordanian request after Qalqilya, FO 371/121535, 'Aid to Jordan'. See also Stuart A. Cohen, 'A Still Stranger Aspect of Suez'.

676. Morris, *Border*, 408-409, Khan Yunis, UN figures record "some 135 local residents" and "140 refugees"; TNA, FO 371/121776, VR1091/158; CIA,

Intelligence Bulletin 30 Dec 1956 (RDP79T00975A002900130001-5); Neff, *Pillars*, 99; NYT, 22 & 24 Feb 57.

Chapter Nine — Postscript: Segue to Today

677. Israel claims East Jerusalem as its sovereign territory, yet makes not even the pretence that its non-Jews are citizens. Regarding the *USS Liberty*, see CIA report 3403-67, dated 9 Nov '67, for the theory that the attack was ordered by Moshe Dayan; theories regarding reasons for the attacks include Dayan's plans to seize the Golan Heights, the desire to keep the US ignorant about an Israeli massacre of Egyptians in the Sinai, and, as with the Lavon Affair, to blame the attack on Egypt. The US government steadfastly blocked any proper inquiry and tried to silence the survivors. See also Scott, *Attack on the Liberty*.

678. Avraham Shalom, head of Shin Bet, 1980-1986, from an interview in the film "The Gatekeepers" (Dror Moreh, 2012); US aid to Egypt is legally contingent on its democratic values, and its peace treaty with Israel; the former is obviously a farce; see, e.g., "US aid to Egypt is not for Egypt but Israel, JJ Goldberg explains," in *Mondoweiss*, 16 Aug 2013.

679. Suárez, Thomas, "UXOs: Did Israel deliberately arm Hamas?," in *Mondoweiss*, 13 Dec 2010; also Email correspondence between the author and a United Nations Mine Action Service Officer, March, 2010.

680. School room desks, books, pasta, and shampoo without conditioner have been among the lengthy list of items Israel blocks from entry into Gaza. The list is not static; it frequently changes. See e.g., Amira Hass, "Israel bans books, music and clothes from entering Gaza," *Haaretz*, 17 May 2009; Gisha (Legal Center for Freedom of Movement), Restrictions on the transfer of goods to Gaza: Obstruction and obfuscation, Jan 2010; "UN agency calls on Israel to lift book blockade of Gaza schools," UN News Center, 10 Sep 2009; "Israel: Stop Blocking School Supplies From Entering Gaza," Human Rights Watch, 11 Oct 2009.

Index

A

Abdullah, King of Jordan 242, 251
Abrahams, Abraham 90, 185, 214
Abu Gosh 280
Acre 64, 132, 135-136, 150, 183, 189, 194, 197-198, 218, 253, 259, 263, 284, 317, 381, 393
Adenauer, Konrad 288
Agudat Ihud 289, 400
Ahiezer (village near Lydda) 308
Ali Alayyan, Fakhriyeh Muhammad 295
Aliyah, ship 231, 389
Allon, Yigal 242-243, 254, 285
Altalena, ship 226
Altman, Arieh (NZO) 80
American Council for Judaism 174, 192, 270, 332
American League for a Free Palestine 262
Anglo-American Commission of Inquiry, and Committee 113, 121, 131, 134, 139, 160
Anglo-Palestine Bank 64
Anti-Terror League 199, 383
Arab Airways 267
Arab Committee of Struggle 229
Arab League 198, 250

Arab Legion 18, 97, 129-130, 194, 278, 291, 294, 301, 313-314, 405
Archbishop of New York 179
Arens, Moshe 80, 354
Armistice Line 14, 15, 275, 278, 280, 286, 289, 291, 301, 305-306, 311, 313, 405
Armon cinema 231
Armon Hotel 172, 177
Astoria, restaurant 208
Athlit Clearance Camp 109, 148
Atlantic, immigrant ship 68
Attlee, Clement 259
Ayelet HaShahar 88
Azzulai, Shimon 167

B

bacteriological warfare 253, 258, 393
Bad Adelschloss Hotel 223
Balfour, Arthur 30, 34, 36, 40, 218, 334, 344, 345, 347, 362
Balfour Declaration 30, 34, 39, 79, 153, 345, 362
Barker, Lieut. Gen. Evelyn 262, 265
Barker, Ronald 65
Beersheba 110, 202, 272, 292
Begin, Menachem 7, 10, 14, 26, 84, 94, 143, 145-146, 193, 206, 226,

270, 271, 340, 342, 371, 390, 396, 399
Beit Dajan 93-94, 155-156, 163, 175
Beit Jala 299
Beit Nuba 295-296
Beit Safafa 188
Beit Shearim 63
Belad es Sheikh 62, 246, 349
Bella, Leo 213-214
Bell, Gertrude 34, 42
Ben Bezalel, Moshe 167
Ben-Gurion, David 11, 24-26, 28, 31-32, 43, 46, 49, 59, 70-72, 82, 83, 89, 92-93, 99, 104, 114-117, 120, 124, 130, 134, 141, 145, 149, 158, 162, 176, 179, 195, 210-211, 226, 237-240, 242-243, 250, 253, 257, 267, 271-272, 275, 281, 285, 289-290, 297, 308-310, 316-317, 331, 334, 340-344, 347-348, 358, 360, 364, 368, 389-390, 395, 400, 404
Bentwich, J. S. 79
Bentwich, Norman 79
Bergson, Peter, pseudonym of Hillel Kook 57, 80, 87, 107, 148, 149, 165, 166, 180, 225, 329, 354, 379
Berlin, Isaiah 353
Bernadotte, Count Folke 135, 265-267, 270, 273, 396, 403
Bernstein. Eduard 29, 343
Betar 192, 381
Bethlehem 175, 220, 236, 299, 300, 341, 349
Beth-Naballa 115
Bevin, Ernest 35, 112-113, 115, 129, 148, 149, 152-153, 162, 202, 255-258, 263, 362-363, 366, 372, 394
Birya 130, 362, 367
Biyar Adas 60
Black Paper of the Jewish Agency and Zionist Terrorism 252
Bloch, Mr. 122
Brando, Marlon 148
Braun, Hanna 2, 28, 285, 330, 342, 343, 398, 399, 403
Brewer, Sam Pope 247
Brith Trumpeldor 270
Brodetsky, Selig 72
Bruce, Inspector 156
Bunche, Ralph 206
Bureij 307, 400

C

Cadogan, Alexander 236, 248
Cafe Ritz 231
Cafferata, Raymond 129
Cairns, Ralph 65
Canada Park 295
Carver, Leslie 308
Chamberlain, Joseph 36
Chevron, HMS 133, 152, 368
Chun Chan Yeng 193
Churchill, Winston 43, 46, 71, 85, 92, 120, 161, 192, 203, 263, 330, 341, 344, 346, 355, 360, 364, 365, 368, 369
CIA 173, 238, 240, 251, 253, 262, 264, 274-277, 284, 303, 308, 313, 315-316, 319-320, 322, 339, 377, 381, 382, 386, 387, 389-390, 393-395, 397, 400, 402-407
Citrus House 174, 207, 378
Clay, Gen. Lucius D. 223
Clayton, Brig. Iltyd 146
Cliansky 111
Coffin, Reverend Henry Sloan 270
Cohen, Robert Waley 72
Collins, H. E. 177-178, 192
Colonial Office 135, 165, 193, 200-201, 261, 368, 382, 388, 394
Committee for a Jewish Army 80-81
Conquest, A. E. 196
Council of Christians and Jews 168
Crane, Charles 43
Cunningham, Sir Alan 126, 128-129, 133, 136, 143, 157, 167-168, 170, 177, 195, 197, 236, 241, 243, 250, 253, 258, 259, 260, 367, 371, 376-378, 385, 390, 393-395

D

Daily Express 23, 161, 375
Daily Herald 164
Daily Telegraph 177-178, 180, 193, 267, 378-379, 385, 395-396
Daniel, Elbert Clifton 205

Davar 59, 146
Davidson, Carter 206
Davika (mortar) 257
Dawayima 268
Dayan, Moshe 277, 303, 407
de Hahn, Yaacov Israel 43
Deir Yassin 256-258, 268, 270, 311, 394
Deitel, Moishe 161
de Reynier, Jacques 256
de Ridder 303, 304
Dobkin, Eliyahu 120
dogs 106-107, 111, 137, 152, 308, 313, 373
Doran, Major Desmond 150
DP camps 12, 28, 119, 121, 160, 176, 209, 222, 224

E

Eagle Aviation 283
Eden, Anthony 263
Eichmann, Adolf 48, 237
EIMAC 322
Eisenhower, Dwight D. 310, 322
El Auja 308, 318
Eldad, Israel 135
Eliav, Yaacov 186, 201
Emmaus 296
Empire Lifeguard, ship 215-216, 386
Empire Rival, ship 148, 227, 372
Epstein, Yitzhak 35, 344
Ernst, Morris 28, 103, 124, 125, 255-256, 264, 330, 343, 360, 364, 366, 394, 395
Evans, Francis 311
Executer, ship 246
Exodus, ship 201-202, 210-212, 227, 330, 385-386, 399

F

Falastin (newspaper) 52-53, 163, 166, 341, 343, 347-348, 371, 375-376, 382, 386, 400
Faradia 269
Farran, Major Roy 209, 252, 261, 330, 385, 393, 395
Farran, Rex 261-262
Feisal, Emir 42, 346

Fejja 62
Festinger, Lea 298-301, 313, 403
Fishman, Rabbi, (Yehuda Leib Maimon) 98
Flesch, Zev 88
Franco, Gen. Francisco 46-47
Fraser, Admiral Lord 263
Fraser, Lord 203
French, Lewis 31, 46, 343
Freund (flatmate of Papanek) 143
Furlonge, Geoffrey 305-306, 311, 404

G

Gammon, Lt. Col. R. J. 314, 317
Gan Hayim 158, 182
Garvey, T. W. 315
Gaza 1, 2, 14-15, 96, 107, 112, 136-137, 182, 184, 188, 217-218, 220-221, 226, 241, 253, 271, 277, 287, 291, 293, 296, 305, 307, 313, 316, 318, 320, 322, 326, 330, 341, 357, 359, 361-362, 393, 400, 407
Ghor Safi 298, 402
Giladi, Naeim 71, 282, 393, 399
Gilbert, Reginald 227
Gillette, Senator Guy, 107,157, 361
Ginzberg, Asher 29, 343
Givat Haim 362
Givat Olga 114, 127, 185
Givat Shaul 93, 105, 155, 159, 167, 257
Glubb, Sir John Bagot 278-279, 287, 295, 305-306, 308, 312, 319, 398-399, 400, 402, 404
Goldschmidt Officers Club 183
Goodlin, Chalmers 272
Gort, Viscount 110
Green Line *(see also Armistice Line)* 273, 275, 278
Greenwood, Arthur 202
Grigg, James 103
Gruenbaum, Yitzhak 82, 98
Gruner, Dov 177, 181, 192, 193, 381
Guggenheimer, Bertha 32, 344

H

Haaretz 43, 296, 352, 381, 399-401, 403, 406, 408

Haavara Transfer Agreement 47
Haboker 86, 237
Hadawi, Sami 248
Hagana 2, 7, 11, 28, 43, 48, 58, 59, 67-69, 71, 79, 82, 88, 95, 98, 106, 108-109, 111-113, 117, 128, 131-132, 134, 137-138, 143-145, 147-148, 153, 156, 159, 167, 170, 180-181, 190, 192, 196, 200-201, 204, 207-208, 212, 216, 220, 225-227, 232, 237, 242-243, 245, 247-248, 250-251, 253-254, 256-258, 260, 263, 269, 285, 342, 347, 350, 352-353, 356, 358, 360, 364, 368, 371-372, 381, 384, 388-389, 392-393, 395, 398-399
Haifa 48, 52-55, 59, 60, 62, 64, 68, 86-87, 89, 94, 104-105, 107, 112, 126, 128-129, 132-133, 135-136, 138, 143, 148, 150-152, 154-155, 156-158, 162-166, 175-176, 180-186, 188-190, 192, 194-198, 200, 207-208, 210, 213, 215-221, 226-228, 231, 240, 242-243, 245-246, 251, 252, 258, 260, 263, 277, 348, 355-359, 361, 367, 369, 372-373, 379, 380, 383, 385-386, 388, 391, 396-398
Haifa Oil Refineries 150
Hamashkif 183
Harris, Monte 265
Hart, Lizzie 193
Hashomer Hatzair 7, 77, 86, 181, 199, 245
Hass, Amira 16, 407
Hayarkon, hotel 138
Hebrew Legion 231
Hecht, Ben 148, 198
Heifetz, Jascha 288
Herut Party 271
Herzl, Theodore 25, 31, 33, 34, 36, 194, 331, 342-343, 344
Herzog, Rabbi 122, 257
Heyd, Uriel 180
hiking parties (surveillance missions) 74-75, 88, 97, 105, 107, 110, 112, 129, 131, 180, 311, 317, 361
Hinkle, T. M. 307
Hirsch, Rosa 174

Histadrut 66, 204, 350
Hitler, Adolf 12, 47, 71, 92, 95, 153, 185, 192, 211, 358, 360
Holocaust 28, 57, 82, 166, 210, 211, 257, 309, 323, 331, 334, 341, 354, 364-365, 385, 404
Homesky, Paul 214
Hoo, Victor 206
Hope Simpson, Sir John 331, 343
Hotel Metropole 172
Hotel Sacher 223
H.R. 2910 (bill) 191
Huberman, Bronislaw 161
Hughes-Onslow, Andrew 97
Hunloke, Henry 79
Hutchison, E. H 299, 301, 303-304, 308-309, 312-313, 331, 402-405

I

Ibn Saud, King Abdel-Aziz 30, 85
ICRC 291
Idna 298, 307
Ilabun 269
International Court of Justice 240
Iqrit 281, 333
Irgun 7, 11, 19, 26, 28, 52-55, 57-60, 62-63, 65-67, 71, 80-81, 84-87, 89-91, 94, 96, 98, 104-108, 110-111, 115-118, 120, 126-137, 139-140, 143-149, 151, 154-167, 170-171, 173-183, 187-192, 194, 197-199, 206-207, 209, 214, 217-222, 225-226, 228-229, 231, 238, 242-243, 245-246, 249, 254, 256-257, 259-260, 262-263, 265-266, 268, 270, 288, 329, 331-332, 340, 342-343, 347-350, 355-357, 359-364, 367-371, 373- 390, 393, 395
Ish-Shadeh, Itzhak 145

J

Jabotinsky, Eri 90
Jabotinsky, Ze'ev 80
Jaffa 42, 43, 52-54, 61-62, 64-65, 84-85, 89, 91, 93-94, 105, 111, 116, 127, 131, 135, 148, 151-152, 155-156, 158, 162-163, 166-167, 182-184, 186, 188, 196, 200, 213,

215, 217-219, 220, 224-226, 231, 242, 245-260, 345-346, 348, 350, 357-359, 362-363, 377, 391
Jerusalem Post 294, 298, 312, 322, 402
Jewish Agency 11, 13, 16, 33, 43, 48, 67-70, 79, 83, 86, 88-89, 94, 98, 106, 108, 109, 111-114, 116-117, 120-121, 130, 134, 137-139, 141, 145, 149, 157, 170, 173, 178, 179-181, 183, 187-188, 190, 195, 204-205, 207, 210, 212, 224, 225, 230, 238, 241, 243, 245-246, 248-252, 255, 260, 265, 283, 304, 329, 331, 349, 351, 356-357, 360, 362-364, 366,-368, 370, 372, 378, 389-390, 393, 397
Jewish Brigade 70, 92, 122, 126, 131-132, 143, 165, 254, 342, 358, 365
Jewish Democratic Front 200, 383
Jewish National Fund (JNF) 19, 29-30, 334, 343, 364
Jewish Regiment 38, 358
Jewish Struggle, The 148, 151, 161, 219, 238, 375
Jish 295, 401
J. N. Camp, Sgt. Maj. 45, 346
Jones, Arthur Creech 162, 178, 191-192
Jones, G. Lewis 285
Jüdische Rundschau 70

K

Kadoorie, Sir Ellis 32, 343
Kafr Bir'im 281
Kafr Qasim 322
Kahanovitch, Yerachmiel 254
Kahn, Julius 42
Kaplan, Eliezer 117, 139, 224, 357, 387
Kaplan, Moyses 214
Kefar Sava 111
Keren Ha Yesod 82
Kfar Hassidim 105
Kfar Saba 54
Kfar Sirkin 167
Khedduri, Sassoon 282
Khirbet Najjar 298
Khisas 242-243, 391
kidnapping of Jewish children 10, 28,

120, 122-124, 173, 252, 286
King-Crane Commission, and Report 44-45, 49, 273, 346
King David Hotel 2, 106, 143, 145-147, 193, 330, 341, 351, 361, 366, 371, 382
Kingdom of Israel 288-289, 400
King, Henry 43
Kiriat Haim 53, 183, 189
Kirkbride, Alec 286, 289, 292, 332, 396, 399-400, 402, 403
Kiryat Motskin 62, 194
Kivutsat Ha Hugim 137
Klear, Hayim 171
Koestler, Arthur 69, 178, 351
Kol Israel 111-112, 134, 138, 143, 151, 260, 362, 368-369
Kollek, Teddy 105, 108, 147, 180, 269, 285, 303, 316, 361, 396
Kook, Hillel *(see Bergson, Peter)*
Korff, Rabbi Baruch 165-166, 193, 202, 226-227, 383, 396
Kunin, Selig 171

L

La Farge, Father John 270
Landau, Annie 43, 333
La Risposta 140
Lavon, Pinhas 69; and 'Lavon Affair', 285, 314-316, 318, 320, 405, 406, 407
Lawrence, T.E. (30, 42, 343
Lazaron, Rabbi 270
Lazarus, Gilberte Elizabeth, (aka Betty Knut) 193, 201-202
Lehi 11, 24, 33, 58-59, 67, 71, 85-88, 90, 93-94, 97-98, 104, 106-108, 110-111, 125-129, 135, 137, 140, 145, 147-148, 150-151, 154-158, 161-165, 167, 169-171, 176, 181-182, 186, 188, 190-192, 193, 196, 200, 208-209, 213, 215, 217, 221, 225-231, 238, 243, 244, 247, 252, 254, 261, 262, 264, 266, 270, 288, 341, 348, 352, 361-363, 368-369, 375-376, 381-384, 386, 389, 400, 402
L.H.I. Bulletin 161, 164-165, 190, 193, 357, 366, 369, 373-376, 381-

382, 386, 390, 403-407
Liberty, USS, ship 325, 407
Lifshitz, Israel 214
Lilienthal, Alfred 8, 332, 339, 354, 366, 381
Livneh, Eliezer 82, 354
London Conference 149, 162, 372
Lovett, Robert 249
Lubya 62
Lydda 59, 65, 91, 96, 105, 111-112, 130, 132, 135-136, 139, 150, 152, 157-158, 163-167, 176, 188, 195-196, 198, 200, 213, 217, 219, 228, 283, 308, 317, 350, 356-359, 361

M

MAC (Mixed Armistice Commission) 291-292, 295-297, 299-304, 306-313, 317, 400-401, 403
MacMichael, Harold 89, 93, 202, 288, 348, 351, 356, 358, 384
Magnes, Judah 109, 149
Mahan Yehuda market 246
Maklef, Gen. Mordechai 296
Malha 298
Manchester Guardian 272, 296, 315, 397
Mapai 224, 250, 277
Mardor, Monya 69
Marks, Simon 72
Marranos 255
Marriott, Cyril 267, 273, 277, 396
Marshall Plan 257
Martin, Sgt. Clifford 212
Martinski, Jacques 200
Masada 69, 351, 367
Masouda Shem-Tov Synagogue 282
McCormick, Anne O'Hare 14, 272
McElroy, John 272
McGhee, George 285
Mea Shearim 60, 64
Medloc train 221, 223-224, 249, 387
Meinertzhagen, Richard 25, 40, 45, 342, 345
Meir, Golda (Meyerson) 149, 212
Melnik, Jacob 25, 342
Memorandum on Acts of Arab Aggression 250, 331, 393

Menuhin, Moshe 8, 161, 332, 339, 343, 366
Meridor, Yacov 104
Mesheq Yagur 141, 143
Milos, immigrant ship 68
Mishmar Force 230
Misrahi, Robert 186
Mixed Armistice Commission *(see MAC)*
Montagu, Edwin 37
Montefiore, C. G. 34
Montefiore, Claude 37
Morris, Benny 16, 289, 310, 391, 403
Mossad 267, 277, 331
Mount Scopus 155, 301, 303-304, 311
Moyne, Lord 57, 97, 98, 103, 161, 267, 360, 365
Mufti, (Haj Amin al-Husseini) 71, 241, 284, 352-353
Mussolini, Benito 58

N

Nablus 97, 105, 107, 135, 283, 286, 306, 357-359, 361
Nahalat Shimon 63
Nahalin 313
Nahum, Rabbi 315
Najd, former name of Sderot 15
Nakam 165, 375
Nasser, Col. Gamal Abdel 315, 320, 407
Nathan, Paul 29
Nazis 7, 12, 27, 28, 47-48, 57-59, 66, 70, 79-80, 82-83, 84-85, 91-93, 95, 98, 103, 109, 113-114, 120, 122, 165-166, 188, 199, 210-211, 219, 231, 236, 239-240, 260, 267, 292-293, 330, 333, 344, 348, 353-354, 358
Near East Air Transport (NEAT) 283
Nes Siyona 66
News Chronicle 178, 378
Newton, Mr. 110
New York Herald-Tribune 198
New York Post 198
New York Times 14, 44, 50, 54, 81, 87, 93, 125, 157-158, 168, 170, 172,

174, 187, 205-206, 228, 242, 245, 249, 272, 310, 339, 374-375, 386
Nixon, John 267
Noel-Baker, Philip 263
Nowers, S. G. 267

O

Observer, The 292, 293, 401
Ocean Vigour, ship 192, 212
O'Dwyer, William 199, 270
Operation Agatha 140, 370
Operation Ali Baba 283
Operation Hiram 269, 296
Operation Musketeer 320-321
Operation Shark 147, 371
Orient v, 83
Orion Cinema 185
Otsray Ha Magifa 139
Ottomans 2, 8, 30, 43, 377

P

Pacific, immigrant ship 68
Paget, Sir Bernard 126
Paice, Sgt. Mervyn 212
Palestine Exploration Fund 26, 342
Palestine Post 112, 113, 159
Palestine Relief Committee 199, 383
Palestine Royal Commission *(see Peel Commission)*
Palmach 11, 79, 109, 117, 126, 128-130, 134, 192, 242, 254-255, 257, 260, 290, 350, 354, 362, 366, 400
Palyam 386
Papanek 143
Pappé, Ilan 8, 9, 16, 246, 333, 339, 343, 345, 356, 390, 391, 392, 393, 396, 398, 399, 404
Paris Peace Conference 42, 43
Park Hotel 246, 252
Parkinson, Sir Charles 31
Partition of Palestine 13-14, 31, 49, 94, 95, 117-118, 148-149, 153, 157, 163, 173, 206, 229, 235-237, 238, 240-242, 249-251, 253, 257, 259-260, 263-264, 269, 272-273, 276-278, 297, 330, 332-333, 341, 358, 359, 376-377, 389, 390
Patria, immigrant ship 68-69, 71, 82,

146, 215, 351, 364
Peel Commission (Palestine Royal Commission) 32, 49-50, 267, 341, 344, 347
Petah Tikvah 88, 224, 388
Philby, Kim 85, 247, 392
Philby Plan 85
Philby, St. John 85
Philip Morris 265
Plan Dalet 229, 268
Political Action Committee for Palestine 165, 226, 376-377, 383, 395
Polkes, Feivel 48, 237
Poniemunski, Chonel 214
President Warfield, ship (see also *Exodus*) 210
Presman, Harry Isaac 213
Prinz, Eric 214
Project Alpha 320
Proskauer, Joseph 39, 366
Protestant Vanguard, The 219, 252
Protocols of the Elders of Zion 219

Q

Qaffin 300
Qalqilya (also Qalqiliya) 94, 151, 163-164, 220, 278, 321, 372, 407
Qataa 94
Qazaza 243
Qibya 309-312, 333, 404
Qiryat Motskin 183
Qiryat Shaul 207

R

Rahman, Sir Abdur 205, 240
Ramat Gan 72, 224
Ramat Hadar. 150
Rass, Jacob 55
Raziel, David 59
Reagan, Ronald 33, 344
Rehavia 52, 63
Reid, Colin 297
Reinhold, Hans (159
Remez, David 179
Repulse, HMS 53
Rex Cinema, Jerusalem 60
Rhodes, P. A. 284, 399
Riley, General William 302-303, 306

Robertson, Sir Brian 224
Roosevelt, Franklin D. 27-28, 85, 103, 124-125, 255, 333, 342, 355, 360, 366, 389-390, 396, 397
Roosevelt, Kermit 235, 239-240, 273
Rosman, Mordechai 211
Ross, Cyril 214, 265
Rossdale, Albert, US Congressman 24
Rothschild, Lord 29, 31, 36, 37, 38, 42-43, 343, 346
Rubowitz, Alexander 209

S

Sacher Hotel 220
Safed 32, 180, 379
Saffa 296
Safsaf 269
Said, Edward 42
Saint Simeon Monastery 259
Sakakini, Hala 248
Salame 170
Salazar y Travesedo, Manuel Allende 247
Salha 269
Salvador, SS, immigrant ship 69
Sandstrom, Emil 205
San Filipo, ship 190
Sarafand 131, 169, 195, 198, 377
Sartre, Jean-Paul 186
Sarwarkeh 200
Scorpion's Pass 312-313, 405
Scriabin, Alexander 193
Sderot, formerly Najd 15
Segev, Tom 9, 16, 333, 342, 344-347, 358-359, 364, 376, 381, 395
Sellers, Dr. Ovid 267
Semiramis Hotel 247, 392
sex workers 177, 229, 378, 389
Shamir, Yitzhak 10, 33, 99, 150, 267, 372
Sharafat 296, 401, 402
Sharett, Moshe 31, 68, 69, 71, 103, 105, 112-113, 116-117, 119, 134, 137, 139, 205, 225, 273, 309, 310, 313, 316-317, 333, 343, 355, 358, 363, 366, 397, 404
Sharon, Ariel 307-310, 329, 404

Sheikh Jarrah 175
Shiloah, Reuven 277
Shoura (terror group in Iraq) 284
Siegel, Paul 46, 346
Sillitoe, Percy 192
Silver, Abba 130, 157
Simpson, Sir John Hope 30, 343
Six Day War 325, 341
Sneh, Moshe 108-109, 110, 114, 117-118, 128, 134, 141, 145, 162, 269, 364, 375, 396
Sons of Liberty Boycott Committee 264
Stanley, Oliver 263
Stern, Avraham 58
Stern Gang *(see Lehi)*
Struma, immigrant ship 69-71, 351
Suez, Suez Crisis 305, 318, 320-323, 325, 330, 332, 407
Sulzberger, Arthur 50, 74, 87, 125
Sulzberger, Mayer 10, 50, 340
Surif 307
Swears & Wells 265
Sykes-Picot Agreement 30
Sykes, Sir Mark 30, 343
Symons, L/Cpl. R. 116
Syrian Orphanage 63, 175
Szyk, Arthur 244

T

Tedder, Lord 263
Tedeschi, Corrado 140
Tel Litwinsky 218, 226, 245
Thwaites, Maj. Gen. William 39
Tiberias 62, 189, 267, 349
Times (The London) 36, 59, 63, 65, 149-150, 162, 168, 180, 241, 340, 349, 352-353, 355-356, 375-376, 379, 388, 393, 396, 399
Tnua (terror group in Iraq) 284
Tobin, Maurice 298
Toynbee, Philip 293, 401
Truman, Harry S 13, 103, 120, 141, 199, 203, 205, 224, 235, 241, 249, 255, 257, 264, 365, 370, 384, 386
Tulkarm 188, 296, 306
Tzrifin Underground *(see Kingdom of Israel)*

U

Ulua, ship 182
Unit 101 307-400
United Jewish Appeal 282
United Zionists-Revisionists of America 185
UNRRA 160, 365
UNRWA 291, 308
UNSCOP 201, 204-207, 210, 223, 240-241, 331, 384, 390
Unsere Stimme 209
UN (United Nations) 10, 13-14, 16, 19, 24, 26, 76, 95, 157, 160, 173, 198, 203, 205, 225, 229-230, 235-236, 238-243, 248-250, 257, 258-259, 261, 264-266, 270-272, 276-280, 286, 288, 291, 295, 296, 297, 298, 300-304, 306-309, 311-313, 316-322, 325-326, 329, 331-332, 342, 389-394, 396-398, 400, 403-405, 407-408
UN Resolution 181 (Partition) 235-236, 240-243, 249-251, 266, 271, 273, 275, 390
US Intelligence in the Middle East 83
Ussishkin, Menachem 31
UXOs (unexploded ordnance) 326

V

Va'ad Leumi 59, 179, 393, 379
Vanunu, Mordechai 86
V-Day 104, 105

W

Wadi Araba 281, 291, 293, 295, 298, 401
Wadi Fukin 307
Wagner, Robert F. 310
Wardiman, Yerovcham 171
Watson, H. D. 44, 346
Weinberg, Aharon 212
Weissenberg, May 65
Weizmann, Chaim 10, 23-24, 35, 37-43, 45, 58, 72, 85-86, 95, 99, 112, 134, 137, 171, 247, 275, 340-341, 343-347, 353, 355, 359, 363, 368-369, 397
Weizmann, Ezer 262
Welles, Sumner 85, 235, 389
Weltsch, Robert 70, 351
Wikeley, T. 314
Wilson, John 304
Wilson, President Woodrow 39, 42, 43, 44, 345, 387
Winchell, Walter 199
Windham, Judge Ralph 177-178, 192
Wise, Stephen 125, 141, 344
Wolf, Lucien 36
World Jewish Congress 284, 315
World Zionist Organization, WZO 9, 19, 82

Y

Yad va-Shem 257, 394
Yalo 295, 296
Yellin-Mor, Nathan 58, 267, 348
Yeshurum Synagogue 183
Yishuv (Jewish settlements) 12-13, 51, 59, 69, 71, 83, 89, 94-95, 107, 112, 118-119, 122, 126, 182, 207, 213, 236-238, 260-261, 361, 370, 388
YMCA 106, 342
Yourgrau, Wolfgang 84

Z

Zertal, Idith 210
Zionist Organization of America (ZOA) 19, 130, 176, 339